The Discourse of Propaganda

The

Discourse of

Propaganda

Case Studies from the Persian Gulf War

and the War on Terror

John Oddo

The Pennsylvania State University Press

University Park, Pennsylvania

Library of Congress Cataloging-in-Publication Data

Names: Oddo, John, 1981– author.
Title: The discourse of propaganda : case studies
    from the Persian Gulf War and the War on
    Terror / John Oddo.
Description: University Park, Pennsylvania :
    The Pennsylvania State University Press,
    [2018] | Includes bibliographical references
    and index.
Summary: "Using case studies from recent
    American military interventions, examines
    propaganda as an intertextual process, one in
    which discourse is recontextualized faithfully
    by multiple parties over time. Explores how
    messages are constructed, performed, and
    recontextualized in new and diverse
    situations"—Provided by publisher.
Identifiers: LCCN 2018023203 | ISBN
    9780271081168 (cloth : alk. paper)
Subjects: LCSH: Propaganda, American—
    Case studies. | Persian Gulf War, 1991—
    United States—Propaganda. | War on
    Terrorism, 2001–2009—Propaganda.
Classification: LCC DS79.739.O33 2018 |
    DDC 956.7044/2—dc23
LC record available at https://lccn.loc.gov
    /2018023203

The Pennsylvania State University Press is a
member of the Association of University Presses.

It is the policy of The Pennsylvania State
University Press to use acid-free paper.
Publications on uncoated stock satisfy the
minimum requirements of American National
Standard for Information Sciences—Permanence
of Paper for Printed Library Material,
ANSI Z39.48–1992.

Contents

Appendixes

Acknowledgments

I want to express my gratitude to the many people who helped me write and publish this book. I thank, first, the entire staff at Penn State University Press, especially Alex Vose and editor Kendra Boileau, who were always attentive and supportive. I am also deeply grateful to the three reviewers who read an earlier version of this text and provided judicious comments.

Next, I thank the people who provided me with unique records and interview data. I am appreciative of the many government employees who processed my Freedom of Information Act (FOIA) requests. And I am very grateful to Dr. David Kay and Ambassador Richard Butler, who generously answered questions and provided valuable insights on television news analysis.

I owe special thanks to several colleagues at Carnegie Mellon University: Barbara Johnstone and Andreea Ritivoi, who read drafts of my work and provided generous feedback; David Kaufer, who listened to me present my argument, always offering patient and insightful remarks; and Suguru Ishizaki, who advised me on book images and obtained for me some hard-to-get tweets. I am indebted, too, to four hard-working research assistants: Les Bennett, Susan Tanner, and Calvin Pollak, who helped me locate and analyze data; and Danielle Lehmann, who helped me design and enhance images. I also gratefully acknowledge that this project was supported by the Falk Fund for Research in the Humanities and the Berkman Faculty Development Fund.

I am grateful to many friends who offered me advice and encouragement: Rich Purcell, Chris Warren, Adam Hodges, Christine Neuwirth, Linda Flower, Danielle Zawodny Wetzel, Necia Werner, Doug Coulson, Joanna Wolfe, and James Wynn. I thank my wonderful students, including those in my Propaganda classes who helped me conceptualize this project. And I especially thank Patricia Dunmire for her discerning comments and unwavering support.

Finally, I thank my entire family, especially my wife, Lindsay, and my children, Amelia and Grace, who strengthen me with their love. I dedicate this book to those who resist propaganda and strive for a more humane discourse.

Introduction

Approaching Propaganda with a Critical Eye

It is evident that a conflict exists between
the principles of democracy—particularly
its concept of the individual—and the processes of propaganda.
　　　　　　　—Jacques Ellul, 1965

Regular readers of the *New York Times* could be forgiven for thinking propaganda is only a problem in foreign dictatorships. So-called rogue states and their propaganda campaigns have been the subject of several recent articles. For example, a 2015 op-ed alerts readers to a "new brand of authoritarian government" emerging in places such as Russia, Turkey, and Venezuela. What is striking about the "new autocrats," the authors write, is that they use "hardly any violence"—instead preferring to "use propaganda, censorship, and other information-based tricks . . . to convince citizens of their superiority over available alternatives" (Guriev and Treisman 2015). Another recent article suggests how such dictatorial propaganda ought to be confronted by the United States. Specifically, the article is about the Voice of America (VOA), the official broadcast network of the United States overseas. This article warns that the VOA may be "floundering at the very moment when America needs to counter sophisticated propaganda" made by "countries like China and Russia and terrorist groups like the Islamic State" (Nixon 2015). In fact, a casual reading of articles since 2012 reveals that the *Times* overwhelmingly associates "propaganda" with authoritarian governments and terrorist groups in foreign countries. Meanwhile, America and the West are said to counteract this propaganda, typically by broadcasting the truth around the world.[1]

This *Times* coverage reflects how Americans typically understand propaganda. Indeed, the coverage hinges on two popular myths, one having to do with who is responsible for propaganda and the other having to do with what propaganda is like. The first myth is that propaganda only happens in totalitarian societies, where the State controls information and prohibits the expression of dissenting views. This myth ignores the fact that propaganda also flourishes in Western democracies—including the United States. Ironically, the existence of Western propaganda is illustrated by the *Times* articles themselves. After all, isn't it strange that the leading newspaper in America consistently reports on propaganda as if it is unique to other countries? Isn't this the kind of self-serving information used to "convince [American] citizens of their [government's] superiority over available alternatives"?

As Jacques Ellul (1965, 132) observes, propaganda is a fact of life in all democratic societies, largely because government officials rely on it to direct public opinion. According to Ellul, democratic governments do not follow popular will; they use propaganda to create popular will. "The point," he writes, "is to make the masses demand of the government what the government has already decided to do." Of course, "the government" is not the only propagandist involved in democratic society. Propaganda also comes from private corporations, think tanks, news agencies, advertisers, public relations firms—just about any elite institution aiming to influence public thought. Less obviously, ordinary citizens also shape how propaganda moves through a democracy. Citizens not only seek out propaganda, looking for ready-made news that can help them stay informed (144–46), but they also help spread propaganda, passing it along to one another and sometimes even pressuring one another to adhere to the prevailing truths of the day. As Huckin (2016, 118) writes, "Propaganda is indeed most effective when it is disseminated unconsciously by the broad public."

The second myth about propaganda is that it necessarily involves disinformation and chicanery, what the *Times*'s op-ed writers characterize as "information-based tricks." In fact, a number of sources insist that propaganda uses specious rhetorical techniques—highly emotional words, deceptive representations, and logical fallacies inhibiting rational thought. Most famously, the Institute for Propaganda Analysis (IPA) published a list (1937) of seven common devices used by propagandists. To this day, the IPA list remains a popular tool for analysts who scrutinize offending texts for things like name-calling, testimonial, and "glittering generalities" (e.g., Marlin 2013; Mazid 2007). However, such inventories of technique have a major weakness: they will detect propaganda in just about any rhetorical act. For instance, in Martin Luther King Jr.'s (1963) written texts, one can find nearly all of the IPA's propaganda devices.[2] But few people would call King's speeches and writings propaganda. For most of us, propaganda is not equivalent to a set of rhetorical techniques. Instead, techniques must be considered in context. Are they being used to sustain unequal power relations, or are they being used to call attention to historical injustices? Who is in power, and who stands to gain?

It is also wrong to assume that propaganda always lies. Some does, but much propaganda is difficult to classify as true or false. (Take the slogan "Free Kuwait," for example.) Other propaganda appears to be factual. It is a fact, for example, that in the 1980s, Iraqi president Saddam Hussein used illegal chemical weapons in a war against Iran. In 2002, this fact was repeated often by the U.S. government as it argued for removing Saddam from power. But such "truthful" assertions can still be misleading. Yes, Saddam used chemical weapons but only with American help: the U.S. government had not only supplied such weapons but had even helped Iraq locate Iranian targets (Borger 2002).

No representation of reality is entirely complete or accurate—so propaganda can never attain the status of absolute truth. And while it is important to consider whether information is factual, an even more critical question for propaganda is whether it circulates widely and plays a dominant role in public discourse. After all, one essential characteristic of successful propaganda is that it propagates. Thus, those studying it should not only attend to the content of messages but also to how those messages spread, how they become mobile, durable, and repeatable. That is the premise of this book. Certainly, I am interested in deceptive rhetorical techniques and other forms of manipulation. But I am even more interested in what enables propaganda to circulate.

On this question, there are two key points. First, propaganda is unlikely to circulate without an institutional and ideological infrastructure to support it. In an American context, this includes the infrastructure of private media—the routines and values of the corporate press, as well as the power relations that give some people access to channels of mass communication. Second, propaganda cannot circulate unless it is portable and detachable. Not every stretch of discourse is equally prone to circulation. Some discourse—for reasons that are formal, semantic, or cultural—will appear more worthy of being repeated. And good propagandists will use rhetorical strategies that induce recontextualization, prompting new audiences to further spread propaganda without altering or undermining it.

How I Conceptualize Propaganda

In this book, I aim to draw upon these observations to stitch together a theory of propaganda and to define those social and rhetorical characteristics that allow it to succeed. I can now state my argument a bit more formally as a set of three essential premises:

- First, propaganda is an *intertextual process* that requires contributions from multiple agents. It can succeed in circulating only if it continually induces new audiences to recognize and recontextualize it on a mass scale. Importantly, the people who create and recontextualize propaganda exist in democracies as well as autocracies. They may be elite actors or ordinary people, powerful agents or "unwitting accomplices" (Huckin 2016, 129) who keep the propaganda alive.

- Second, propaganda is *manipulative* without necessarily being false. Propaganda can include misleading rhetorical techniques and disinformation, but manipulation can take many other forms as well. Indeed, people may be manipulated simply because one truth becomes so dominant that other relevant truths are overwhelmed and obscured. In other words, propaganda may be accurate, factual, and logical—yet still hegemonic and therefore coercive.
- Third, discourse best qualifies as propaganda if it *harms the Many and serves the Few*. We need not label as propaganda every case of mass-recontextualized discourse, even when that discourse includes so-called propaganda devices. No scholar refers to Martin Luther King Jr.'s speeches as propaganda precisely because these speeches contributed to a more just and equitable society. Propaganda, by definition it seems, works in the opposite direction: it consolidates the power of some groups while damaging the interests and well-being of other (typically less powerful) groups. This is true no matter who is spreading the propaganda or what their intentions might be.

In support of this argument, this book examines cases of war propaganda, specifically domestic American propaganda used to justify the Persian Gulf War (1990–91) and the "Global War on Terror" (2001–present). With these case studies, I aim to clarify key functions of contemporary war discourse and illustrate the utility of theorizing propaganda as an intertextual process. I ask the following questions: What are the persuasive properties of war propaganda? What techniques are used to ensure a message will be heard, believed, and repeated by others? How is this propaganda kept alive in the media ecosystem? How are propaganda messages recontextualized in ways that ensure their continued viability?

In answering these questions, this book helps uncover the mechanisms by which propaganda is circulated: the agents, texts, and cultural practices that allow a message to both persuade and proliferate. It reveals that propaganda is spread not just by politicians and news organizations but also by interest groups, corporations, and ordinary citizens, who wittingly or unwittingly keep the propaganda alive.[3] In addition, the book firmly ties propaganda to current notions of intertextuality and emphasizes how makers of propaganda signal that their discourse is detachable and repeatable, inducing people to recontextualize the propaganda in new contexts and for new audiences. Finally, the book draws attention to an issue of critical importance: propaganda's threat to democracy. Indeed, this book raises serious questions about the degree to which American citizens can meaningfully participate in democratic politics, especially those politics that have thrust the country into a state of perpetual war.

My Goals for This Book

As Jowett and O'Donnell (2015, 1) report, propaganda has been studied in many disciplines: history, journalism, political science, psychology, rhetoric, and communication. I hope to contribute new knowledge to scholars in all these areas, though I approach propaganda from my position in the field of critical discourse studies (CDS).[4] Curiously, in CDS, propaganda has received relatively little attention, despite the field's stated interest in discursive power abuse and illegitimate forms of persuasion.[5] In fact, a search of the top journals publishing CDS reveals that very few articles include "propaganda" in their titles or keywords.[6] And the articles that do refer to propaganda generally fail to define the term, let alone offer a theory for it.

However, CDS does offer a number of valuable concepts that can inform how propaganda is understood, concepts such as manipulation (Van Dijk 2006), textual silence (Huckin 2002, 2010), mediation (Chouliaraki 2006; Graham 2004), legitimation (e.g., Van Leeuwen 2007; Cap 2006), and intertextual reproduction (Dunmire 2011; Fairclough 1995; Hodges 2011). While these concepts bear a crucial relationship to propaganda, none is identical to it. My goal, then, is to build upon insights from CDS (and discourse studies more generally) to develop an explicit definition of propaganda. Though my definition is motivated by critical theories of language and power, it should be of interest to anyone studying propaganda.

A related goal of this book is to suggest different methods for propaganda analysis. Several studies of propaganda fix upon a single text—say, a political ad or a presidential oration (e.g., Mackay 2015; Mazid 2007). While such focused research can be enlightening, I think it overlooks the intertextual character of propaganda. Indeed, by treating propaganda as an intertextual process, I am strongly suggesting that it ought to be studied intertextually. Propaganda does not happen in one discrete (con)text. Instead, by definition, successful propaganda spreads out across many texts and contexts. Such an understanding of propaganda requires that we pay greater attention to enduring media campaigns rather than short-lived discourse moments. As Carvalho (2008, 164) suggests, "Most studies of media discourse are like snapshots examining some news items in detail but covering a short time span. . . . While this may be relevant for some events, most public issues have a significantly long 'life,' which is tied to representations in the media." An intertextual focus allows us to examine how dominant meanings develop over time and how stories, themes, and slogans are recontextualized again and again—so often and so widely that they become recognizable as propaganda. By looking beyond individual texts, we also gain insight into the more persistent (and typically more significant) efforts to manipulate popular consciousness. We observe how meanings both emerge and remain viable in media ecosystems, sustaining public attention and potentially securing consent for illegitimate practices.

Finally, by defining propaganda in terms of intertextuality, I aim to draw attention to both the contextual factors that give rise to propaganda and the linguistic-discursive factors that make certain texts more available for reuse. In fact, most propaganda scholarship focuses on the former—the historical development of propaganda campaigns and the extralinguistic variables that contribute to circulation (e.g., Parry-Giles 1996; Sweeney 2012). To be clear, discourse must be understood in context, and I fully support examining "the historical-cultural processes" that allow propaganda to succeed (Parry-Giles 1996, 162). Still, I think it is equally important to examine the rhetorical and sociolinguistic details of propaganda—the words, images, and sounds, and the processes of entextualization and recontextualization. Only then can we understand how propaganda addresses audiences and gains momentum. Thus, a major goal of my book is to focus on *discourse*, especially discursive properties that render propaganda detachable and subject to repetition.

Of course, in outlining structures and processes of propaganda, I borrow extensively from others (Ellul 1965; Huckin 2016; Van Dijk 2006). As Bakhtin (1986) reminds us, every new contribution builds on what came before, and mine is no different. As I enter this scholarly dialogue, I hope to add qualifications and amendments to existing discussions of propaganda. At the same time, I expect others to examine critically my claims about propaganda and to revise and amend them based on competing theoretical principles and new empirical evidence.

Still, I am hopeful that scholars of history, rhetoric, media, and discourse studies will benefit from both my theoretical outline and the case studies of propaganda used to justify recent American wars. This book aims to provide a fuller picture of how such propaganda is produced and sustained in a democratic society and how it is kept alive across texts and rhetorical performances. Simultaneously, this book challenges readers to consider the pernicious consequences of propaganda and the uncertain prospects for civic rule over political affairs.

A Note on My Approach

In choosing my data for this project, I had to make some assumptions about what propaganda is like. Particularly, I assumed from the beginning that propaganda is identifiable partly because it propagates. And, based on previous scholarship (e.g., Ellul 1965), I also assumed that propaganda is harmful. Some might object that making these assumptions is problematic, especially the latter assumption, since it requires the researcher's evaluative judgment. But I would submit that it is impossible to study discourse phenomena without making such evaluations. For example, one cannot study instances of political rhetoric without first judging what is rhetorical and what is political. In any case, my main goal in this project was not to distinguish propaganda from nonpropaganda but rather to explain how propaganda works—that is, what makes it effective. Thus, I chose cases where apparently harmful discourse had clearly succeeded in propagating and tried to explain this success.[7]

In pursuing this line of inquiry, I came to understand that propaganda discourse is often designed to be propagated. And I further observed that such propagation always involves multiple parties and always unfolds through processes of recontextualization. However, existing theories of propaganda did not account for these observations. So, in trying to describe how propaganda works, I discovered I had something to say about how propaganda ought to be defined. Ultimately, then, my theory of propaganda is based on the case studies in subsequent chapters. I arrived at it only after conducting analyses of discourse. One could say that in trying to learn how propaganda works, I came to better understand what propaganda actually is.

Of course, my project is not merely descriptive. In defining propaganda as harmful, I am quite consciously taking a critical stance. In fact, I regard propaganda analysis as a form of critical discourse analysis. Accordingly, analysts are not detached and neutral but critical of the sociopolitical events they observe. Critical analysts explicitly begin with "prevailing social problems" and take "the perspective of those who suffer most" (Van Dijk 1986, 4). They are specifically interested in relations of power and dominance, and their analyses often expose how people use language to legitimize social injustice (Fairclough 2003; Van Dijk 1993).

Again, this may strike some readers as a problem. After all, how can one be trusted to accurately examine discourse if that person has political commitments and goals? The simple answer is "ideological commitment . . . does not equal analytical distortion" (Carvalho 2008, 162). We can have an interest in social justice yet still design sound studies and remain scrupulous in our analysis and reporting of the data. Essentially, this means we choose systematic methods, we don't cherry-pick to reach tendentious conclusions, and we remain circumspect about our claims.

However, we must dispense with the idea that there is such a thing as an "objective" discourse analysis. As Hodges and Nilep (2007, 4) emphasize, "Analysts are also participants in the world under study." They themselves occupy social and ideological positions, and their own understanding of context, history, and the public good necessarily informs their research. This is the case not only in humanities scholarship but in other disciplines, too. As the late historian Howard Zinn (2001, 185) explains, even "hard" scientific research is politically interested, since scientists, like everyone else, determine what to study based on notions of social value. Scientists arguably aim to maximize happiness by extending control over the physical environment and eliminating forms of pollution and disease. Similarly, critical discourse analysts aim to maximize human happiness by extending democratic control over the political environment and eliminating war, poverty, discrimination, and other social ills. As long as our values only determine the questions we ask—and not the answers we supply— we need not be troubled by them (184). To the contrary, we should unabashedly declare our values and justify our research in part by explaining how it aims at the social good.

In this spirit, I wish to unabashedly declare my own values and interests. First, as an American citizen, I am interested in democracy—more specifically, meaningful participation in democratic life. I object to propaganda insofar as it (1) narrows the range of choices available to citizens, (2) prevents them from adequately judging what is true, or (3) reduces their power to influence public affairs. Second, as an advocate for peace, I am interested in eliminating most forms of violence—especially wars of aggression, wars of questionable legality, and wars that are justified on false premises. I am not a pacifist, and I believe that, under rare circumstances, a focused act of violence may be necessary to stop "a monstrous and immediate evil" (Zinn 2007). However, as Zinn (2007) writes, "War by its nature is unfocused, indiscriminate, and . . . inevitably involves the deaths of large numbers of people and the suffering of even more." Even "targeted" drone strikes "kill vastly more people than their targets" (Ackerman 2014). Moreover, war is simply unreliable: "There is no likelihood that it will achieve its desired end" (Zinn 2007). Indeed, war often exacerbates the very problems it is meant to resolve.

In this book, I try to be as transparent as possible about my understanding of sociohistorical context and how that understanding informs my beliefs. I don't expect every reader to share my political views. But I hope readers appreciate that there is no objective vantage point from which I—or anyone else—can operate. Thus, at the very least, my political views are available for examination. And I am confident that even readers who disagree with those views will still find my discourse analyses to be systematic and grounded in empirical data. (See appendix A for more about my understanding of discourse and how I study it.)

Overview of the Chapters to Follow

I conduct three case studies of American war propaganda, centering on the first Gulf War and the ongoing War on Terror. The book is divided into four main parts.

Part 1 defines propaganda and provides a brief history of the recent American wars where it played an important role. In chapter 1, I review key theories and definitions of propaganda before developing my own view of propaganda as an intertextual process that, when successful, replicates and recontextualizes the "same" message on an enormous scale. No one person controls propaganda; it must change hands as it moves along an intertextual chain. To be considered propaganda, I also argue, a message must harm a democratic citizenry by manipulating public debate and promoting unequal power arrangements.

Chapter 2 sketches the history of recent U.S. wars in the Middle East, especially the two wars in Iraq (1990–91; 2003–11), where I find discrepancies between the stated justifications for war and privately held rationales. I highlight the damage these wars caused—destruction and human suffering, disintegration of traditional societies, and violations of international law—and conclude that it is reasonable to describe the discourse that led to them as propaganda.

Part 2 examines the circulation of the "incubator story," a false story told before the first Gulf War that portrayed Iraqi soldiers ripping premature Kuwaiti infants from their incubators. Chapter 3 focuses on one important telling of this atrocity story, a performance in which a fifteen-year-old girl named Nayirah signaled that her narrative could be detached and recontextualized by the media. I go on to examine how American journalists reported on Nayirah's story and strengthened its status as a factual, eyewitness account.

In chapter 4, I continue my exploration of the incubator story, tracing its intertextual development throughout the period before the 1990–91 Gulf War. I follow several iterations of the story as it was retold before and after Nayirah's performance, and I try to explain the factors that led the press to report on it. Both American elites and insiders close to the events in Kuwait continually reenacted the story from positions of authority, creating detachable versions of the narrative that were ready-made for recontextualization in the news. Meanwhile, those who called the incubator story into question were not perceived to have authoritative voices or a discourse "shareable" within mainstream media.

In part 3, I investigate the role of TV news analysts during the run-up to the 2003 Iraq War. Specifically, I examine discourse from two groups of analysts: a group consisting of former U.S. military generals and a group consisting of former U.N. weapons inspectors. Chapter 5 reveals how many of these supposedly independent news analysts were connected to entities with a vested interest in war. Drawing on investigative reports, documents obtained through Freedom of Information Act requests, and personal interviews, I show how the U.S. government courted analysts and induced them into favorably recontextualizing its claims.

Chapter 6 continues my study of TV news analysts before the Iraq War. First, I examine how the networks entextualized analyst discourse and enacted for the analysts an "expert voice." I show how language and visuals worked together, indexing that analyst talk was not only neutral and authoritative but also distinct (and detachable) from the rest of the news broadcasts. I find the analysts' discourse was typified by a pro-administration slant, all but ensuring that the expert voice would be a voice for war.

In chapter 7, I follow the intertextual trajectory of a pro-war talking point, exploring the Bush administration's 2002 claim that Iraq had obtained aluminum tubes designed for a nuclear weapon. In fact, the intended use of these tubes was hotly debated in the U.S. intelligence community. The question I seek to answer is: how did discourse about the tubes change as it was recontextualized first in private intelligence documents and later in public speeches and news reports? I show that, in the hands of the press, the government's one-sided claims were uncritically repeated, recontextualized, and reified, while alternative viewpoints were consistently ignored. Indeed, the most prominent news analyst on American television affirmed the tubes propaganda, endowing it with even greater credibility.

Part 4 investigates the wartime slogan "Support Our Troops," exploring why it succeeds as propaganda. Chapter 8 examines how the slogan's linguistic qualities allow it to function as a memorable and decontextualizable text. I suggest that the slogan's poetic features and grammatical mood help ensure its future recontextualization. I also study the history of the slogan and the indexical associations that have attached to it, revealing how the slogan emerged as a response to the antiwar movement and how it has been juxtaposed with larger American narratives that avert policy questions, lionize the troops, and portray dissent as treason.

In chapter 9, I examine how the "Support Our Troops" slogan has been recontextualized by different groups, first (from the top down) by high-profile American politicians and next (horizontally) by ordinary citizens. I investigate the semiotics of "Support Our Troops" merchandise and how public displays of such merchandise can exert social pressure. And I analyze how the slogan has been used by ordinary Twitter users, who not only recycle prevailing myths about troops but who work to discipline the online community, integrating people into proper wartime roles.

In the conclusion, I offer some final remarks on propaganda, review my theory, and identify its potential strengths. I also consider whether critical scholars have overstated the problem of propaganda, ignoring the public's ability to resist attempts at manipulation. Finally, I offer some suggestions on how citizens might respond to propaganda and perhaps counteract its negative influence.

Defining Propaganda and Historicizing

America's Wars in the Middle East

1

1. Theorizing Propaganda
Intertextuality, Manipulation, and Power

But the most brilliant propagandist technique will yield no success unless one fundamental principle is borne in mind constantly and with unflagging attention. It must confine itself to a few points and repeat them over and over.

—Adolf Hitler, 1924

Leonard Doob (1989, 375) suggests that "a clear-cut definition of propaganda is neither possible nor desirable." However, I think it's worthwhile to clarify what propaganda is, even as I recognize the difficulty. There seem to be two main obstacles to defining propaganda. First, it is difficult to distinguish propaganda from other discourse. For example, propaganda is closely related to rhetoric, since it involves the use of signs to induce persuasion. But it's hard to say what makes propaganda different from other kinds of rhetoric. A second obstacle is the fact that propaganda has come to be associated with ethical impropriety. To be sure, not all scholars think that propaganda is inherently wrong. But deception and manipulation are almost always suggested by the term, and this has been generally true since the end of World War I. But how do we decide what (un)ethical discourse entails? In this chapter, I attempt to deal with some of the pitfalls of conceptualizing propaganda and, ultimately, advance my own theory.

A Brief History of Propaganda

Before the sixteenth century, *propaganda* was a Latin term describing biological reproduction. In the late 1500s, however, the Catholic Church began to use the term in its effort "to spread Catholic doctrines in non-Christian lands" (Fellows 1959, 182).

In 1622, Pope Gregory XV formally established the Sacra Congregatio de Propaganda Fide (Sacred Congregation for the Propagation of the Faith), "which was charged with carrying 'the faith' to the New World and with reviving and strengthening it in Europe as a means of countering the Protestant revolution" (Jowett and O'Donnell 2015, 82). Well into the nineteenth century, propaganda was still associated primarily with Catholic evangelism. However, by the mid-1800s, "propaganda" was beginning to take on political connotations. For example, in 1852, Millard Fillmore said the historical goal of America was "to become a 'propagandist' of free principles." Others occasionally suggested propaganda was a sinister activity. An 1843 dictionary defines it as "the spread of opinions and principles which are viewed by most governments with horror and aversion" (quoted in Fellows 1959, 183).

Still, at the turn of the twentieth century, the word "propaganda" was rarely used (Fellows 1959, 184; Miller 2005, 11). It wasn't until World War I (1914–18) that "propaganda" became a popular term for systematic campaigns aimed at mass manipulation. Miller (2005, 14) observes that Allied governments "besmirched the word by using it only in dark reference to *the enemy*." Thus, the Germans were said to be deceiving their people through outrageous propaganda. Meanwhile, America and Britain were countering German lies with what George Creel (1920, 5), director of the U.S. Committee on Public Information, called the "straightforward presentation of facts." Following the war, however, people learned the Allied governments had themselves used all sorts of prevarication to demonize the "Huns." Miller (2005, 15) describes the public reaction: "As [the American and British people] learned more and more about the outright lies, exaggerations and half truths used on them by their own governments, both populations came, understandably, to see 'propaganda' as a weapon even *more* perfidious than they had thought when they had not perceived themselves as its real target."

Following the Great War, attempts to reclaim a positive meaning for "propaganda" largely failed. For example, in 1928, public relations specialist Edward Bernays defined "propaganda" as a neutral form of mass persuasion, one that could be used for good or ill. But the public, still stunned by revelations of World War I lies, rejected his efforts to "rid the word of its bad smell" (Miller 2005, 15). In spite of his failure to win over converts, Bernays remains an important figure as he transparently describes the deliberate propagandist's view of democracy. According to Bernays ([1928] 2015), democratic society is ruled by a few "invisible governors" (37) who "pull the wires which control the public mind" (38). It is necessary and inevitable that "intelligent minorities" (57) manipulate "the herd" (126). For without their leadership, there would be "nothing but confusion" (38). Indeed, for Bernays, propaganda is the only way to ensure the "reasonable smoothness" of the free market (39) and the "orderly functioning of our group life" (38).

Positive uses of "propaganda" declined after World War I, but the elitist view expressed so candidly by Bernays—that the public should be ruled by a benign minority of experts—has remained in force ever since. Thus, even as groups such as the Institute for Propaganda Analysis (1937) taught people "how to detect propaganda," governments redoubled their efforts to manage the public mind. By World War II, "certain persuasive activities were highly organized and developed under the leadership of experts, seeking maximum application of available scientific knowledge to the influencing of opinion" (Fellows 1959, 185). Indeed, while the U.S. government decried communist and Nazi propaganda, it increasingly employed strategies from advertising and public relations to create its own domestic propaganda campaigns, as well as "psychological warfare" against enemies. Meanwhile, interest groups and corporations also expanded their power over mass media, seeking to influence voters and consumers.

None of this was lost on American academics, who, in the 1920s and 1930s, began to examine propaganda and its dangers. As Sproule (1987, 1989, 1991) observes, American intellectuals were initially alarmed about the potential for propaganda to upend democracy. Thus, most early propaganda analysis was decidedly anti propaganda: critical, empirical case studies aimed at helping people resist propaganda's allure. However, as World War II approached, opinion leaders became less interested in disabling propaganda and more interested in mobilizing people for war. Meanwhile, the paradigm of critical propaganda studies was superseded by a paradigm of communication research based on "neutral" quantitative and experimental methods. Communication researchers now aimed to make their work noncontroversial and useful to powerful agents interested in influencing the public.

However, the "social dislocations of the 1960s and 70s again made issues of institutional manipulation salient to American experience" (Sproule 1989, 226). Several U.S. scholars criticized government attempts to manipulate people through techniques such as audience segmentation, market research surveys, and pseudorational advertising (e.g., McGinniss 1969). However, the most vital work on propaganda to come out of this era is that of French scholar Jacques Ellul. Ellul (1965, 242) rejected the claim that "propaganda is merely a neutral instrument" useful for democratic ends. Instead, he pointed to a "private monopoly" in mass communication and warned that the trend in democracies was "in the direction of a very few, very powerful companies controlling all the propaganda media" (236, 237). Such a climate threatens freedom of expression, Ellul argued, as democratic debate is dominated by those with access to mass media. Ellul noted such elite propaganda is often "rational and factual" (85) but is still toxic since it limits one's ability to "choose freely" and always assumes the superiority of the reigning regime (87).

Ellul also reconceived how propaganda circulates. He argued that propaganda need not move vertically from powerful institutions to the public. Instead, he supplemented this classical account with a view of sociological propaganda, a propaganda that "aims . . . at an entire style of life" (62–63), rather than one opinion or course of action. Such propaganda is not rapid and intentional; it acts "gently" and "slowly"

(66). Indeed, this propaganda may move horizontally among people as they "unwittingly" reinforce "doctrines on what is *good or bad*" (64, 65). Regardless of its form, however, Ellul remained convinced propaganda violates principles of democracy and further entrenches the supremacy of elite forces. In his view, "all propaganda ends up as a means by which the prevailing powers manipulate the masses" (241).

Contemporary Definitions of Propaganda

From this brief history, we see there has always been some disagreement about propaganda and its traits. Is it, as Bernays ([1928] 2005) suggests, a neutral form of mass communication that facilitates the smooth running of democratic society? Or is it a repressive form of communication that ultimately violates democratic principles? Is it the deliberate dissemination of lies by institutional elites? Or could propaganda be unintentional and rational? Could it even be spread horizontally by ordinary people?

Over the last few decades, "the level of interest in propaganda among scholars in many academic fields . . . has increased substantially" (Jowett and O'Donnell 2015, xiii). But researchers are still grappling with the same questions. Table 1 presents several definitions of propaganda by leading academics. In the right-hand column, I assign numbers to the definitions, each numeral associated with what I see as a potential shortcoming:

1. The definition limits propaganda to only institutional sources.
2. The definition implies a bounded rhetorical situation where a propagandist deliberately targets a recipient to achieve a self-serving purpose.
3. The definition treats propaganda as intentionally and deliberately harmful.

There is much to recommend these definitions. Indeed, for reasons I explain below, I endorse the views that propaganda reaches "masses of people" (Parry-Giles 2002, xxvi) and tends to hinder our best judgment (Marlin 2013, 12). However, I disagree with the view offered by most scholars that propaganda *necessarily* targets audiences so that some source can achieve a self-serving or harmful goal. To understand why I find this view problematic, I explore two definitions in greater detail: Jowett and O'Donnell's (2015) and Huckin's (2016). I focus on these authors for two reasons. First, unlike some others, they fully explain their definitions. Second, they are principally interested, as I am, in defining propaganda based on theories of communication, rhetoric, and discourse (as opposed to, say, social psychology).

Jowett and O'Donnell have written what is probably the most popular book on propaganda, now in its sixth edition. As such, their definition is very influential: "Propaganda is the deliberate, systematic attempt to shape perceptions, manipulate

Table 1 Contemporary definitions of propaganda

Source	Definition	Shortcoming
Sproule (1994, 8)	"Propaganda represents the work of large organizations or groups to win over the public for special interests through a massive orchestration of attractive conclusions packaged to conceal both their persuasive purpose and lack of sound supporting reasons."	1, 2
Carey (1997, 20)	"By 'propaganda,' I refer to communication where the form or content is selected with the single-minded purpose of bringing some target audience to adopt attitudes and beliefs chosen in advance by the sponsors of the communication. . . . [T]he purpose [of propaganda] is to close [minds] to the possibility of any conclusion but one."	2
Pratkanis and Aronson (2001, 11)	"The word *propaganda* has . . . evolved to mean mass 'suggestion' or 'influence' through the manipulation of symbols and psychology of the individual. . . . [I]t is the communication of a point of view with the ultimate goal of having the recipient of the appeal come to 'voluntarily' accept this position as if it were his or her own."	2
Parry-Giles (2002, xxvi)	"'Propaganda' is conceived of as strategically devised messages that are disseminated to masses of people by an institution for the purpose of generating action benefiting its source."	1, 2
Marlin (2013, 12)	"The organized attempt through communication to affect belief or action or inculcate attitudes in a large audience in ways that circumvent or suppress an individual's adequately informed, rational, reflective judgment."	3
Jowett and O'Donnell (2015, 7)	"Propaganda is the deliberate, systematic attempt to shape perceptions, manipulate cognitions, and direct behavior to achieve a response that furthers the desired intent of the propagandist."	2

cognitions, and direct behavior to achieve a response that furthers the desired intent of the propagandist" (Jowett and O'Donnell 2015, 7). The authors stress that the last words of their definition ("the desired intent of the propagandist") are the most important, "for the one who benefits from the audience's response, if the response is the desired one, is the propagandist and not necessarily members of the audience" (15). Notice that, in this view, there is a clear distinction between "the propagandist" and "the audience."

Reinforcing this point, the authors offer a "model of propaganda" based largely on Westley and MacLean's (1977) theory of communication (Jowett and O'Donnell 2015, 34–35). Here, communication is defined as "a process in which a sender transmits a message to a receiver through a channel" (34). More specifically, propaganda involves a sender (A) who communicates with a receiver (B) about some message (X). The sender and receiver need not be individuals; either A or B can be a group or even an entire social system. Sometimes the communication between A and B is direct and face-to-face, but it may also involve a gatekeeper (C). The gatekeeper acts as an intermediary; it could be an agent, such as a journalist, or technology, such as a computer. In a mediated interaction, A communicates to B through C about X. The audience (B) will either respond to the sender's message through "feedback" or otherwise undergo "effects" (35). Again, what distinguishes propaganda is that it is expressly aimed at furthering "the desired intent" of A, that is, the propagandist: "The purpose of propaganda is to promote a partisan or competitive cause in the best interest of the propagandist, but not necessarily in the best interest of the recipient" (36).

The problem with Jowett and O'Donnell's definition is that it oversimplifies the process of communication, reducing it to a discrete interaction between A and B, while overlooking the realities of intertextual discourse. We can expose this problem by taking a hypothetical, but by no means far-fetched, example of a propaganda event. Let's say that after developing intelligence about a foreign threat, the U.S. government decides (for selfish reasons) that it must wage war against an enemy. The president holds a press conference that is recorded but not broadcast live. In it, he cites government intelligence files and argues that war is necessary, peppering his appeal with misleading and unwarranted claims. Later, journalists issue reports about the press conference, re-presenting many of the president's claims in mainstream newspapers. Many readers of these reports accept the president's claims and express support for the war on social media.

At first blush, this scenario seems to fit Jowett and O'Donnell's model. A sender (the president) sends a message (an argument for war) to a receiver (the public) through a gatekeeper (the newspapers). Upon closer inspection, however, the model appears inadequate. Most glaringly, it assumes that the message is something like a rigid object, one that originates with a single source only to be sent along to the next party. The model does not account for how the source assembles this message, how the message is stitched together from other texts. In our hypothetical case, for instance, the president is deemed the sender. But this is only true in a crude sense. For before he could act as the sender, the president first functioned as an audience member who read and interpreted intelligence reports. His own discourse—his own argument for war—largely depends on how he makes meaning out of prior texts and communicates with other sources. But according to the model, this is not part of the communication process.

Also, in the model, the message simply passes through the media gatekeepers without changing. Journalists are rather like conduits for the sender's information. But journalists are not mere conduits. Indeed, in our scenario, they are the president's first audience, the first to hear the president's address. Furthermore, their reaction amounts to more than "feedback" or the experience of vague "effects." Their response is active and interpretive: they recontextualize and transform the president's claims as they produce news reports for the public. In this case, the public interfaces only with news reports—with re-presentations of the president's words. And these members of the public will also do more than reply with "feedback." They, too, may recontextualize and transform the discourse; they, too, may participate in spreading the propaganda on Twitter or Facebook or in mundane conversation.

Even from this sketch, we can see propaganda is a distributed activity—a dialogic process.[1] Someone who is at one moment the addressee, the receiver of propaganda, becomes in the next moment the addresser, the one who spreads propaganda to a new audience. Once we acknowledge that this is always the case—that there is no such thing as an A-B-C model of communication, then we can begin to see other problems with Jowett and O'Donnell's definition. For instance, it becomes impossible to distinguish between the propagandist and the audience. In our example, is the propagandist the president, or is it the press? The message could only spread with both of them, and it continues to spread without them as members of the public further circulate the message "downstream." If all of these parties are responsible for spreading propaganda, then they are all propagandists. And there is simply no way to talk about "the desired intent of *the* propagandist," for the different parties may have entirely different intentions. Sure, the president may want to manipulate people into war. But is this also the intention of the press? Is it also the deliberate intention of your Aunt Grace, who sends you a link to the president's speech on Facebook? Of course not. The intentions vary depending on the person, as does the degree of responsibility for the circulation of the message.

Elsewhere in their work, Jowett and O'Donnell (2015, 389) hint at a more intertextual understanding of discourse by referring to propaganda as "a process within a social system." They describe a "multistep flow of communication," whereby propaganda is spread not only by "propaganda agents" but also by opinion leaders and other "people who facilitate rumors innocently or deliberately throughout a social network" (395). However, evidence that people may "innocently" spread propaganda, furthering someone else's interests, does not lead the authors to revise their definition, which insists that propaganda is self-serving.

Huckin (2016) describes propaganda more broadly and distinguishes, as Ellul (1965) does, between different types. First, in his formal definition, Huckin refers to what might be called classic or vertical propaganda. He asserts that propaganda is "addressed to a mass audience by parties who thereby gain advantage" (Huckin 2016, 126), adding that propaganda is always created "in the source's interest" (127). Accordingly, the agents behind propaganda "intentionally *design* and *create* information which they then *disseminate* to a certain audience to gain *advantage*" (129). Here, Huckin appears to provide a definition similar to Jowett and O'Donnell's, as he, too, describes a single propaganda "source" with one self-serving "interest," rather than a multitude of sources with competing interests and varying degrees of selfishness.

However, Huckin extends his definition by also acknowledging horizontal propaganda, which is spread collectively by a diffusion of participants who may not gain any real benefit. Such propaganda is "disseminated by the broad public, which ironically is also its most impacted victim" (118). According to Huckin, when ordinary people spread propaganda, they still think they are gaining some advantage. However, even as they disseminate the propaganda deliberately, they may do so unconsciously, without realizing they are acting in self-defeating ways. Thus, for Huckin, the victims of propaganda are often "unwitting accomplices" (129), who disseminate propaganda "collectively and unconsciously" (131).

I would not insist, as Huckin does, that even unwitting propagandists seek to gain an advantage. Some surely spread propaganda innocently without seeking any benefit. In any case, it's important to stress that rewards change as propaganda moves across parties and that the same propaganda message may be spread by different people seeking different goals and different advantages. Less significantly, I would quibble with Huckin's assessment that propaganda, by definition, "addresses a mass audience." Granted, much propaganda directly addresses masses of people, especially propaganda spread through broadcast media. However, some propaganda is addressed to very small audiences, for example in face-to-face talk or on platforms allowing for one-to-one communication. Of course, to be successful, such propaganda must circulate beyond these small circles and eventually reach a mass audience, even though it may be addressed to just a few people at a time.

This is why I avoid Huckin's term "dissemination" to describe how propaganda moves. To me, dissemination implies one source scattering something in every direction, often a media institution delivering identical content to a mass audience.[2] Again, there are moments when propaganda is instantaneously spread this way. But even in these cases, the disseminator usually broadcasts a propaganda message it received from another source. Moreover, after the moment of mass broadcast, millions of people may rearticulate and reshape the propaganda, variously transforming it for smaller audiences, without ever again disseminating the original message to a mass audience. As I define it, propaganda is never solely the work of a centralized author disseminating identical content in every direction. Instead, propaganda only truly succeeds if it changes hands; it must travel from one source and one context to another, shifting its meaning along the way. Thus, I prefer terms such as "recontextualization" and "mass-recontextualization," which better capture how propaganda is borrowed, reused, and recycled.

Despite our differences, Huckin's (2016) thinking on propaganda is very much in line with my own. He draws important attention to different sources and trajectories of propaganda, showing that it can move vertically or horizontally and that it derives from both elites and the broad public. Following his discussion, I find it useful to distinguish between two different kinds of propagandists. First, there are *deliberate propagandists*, who consciously design manipulative and self-serving discourse and who seek to get that discourse recontextualized on a mass scale.[3] Second, there are *unwitting propagandists*, who spread propaganda downstream, without necessarily having first designed it, without necessarily seeking to influence a mass audience, and without necessarily seeking to manipulate anyone for selfish ends.[4] A deliberate propagandist might be a government official who tells self-serving lies during a press conference. Meanwhile, an unwitting propagandist might be the reporter who uncritically prints the official's speech or the Twitter user who shares the reporter's story with a dozen followers.

I think we can clarify how all propaganda works by adopting an intertextual perspective. Such a perspective accounts for both classical top-down propaganda and unwitting sociological propaganda. It allows for the possibility that propaganda can serve the interests of the Few, without insisting that every propagandist seeks a selfish advantage.

Theorizing Propaganda from an Intertextual Perspective

Intertextuality is the notion that texts are interrelated, that any text is composed of other texts and bears traces of them (Fairclough 2003, 39). More broadly, it means that any text's meaning depends on other texts. We often understand what a text is "saying" because we recognize in it generic meanings we've observed before (Thibault 1991). In this regard, propaganda is inherently intertextual. Take, for example, a political ad insinuating Barack Obama is a Muslim (Krakauer 2010). We may label the ad as propaganda—not just because it is misleading and Islam-ophobic but because it is not the only one of its kind. There are identical ads, and copious other texts, that share the same generic meaning and constitute a larger propaganda campaign.

It is wrong, however, to treat intertextuality as a static relationship between texts. Instead, it is helpful to view it as a communicative process. After all, when two texts share the same meaning, it is because the person who designed the second text recontextualized a meaning from the first—knowingly or unknowingly extracting some element from the "original" and repurposing it in a new context. Such recon-textualization can happen unknowingly because we may rearticulate preexisting meanings without intending to or without realizing that what we've said has been said before. The agent who recontextualizes discourse need not have the same inten-tion as the original source. Indeed, recontextualizing agents transform original dis-course (Linell 1998), reshaping original meanings to meet the demands of new rhetorical situations.

We can also consider this communicative process from the perspective of the "original" speaker. This speaker is part of a "living dialogue" with future interlocutors and aims discourse at a future response (Bakhtin 1981, 280). As Bakhtin explains, the original discourse is "directly, blatantly oriented toward a future answer-word: it provokes an answer, anticipates it and structures itself in the answer's direction" (280). All discourse has this anticipatory property, signaling what response is desired and expected (Halliday and Matthiessen 2004, 108). For example, if I offer informa-tion in a declarative assertion, I signal my expectation that my addressee will acknowledge (and not contradict) me (108).

What makes much propaganda discourse special is that the desired response is not just acknowledgment but repetition. Such propaganda is designed to be recontextualized extensively and with some degree of semantic consistency. Deliberate propagandists, in particular, want their discourse to be replicated: repeated broadly and without much change to the "original" sense.

Ridolfo and DeVoss (2009) capture this future-oriented thinking with their concept of rhetorical velocity. As they explain, "Rhetorical velocity is the strategic theorizing for how a text might be recomposed . . . by third parties, and how this recomposing may be useful or not to the short- or long-term rhetorical objectives of the rhetorician." Those interested in rhetorical velocity—for our purposes, deliberate propagandists—consider "the speed at which information . . . travels . . . across physical and virtual spaces." They contemplate "the working conditions of the third party and what type of text it would be useful (or not) to provide." They think about which segments of their discourse will be useful for someone else's media production. And they consider future times and places of "recomposition"— the conditions under which their discourse will be recontextualized by someone else. Ultimately, deliberate propagandists try to facilitate a future text trajectory favorable to them, maximizing the possibility that others will circulate their discourse, while ensuring that any recontextualization will be beneficial to their own objectives.

Of course, even unwitting propagandists, who don't necessarily intend to maximize rhetorical velocity, may design discourse that gets repeated broadly. We need not insist that every propagandist deliberately crafts messages so that others will reuse them. Instead, we may ask more generally: how do propagandists create discourse, whether strategically or unintentionally, that is likely to be recontextualized? Bauman and Briggs (1990) offer some useful suggestions. They note that before a stretch of discourse can be recontextualized, it must first be entextualized. That is, it must be recognized as text: something that is "extractable" and "decontextualizable," something "that can be lifted out of its interactional setting" (73). Importantly, Bauman and Briggs argue, a speaker can "render stretches of discourse discontinuous with their discursive surround, thus making them into coherent, effective, and memorable texts" (73–74). They can endow their discourse with "prepared-for detachability" (74), signaling to audiences that certain stretches of linguistic production are potentially reusable.

Such signals can be explicit, as speakers may provide "instructions about how . . . discourse is to be approached as text" (Urban 1996, 33). For example, one can use metalinguistic cues that help objectify a stretch of discourse and suggest its repeatability (e.g., "A point that bears repeating is . . ."). Other cues, however, may suggest something is not "copiable" or "shareable" in a new context (24): false starts, hesitations, or speaking errors. As Bauman and Briggs (1990) stress, performative semiotics play an important role in rendering discourse extractable. Many poetic devices—parallelism, repetition, vocal stress, dramatic pausing—call attention to themselves and make decontextualization more likely. Other performative features may make a text more memorable and comprehensible. For example, as Van Dijk (2006) explains, listeners more easily understand speech pronounced slowly and distinctly, with simple syntax and vocabulary. Those who speak accordingly maximize comprehension and may induce listeners to re-present their meanings. Likewise, "if speakers wish to hamper understanding"—and prevent others from remembering and repeating their discourse—they will "speak faster and less distinctly, with more complex sentences [and] abstruse words" (366).

Multimodal signals may also indicate which discourse is unique and potentially removable—a border drawn around words, a change in music. Often textual layout is used strategically to help audiences see something as more important and memorable than surrounding discourse. For example, bold and salient text, such as a newspaper headline, is used to express "semantic macrostructures" and is thus more likely to be noticed, recalled, and, presumably, repeated (365). The physical form of a message can also impact its portability. A "Support Our Troops" magnet is recontextualizable not only because of it language but because the slogan is inscribed on material that can be removed and redisplayed in multiple contexts.

As Urban argues, "Some kinds of discourse are intrinsically more shareable than others." A metadiscursive cue (e.g., "My claim is") is less repeatable than what comes after it (e.g., "propaganda is intertextual"). However, whether "some kinds of discourse make for better culture" is ultimately a question of whose culture one is trying to enter (Urban 1996, 24). A politician trying to be heard in the culture of journalism finds that certain discourse is more likely to be recognized as valuable and repeatable (Cramer 2013). Specifically, TV news producers value discourse that is pithy, sensational, and striking, such as sound bites that contain intense evaluation and highlight conflict and drama. These are "desired qualities" in the press (Bauman and Briggs 1990, 77), and politicians often seek to index them. But such qualities may be less desirable in different contexts. A pithy insult may not be counted as shareable for a pastor delivering a sermon.

However, purely linguistic features are never enough to guarantee a stretch of discourse will be recontextualized favorably. My Uncle Frank may produce political zingers till the cows come home, but he is very unlikely to have his discourse published in the *New York Times*. And even if, miraculously, his discourse was published in the *Times*, it is quite unlikely that his words would make the front page and quite likely that they would be challenged, distorted, and undermined. In many (if not most) contexts, discourse is viewed as replicable not because of what is said but because of who is saying it. Certain speakers claim a more powerful voice, which Blommaert (2005, 68) helpfully defines as the "capacity to generate an uptake of one's words as close as possible to one's desired contextualisation." In other words, voice is the power to be understood in the ways you intend. As such, it is also the "*capacity for semiotic mobility*" (69; emphasis in original)—the power to have your desired meanings travel across time and space.

Here we see why, while theoretically anyone can spread propaganda, powerful actors have a distinct advantage. They have access to texts and contexts that many of the rest of us don't. "Symbolic elites"—politicians, journalists, business leaders, and public intellectuals—have "preferential access to mass media and public discourse." Their words are more shareable in mass-media contexts: news, books, TV programs, advertising, and so on (Van Dijk 2006, 362). And so, their "valued meanings" are often mediated, "carried over and historically propagated," while "other meanings are devalued and 'filtered out'" (Graham 2004, 57).

Put another way, symbolic elites are best equipped to "keep control over entextualisation processes" (Blommaert 2005, 78). Granted, no one has total control over how audiences recontextualize their discourse. But elites are often assumed to have an authoritative voice, so their discourse is "maximally protected from compromising transformation" (Bauman and Briggs 1990, 77) and is more impervious to being challenged and undermined. Politicians, for example, may induce the press to faithfully recontextualize their propaganda because their voices are deemed inherently repeatable. Indeed, official voices are so desirable that journalists typically calibrate their news coverage according to the range of government debate (Bennett 1990). When debate is limited, "the press becomes more a government mouthpiece" that consistently repeats the voices of Washington (Bennett, Lawrence, and Livingston 2007, 39).

Meanwhile, the voices of ordinary people are rarely deemed worthy of recontextualization in the news (68–70) and are less protected from being unfavorably transformed. Journalists might distort what ordinary people say, yet the journalists' interpretation may become "common sense." This speaks to a general principle: the more powerful you are, the better able you are to recontextualize someone else's discourse however you like while ensuring that your recontextualization "counts as legitimate" (Bauman and Briggs 1990, 77).

Besides cultural prestige, elite actors also have the materials "to create favourable conditions for a desired uptake" (Blommaert 2005, 68). As Bernays ([1928] 2005, 119) explains, elites are capable of "creating circumstances" that ensure propaganda resonates. For example, they can provide incentives, whether monetary or otherwise, to agents who spread their propaganda: public relations specialists, opinion leaders, or activists. Some refer to this incentivizing as "subpropaganda" or "facilitative communication"—granting favors or creating "a friendly atmosphere toward those who may be needed" to spread a message (Jowett and O'Donnell 2015, 31).

In our terms, these are simply ways of inducing an audience to recontextualize one's discourse favorably. Indeed, paying people to replicate your propaganda can be much more efficient than prompting them exclusively through language. This is why the "invisible government," Bernays explains, "tends to be concentrated in the hands of the few." It is "because of the expense of manipulating the social machinery which controls the opinions and habits of the masses. To advertise on a scale which will reach fifty million persons is expensive. To reach and persuade the group leaders who dictate the public's thoughts and actions is likewise expensive" (Bernays [1928] 2005, 63). Bernays overstates how much elites control the public mind, but we should not discount his observations about their financial power to induce "deputies and lesser troops" into recontextualizing desired meanings (Miller 2005, 22).

Ultimately, many factors influence whether a stretch of discourse will become propaganda. First, to succeed as propaganda, discourse must be considered detachable and repeatable. (See appendix B for details). In other words, propaganda will entail semiotic signals—whether contextual or rhetorical—that suggest that some stretch of discourse is comparatively more worthy of recontextualization, that it ought to be considered more reusable than surrounding discourse or competing discourse in the intertextual universe. Discourse can seem detachable and reusable either because of its design and content or because of extralinguistic factors, such as the agents and resources behind it. Generally, elites are most capable of signaling their discourse is shareable in mass media. They often induce extensive recontextualization, especially if they design their discourse effectively and, even more so, if they pay others to repeat it.

However, even symbolic elites cannot guarantee that their messages will circulate, since the effectiveness of any propaganda claim ultimately depends on "the interpretive web into which it enters" (Hodges 2008a, 10). Propaganda stays alive, carrying on its intertextual journey, only if audiences continue to recontextualize it downstream. Indeed, we can imagine a continuum of recontextualization practices that lead variously to propaganda success or failure. On one end of the scale is failed propaganda, wherein the message is either ignored or unfavorably recontextualized.[5] In cases of failure, the deliberate propagandist must either give up or try again (and again) to induce a positive uptake. In more successful cases, propaganda is recontextualized favorably: the message is re-presented as fact, it is legitimized, or better yet, it is taken for granted as an assumption as it becomes an unquestioned "black box" (Latour 1987). Of course, we must also consider the scale and duration of recontextualization. A message is most likely to flourish as propaganda when it is recontextualized repeatedly by (and for) huge numbers of people, especially if it is continually recontextualized over a long duration.

Figure 1 shows the range of possibilities. Here, we imagine a slogan—"Support Our Troops"—whose destiny as propaganda depends on an intertextual process. The slogan succeeds as propaganda as it tends toward the bottom of the diagram—as it is faithfully recontextualized by many parties, across media platforms, day after day.

Propaganda may be circulated by politicians boosting policies, public relations firms and advertisers maximizing profits, journalists selling newspapers, or ordinary people seeking nothing more than the exchange of ideas. It may move vertically from

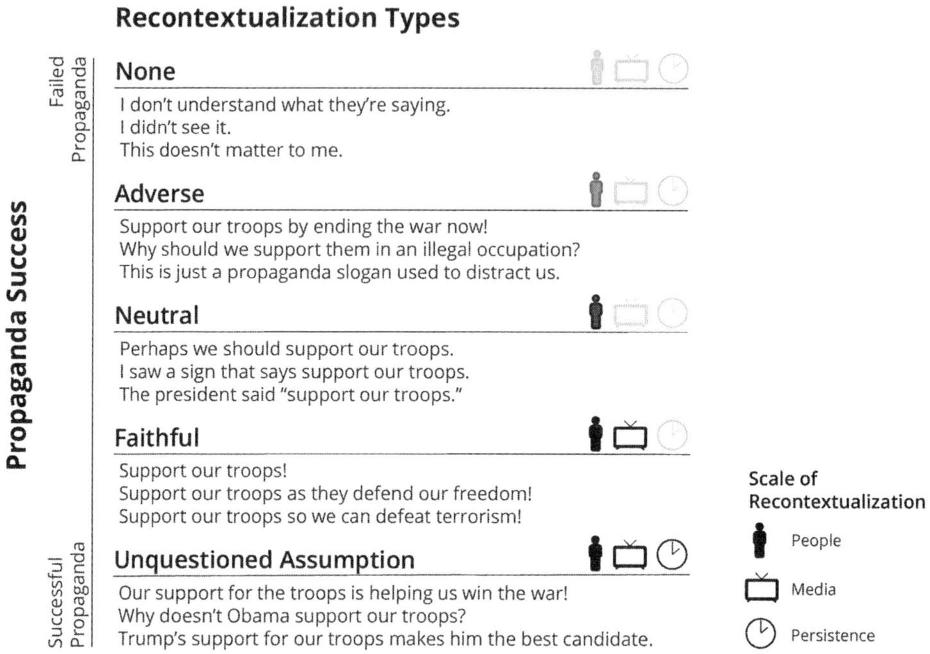

Recontextualization Types

Propaganda Success

Failed Propaganda

None

I don't understand what they're saying.
I didn't see it.
This doesn't matter to me.

Adverse

Support our troops by ending the war now!
Why should we support them in an illegal occupation?
This is just a propaganda slogan used to distract us.

Neutral

Perhaps we should support our troops.
I saw a sign that says support our troops.
The president said "support our troops."

Faithful

Support our troops!
Support our troops as they defend our freedom!
Support our troops so we can defeat terrorism!

Unquestioned Assumption

Our support for the troops is helping us win the war!
Why doesn't Obama support our troops?
Trump's support for our troops makes him the best candidate.

Successful Propaganda

Scale of Recontextualization

- People
- Media
- Persistence

Figure 1 Propaganda success depends on type and scale of recontextualization

leaders to the public or horizontally across a social network. But in all cases, it requires intertextual dialogue. No person or group can do it alone. To achieve "semiotic mobility" the propaganda must change hands (Blommaert 2005, 69). It must continually induce new audiences to entextualize and recontextualize some meaning, keeping that meaning more or less resistant to compromising change.

Manipulation as Key Feature of Propaganda Discourse

One might define "propaganda" exclusively as discourse that is faithfully recontextualized on a mass scale. This simple definition has the advantage of being neutral. It avoids passing judgment and focuses on what can be measured empirically: whether discourse propagates. While such a neutral definition has its merits, I believe propaganda should also be defined in political and ethical terms. After all, "propaganda" has historically meant not just far-reaching discourse but discourse that is immoral. And I don't think we can, or should, purge the word of its negative associations. Indeed, if we accept that "propaganda" implies bad rhetoric, then we need to wade into the murky waters of morality when defining it, touching upon questions of right and wrong, while acknowledging that there are no universal values and that there are different views of the political good.

With this in mind, I extend my definition of "propaganda" to include not just discourse that succeeds in inducing mass-recontextualization but discourse that also manipulates people. Before going further, I should make several points. First, it is useful to imagine manipulative discourse on a spectrum. On one end is open, democratic dialogue that welcomes different perspectives and champions the will to truth. On the other end is autocratic monologue that conceals opposing viewpoints (or declares them worthless), practices deceit and censorship, and respects only the will to power. Across the middle is everything from a slight overstatement to the self-interested framing of a controversy or misleading arguments that nudge audiences toward prechosen conclusions. Insofar as widely circulated discourse tends toward egregious manipulation, we can confidently call it propaganda, but there are borderline cases.

Next, discourse can be manipulative without a conscious manipulator. Again, manipulators (or deliberate propagandists) certainly exist. But manipulative discourse can spread without a Machiavellian ringleader. Indeed, manipulation can simply involve one perspective becoming so dominant that other perspectives go unnoticed. This does not necessitate a conspiracy by an external agent but a propaganda system wherein certain truth claims are more shareable than others. That said, dominant groups have "an inherent advantage" in circulating manipulative discourse, "especially during crisis periods in which anticritical trends [are] in force" (Sproule 1989, 236). Meanwhile, others face significant constraints, often lacking "sufficient control of media and other instruments of power" (Stanley 2015, 162).

Finally, as Van Dijk (2006, 372) argues, we must go beyond linguistic techniques when evaluating manipulation. A technique that is manipulative in one context may not be in another. Indeed, not everyone is equally susceptible to manipulation. Even deliberate propagandists cannot simply "infuse their messages into a passive or irrational public" (Sproule 1989, 236). Some will be "impervious to manipulation" and will expose and counter manipulative claims (Van Dijk 2006, 375). Thus, analysts need to address how discourse is interpreted in real situations. Furthermore, when considering manipulation, they should factor in the social consequences of discourse and how it contributes to existing relations of power and domination. I return to this point later in the chapter, but first, I review some overlapping categories of manipulative language.[6]

Positive Self-Representation and Negative Other Representation

Perhaps the most powerful mechanism of manipulation is the overall strategy of positive self-presentation and negative other-presentation (Van Dijk 2006, 373). This semantic strategy relies on a dichotomy between "Us" and "Them": our positive characteristics and their negative ones are emphasized, while our negative characteristics and their positive ones are ignored. Such ideological polarization is evident in all propaganda (Van Dijk 1998), but it is especially evident in war propaganda (Ivie 1980; Van Dijk 2006; Hodges 2015), where we are framed as "good and innocent protagonists" forced to fight their "evil aggressors" (Oddo 2011, 289).

Hart explains that this polarizing discourse is effective largely because of evolutionary psychology. Human cognition has evolved such that we are "biologically prepared" to consider out-group members a potential threat to survival (Hart 2010, 52–54). This is not to say, however, that prejudice against "Them" is innate. Instead, inborn cognitive mechanisms are exploited by language users who associate an out-group with an inflated sense of "negativity or threat" (60).

Emotional Coercion

Contrary to popular belief, emotions are not opposed to rational thought; instead, they are "an integral part of cognitive processing" (Hart 2010, 80). In fact, speakers can activate our emotions to help us make good, prosocial decisions. By appealing to your sense of empathy, one can motivate you to help someone in need. By shouting "Look out!" one can activate your "fear module" (80) and spur you to avoid an incoming foul ball. The problem is that discourse may also be used in Machiavellian ways, as people "falsely induce" emotions for their own advantage (81). For example, Hart (2010) reports, people can exploit emotional vocabulary to activate fear and anger, coercing a negative reaction even when there is little to be fearful or angry about. One neurological study found that when people are presented with threat-connoting words—such as "danger," "damage," "destroy," and "intrude"—their amygdalae are activated (Isenberg et al. 1999). Bear in mind these words alone activated the brain's emotional center. One can only imagine what cognitive effect such words have when used repeatedly to characterize an out-group.

Closely related to emotionally tinged language are proximization strategies, which work by construing a "deictic center," a point in space occupied by speaker and addressee (Cap 2006, 2013). This deictic center can be represented as either "close to" or "distant from" other actors and events. According to Cap (2006, 2013), proximization strategies are exploited especially in war propaganda, in which the enemy is construed as (1) threatening our physical space, (2) poised to attack in time, and (3) impinging upon our cherished values. Such discourse "reinforces emotive coercion," insofar as it presents a remote or nonexistent threat as close at hand (Hart 2010, 85).

Misleading Representations and Arguments

Propaganda can also manipulate if it misleads people through lies, half-truths, and fallacious reasoning. First, there is out-and-out fabrication, where the propagandist construes reality in ways that are demonstrably false. More common is distortion, where the speaker does not tell an outright lie but may exaggerate via hyperbole or minimize the reality of a situation through euphemism. Somewhere in between fabrication and distortion lies doublespeak, a term derived from George Orwell's (1949) classic novel *1984*.[7] Doublespeak occurs when something is named precisely to give a false impression of what it actually is—for example, when presidential aide Kellyanne Conway used the phrase "alternative facts" to describe what were, in reality, the Trump administration's shameless lies.

Another key strategy is "manipulative silence," whereby an agent withholds crucial information that, if disclosed, would alter one's perception of events (Huckin 2002, 351; 2010). Using silence, a propagandist can avoid offering false assertions yet still mislead the audience. For example, Franklin Delano Roosevelt (1941) did not lie when he said a German submarine had torpedoed an American ship, the USS *Greer*. However, he omitted that the *Greer* had been attacking the submarine for three hours before the Germans fired back (Oddo 2011, 292). As G. K. Chesterton said, "Selection is the fine art of falsity. . . . [G]ive me the right to pick out anything and I shall not need to invent anything" (quoted in Marlin 2013, xvii).

Aside from false and selective representations, there are also misleading arguments, a statement or group of statements implying a false conclusion or otherwise pressuring audiences to perform some unwarranted action.[8] Even a string of factual assertions can lead people to make false inferences. For example, to justify the 2003 Iraq War, President George W. Bush (2002b) used arguments by transitivity to implicate Saddam Hussein in the terrorist attacks of September 11, 2001. According to Perelman and Olbrechts-Tyteca (1969, 227), arguments by transitivity make it possible to infer that because a relationship exists between A and B and between B and C, a relationship also exists between A and C. In Bush's address, the argument takes the following form: Iraq is related to al-Qaeda, al-Qaeda is related to the 9/11 attacks; therefore, Iraq is related to the 9/11 attacks: "We know that Iraq and the al Qaeda terrorist network share a common enemy—the United States of America. We know that Iraq and al Qaeda have had high-level contacts that go back a decade. Some al Qaeda leaders who fled Afghanistan went to Iraq. . . . We've learned that Iraq has trained al Qaeda members in bomb-making and poisons and deadly gases. And we know that after September the 11th, Saddam Hussein's regime gleefully celebrated the terrorist attacks on America" (Bush 2002b). Here, Bush falls short of explicitly concluding that Iraq was involved in the 9/11 attacks. Instead, he entices listeners to draw this conclusion on their own. Thus, he could plausibly deny he made false assertions before the war, even as he misled 64 percent of Americans into believing Saddam Hussein helped terrorists conduct the 9/11 strikes (Pew Research Center 2002).

Manipulation of Dialogic Space

Ideally, any democratic debate should welcome "diverse reasonable perspectives" (Stanley 2015, 107), especially the perspectives of citizens who are directly affected by the policy under discussion. Stanley extends this principle as holding between citizens of different nations. When the actions of one nation impinge upon the citizens of another, it is important to hear those other citizens' perspectives. Thus, when America launches a war in another country, Stanley argues, American citizens should have the opportunity to hear from "a member of a population being invaded and . . . bombed." Instead, "a paradigm way that propaganda in a democratic society manifests is by representing [some] perspectives . . . as unworthy of consideration" (122).

Of course, alternative perspectives can be actively discredited (Oddo 2014a). For example, one can call "Them" liars and manipulators as a way of suggesting their views are suspicious and unworthy of examination. But propaganda may also work more subtly, by closing down the space for dialogic alternatives (Martin and White 2005). This can involve:

- flatly negating an alternative assertion (e.g., "Iraqi officials deny accusations of ties with Al Qaida. These denials are simply *not credible*" [Powell 2003]);
- "fending off" a competing view by countering it with a preferred locution (e.g., "There has been a tendency to emphasize the weapons of mass destruction issue, *but . . . the real thing* that has concerned the President . . . is the connection between terrorism and weapons of mass destruction" [Wolfowitz 2003]); or
- proclaiming the special warrantability of your own view (e.g., "*We know* that [Saddam] has a long-standing relationship with various terrorist groups, including the al Qaeda organization" [Cheney 2003]).

Even more significantly, one can avoid any reference to an alternative viewpoint, completely excluding different perspectives while presenting one's own assertions as categorical facts (Fairclough 2003, 41).

This brings us back to Huckin's (2002, 2010) notion of manipulative silence, as propaganda can involve the omission of not only individual voices but also entire discourses. Indeed, we may find that some intertextual systems provide little or no dialogic space for disagreeable worldviews. Orwell (1949) describes the process of systematic omission in *1984*, as the government of Oceania methodically erases meanings—voices, people, events—from its history books and press reports. Simultaneously, the government invents a new language, Newspeak, whose chief function is to eliminate words from the old language. As Orwell explains it, "the whole aim of Newspeak is to narrow the range of thought" (52). Specifically, "heretical thought" and "unorthodox opinions" become "literally unthinkable" (300, 310), precisely because no words exist to express them.

Of course, in America, no central authority is eliminating English words. But the notion of "narrowing the range of thought" remains important, particularly in the context of journalism. A key question is whether news reports include a diversity of viewpoints or if certain frames are being systematically ignored or underrepresented. Entman (2004, 48) argues that, in a free press, news discourse ought to exhibit "frame parity," where "two (or more) interpretations" of an issue receive "something like equal play." So, for instance, a pro-war frame advanced by a presidential administration ought to be opposed in the press by an "equally well-developed" antiwar frame. Ideally, this counterframe would have "as much magnitude and resonance as the administration's" (48), but, in practice, Entman finds one frame usually dominates. The alternative view may be presented but only in "ill-digested and scattered morsels" (17).

Herman and Chomsky (2002) make a similar observation. They argue that news content is generally shaped by "filters" that tend to produce propagandistic reporting: (1) corporate ownership, (2) dependence on advertising revenue, (3) reliance on official sources, (4) discipline from government, and (5) conformity with the dominant ideology. These filters work to narrow the range of democratic debate, keeping "dissent and inconvenient information . . . within bounds and at the margins" while ultimately ensuring "the domination of the official agenda" (xii). In other words, dissenting voices may be recontextualized in mainstream media but less often and in more delegitimizing ways. In fact, Chomsky (1992, 68) argues, instead of State-run propaganda, America has a "privatized system of propaganda," involving the media, intellectuals, and other opinion leaders. This privatized system is not as all-controlling as a totalitarian system (Herman and Chomsky 2002, xii), but, Chomsky says, it produces the similar result of reducing "the entire spectrum of thinkable thoughts" (1992, 73).

Propaganda as Defined by Societal Consequences

In Brazil, the Ministry of Health requires tobacco companies to issue warning labels on cigarette packages (Freeman 2010). One label shows a human torso after an autopsy. The corpse is ripped open, exposing bloody organs underneath the skin, and there is a hole in the throat, evidently from a tracheotomy. Above, in bold white letters, is the word "DEATH," and below is a caption: "Use of this product leads to death from lung cancer and emphysema."[9] This warning is circulated broadly and intertextually. In a sense, the Brazilian government has induced tobacco companies to recontextualize the government's meaning on a massive scale. Arguably, the warning is also manipulative. The image is emotionally coercive, triggering deep-rooted instincts of fear and disgust. And the text is somewhat misleading. Cigarettes do not simply "lead to death." Presumably, one would need to smoke them regularly. And even then, death from lung cancer and emphysema is not guaranteed. In short, the assertion is too categorical; it leaves no space for dialogic alternatives that might qualify its claim. Are such warning labels therefore propaganda?

Before contemplating an answer, let's consider another case. Recently in the United States, there have been demonstrations carrying the banner "Black Lives Matter" (BLM). The BLM slogan has been recontextualized widely—not only on picket signs but also on T-shirts and bumper stickers and as a popular hashtag on Twitter. It has been especially visible in the aftermath of high-profile cases in which police officers (or others) have shot and killed unarmed African Americans, only to escape penalty.

Again, the slogan has circulated extensively through processes of entextualization and recontextualization; it has propagated. And one could argue that it is manipulative. For example, the slogan may pressure people into accepting the demands of the BLM movement, simply so they can avoid unfair criticism. After all, to insist black lives matter is to imply that others believe black lives *don't* matter. Thus, some might have reasonable arguments against the movement's demands but might inhibit expression of such arguments because they fear being accused of undervaluing black lives. In addition, one could object to the slogan when it is used in mass demonstrations. Arguably, such demonstrations are manipulative since they preclude rational discussion and the exchange of "diverse reasonable perspectives" (Stanley 2015, 107). Shouting a slogan violates norms of democratic debate. Indeed, the protest chant fails to treat listeners as equal "coparticipant[s] in decision-making" and clearly "seeks to limit the field of choice open to the audience" (Bennett and O'Rourke 2006, 66–67). So, is the BLM slogan propaganda?

Democratic Propaganda?

According to Stanley (2015, 59), both the BLM slogan and the antismoking warning labels are propaganda, specifically "democratically acceptable" propaganda. This is "a kind of propaganda that is politically necessary . . . to overcome fundamental obstacles to the realization of democratic ideals" (109–10). Regarding the cigarette labels, Stanley argues, the Ministry of Health is performing a democratic duty, since it is tasked with safeguarding the health of citizens who may not appreciate the dangers of tobacco. The citizens, he says, have "tacitly granted . . . permission to the ministry of health to take such steps" (59). Insofar as the labels are sanctioned by citizens and used to deter a known health risk, they are "democratically acceptable" (59).

Stanley would also argue that the BLM slogan is legitimate propaganda. Granted, the slogan may pressure audiences, but this may be necessary to "force a dominant majority to expand the domain of respect and empathy to include a persecuted and ignored minority" (111). Indeed, the slogan draws attention to white supremacy and the systematic targeting of African Americans. As one slogan creator explains, "Black Lives Matter" seeks to affirm the human rights and dignity of black people in the face of disproportionate poverty, mass incarceration, and "extrajudicial killings . . . by police and vigilantes" (Garza 2014). It aims to secure for black people the same democratic and human rights already enjoyed by the white majority.

It may also be true that, when used in a mass protest, the slogan violates norms of rational debate. But, as Stanley (2015, 115) further observes, "there is no obvious way that members of the group whose perspectives are invisible could use reasonable claims in public political discourse to compel their fellow citizens into recognizing their perspectives." In other words, the perspectives of African Americans would not be heard were it not for mass demonstrations. The demonstrations help put "invisible" perspectives on the agenda, provoking democratic discussion about policies affecting a disenfranchised group.

We can infer from Stanley's (2015) work that democratically acceptable propaganda has several characteristics:

- It serves the public interest by drawing attention to either an indisputable danger or the views of a marginalized or victimized group. The latter case serves the public interest because it helps "make an allegedly democratic state into a genuinely democratic state" (119).
- The discourse comes from either democratically accountable groups who have been sanctioned by the people or marginalized groups whose perspectives have been ignored. A warning about public health is legitimate if it comes from a government body that is accepted by citizens, even-handedly draws from the best available research, releases evidence for its claims, and is answerable for misconduct. A protest is acceptable if it gives voice to a marginalized perspective. It would be less acceptable if it were, say, secretly organized by self-interested elites.
- The discourse does not mislead. Granted, there may be some embellishment or stridency. Speakers might exaggerate or pressure audiences. However, they don't fabricate or steer people toward false conclusions. Thus, the cigarette label may overstate the case that smoking causes death, but the label is not really misleading. After all, overwhelming evidence supports the somewhat more modest assertion that regular smoking typically leads to disease and death. And, arguably, some overstatement and emotional coercion is necessary to catch the attention of people who are addicted to cigarettes and, thus, are unable to make fully rational decisions (313 n. 29).

I generally agree with Stanley that we should try to distinguish between democratic propaganda and illegitimate propaganda. However, I don't think the word "propaganda" should even be used for democratically acceptable communication. Rather than call it propaganda, which has such negative connotations, I prefer Stanley's other term for such discourse: "civic rhetoric" (5). Civic rhetoric may be recontextualized extensively, reaching vast numbers of people. It may even be to some degree coercive. But in my view, it is not propaganda because it is democratic, serving the public interest and encouraging the realization of human and constitutional rights.

Dominance by the Few

By contrast, we can say that propaganda—in addition to being widespread and manipulative—is undemocratic, serving the interests of the Few while harming the interests of the Many. When I say "the Few," I do not mean a numerical minority. For example, African Americans may be fewer than the white majority, but they are not the Few. Instead, the Few tend to be dominant groups who have enormous social and material power (or groups trying to ascend to power by exploiting and victimizing more marginalized communities). Following Van Dijk (2006, 364), we can say that propaganda is illegitimate in a democracy because "it is in the best interests of" these more dominant groups and "hurts the interests of less powerful groups and speakers." This means propaganda is not defined by the intentions of the communicator or by the "conscious awareness of manipulation by the recipients." Instead, it is defined "in terms of societal consequences" (364). It is propaganda if it consolidates the power of one group while harming the interests of subordinate groups.

That said, the difference between propaganda and civic rhetoric is not always clear-cut. Again, it is helpful to imagine not a binary distinction but a spectrum of discourse ranging from the egregiously bad to the sublimely good. On one end of the cline is discourse that nearly everyone recognizes as antidemocratic propaganda: clear cases of dishonesty, racism, and tyranny that harm vulnerable members of society. On the other end is discourse that nearly everyone recognizes as egalitarian civic rhetoric: widely accepted statements about equality, fairness, and justice. In the middle are disputed cases: discourse that some see as ethical and just but others see as harmful. However, even if we imagine this spectrum, we inevitably run into problems. Most of what is called propaganda falls into the muddled middle of the continuum. And even at the poles, there are always detractors: while most people see Martin Luther King Jr.'s speeches as civic rhetoric, some regard them as vile propaganda. Indeed, every case presented as propaganda in this book will surely strike some readers as entirely justified rhetoric.

A reasonable person might wonder: Who gets to decide when discourse is democratically acceptable? Conversely, who gets to decide what social harm is, who has been harmed, and if propaganda has contributed to the harm? Does a scholar, for example, have the right to decide what is harmful, or is this just imposing one's viewpoint on the world? My answer is straightforward. Scholars cannot decide for everyone when discourse is harmful and for whom. No one can. However, I believe that scholars can and should argue that certain discourse is destructive and that certain people are victimized as a result. Why? Because to be a scholar is to engage with the world, and that engagement includes making claims about what is beneficial or detrimental. This does not mean any scholar has the final word on the subject; others can and will disagree. Indeed, readers are free to dispute my arguments, but to avoid making them or to disguise them in the language of scholarly detachment are solutions I find untenable.

The best any of us can do, I think, is to make our assumptions and values clear. For example, I assume there is an asymmetry of power in the United States—inequality whereby dominant groups exert undue control over sociopolitical affairs. Some readers may find this assumption unwarranted. So, I will do my best to support this claim with evidence: Over the past thirty years, a huge share of U.S. economic growth has gone to the top one hundredth of 1 percent of income earners, "who now make an average of $27 million per household," while average income for the bottom 90 percent is $31,244 (Gilson and Perot 2011). The thirty richest people in America own as much as half of the U.S. population: "That's 30 people owning as much as 157,000,000 people" (Buchheit 2014). The wealth gap is correlated with divergent outcomes in health and education, as the rich enjoy better health and superior schools (Porter 2013).

Crucially, the wealth gap also gives the richest Americans vastly more political power. In a statistical study of over 1,700 issues, Gilens and Page (2014, 565) find that average citizens have virtually "no independent influence" on U.S. policy, but economic elites and business interests have "substantial independent impacts." Elite money dominates elections (Gold and Narayanswamy 2015), and interest groups have unmatched power to lobby politicians and propagandize to the public (Drutman 2015; Quinn and Young 2015). Some corporate interest groups actually write public legislation, often getting this legislation passed by politicians whose campaigns they support (Moyers 2012). Meanwhile, there is a revolving door between government and the private sector, so politicians are frequently guaranteed corporate jobs after leaving office (and after they have done the bidding of their future employers). There is also a "reverse revolving door," whereby corporate insiders receive bonuses when they leave their jobs for positions in government (Fang 2013). As Gilens and Page (2014, 567) put it, "All but the most dedicated skeptic is likely to perceive interest-group influence at work." Indeed, they continue, "ordinary citizens get what they want from government only when they happen to agree with elites or interest groups that are really calling the shots" (573).

Corporate dominance is especially apparent in mass communication and mainstream journalism. As of 2013, six corporations controlled 90 percent of American media (Lutz 2012). These corporations often maximize profits by focusing on uncritical entertainment that keeps advertisers and CEOs happy (Jackson 2014). Investigative watchdog journalism costs more than routine stories on Washington politics, so the press over-depends on government sources, without reflecting the views of ordinary citizens (Bennett, Lawrence, and Livingston 2007; Entman 2004; Herman and Chomsky 2002). The result is too often a "monochromatic media" (Wolin 2008, 7) that is "inherently contradictory to the values of democracy" (Morrison 2011).

Finally, the power of the State has also grown enormously, jeopardizing the ideal of government by, for, and of the people. Granted, the U.S. government was never designed to offer citizens direct sovereignty over political affairs. As Gilens and Page (2014, 573) write, "Because of the impediments to majority rule that were deliberately built into the U.S. political system . . . the system has a substantial status quo bias."

However, the U.S. government has gone beyond "status quo bias," securing for itself a number of "extraconstitutional" powers (Wolin 2008, 43).

According to Sheldon Wolin (2008, 46), the government may even be headed toward a new kind of totalitarianism, which he calls "inverted totalitarianism." Wolin argues that participatory, social democracy has been replaced by "managed democracy" (47), where citizens vote in contrived elections or offer opinions on polls but otherwise do not participate in directing the nation's political affairs. Meanwhile, as the United States has emerged as a superpower—a power never authorized by the Constitution—it has also enacted apparently authoritarian policies, which are always justified in the name of security. Domination abroad is mirrored by domination at home (192): wiretapping of private communications; indefinite detention of criminal suspects; mass incarceration of huge segments of the population; programs dedicated to torturing alleged enemies; undeclared wars; extrajudicial killings of both foreign "militants" and American citizens (including those killed by increasingly militarized police forces); "phobia about leaks to the press"; prosecution of whistleblowers; and a "zeal for stamping documents from the distant past as 'classified,' and thus shaping future interpretations" of history (133).

War Propaganda and the Interests of the Many

Examining this list of Orwellian practices, one may better understand how Wolin concludes that the U.S. government is moving toward a new "species of totalitarianism" (52). At the very least, it is clear that the emerging "union of corporate and state power" represents a real menace to democracy (137). Propaganda is the name assigned to discourse that reinforces or supports such antidemocratic tendencies. More specifically, successful propaganda may be defined as mass-recontextualized and manipulative discourse that promotes the power of the Few while harming the interests of the Many. Of course, the Many may help spread propaganda, even as they are harmed by it. Meanwhile, the Few who benefit from propaganda could be already powerful groups (governments, corporate oligarchs, public relations professionals, advertisers, and so on) or groups (white supremacists, for example) trying to ascend to power by victimizing "Others."

As noted, no person can unilaterally decide when discourse violates the interests of the Many, and any argument about what qualifies as propaganda is bound to be disputed. This is particularly true with war discourse, which always claims to be protecting vulnerable citizens from an enemy threat and, therefore, serving the public interest. Thus, I want to be very clear about how I try to assess when call-to-arms discourse amounts to harmful propaganda. As I see it, the government can make legitimate claims about the need for violence. As in the case of cigarette warnings, it may be necessary to disseminate powerful discourse in order to raise the alarm about a true threat to public safety. However, discourse used to justify war may be antidemocratic propaganda if it conceals or fails to account for the perspectives of those most impacted by the proposed violence (e.g., citizens of another country). Moreover, as soon as that discourse lies, omits crucial details, or vastly exaggerates the threat, I believe it devolves into propaganda. Recall that the cigarette labels were justified only because tobacco poses a broad and irrefutable threat to public safety. This is not always the case when it comes to the threat posed by so-called enemies, who may have neither the intention nor the ability to pose a significant danger to U.S. citizens.

Furthermore, regardless of the stated justifications, I try to consider what happens as a result of war. Indeed, war may have a "just cause" yet still be executed and enabled through unjust means (Zinn 2007). When a war kills civilians whose perspectives remain invisible, provokes hatred and terrorism, enriches corporate profiteers, and expands the extraconstitutional powers of the government, then the discourse that called the war into being may rightly be called propaganda. Indeed, it may be hard to make war without propaganda, as war so often contributes to human misery, literally harming citizens wherever it is fought.

A key feature of successful propaganda is that it propagates, reaching enormous numbers of people. Such propagation is, of necessity, an intertextual process: a message cannot reach masses of people unless it is recontextualized on a mass scale. The propagandist, whether deliberate or unwitting, must design discourse that induces a favorable uptake. That is, the propagandist must induce audiences to entextualize and perpetuate the propaganda. By "entextualize," I mean identify a given stretch of discourse as removable and potentially reusable. And by "perpetuate," I mean recontextualize that discourse, thereby giving it new life.

Symbolic elites are more likely to have their discourse counted as valuable and, thus, repeatable. For instance, the president may induce journalists to recontextualize his words on a huge scale—not only because his words intrinsically possess "prepared-for detachability" (Bauman and Briggs 1990, 74), but because they are regarded as authoritative. Meanwhile, news reports of presidential discourse are likely to be recontextualized by the public. This is so not only because the press uses detachable and memorable headlines but also because journalism is valuable in a democracy. News discourse is the authoritative resource for those wishing to be informed, which helps ensure that it, too, is recontextualized without being undermined.

Of course, the intertextual process need not "cascade" downward from elites to the public (Entman 2004). Ordinary citizens may also circulate propaganda, inducing new audiences to recontextualize some meaning "throughout a social network" (Jowett and O'Donnell 2015, 395). As Huckin (2016, 130) argues, this happens regularly as citizens disseminate normative meanings and collectively recontextualize the presuppositions of society. When it comes to foreign policy discourse, however, citizens are less able to control which claims have legitimacy. They don't have access to key information (intelligence files, national security meetings, and so on). Thus, they are less likely to deliberately create war propaganda for self-serving ends and are more likely to be unwitting propagandists, recontextualizing war discourse originally designed by political and media elites. If they do challenge war propaganda, those challenges are unlikely to be shareable in mainstream media.

In my view, another essential feature of propaganda is that it is manipulative. Propaganda will almost always have a semantic undercurrent suggesting that our group is superior to, and threatened by, their group (Van Dijk 2006). Furthermore, propaganda can manipulate people through emotional coercion, misrepresentation, selective omission, and the closing down of dialogic space such that some perspectives become less discernible, if not invisible.

Some degree of manipulation may be legitimate if it is used for democratically sanctioned purposes. Perhaps there is a kind of civic rhetoric that shares formal features with propaganda (e.g., wide circulation, emotional language) but has a noble purpose: securing unfulfilled democratic potential. Nevertheless, certain forms of manipulation are so egregious that they automatically indicate propaganda. For example, lying or implicating a false conclusion is incompatible with democratic life (Stanley 2015; Wolin 2008). By "lying," I don't mean a slight overstatement of a well-established conclusion (e.g., "Smoking causes cancer"). I mean the deliberate misrepresentation of reality. As Wolin (2008, 261) explains, "Self-government is, literally, deformed by lying; it cannot function when those in office assume as a matter of course that, when necessary or advantageous, they can mislead the citizenry." Indeed, "lying is the expression of a will to power" (263)—a form of domination, not democratic deliberation.

The dehumanization of subordinate groups also indicates propaganda. We are all familiar with discourse targeting minorities, whether it is Jewish people, African Americans, Muslims, or immigrants. This discourse is obviously propaganda insofar as it declares that such people are less than human, that they present a threat, or that they are the source of the majority's problems. Such scapegoating and demagoguery place citizens outside the polity, depriving them of respect (Burke 1954; Roberts-Miller 2005). Indeed, scapegoating is traditionally viewed as a fascist technique, and its continued presence in allegedly democratic discourse is most disturbing (see, for example, Donald Trump's presidency).

Lies and demagoguery are tell-tale signs of propaganda because they epitomize the last of propaganda's essential characteristics: it is hostile to democracy. As I see it, propaganda is partly defined by its societal consequences—specifically, its tendency to empower dominant groups while threatening the interests of less powerful ones. To accept this characteristic of propaganda, one must also accept that society is plagued by an inequitable distribution of wealth and political power. One must acknowledge the "increasingly unequal struggle between an unrealized democracy and an antidemocracy that dare not speak its name" (Wolin 2008, 213).

Propaganda enhances the antidemocracy, even as it claims to secure democratic aims. It is never benign and always pernicious, for it ultimately reduces the sovereignty of the people and often requires that certain people forfeit their lives.

2. The Persian Gulf War and the War on Terror

A Brief History

The propagandist's purpose is to make
one set of people forget that certain other
sets of people are human.

—Aldous Huxley, 1936

U.S. foreign policy is often described in radiant terms: America is the benign super-power, aspiring only for global peace and security (Bacevich 2010, 12–14). However, such descriptions conceal that the United States also seeks control of world affairs, a pursuit that has arguably led not to worldwide security but unending conflict. As Bacevich explains, America has continuously adopted "a national security strategy that relies on global military presence and global power projection to underwrite a policy of global interventionism. Touted as essential to peace, adherence to that strategy has propelled the United States into a condition approximating perpetual war" (16). Bacevich is not alone in suggesting that, for the past sixty years, U.S. foreign policy has promoted military expansion as a means to secure power and maintain global dominance (Chomsky 2003; Zinn 2003; Blum 2004; Kinzer 2006).

One might say, then, that American wars are generally unjust because they are premised on an unjust foreign policy, one that openly advocates for control of the entire world. While I find this general argument compelling, my goal in this chapter is more concrete: to show how specific U.S. wars have had specific antidemocratic consequences. Again, my claim is that insofar as these wars harmed the interests of the Many, then the discourse that called them into being is propaganda. Here, it is incumbent upon me to make the case that recent wars were indeed harmful and unjust, in spite of rhetoric to the contrary. Simultaneously, I provide historical context for the propaganda analyses in the chapters to follow.

My focus is on the U.S. campaigns in the Persian Gulf War (1990–91) and the "Global War on Terror" (fought in Afghanistan 2001–14 and Iraq 2003–11). I suggest that both were unjust and antidemocratic for two reasons. First, the American public was misinformed about the actual reasons for fighting. In fact, political leaders often distorted "security threats" and failed to disclose whether U.S. foreign policy itself had provoked anti-American aggression. Second, I find the wars unjust because their architects repeatedly defied constitutional and international law. In the name of national security, the U.S. government expanded its domestic power, often claiming authority not granted in the Constitution. Meanwhile, as the government brutalized America's "enemies" abroad, it also ignored the perspectives and well-being of vulnerable noncombatants. Indeed, the wars' most antidemocratic feature was that they denied others an equal "right to life . . . and security of person" (U.N. General Assembly 1948). To demonstrate this, I highlight how U.S. violence produced unnecessary civilian suffering, including death, destruction, and terror. This suffering directly contradicts the clichés of war propaganda, specifically the old platitude that war advances the cause of liberty.

The Persian Gulf War

Saddam Becomes an Enemy

Former Iraqi president Saddam Hussein was not always America's enemy. In fact, in the early 1980s, Saddam was considered a strategic ally, if not a friend, of the United States. The partnership began mainly as a result of Iran's revolution in 1979, when, much to the chagrin of the American government, rebels finally overthrew Mohammad Reza Shah Pahlavi. Mohammad Reza had been brutalizing the Iranian people for years (Blum 2004, 70–72), and the United States, which had installed him as shah, had continued to support him throughout his oppressive rule (Zinn, Konopacki, and Buhle 2008, 232–53).[1] Still the U.S. government was unprepared for both the revolution and subsequent anti-American backlash. Officials watched in horror as Iranian protesters stormed the U.S. embassy in Tehran and took American diplomats hostage.

Suddenly, the U.S. government had to contend with an unfriendly Iranian regime, but this newfound enemy might still be checked with a little help from Iran's regional adversary, Iraq. From the U.S. point of view, Saddam Hussein and his Sunni government represented a bulwark against Iran's revolutionary Shiites. Thus, in 1980, America did not prevent—and may have encouraged—Iraq when it launched an attack on Iran (Blum 2004, 332). This set off a deadly eight-year war, during which the United States provided Iraq with weapons, training, and intelligence, including reports of Iranian troop movements (Kinzer 2006, 287). To be sure, Saddam was known to be an "odious, repressive beastly thug" (Blum 2004, 332), but now that he was fighting the Iranians, his crimes were more easily overlooked. In 1980, he was even given the key to the city of Detroit (Brooks 2003).

After the bloody war with Iran, Iraq was deeply in debt and increasingly resentful of rich lender nations such as Kuwait. Saddam charged that Kuwait had stolen $2.4 million of oil by illegally slant-drilling from the Rumailia oil field (Blum 2004, 321). He was also indignant that Kuwait and the United Arab Emirates were exceeding established oil production quotas, driving oil prices down and effectively preventing Iraq from an economic recovery (321). Iraq's bitterness with Kuwait was only exacerbated by the fact that Kuwait had been part of Iraq until World War I, when it was arbitrarily partitioned off by the British Empire. As Kagan (2014) notes, "Leaders in Baghdad had long regarded it as an Iraqi province." Now Saddam demanded that territory be returned to Iraq. Specifically, he wanted "possession of two Gulf islands which blocked Iraq's access to the Gulf as well as undisputed control of the Rumailia oilfield" (Blum 2004, 321). In early July 1990, he amassed troops along the Kuwaiti border.

The United States, still on good terms with Iraq, gave Saddam mixed signals about a possible invasion. On one hand, American leaders cautioned Iraq about the use of force. On the other, they repeatedly said that the United States had no defense treaties with Kuwait and no commitment to come to its aid. On July 25, 1990, Saddam met with American ambassador April Glaspie to discuss the situation. As Kinzer (2006, 287) writes, "The Americans had not objected when he attacked Iran a decade before, and he wanted to be sure they would not object this time either." Glaspie expressed concern about Iraq's massive troop buildup but told Saddam that America had "no opinion on the Arab-Arab conflicts, like your border dispute with Kuwait" (Blum 2004, 322). Eight days later, Saddam sent his army to invade Kuwait and annexed the country in a violent takeover. According to the Central Intelligence Agency (CIA), Saddam believed America had given him a "green light"; he was "sincerely surprised" when the United States reacted by mobilizing its military (324).

Characterizing Saddam's aggression as entirely unprovoked, President George H. W. Bush ordered Iraq's immediate and unconditional withdrawal from Kuwait. Within days, Bush launched Operation Desert Shield, amassing thousands of American troops in Saudi Arabia along the Iraqi border—allegedly to protect the Saudis from Saddam's next planned assault. To justify this move, Bush claimed Saddam had placed one hundred thousand soldiers along the border, but investigative reporters for the *St. Petersburg Times* found no evidence to corroborate this allegation (Kellner 2004b, 140). In fact, Bush had pressured Saudi Arabia into allowing American troops to be stationed there, even though neither the Saudis nor the Americans expected an Iraqi attack (Blum 2004, 331).

Next, Bush persuaded members of the United Nations to accept resolutions, including one that imposed crippling economic sanctions on Iraq and another that authorized an international coalition to force Iraqi soldiers out of Kuwait (326–27).

According to Blum, the resolutions provided the president with a "figleaf of 'multi-national' respectability" for "what was essentially an America mission, an American war" (326). As the sanctions were given "time to work," Bush struggled to persuade the American people of the probable need for violence. As noted, the claims of Iraq's troop buildup near Saudi Arabia were disputed. And Americans were unimpressed by Bush's complaint that Iraq was disrupting international oil markets. The president had more luck with the public when he emphasized Iraq's "naked aggression" and made outrageous comparisons between Saddam and Hitler. But his most persuasive argument was that Iraq was close to acquiring a nuclear weapon.

Arguably, none of Bush's stated justifications for war held up to scrutiny. The apparent outrage over Saddam's "naked aggression" seemed insincere, considering that no such outrage had been expressed when Saddam had displayed "naked aggression" toward Iran ten years earlier (332). And denunciations of Iraq's savagery were equally ironic given that Kuwait and Saudi Arabia were also brutal dictatorships with horrible human rights records (332). Finally, though Iraq did pose a potential nuclear threat, so did a lot of other countries, and Iraq was apparently still five to ten years away from a usable weapon (333).

The public seemed to sense that the case for war was questionable. As late as November 1990, most still favored sanctions over military intervention (Kagan 2014), and even as the war became increasingly likely, the public remained divided (Zinn 2003, 597). In January 1991, the president was compelled to seek congressional approval. Congress was not asked to declare war as called for by the Constitution but to authorize the president to make war at his discretion (596). After a robust debate, the congressional resolution for military force passed by a slim vote—helped along by false stories of Iraqi atrocities, appeals to support the troops, and other pro-war propaganda from the corporate press (Kellner 1992, 2004b; Zinn 2003, 595).

Still, there was time to avert a catastrophe. The United Nations had given Saddam until January 15, 1991, to pull out of Kuwait. Saddam, however, was too proud and stubborn to accept the United Nations' terms. Instead, he offered a face-saving compromise: "On the 11th, Arab diplomats at the U.N. said . . . that Saddam planned an initiative soon after the 15th that would express his willingness 'in principle' to pull out of Kuwait in return for international guarantees that Iraq would not be attacked, an international conference to address Palestinian griev-ances, and negotiations on disputes between Iraq and Kuwait. The Iraqi leader, the diplomats said, wanted to wait a day or two after the deadline had passed to demonstrate that he had not been intimidated" (Blum 2004, 329). In fact, this was not Saddam's first attempt to broker a deal. Back in August and again in October, he had signaled his willingness to withdraw from Kuwait in exchange for control of some key oil fields and an end to the sanctions against his country (327). The Bush administration first denied these offers had been made, then flatly rejected their merits. Saddam's last-minute offer in January was similarly rebuffed, as were other efforts at negotiation proposed by members of the U.N. Security Council (328–29).

Why was the administration so bent on war? Several historians believe that Bush's actual reasons for fighting were hidden from the public. With his poll numbers sagging and Democrats making gains in Congress, the president's staff reportedly believed a short, decisive victory might help him win reelection (Zinn 2003, 595). Such a victory would also display power to the rest of the world and quell any lingering doubts from the Vietnam era about America's resolve to wage war (Zinn 2003, 600; Chomsky 1991). Second, Blum (2004, 321) argues, Bush wanted to prevent cuts to the defense budget. Now that the Cold War was over and the threat of the Soviet Union apparently dissolved, Congress was threatening huge reductions in military spending. Bush—who had allies in the "military-industrial-intelligence complex" (320)—allegedly aimed to prove that America still needed a powerful military (321). Saddam's invasion of Kuwait provided just the right event to spur considerable defense spending (325–26).

Third, Bush apparently wanted American control over Middle East oil (Blum 2004, 330–31; Zinn 2003, 595). As Chomsky (1991) argues, the goal was "not to keep oil prices low, but to keep Washington, Wall Street, and their allies in charge of setting oil prices." Finally, Blum (2004, 333) claims, Bush wished to expand the reach of American empire by installing a system of military "superbases" in Saudi Arabia. These military bases would enhance America's ability to project power in the Middle East—and further advance the grand strategy of a "new world order" led by the United States (Dunmire 2011).

Desert Storm

On January 18, 1991, the United States launched its air war in Iraq, dubbing the operation "Desert Storm." The Iraqi army, which had been touted as a "formidable military power," turned out to be less than capable, especially as "the U.S. Air Force had total control of the air, and could bomb at will" (Zinn 2003, 596). For forty-three days, the United States relentlessly attacked, "dropping 177 million pounds of bombs on the people of Iraq in the most concentrated aerial onslaught in the history of the world" (Blum 2004, 320). U.S. leaders boasted that their laser-guided munitions, or "smart bombs," could hit targets with surgical precision. In reality, about 40 percent of these missed the mark, and the more widely used "dumb bombs" missed 70 percent of the time (Zinn 2003, 597; Pershing and Yocum 1996, 53 n. 14).

For Iraqis, the results were devastating. U.S. warplanes hit chemical weapons facilities, releasing toxic vapors that killed scores of innocent people (Blum 2004, 334). Shells made of depleted uranium left radioactive dust clouds. American bombs hit "apartment houses, crowded markets, bridges filled with pedestrians and civilian vehicles, and a busy central bus station" (334). One bomb alleged to have hit a "biological warfare facility" had actually hit a baby food factory (334). Another bomb hit a seventy-three-room hotel in south Baghdad. "They hit the hotel, full of families," said a witness, "and then they came back to hit it again" (quoted in Zinn 2003, 597). Other bombs crippled Iraq's electrical system, reducing the food and water supply and flooding houses with raw sewage (Blum 2004, 335).

In February, after military targets had been destroyed, the United States continued to drop bombs, at one point hitting an air raid shelter and killing 1,500 civilians. A journalist at the scene described how rescue workers "vomited from the stench of the still-smoldering bodies," many of which had been "charred into blackness" (quoted in Blum 2004, 335). Iraqis who were trying to flee into neighboring Jordan were killed on the highway leaving Baghdad: "Buses, taxis, and private cars were repeatedly assaulted, literally without mercy, by rockets, cluster bombs and machine guns; usually in broad daylight, the targets clearly civilian." Following the war, "the Pentagon admitted that non-military facilities had been extensively targeted for political purposes" (335).

The ground war was no less dreadful. Tanks equipped with plows trapped Iraqi soldiers in trenches, where they were shot and covered under mounds of sand. Thousands were buried this way—many of them still alive. Iraqis trying to surrender were nevertheless fired upon (334). As the ragged Iraqi army was retreating from Kuwait, American planes assailed them with bombs and rockets, which also hit civilian vehicles and refugees (336). According to journalist Seymour Hersh (2000), the American attacks even persisted after a ceasefire had been called, as American forces led by General Barry McCaffrey cut off retreating Iraqi troops and destroyed their convoy. As a condition for granting this ceasefire, President Bush had insisted that Saddam comply with all twelve U.N. resolutions. "In evaluating Bush's legalistic demands," argues Blum (2004, 337), "it should be kept in mind that the policy and practice of the American war had repeatedly violated the letter and spirit of the United Nations Charter, the Geneva Conventions, the Nuremberg Tribunal, the protocols of the International Committee of the Red Cross, and the U.S. Constitution, amongst other cherished documents."

Throughout the campaign, the American press mostly ran patriotic stories on the brilliance of the U.S. military, ignoring the civilian carnage and conveying the government narrative of sophisticated, high-tech violence (Kellner 1992, 2004b; Zinn 2003, 598). Returning U.S. troops were welcomed home as heroes and were celebrated both in the press and in yellow ribbon parades. Meanwhile, 100,000 Iraqi troops and 33,000 civilians lay dead (Pershing and Yocom 1996, 52). The United Nations described "near-apocalyptic results on [Iraq's] infrastructure," adding that "most modern means of life support [had] been destroyed or rendered tenuous" (quoted in Zinn 2003, 599). Another report from a Harvard medical team predicted at least 170,000 more children would die in the coming year from infectious diseases carried by raw sewage (Blum 2004, 335). Over the next decade, Iraq deteriorated further under economic sanctions that "reportedly caused the deaths of

1.25 million people, including more than 500,000 children" (Zinn, Konopacki, and Buhle 2008, 256).

The United States had spent $61.1 billion to destroy Iraq—"the equivalent of spending one million dollars a day for a period of over 167 years" (Pershing and Yocom 1996, 53). The "350 million dollars spent on two days of air combat equaled more than UNICEF's entire 1990–91 budgeted expenditures" (53 n. 15). Few Americans seemed to care. Saddam Hussein—the strategic ally turned enemy—had been humiliated. And President Bush, now a very popular man, had brought his country a victory.

The War on Terror

Empowering Terrorists

On September 11, 2001, nineteen men belonging to a radical organization called al-Qaeda hijacked commercial jets and crashed them into the World Trade Center in New York City and the Pentagon building in Washington, D.C.[2] More than three thousand innocent people were killed in the worst terrorist assault ever perpetrated on U.S. soil. As in the case of the Iranian hostage crisis, the American public was shocked and mystified by a group of Muslim radicals who had seemingly attacked their country out of the blue. Many wondered, "Why do they hate us?" President George W. Bush (2001a) provided one possible answer, telling the American people that the attackers "hate our freedoms." But a Pentagon report probably came much closer to the truth: "Muslims do not 'hate our freedom,'" it said, "they hate our policies" (Defense Science Board 2004, 40). Indeed, the atrocity of September 11, 2001, may be considered "blowback," an unintended consequence of America's covert operations in the Middle East (Johnson 2004).

Late in 1979, as the United States was still reeling from the Iranian Revolution and warming up to the brutal regime of Saddam Hussein, the Soviet Union was busy fighting a bloody war in Afghanistan and trying to quell a group of insurgents called the mujahideen. The mujahideen were fundamentalist "holy warriors," and they were attacking Kabul's left-wing government not only because it threatened their ultraconservative traditions but because it threatened to divest them of their property (Blum 2004, 340–41). Worried that these anticommunist Muslims might take over Afghanistan, the Soviets sent in an occupying army (342; Kinzer 2006, 266).

The United States saw this as a great opportunity—a way to hand the Soviets their own Vietnam-like quagmire. Initiating the most expensive operation in its history, the CIA made plans to aid the mujahideen rebels. To do it, intelligence officials struck a deal with General Zia-ul-Haq, Pakistan's military dictator, who was pursuing his own version of radical Islam (as well as nuclear weaponry) (Kinzer 2006, 265). According to the deal, the CIA would channel funds and weapons to the mujahideen through Pakistan's Inter-Services Intelligence (ISI) agency, leaving the

ISI "to decide which of the various Afghan guerilla groups should be the beneficiaries" (Blum 2004, 345–46). Predictably, the ISI "favored those who shared Zia's commitment to fundamentalist Islam. While the Americans looked on happily, the ISI sent hundreds of millions of dollars to obscurantist warlords," including one who "dreamed of turning Afghanistan into a pure Islamic state, and liked to lead his followers in lusty chants of 'Death to America!'" (Kinzer 2006, 267).

Remarkably, the Americans never considered the long-term consequences of arming and funding radical anti-American extremists who were already known to have committed terrorist attacks (265; Blum 2004, 344–45). Some of these extremists were not even from Afghanistan, as the ISI recruited radicals from other countries to take part in the rebellion. One outsider "who thrived in this milieu" was Osama bin Laden, a Saudi millionaire who joined the insurgency in Afghanistan and met like-minded jihadists from around the world (Kinzer 2006, 270).

In 1989, the Soviets were finally defeated by the U.S.-backed mujahideen, and the Red Army withdrew from Afghanistan. During the war, one million Afghans had been killed, three million more had been disabled, and five million had been forced to flee (Blum 2004, 351). The U.S. government was elated. They had finally triumphed over the Russians.

As the United States turned its attention to new threats—Saddam Hussein, for example—Afghanistan was thrown into utter turmoil. Yes, the Soviets were finally gone, but the Pakistani government retained significant control over Afghan affairs (Kinzer 2006, 271). Meanwhile, mujahideen warlords turned against one another in violent struggles for power, killing thousands of Afghans in a lengthy civil war (Blum 2004, 351). Eventually, Pakistan organized a group of fundamentalists known as the Taliban and helped them wrest control of Kabul. In fact, the Taliban owed much of their success to the United States, as some of them "had learned the art of war during the 1980s at camps paid for by the CIA," and "many others became radicalized in the profundamentalist climate that the CIA encouraged" (Kinzer 2006, 272).

By all accounts, the Taliban government was brutal and despotic—outlawing free expression, subjugating women, and meting out all sorts of cruelty. The Taliban permitted al-Qaeda to recruit terrorists in Afghanistan, including some former mujahideen members who carried out the 1993 bombing of the World Trade Center (Blum 2004, 352). Later, the Taliban also allowed the return of Osama bin Laden, who promptly expanded al-Qaeda's operations and declared war on the United States. And yet America maintained good relations with the terrorist-friendly Taliban regime (Kinzer 2006, 273). As Kinzer explains, a U.S. oil company called Unocal wanted to build a natural gas pipeline through Afghanistan, and the Taliban were seen as a government that could keep the necessary order for this $2 billion project (273–74). And so the Taliban's crimes—"amputations, floggings, and public executions" (274)—were tolerated, as American foreign policy "was publicly and inextricably linked to the financial goals of an oil company" (Coll 2004, 330).

Fighting Terrorists

After a disputed 2000 election, President George W. Bush took office, apparently with little knowledge of Afghanistan and al-Qaeda. Bush was focused on ousting Saddam Hussein from Iraq, and he ignored "repeated warnings that devastating [al-Qaeda] attacks were imminent" (Kinzer 2006, 276). When the 9/11 strikes rattled the nation, Bush temporarily dropped his plans for war in Baghdad and declared, instead, a "war on terror." In framing the 9/11 attacks as an "act of war" rather than a crime, the president essentially ruled out using limited force to apprehend and try terrorist suspects (Hodges 2011, 23–30). Instead, he would mobilize the American military for a vast campaign. Though he did not seek legal authority from the United Nations, the president obtained a resolution from Congress giving him incredible discretion to wage war wherever he pleased.[3] Only one lawmaker voted against the bill, despite the fact it lacked "the declaration of war that the Constitution required" (Zinn 2003, 678). (Weeks later, Congress would also pass the Patriot Act, giving the government greater power to spy on its own citizens.)

For the first phase of the War on Terror, Bush proposed a massive air campaign in Afghanistan, where Osama bin Laden was thought to be hiding. Just as there had been no real debate in Congress, there was no real debate in the mainstream press (Kellner 2004a; Wolin 2008). So overwhelming was the elite consensus, Americans might have been shocked to learn that almost every other nation opposed a military solution. Polls showed "clear and sizable majorities" around the world favoring "extradition and trial of suspects" instead of an invasion, "yet such polls [were] ignored by the media" (Miller 2001).

Likewise, the mainstream media failed to challenge the contention that the terrorists had attacked because "they hate freedom." More plausible reasons for the attack had been recited frequently not only by al-Qaeda but by millions across the Middle East. They were angry because the United States had developed military bases in Saudi Arabia, had helped impose sanctions that killed hundreds of thousands of Iraqis, had supported Israel, and had sustained brutal dictatorships across the region. Of course, none of this justified the terrorist assault on innocent Americans. But U.S. elites might have considered whether a new bombing campaign was likely to resolve—rather than intensify—the basic grievances that inspired anti-American hatred.

To avert a war, the Taliban were prepared to turn over Osama bin Laden to a third party—if the United States provided evidence that bin Laden was involved in the 9/11 attacks (Frantz 2001). But America was in no mood to negotiate; it wanted revenge. According to Richard A. Clarke (2004, 24), a counterterrorism official in the Bush administration, the president was warned that international law forbade using force for the purpose of retribution, but Bush was not interested: "I don't care what the international lawyers say, we are going to kick some ass." Bush also ignored the opinions of respected parties within Afghanistan. Major aid organizations there opposed the war and warned "that millions were on the verge of starvation and that the consequences might be horrendous" (Chomsky 2016). Even a respected anti-Taliban leader condemned the American bombing campaign, complaining it would lead to suffering and disrupt efforts to overthrow the Taliban from within (Chomsky 2016).

Still, the American assault came. Initially, U.S. "military planners struggled to find targets they could hit in a country that had been blasted to ruin by years of war" (Kinzer 2006, 277). Bombs were aimed at the Taliban's primitive air defenses and military bases (278), but they often hit areas populated with civilians. For instance, U.S. forces twice bombed a Red Cross building—even though it was marked with a giant red cross—and tried to bomb the building a third time, only to hit a residential neighborhood instead (Zinn 2002, 83). Afghan refugees told reporters how Americans had bombed them even as they tried to flee. The warplanes had killed twenty people, including nine children, they said, and had left the injured "screaming in vain for help" (quoted in Zinn 2002, 86).

By 2002, U.S. bombs had directly killed between 3,100 and 3,600 civilians (Herold 2003). Thousands more died from starvation and illness (Conetta 2002), while perhaps another million were forced to flee (Zinn 2002, 11). That year, according to the *Guardian*, 100 people died every day from starvation and exposure at a single refugee camp near Herat (cited in Zinn 2002, 11). By 2014, one estimate claimed, the war had directly killed 149,000 people in Afghanistan and Pakistan, including over 26,000 Afghan civilians (Taylor 2015). Another estimate suggests that the number of civilians killed is much higher—between 106,000 and 170,000 (Guilliard et al. 2015, 78).

In addition to the cost in human lives, the war in Afghanistan had cost a staggering amount of money, roughly $685 billion (Thomspon 2015). For this investment, the United States did topple the Taliban government and gained more military bases in the process (Blum 2004, 383). But the War on Terror had done little to diminish terrorism. Indeed, through its relentless violence, the United States itself had terrorized the people of an impoverished country.

Another War in Iraq

Containing Saddam

In 2002, George W. Bush would declare that Afghanistan was merely the first front in the War on Terror. The second front would be Iraq. According to the president, the time had finally come to deal with Saddam Hussein. By this time, Saddam was a familiar enemy. In fact, "the need to deal with Saddam" had been an American talking point ever since the end of the original Gulf War.

Back in 1991, President George H. W. Bush had elected not to march on Baghdad and instead sought to contain Saddam through international pressure. Specifically, the elder Bush urged the U.N. Security Council to pass Resolution 687, which established in Iraq a new inspection regime: the United Nations Special Commission.[4]

UNSCOM, as the group was known, was charged with forcing Iraq to destroy proscribed facilities and munitions, especially weapons of mass destruction (WMD). Though its inspectors managed to recover some weapons, UNSCOM also faced regular obstruction from the Iraqi government, which never fully cooperated and even worked to conceal some of its weapons technology.

To many Americans, this Iraqi obstruction was simply more evidence of Saddam's treachery, but the Iraqis maintained they had good reason to avoid cooperating with the inspectors. For example, officials in Iraq frequently suggested the inspectorate was biased against them—a charge that may have had some credence. Indeed, the United Nations' own humanitarian mission in Iraq publicly accused the inspectors of being "non-neutral" and "deliberately provocative" and even referred to the inspections regime as "UN-SCUM" (Varadarajan 1998). More consequentially, Saddam worried that the inspectors—who typically came from Western countries that had participated in the Gulf War—would pass sensitive military intelligence to America and Israel, which still wanted to topple him.

As it turns out, Saddam's worry was well founded. For even as the first President Bush publicly called for a lawful process of U.N. inspections, he privately pursued extralegal covert operations to depose the Iraqi leader. As early as May 1991, he directed the CIA to "create the conditions for the removal of Saddam Hussein" (Mayer 2004). In 1998—with inspections still going on—President Clinton signed a law making "regime change" in Iraq official U.S. policy. Thus, America was not simply interested in "Iraqi compliance" with UNSCOM inspections; it wanted to replace Saddam's government. And some members of the inspection team were not opposed to helping the CIA achieve this goal (Kay 1999).

It wasn't long before the CIA was actively using UNSCOM to advance its objective of regime change. According to the *Washington Post*, U.S. intelligence services infiltrated UNCSCOM and, for three years, eavesdropped "on the Iraqi military without the knowledge of the U.N. agency that it used to disguise its work" (Gellman 1999). Using the United Nations as cover, the United States reportedly spied on Saddam's inner circle and may have used this intelligence in 1998, when it dropped bombs on Iraq in Operation Desert Fox (Hedges 1999).

Supposedly, Desert Fox targeted Iraq's weapons facilities as punishment for Saddam's failure to comply with inspectors. But evidence suggests that the attack was orchestrated to take out Iraqi leaders (Arkin 1999; Gellman 1998; Mason 2013). In any case, it was civilians who once again suffered the most: about two hundred were killed in the seventy-hour bombing campaign (Tirman 2011, 210; Zinn 2011, 237–38). Like others before it, the Desert Fox attack had failed to "punish" Saddam. Instead, it effectively ended UNSCOM's presence in Iraq. Later, many would claim that Saddam had "kicked the inspectors out," but it was the Clinton administration that had instructed inspectors to leave in order to protect them from American missiles. Their departure proved significant. Though plagued by problems, UNSCOM had been the only entity capable of assessing Iraq's weapons programs. Now no one knew for sure what Iraq was up to, and the United States could exploit this uncertainty to make a case for war.

The Case for Regime Change

When George W. Bush took office, he was already prepared to wage war in Iraq. In fact, Bush sought a preventive war that might eliminate Saddam Hussein before he could pose a serious threat (Dunmire 2009). The trick was to persuade the public that regime change was necessary *now*, even though the supposed threat from Iraq was far in the future. The president found a pretext for war in the terrorist attacks of September 11, 2001. Within months of the attacks, the administration began suggesting to a terrified public that Saddam Hussein was linked to al-Qaeda and was poised to pass WMD to terrorist operatives. In reality, Saddam had already dismantled his WMD stockpiles, and the Iraqi government had no meaningful relationship with al-Qaeda. Again, the stated reasons for war appeared to be "smokescreens designed to hide" more fundamental reasons. These included an interest in regional oil and military bases (Falk and Friel 2004, 4) and "an intense desire for . . . final victory over" Saddam (Kinzer 2006, 293).

The Bush propaganda campaign was relentless, as the administration inundated the public with detailed descriptions of Iraq's nonexistent weapons and frightening images of the "mushroom cloud" that might hang over the world if terrorists were to deploy a nuclear weapon supplied by Saddam. According to a study by the Center for Public Integrity, President Bush and other top-level officials "made at least 935 false statements in the two years following September 11, 2001, about the national security threat posed by Saddam Hussein's Iraq." The authors of the study also point out that "much of the wall-to-wall media coverage provided additional, 'independent' validation of the Bush administration's false statements" (Lewis and Reading-Smith 2008). Other studies have confirmed that the mainstream press uncritically repeated the administration's dire claims (Bennett, Lawrence, and Livingston 2007)—and in some cases worked to render those claims even more persuasive (Oddo 2013, 2014a).

Ultimately, majorities of the American public were misled into believing that Saddam Hussein had acquired nuclear weapons and had even helped orchestrate the 9/11 attacks (Pew Research Center 2002). Meanwhile, Congress once again gave the president extraconstitutional authority to wage war, as both Democrats and Republicans united against a country that had neither attacked the United States nor threatened to do so.

With its rhetoric having the desired effect at home, the Bush administration also took the show on the road and tried to win international legitimacy through the U.N. Security Council. In November 2002, Bush persuaded the council to reinstate weapons inspectors in Iraq and give them unprecedented access to Saddam's facilities. For the next several months, inspectors examined site after site but turned up no evidence of massive WMD programs. According to Bush, this only proved how cleverly Iraq was engaging in "denial and deception."

In January 2003, the inspectors reported they had still found no significant evidence of WMD but needed more time to confirm Iraq's disarmament (Anderson 2011, 121). Instead of allowing for more time, the president "short-circuited" the U.N. process by mobilizing the U.S. military "before the inspections [would have] rendered an attack unwarranted" (O'Sullivan 2009, 175). Ignoring a worldwide antiwar protest (McFadden 2003) and without authorization from the U.N. Security Council, the president launched Operation Iraqi Freedom.

Shock and Awe

The war began earlier than planned, on March 19, 2003, when U.S. intelligence officials received a tip about Saddam's whereabouts and sought to end his life with a "decapitation strike" (Kinzer 2006, 297). American bombs and cruise missiles rained down on a farmhouse on the outskirts of Baghdad. As it turned out, Saddam was not there—and hadn't been there since 1995. Instead, the so-called decapitation strike "killed one civilian and injured fourteen others, including nine women and one child" (*Second Gulf War* 2009). This strike was emblematic of a larger pattern. In the first months of the war—the "shock and awe" phase—the United States launched some fifty airstrikes at "high-value targets," including Saddam and his henchmen. The "precision-guided weapons" were often touted as successful by the administration and the press, but instead of killing their intended targets, they killed enormous numbers of civilians (Glaister 2004). According to the Iraq Body Count (2012), "On a per-day basis, the highest intensity of civilian killings over a sustained period occurred during the first three 'Shock and Awe' weeks of the 2003 invasion, when civilian deaths averaged 319 per day and totalled over 6,716 by April 9th, nearly all attributable to US-led coalition-forces." As bombs pounded Baghdad in March 2003—undoubtedly terrorizing the people below—Secretary of Defense Donald Rumsfeld reassured the American public: "It looks like it's a bombing of a city, but it isn't" (quoted in Blum 2004, 390).

Following the air raids, American forces swept into the Iraqi capital, meeting hardly any resistance from Saddam's "pitiful shell" of a military, much of which had deserted (Kinzer 2006, 290, 297). Iraqi soldiers overlooking the American march to Baghdad were burned to death in "massive fireballs" ignited by an incendiary substance "remarkably similar" to napalm (Murdoch 2013). Meanwhile, Saddam himself fled Baghdad, and his brutal regime collapsed. Iraq had been "liberated."

On May 1, 2003, President Bush triumphantly stepped out of a fighter jet and onto the USS *Abraham Lincoln*. To the delight of the press, the president was dressed in a pilot's flight suit, his codpiece bulging. Later, under a banner reading "Mission Accomplished," he announced that "major combat operations" in Iraq had ended. But following this apparent victory, Iraq turned into a "cauldron of violent anarchy and a magnet for fanatics around the world" (Kinzer 2006, 312–13). People faced shortages of electricity, clean water, and food, and soon looting and riots were breaking out around the country (Tirman 2011, 229). The U.S. military—now an occupying army—could not meet the demands of a desperate public, nor could it control a growing insurgency. Before long, the country devolved into sectarian war.

Amidst the chaos, innocent people suffered the most. In 2004, as Blum (2010) reports, American forces flattened the city of Fallujah "using white phosphorous shells, depleted uranium, napalm, cluster bombs, neutron bombs, laser weapons, weapons using directed energy, weapons using high-powered microwave technology, and other marvelous inventions in the Pentagon's science-fiction arsenal." Fallujah became so toxic that, by 2010, "the level of heart defects among newborn babies [was] said to be 13 times higher than in Europe." A BBC correspondent "saw children in the city who were suffering from paralysis or brain damage, and a photograph of one baby who was born with three heads" (Blum 2010).

Only a year into the invasion, a U.N. survey had already found that the Iraqi population was enduring "war-related injuries, chronic malnutrition, low life expectancy, declining health, declining literacy, and significant setbacks in women's rights" (quoted in Tirman 2011, 243). Millions were forced to flee to refugee camps, where the prospects for a healthy life were still terrible. In 2006, a father described what it was like having to send his children away to escape the violence: "Most of the time you are sick with worry over their safety and well-being. The knowledge that they are in constant danger consumes you. It eats you alive. You then realize that it is your love for them that is killing you. You begin to hate that love" (quoted in Tirman 2011, 248).

On the ground in Iraq, overwhelmed American troops resorted to harsh forms of martial security. Trying to restore order, they frequently ended up killing unarmed Iraqis at checkpoints and during house raids. Perhaps 120,000 "Iraqi men and boys were arrested in front of their families and sent to detention camps or prisons like Abu Ghraib without any evidence of wrongdoing" (Tirman 2011, 230). Prisoners at Abu Ghraib were tortured and abused; female detainees reported being threatened with rape (253).

Meanwhile, the situation in Iraq remained a nightmare. Al-Qaeda, which had not existed in Iraq before the invasion, now materialized as a result of the American occupation. The Iraqi people faced violence from both local insurgents and U.S. forces. Thousands died from suicide attacks, improvised explosive devices, and aerial bombardment. Popular opinion in Iraq was decidedly against America's military presence. As Chomsky (2016) reports, "Pentagon and British Ministry of Defense polls found that only 3% of Iraqis regarded the U.S. security role in their neighborhood as legitimate, less than 1% believed that 'coalition' (U.S.-UK) forces were good for their security, 80% opposed the presence of coalition forces in the country, and a majority supported attacks on coalition troops." Rather than withdrawing forces in response to popular will, in 2007, Bush orchestrated a "surge" of more troops. The level of violence in Iraq subsided but remained shockingly high (Bacevich 2010, 202). Indeed, the bloodshed continued even as America formally ended the war in 2011.

During the Iraq War, the United States spent roughly $815 billion (Thompson 2015), but it is difficult to calculate the true cost of the violence. Perhaps half a million Iraqis were killed (Sheridan 2013); millions more displaced (Dewachi 2011). Iraq—which had no caches of WMD and no plans to supply such weapons to terrorists—was now a hotbed of terrorist activity. Part two of the War on Terror had once again generated more of it (Bergen and Cruickshank 2007)—including the U.S. terrorism of "shock and awe."

In my view, the legitimation and execution of the Persian Gulf War and the Global War on Terror hinged on the exercise of antidemocratic power, which was enabled by U.S. war discourse at the time. The wars were marketed on dubious grounds, as the political and media establishment overstated enemy threats and failed to disclose information about the real reasons for conflict. American citizens were denied the chance to provide informed consent for proposed military campaigns. At times, the public interest was subordinated to the profit interest of oil, defense, and media corporations. Furthermore, the U.S. government failed to abide by constitutional mandates, waging war without congressional declaration and creating invasive programs of mass surveillance. On a global scale, the United States violated international law and fundamental human rights by enacting policies of torture and indefinite detention. Above all, it chose military means that punished the innocent and subjected civilians to death, disease, and degradation.

Beyond these concrete injuries, the United States also continued an antidemocratic foreign policy centered on global domination. This is a stated policy, couched in military phrases such as "full-spectrum dominance" or in euphemistic strategy documents asserting U.S. readiness "to project power globally . . . in multiple theaters" (U.S. National Security Council 2015, 8). I hope the reader will keep this context in mind as I examine instances of American war propaganda in subsequent chapters. As I see it, this propaganda fueled American empire and helped give rise to a superpower incompatible with republican democracy and the right to live in peace.

Manufacturing an Atrocity

3. How the Incubator Story Became News

The Power of Performative Semiotics

If I wanted to lie . . . I wouldn't choose my daughter to do so. I could easily buy other people to do it.

—Sheikh Saud Nasir al-Sabah,
Kuwaiti ambassador
to the United States, 1992

When political leaders want to craft a persuasive campaign for war, they follow a simple and time-honored principle: demonize the enemy. Indeed, constructing a savage foe is an obligatory strategy in call-to-arms discourse—and a very effective one (Ivie 1980; Graham, Keenan, and Dowd 2004; Oddo 2011). As Hermann Göring, creator of the Gestapo, famously observed, human beings naturally don't want to go to war and risk their lives for some dubious cause. But if their political leaders can convince them that the enemy is a monster bent on destroying civilization, then it becomes rather easy to "drag the people along" (quoted in Gilbert 1947, 278–79).

One good way to highlight the enemy's depravity is to tell "atrocity stories," narratives that purportedly recount massacres, mutilations, and other cruelties against the weak and vulnerable (Jowett and O'Donnell 2015, 246). The more graphic and grotesque the alleged atrocity, the more effective the story will be. For example, during World War I, British pamphleteers sought to establish the ruthlessness of German forces by describing the Germans' cold-blooded slaughter of Belgian civilians. The pamphlets describe how soldiers bayoneted pregnant women, gouged out the eyes of young men, and even attacked defenseless children. One pamphlet titled *The Kaiser and His Barbarians* includes sixty-four pages of atrocity propaganda, including reports of German assaults on babies. "In one Belgian village," the pamphlet asserts, "the priest . . . saw a six-months-old baby carried on the point of a bayonet by a German soldier. Another baby of seven weeks was snatched from its father's arms and dashed to the ground. Yet another baby, whose mother resisted the efforts of some drunken Uhlans to seize the child, had its poor little hands slashed off by a sword" (Willis 1914, 51). As it turns out, these allegations of massacred babies were without substance. But this did not stop the Bryce Committee, a British group charged with investigating German atrocities, from issuing a 1915 report that verified the sensational accounts. The committee failed to interview a single witness and, instead, published unsworn testimony and hearsay as fact (Knightley 2004, 88). Still, its report was subsequently publicized (and praised) in newspapers around the world, including a *New York Times* (1915) piece titled "German Atrocities Are Proved." As Knightley (2004, 114) remarks, by the time the baby-killing stories were discredited, they had already served their purpose: strengthening the resolve of British and French troops while weakening the American public's resistance to entering the war.

The German invasion of Belgium must have seemed like ancient history when, in August 1990, Saddam Hussein's troops stormed into Kuwait. But the atrocity stories that cropped up during the Iraqi raid were eerily similar to those that had appeared during the Great War. Again, there were accounts of young men with their eyes gouged out, pregnant women pierced by bayonets, and atrocities against babies. Specifically, it was alleged that, while raiding Kuwait's hospitals for equipment, Iraqi soldiers had torn premature babies from their incubators, leaving them to suffer and die.

This "incubator story," as I will refer to it, was also untrue (Abu-Hamad 1992; MacArthur 1992). And yet, as I show in this chapter and the next, it succeeded spectacularly as propaganda, traveling through the corridors of the Washington power establishment, across channels of American news media, and into living rooms around the country. Here, I examine one particularly persuasive version of the incubator narrative, a public performance by a fifteen-year-old Kuwaiti girl named Nayirah. In fact, Nayirah's performance of the incubator story is widely cited as one of the most significant rhetorical acts of the prewar period (MacArthur 1992; Walton 1995; Rowse 1992).

Broadly, I wish to examine what made Nayirah's performance such an effective piece of propaganda. Here, I assume effective propaganda is replicated on a mass scale. More specifically, effective propaganda is designed in ways that ensure it will be favorably and broadly recontextualized. It is endowed with "prepared-for detachability" (Bauman and Briggs 1990, 74) and imbued with "desired qualities" that make it attractive to a recontextualizing agent. Ultimately, the most effective propaganda induces media audiences to recognize it as a portable, valuable, and authoritative text that is worthy of being recontextualized without "compromising transformation" (77). To investigate Nayirah's performance of the incubator story, I follow an approach to micro-rhetorical analysis described in earlier work (Oddo 2013, 2014a). This approach involves a close analysis of linguistic discourse, multimodal semiotics, and intertextual relations between a public address and subsequent news reports. Using this method, I find that several factors contributed to the success of Nayirah's incubator story. First, governments and public relations firms secretly colluded and orchestrated Nayirah's performance, constructing an authoritative setting for her speech, complete with indexical references to a formal legal hearing. In addition, Nayirah herself performed and embodied an ensemble of multimodal signs—speech, gaze, facial expressions—all designed to entextualize her narrative and render it shareable in mainstream news (Urban 1996, 24). Her performance included high drama, intense and moralized diction, the visual accoutrements of sworn eyewitness testimony, and simulations of seemingly authentic emotion—all "desired qualities" that made it virtually irresistible to the corporate press (Bauman and Briggs 1990, 77). Thus, the incubator story was recontextualized, not just by Nayirah but also by "impartial" reporters who unwittingly added to the facticity and credibility of the tale.

Citizens for a Free Kuwait

The publication of the incubator story in America was not an accident but a direct result of an enormous propaganda operation by a foreign government working in concert with U.S. elites. Specifically, the government of Kuwait sought to steer U.S. public opinion toward a war with Saddam Hussein. Indeed, days after Iraq's invasion, Kuwaiti leaders launched a front group in America called Citizens for a Free Kuwait (CFK). Despite its title, CFK was hardly composed of concerned "citizens," as 99 percent of its funding came from Kuwaiti officials (MacArthur 1992, 47).

On August 10, 1990, CFK hired the American public relations firm Hill & Knowlton (H&K) to publicize Kuwait's suffering and generate U.S. support for war. At the time, H&K was a giant in the public relations industry and was well connected in Washington politics (MacArthur 1992). For example, Craig Fuller, who headed the Kuwaiti account for H&K, had served as chief of staff for George H. W. Bush when he was vice president (O'Dwyer's PR Services Report 1991, 8). When Bush became president, Fuller remained a close ally and began running the Free Kuwait campaign in consultation with the White House. Thus, though the H&K campaign was funded by the Kuwaiti government, it was also supported by the Bush administration in what amounted to a "coordinated communication effort" (Manheim 1994, 144). Fuller frequently visited the White House to, in his words, "find out how we could be supportive with respect to the President's program" (quoted in MacArthur 1992, 49).

The H&K operation was the "largest foreign-funded campaign ever aimed at manipulating American public opinion," costing CFK nearly $11 million (Stauber and Rampton 1995, 169). The money was well spent. H&K quickly publicized the Kuwaiti cause throughout the United States. It organized a National Free Kuwait Day and a National Day of Prayer for Kuwait (Rowse 1991; MacArthur 1992). It distributed thousands of "Free Kuwait" bumper stickers and T-shirts and organized public rallies and speaking engagements. And it arranged media interviews, providing news releases and information kits to journalists. At every turn, H&K closely observed how its campaign was playing, monitoring whether speakers and messages were having the desired effects (Manheim 1994; Rowse 1991).

When CFK first hired H&K, most American citizens and lawmakers opposed war in Iraq (Kellner 1992, 70) and distrusted President Bush's justifications for involvement. Indeed, Bush (1990a) had initially premised intervention on the idea of controlling the flow of Middle East oil and protecting economic interests in Saudi Arabia. But most Americans were unmoved by the economic reasons for war, and the phrase "No Blood for Oil" quickly became a slogan among peace activists.

Thus, H&K's strategy was to elicit sympathy for Kuwait by shifting the focus to the horrors of Iraq's occupation (Jamieson and Waldman 2003, 17). Arguments about oil were replaced with graphic depictions of "the rape of Kuwait." Saddam Hussein, once a friend of the Bush administration, was now demonized as the "Butcher of Baghdad" and described as a virtual clone of Hitler. And atrocity stories were publicized, illustrating Iraq's crimes against humanity.

Finding a Washington Audience and Concealing the Identity of the "Star Witness"

The incubator atrocity was seen as a perfect vehicle for dramatizing Iraq's evil and Kuwait's suffering (Jamieson and Waldman 2003, 17). By October 1990, the story had already appeared in the press, but it had not yet ascended to the level of a major news item.[1] That all changed on October 10, when the U.S. Congressional Human Rights Caucus (HRC) held a hearing on Iraqi atrocities in Kuwait (U.S. Congressional Human Rights Caucus 1990). The HRC, co-chaired by Representatives Tom Lantos and John Porter, had a friendly relationship with H&K and CFK, after receiving money from them for lodging, travel, and election campaigning (MacArthur 1992, 60–61). In fact, the caucus hearing had effectively been planned by members of the CFK team. H&K both provided "eyewitnesses" and coached them on their testimony (MacArthur 1992; Rowse 1991).

For nearly two hours, these "witnesses" told disturbing (if unverifiable) tales of Iraqi misconduct. A man using the name "Abdullah" claimed he saw soldiers execute two teenage boys in front of their mother. A woman named Deborah Hadi said she saw soldiers sodomize youngsters with broken bottles and later bayonet a pregnant woman at a maternity hospital. Finally, fifteen-year-old "Nayirah" was called upon to share her harrowing tale. As with several other witnesses, Rep. Porter said, Nayirah's full name could not be revealed to the media because of "the need to protect her family" from retaliation back in Kuwait.

However, the real reason for withholding Nayirah's name was more sinister. Nayirah was the daughter of the Kuwaiti ambassador to the United States, Sheikh Saud Nasir al-Sabah (MacArthur 1992). She was a member of the Kuwaiti royal family, and as such, she had a vested interest in promoting war against Iraq, even if it meant lying (Walton 1995). No one at the HRC revealed Nayirah's true identity, and Nayirah herself gave no indication that she was anything but an ordinary Kuwaiti girl. Thus, "manipulative silence" was a crucial factor in spreading the incubator tale (Huckin 2002). In order to make the allegation credible—and, therefore, shareable in news reports—the true identity of the speaker was strategically left unsaid.

But the decision to conceal Nayirah's name was only one factor that allowed the incubator story to be recontextualized. To guarantee a successful "uptake" of the tale (Blommaert 2005), it also had to be clothed in the symbolic garb of an official congressional hearing. And, of course, Nayirah had to successfully perform the incubator testimony, deploying various semiotic resources to provoke an emotional reaction and convey narrative authenticity. Below, I investigate the semiotic resources at play during her performance.

Staging Nayirah's Story

Much of the persuasive impact of Nayirah's testimony can be attributed to the visual semiotics of the hearing chambers as well as the symbolic significance of Nayirah's personal appearance. As shown in figures 2A and 2B, a number of design elements indexed that this event should be interpreted as an official congressional hearing. Figure 2A shows the long, rectangular table where the panelists sat. (Nayirah is seated on the right side of the image, farthest from the camera.) The panelists are given placards specifying their names, and the table is equipped with microphones. All of these features index the relative importance of these panelists, who, unlike the spectators sitting in back, have been given the privilege to speak and be heard. The panelists' relative importance is also indexed by their proximity to the congressional representatives they face. As shown in figure 2B, HRC members also sit at a table equipped with microphones and name placards, on an elevated dais resting under a blue banner that reads "Congressional Human Rights Caucus." These signs indicate the power of the lawmakers, who literally preside over the hearing, regulating who gets to speak and when. Indeed, all chairs in the room are pointed at the dais where the lawmakers sit, making them the focal point of the proceedings. Among these lawmakers, Tom Lantos (third from the right in figure 2B) and John Porter (second from the right) are designated as especially powerful. They sit at the center of the platform, directly under the banner, which also identifies them by name and institutional title. Of course, language also helps to categorize the activity and relevant participant roles. The event is referred to as a "hearing"; the lawmakers are

Figures 2a, b Images from HRC hearing

always identified by their official titles, last names, and honorifics ("Representative Morella," "Mister Chairman," etc.); and panelists are consistently called "witnesses" and asked to "testify."

Thus, a configuration of multimodal signs indexes a formal legal hearing. This may seem like an obvious point, but we must not overlook how much labor went into creating these optics and how they function to regulate interpretations of the event. Indeed, it is only in the context of a congressional hearing that Nayirah's words can carry the conviction of a legal promise. Onlookers instantly recognize the signs— lawmakers perched on their dais, witnesses who testify from below—and infer that the witnesses have taken an oath and, thus, that their testimony is legally binding. However, the Human Rights Caucus is not a committee of Congress and, therefore, is not obliged to swear in its witnesses. We find the trappings of a legally binding hearing, without any legal consequences—for example, penalties for lying. Despite the lack of formal oaths, the clever staging drew enormous media attention. Reportedly, there were fifteen television camera crews and a host of print reporters on hand (Rowse 1991). Thus, it is not just what Nayirah says but where she says it that counts. If she had spoken at a different venue—say, a school board meeting in Loup City, Nebraska—then her statement would have been viewed quite differently. Perhaps, it would not have been viewed at all.

Nayirah's Performance: Embodying the Eyewitness and Simulating Grief

Nayirah's talk is ostensibly a narrative of personal experience (Labov and Waletzky 1997; Labov 1972), one that has a number of recognizable elements:

- an *abstract* that signals an upcoming story and the narrator's right to tell it;
- an *orientation* that introduces the characters, setting, and initial situation;

- *complicating action* that relates the story's plot in a series of suspenseful events;
- a *resolution* that describes what finally happened to end the tension;
- *evaluation* that indicates the stance of the narrator and the point of the story; and
- a *coda* that marks the story's end and returns listeners to the present. (Labov 1972)

I use these terms in this analysis as they help reveal the structure and functions of Nayirah's story (Johnstone 2005; 2008, 92–96). However, I also consider extralinguistic factors, including Nayirah's physical appearance. Remember, Nayirah was chosen to tell the incubator story because she looked the part. Her physical characteristics, then, aren't just biological facts but "motivated" signs that were selected according to the ideological interests of the producer, CFK (Kress 1993, 173). Excerpt 3.1 transcribes the abstract of Nayirah's talk and accounts for details of verbal and visual discourse. Time (in seconds) is indicated in column 1, a snapshot of a corresponding visual frame is provided in column 2, and the audio soundtrack—in this case Nayirah's voice—is transcribed in column 3.[2]

Nayirah not only bears the marks of a witness but a witness of a particular kind.[3] Her physical characteristics—dark hair and eyes, olive (moderate brown) skin, and facial structure—are consistent with Western perceptions of a "Middle Eastern" look.[4] That is, Nayirah has both the name and the appearance of a "real" Kuwaiti, which adds to the perceived authenticity of her narrative.[5] Nayirah further establishes her national identity by saying she "just came out of Kuwait." Here, the adverb "just" intensifies Nayirah's spatiotemporal proximity to events in the Middle East, suggesting not only that Nayirah is from Kuwait but that she is only recently removed and, thus, is better able to describe current conditions there.

Excerpt 3.1

Time	Frame	Soundtrack*
21–25		Mister Chairman and members of the committee my name is Nayirah and I just came out of Kuwait.

*To save space, I delete several visual frames. I use this convention often throughout this book, marking condensed transcripts with a star (*) in the soundtrack.

Excerpt 3.2

Time	Frame	Soundtrack*
52–70		~I may have wished sometime that I could be an ~~adult~~ (1.5) ~~that I could grow up quickly~~. (2.6) (.hhh) ~What I saw happening to the children of Kuwait and to my country has changed my life forever~. (1.1) ~has changed the life of (.) all Kuwaitis (.) young and old~. (1.1) ~~We are <u>child</u>ren no more~~.

Aside from indexing her regional identity, Nayirah's appearance also indicates her youth. She is fifteen years old and has all the physical characteristics one would expect from someone her age: a wrinkle-free face, taut eyebrows, tight muscle tone, and so on. In fact, Nayirah's youthful appearance provides a crucial context for her verbal testimony. As shown in excerpt 3.2, Nayirah frequently identifies herself by her age, constructing an evaluative thread in which her youthful innocence has been destroyed along with the lives of Kuwaiti children and the supposed purity of her country. In the soundtrack of excerpt 3.2, *underlining* represents extra prominence on stressed syllables. Numbers in parentheses represent pauses measured in seconds and tenths of seconds. Micropauses, too short to measure, are represented by a period in parentheses. ~Tildes~ indicate a wobbly voice. And (.hhh) indicates an audible in-breath.

Nayirah uses the desiderative mental process "wished" to indicate her past desire to be "an adult." Thus, she indexes a time during which she identified herself as youthful, that is, not yet grown up. Crucially, while Nayirah's words signal a past feeling of positive emotion ("wished"), the tenor of her speaking voice indicates a present feeling of sadness. Throughout this excerpt, Nayirah's voice is trembling, and the tremulousness increases sharply just as she utters the word "adult." Audiences immediately understand that Nayirah has experienced some trauma, some event that has caused her to interpret her past wish to "grow up" with sadness. Following an audible in-breath, Nayirah uses a transformative process ("changed") to specify her trauma. Here an abstract actor ("what I saw happening to the children of Kuwait") is represented as having transformed an equally abstract goal ("my life," later extended to include "the life of all Kuwaitis"). In this way, Nayirah's personal sensory experience ("what *I* saw") is construed as having had not only a maximally durable impact on her ("changed *my* life *forever*") but also a maximally far-reaching impact on her country ("changed the life of *all Kuwaitis*").

While Nayirah fails to specify what she saw happening, she does specify whom it happened to in a pair of coordinated prepositional phrases: "to the children of Kuwait and to my country." Here, Nayirah pairs a local happening with a national happening, syntactically linking an apparent assault on children with the assault on the country of Kuwait. Nayirah concludes with this evaluative comment spoken in a particularly wobbly voice: "We are children no more." By using the first-person plural pronoun "we," Nayirah seeks to join herself with all Kuwaitis—and, interestingly, she defines this group by forcefully negating the youthful identity "we" once possessed ("We are *children no more*"). In this way, Nayirah suggests she is sad (as indexed by her wobbly voice) not only because she witnessed the loss of innocent children but because she and her country experienced the spiritual loss of childhood innocence. Needless to say, this is a sophisticated rhetorical performance that succeeds largely because of Nayirah's youthful appearance. The propaganda is effective—that is, believable and decontextualizable—only if the speaker embodies the "childhood" she claims to have lost.

Nayirah's opening statements invite the question: what did she see happening to the children of Kuwait that so affected her? Indeed, Nayirah's evaluative clauses build narrative suspense that is relieved when she tells the incubator story. During the orientation for this story, Nayirah explains that she "stayed behind" in Kuwait and "volunteered at the al-'Addan Hospital" because she "wanted to do something for [her] country." She frames herself as both patriot and humanitarian, one who remains in Kuwait despite the danger because of her love of country and her desire for altruism ("I wanted to do something *for my country, I volunteered*"). Nayirah then moves into the plot of the incubator story. As shown in excerpt 3.3, her performance is remarkable for its linguistic and paralinguistic qualities. Again, some transcription conventions should be noted up front: Upward arrows indicate a sharp increase in pitch. Noticeably soft speech is enclosed in degree signs. Sobbing is transcribed with (.HIH), and wet sniffs are transcribed with (.shih).

Nayirah is the first speaker at the hearing to say she directly perceived the theft of incubators in Kuwait ("I saw"). Thus, she positions herself as the ultimate insider, an actual eyewitness. In addition, Nayirah uses sophisticated and elegant rhetorical schemes. This is best observed if one puts the central clauses of her narrative in poetic form:

Thĕy tóok thĕ bábĭes óut ŏf thĕ íncŭbátŏrs
tóok thĕ íncŭbátŏrs
ănd left thĕ chíldrĕn tŏ díe ŏn thĕ cold flóor.

Excerpt 3.3

Time	Frame	Soundtrack
156–58		~While I was there I saw the Iraqi soldiers~ ~~c- come into the hospital with guns.~~
159		
160–61		~~~They took the babies out ~~~of the incubators~~~.
163–65		

Time	Frame		Soundtrack*

166–68

(.shih)
~~~took the incubators~~~
[*cameras clicking*]
~~~and left the children to die on the~~~

169

~~~↑°cold°↑°floor°~~~ .

170–73

(.shih)(.shih)
[*gulp*]

174

~~It was horrifying~~.
(.HIH)

First, note the parallelism in syllable length. The first clause has twelve syllables, the second has six, and the last has eleven. Thus, there is an almost mathematical symmetry (2:1:2), whereby the first and third clauses are balanced against each other. There is also grammatical parallelism, where "they" (i.e., the Iraqi soldiers) is carried over elliptically as the grammatical subject in three consecutive clauses. This series of three clauses has an internal logic (*incrementum*), as they are arranged in chronological order. Indeed, listeners get the sense that Nayirah is not only listing events in the order they occurred but building toward a finale. The sense of momentum is also a product of the anaphora in the first two clauses of complicating action, each of which begins with the phrase "they took." Listeners must hold their "mental breath" for the third clause, the resolution, which is both the final event in the chronological sequence and (potentially) the last clause to fulfill the expected pattern: They took A; they took B; *they took C.*

The pattern, however, is not fulfilled in the final clause, as listeners are told not that the Iraqis *took* something, but that the Iraqis "*left* the children to die on the cold floor." Listeners may experience a jolt from this violation of the anaphoric pattern, a jolt that complements the shock experienced when they learn of the soldiers' outrageous crime. The jolt is strengthened by the fact that the final clause ends emphatically with a jarring sound pattern, two consecutive stressed syllables with a similar vowel sound [o]: "cold floor." Once again, the musical discord serves as an icon for the emotional discord. The phrase "cold floor" also provides an evaluative description of the scene, helping listeners understand that the act was not just shocking (leaving babies to die) but downright evil (leaving babies to die in a place devoid of warmth and comfort). Nayirah appropriately concludes the story with a summative evaluative comment, signaling the intensity of her dread and disgust: "It was *horrifying.*"

But the real power of Nayirah's testimony comes not from her rhetorical schemes or word choices but her multisemiotic display of grief. Nayirah slows her tempo as she relates the incubator allegation, pausing dramatically between bursts of speech. In fact, after Nayirah says "They took the babies out of the incubators," she pauses for 3.4 seconds before uttering another word. Then, after she delivers the news that the soldiers "left the children to die on the cold floor," she pauses for an additional 4.0 seconds before speaking. These lengthy moments of silence stand out in the testimony, building narrative suspense while suggesting the difficulty that Nayirah has as she tries to relate traumatic events.

The pauses are also interesting because they offer moments for Nayirah to display visual signs of sadness. For instance, Nayirah changes the direction of her gaze when she pauses in frames 163–65, staring down and to the left, while focusing on nothing in particular.[6] This "disengaged" gaze communicates withdrawal or inner cognition (Baldry and Thibault 2005, 201), suggesting that Nayirah is recalling and perhaps reliving a past experience. Nayirah's facial expression also changes during the pauses. At the beginning of the narrative (frames 156–58), Nayirah's expression is fairly neutral: her eyebrows are level, and the corners of her lips are not turned in either vertical direction. However, as Nayirah pauses in frames 163–65, her facial expression clearly changes. Here, just as she is about to deliver the meat of her story, Nayirah begins to raise the inner corners of her eyebrows, while depressing the corners of her lips into a frown. (The raised inner brows and frown are unmistakable by frame 169.) Both expressions indicate sadness (Tian, Kanade, and Cohn 2005, 253). Even more telling, Nayirah appears to be crying actual tears. Though difficult to see in the transcript, there is moisture on Nayirah's right cheek in frames 163–65. Meanwhile, on her other cheek, Nayirah apparently wipes tears away with her left hand (frames 166–68). Other physiological signs of crying include the wet sniff in frames 166–68 and the pair of wet sniffs (followed by a gulp) in frames 170–73.

Finally, the quality of Nayirah's voice also signals intense emotional distress. As shown in frames 156–58, Nayirah's voice is wobbling even as she begins her incubator narrative. But the tremulousness of her voice increases dramatically as she relates the details of the crime, reaching a noticeable peak in frames 160–61 and 166–69. Moreover, just as Nayirah utters the climactic phrase "cold floor," her pitch rises sharply while the volume of her voice decreases appreciably. It is almost as if Nayirah can barely get the words out in her state of anguish. The heightened pitch and vocal tremble subside as Nayirah deems that the events she witnessed were "horrifying." Still, she manages to conclude her story with yet another clear indicator of sorrow: an inhaled sob (.HIH) in frame 174.

Nayirah's display of grief has one obvious consequence: it stirs passions in her audience. As Aristotle (2007, 2.8.1386b) observed long ago, emotional appeals—called appeals to pathos—can have a hypnotic effect on audiences, especially when the speaker is able "by gestures and cries and display of feeling" to bring her suffering "before the eyes" of the listener. Nayirah's tearful performance certainly excites pity. However, whipping up emotions is just one rhetorical function of her performance. Nayirah's display of grief also augments her credibility. Just think about what would have happened if Nayirah's emotional performance fell flat—if she had failed to cry or, worse, if she had looked like someone faking it. Nayirah would have been exposed as a fraud and the incubator story a lie. But Nayirah's emotional outpouring appears real and spontaneous. This makes her voice both dramatic and authoritative—and, thus, desirable and recontextualizable in news narratives.

Take, for example, her facial expressions. It is difficult, even for trained actors, to deliberately depress the corners of their lips while raising their inner eyebrows. In fact, these signals are often scrutinized by lie detection experts to judge whether someone is being honest (Ekman and Rosenberg 1997). Nayirah not only produces these sad facial expressions but adds other signals—wet sniffs, tears, gulps—that smack of authentic anguish. These signals are what Peirce referred to as affective interpretants, involuntary signs that convey meaning without intention (Peirce 1955,

277; Kockelman 2005, 274). And since the emotional semiotics appear unintentional, they are taken to be revelatory of the truth. The emotions are real, the audience reasons, so the events that inspired them must also be real. Genuine feeling equals genuine testimony. Pathos equals ethos.[7]

But there's more. Nayirah's emotional semiotics also help ensure her story is perceived as a newsworthy sound bite, an "extractable" text (Bauman and Briggs 1990, 73). It's worth noting that a narrative of personal experience already has prepared-for detachability (74), since it has a discernible beginning and end (Labov 1972). But Nayirah further entextualizes her incubator story by reaching an emotional crescendo as she delivers the complicating action and resolution, effectively setting these clauses apart from the rest of her discourse. Everything—the increased tremble in her voice, her detached gaze, her lengthy pauses—signals to journalists that this stretch of speech is removable from its local context and shareable in the context of contemporary news melodrama (Urban 1996, 24). When we also consider the poetics of her narrative—momentum-building anaphora, vivid diction—we see that Nayirah provided journalists with additional cues that the incubator story was a discrete and portable text. This was a performance designed to be noticed and reused.

Nayirah's emotional climax also helps explain why her story was more attractive to the press than other reportable atrocity narratives. In fact, two other speakers at the hearing delivered versions of the incubator story: Chair Tom Lantos and Representative Constance Morella. If the generic content of the story—that Iraqi soldiers removed babies from incubators—was the driving force behind its success, then either Lantos's or Morella's version might have been reported instead of Nayirah's. But their versions of the story were less repeatable, precisely because they lacked the performative semiotics Nayirah so naturally displayed.

Only Nayirah looks the part; she is appropriately "Middle Eastern." Only Nayirah provides a firsthand account of the incubator tale. And crucially, only Nayirah conveys a spontaneous eruption of "real" emotion.[8] And this is likely what saved her (and the Citizens for a Free Kuwait) from a public disaster. Indeed, had Nayirah delivered an unemotional performance and calmly read her statement, then people watching might have detected the rather conspicuous artifice of her rhetoric, a clear sign of a professional public relations campaign. For example, in the coda at the end of her speech—the only other place where she maximizes the wobble in her voice—Nayirah declares:

> I am glad I am fifteen
> <u>old</u> enough to remember Kuwait before Saddam Hussein *destroyed* it
> and <u>young</u> enough to *rebuild* it.

Note the sophisticated parallelism—specifically, antithesis, where antonymous meanings (<u>underlined</u> and *italicized*) are balanced against each other in corresponding phrases. Nayirah's conclusion also rearticulates the youthful identity theme she developed earlier. The elegant parallelisms and recurring motifs are poetic, but they also seem strange coming from a teenage girl, especially a girl presumably speaking in her second language. Indeed, Nayirah's testimony evinces "double-voiced" discourse (Bakhtin 1981) that simultaneously signals the authentic recollection of a young witness and the artful rhetoric of a seasoned politician. In short, her prose suggests the kind of polish we associate with professional speech writing. But because Nayirah is so emotional, so *convincingly* emotional, such signs of professional craft are rendered less visible, and her speech is rendered more repeatable.

Thrusting Nayirah into the News

Even if Nayirah projected the right signals—even if she looked the part, adopted the voice of an eyewitness, and camouflaged her public relations training in an emotional tour de force—her narrative might yet have failed. Her performance, no matter how moving, could only thrive with the aid of journalists. As Latour (1987, 40) reminds us, a claim is powerless unless it is subsequently referred to by new rhetors in new contexts. If even the most convincing claim fails to get repeated, then it is as if that claim never existed. Thus, journalists not only had to recognize Nayirah's story as a decontextualizable snatch of discourse, they also had to report her story, finding room for it in already-packed news narratives. Moreover, reporters had to construct the right uptake of Nayirah's incubator allegation (Blommaert 2005), recontextualizing and reinterpreting it in ways that favored the Free Kuwait campaign.

One good way to get journalists to report your story is to make it easily accessible. In this case, having an official venue in Washington certainly eased the burden on the press, but H&K took additional measures. It spent hundreds of thousands of dollars creating and distributing video news releases (VNRs), made-for-TV videos that look and sound like real newscasts (Rowse 1991). Nayirah's testimony was just one event that was prepackaged and distributed to major television news networks in the form of a VNR. Excerpt 3.4 shows a few frames from this VNR (excerpted from Docherty 1992), illustrating how H&K demarcated and described Nayirah's testimony.

The VNR helps entextualize Nayirah's discourse by drawing boundaries around her testimony and defining it as usable text (Silverstein and Urban 1996, 1). Moreover, the VNR categorizes speakers, topics, and forms of expression. In frame 2, for example, the VNR declares that "accounts of atrocities in Iraq continue to mount." The speech act noun "accounts" backgrounds the identity of the actors responsible for the allegations and assigns the allegations authority (compare "accounts" to "claims"). Meanwhile, the prepositional phrase "of Iraqi atrocities in Kuwait" not only specifies the topic of the speech act but moralizes the behavior of key agents— signaling that an enemy ("Iraq") is responsible for exceptionally unethical acts

Time	Frame	Soundtrack*
1	VIDEO NEWS RELEASE HUMAN RIGHTS CAUCUS IRAQI ATROCITIES IN KUWAIT	
2	Accounts of Iraqi atrocities in Kuwait continue to mount. In Washington. The Congressional Human Rights Caucus heard testimony today from several recent escapees from Kuwait who describe widespread torture. rape. and killing.	
4	Nayirah. Age 15 Kuwaiti Escapee	

("atrocities"). Finally, the metaphorical verb phrase "continue to mount" suggests the atrocity stories are autonomously accumulating rather than, say, being propagated by elites with a vested interest.

Other word choices classify the speakers and speech forms at the hearing in ways favorable to the CFK campaign. Note, for instance, the use of "testimony," a word that likely suggests a legally binding oath, even though no such oath was taken at the HRC. And speakers, including Nayirah, are referred to as "escapees," a word that presupposes a past condition of danger (presumably Iraqi danger) so serious that it caused people to escape. In short, the VNR helps contextualize Nayirah's speech in ideological ways by promoting the notion that she was just one witness to describe "mounting" human rights violations, that her speech represented eyewitness testimony, and that she herself was victimized (i.e., forced to flee).

Interestingly, the VNR also includes discourse indexing its own context of production. It refers to itself as a "video news release" and, in another frame (not pictured), enumerates several kinds of content (sound bites, setup, and cutaways) that require advanced video production and editing technology. Moreover, in an earlier screen display (not featured in excerpt 3.4), the VNR explicitly identifies the agents who created it: "The following material is offered for your unrestricted use by Hill & Knowlton on behalf of its client Citizens for a Free Kuwait." Thus, the television news networks received unequivocal notice that the video content had been produced by a public relations firm using state-of-the art equipment.

However, few (if any) journalists using this VNR footage would disclose where it came from. As Cramer (2013, 78) explains, journalists avoid publishing details about the production and development of their news accounts because divulging such information "would tend to erode the perceived authority of the accounts, and by extension, the news organization." Certainly, identifying that your news content was produced by a public relations firm would be the ethical thing to do, but it would also represent an admission that you did not work to locate the news story yourself.

On October 10, 1990, *NBC Nightly News* aired a story on the HRC hearing that did not include the kinds of explanatory video shots from excerpt 3.4.[9] Perhaps this is because NBC did not use the VNR footage, or perhaps it is because NBC simply erased any signs that it had. Excerpt 3.5 transcribes NBC's recontextualization of Nayirah's testimony.

Tom Brokaw begins with a voice-over description of the setting for Nayirah's speech, a description complemented with a distant visual shot of the banner at the HRC hearing. Interestingly, Brokaw does not identify the HRC as responsible for the event but instead specifies "U.S. Congress" as the responsible actor. Thus, viewers are led to believe that the hearing was official business of the entire U.S. Congress, when, in reality, it was just a caucus hearing, without any legal consequences. Brokaw emphatically describes the hearing as "<u>high</u>ly emotional," as a close shot of crying women appears on screen. In doing so, he positions the viewer to accept that the hearing was indeed emotional (as opposed to, say, melodramatic) and predisposes audiences to regard Nayirah's testimony as something that should elicit sympathy. Even more telling, though, is the reporting clause in which Brokaw attributes the hearing discourse to its sources: "Witnesses describing the bru<u>tal</u>ity of Iraqi occupying forces." Brokaw attributes the discourse to "witnesses," positioning audiences to take for granted that speakers actually witnessed something and, perhaps, reinforcing the false idea that their speech represents sworn testimony. And with the nominal

Excerpt 3.5

Time	Frame	Soundtrack*
21–22		**[Brokaw:]** U.S. Congress held a <u>highly</u>
23–29		emotional hearing today on Iraqi atrocities in Ku<u>wait</u>. <u>Wit</u>nesses describing the bru<u>tal</u>ity of the Iraqi occupying forces.
30–33		I saw the Iraqi soldiers ~~c- come into the hospital with guns.~~ (1.0) ~~~They took the babies out of the incubators~~~. (2.6) (.shih)
34–47		~~~took the incubators and left the children to die on the ↑°cold°↑°floor°~~~ (2.5) (.shih)(.shih) [*gulp*] ~~It was horrifying~~. (.HIH)

Time	Frame		Soundtrack*
48–49			(1.8)
50–58			Those atrocities by Iraq have forced hundreds of thousands of Kuwaitis to escape into neighboring Saudi Arabia where they can only ponder the future of their country now.

phrase "the brutality of the Iraqi occupying forces," he presupposes that what the witnesses saw was actual brutality. Even before viewers hear Nayirah speak, they have been prepared to accept her discourse as an eyewitness account of a brutal act.

Perhaps not surprisingly, NBC opted to display the portion of Nayirah's incubator story I analyzed above in exccrpt 3.3. Nayirah's performative semiotics apparently succeeded in making this part of her testimony detachable and reportable.[10] That itself was a victory for the Free Kuwait campaign. But Brokaw's recontextualization of Nayirah's testimony enhances both its emotional impact and its presumed veracity. Just after Nayirah's clip, Brokaw pauses for almost two seconds, first gazing off camera to his left before finally settling his gaze on the viewer (48–49). This conspicuous pause may be interpreted as an evaluative display of contemplation after shocking testimony. More importantly, Brokaw's words in frames 50–58 further transform Nayirah's claims into categorical facts. Specifically, in the phrase "those atrocities by Iraq," Brokaw again presupposes that Iraq is responsible for atrocities, thus presenting his negative evaluation of Iraqi behavior as a universally held truth. And, crucially, the deictic "those" points backward to Nayirah's freshly completed story. Thus, viewers are positioned to understand Nayirah's performance as a self-evident representation of an Iraqi atrocity.

A similar recontextualization strategy is evident in the National Public Radio (NPR) news program *All Things Considered*: "Today the Congressional Human Rights Caucus heard testimony from Kuwaitis and Americans who fled Kuwait after the August 2 invasion. The witnesses told of atrocities they saw committed there by Iraqi soldiers. We caution our listeners that their stories are graphic descriptions of violent events and may be painful to listen to" (Adams 1990a) The host, Noah Adams, is more careful to identify the HRC (and not all of Congress) as the sponsor for the hearing. But once again, the reporter refers to "testimony" and "witnesses," suggesting a legally binding oath. The witnesses are again presented as having directly observed Iraqi crimes ("told of *atrocities they saw*") rather than presented as claiming to have observed crimes. And once again, the reporter prepares the audience to regard the HRC discourse as highly emotional. In fact, Adams directly warns listeners that the stories represent "graphic descriptions of violent events" that "may be painful to listen to." In this way, NPR guides its listeners to regard the HRC testimony not only as evidence-based "descriptions" but as descriptions likely to cause "pain." This may seem like a natural way to introduce atrocity material, but bear in mind that the reporters could have made different choices. Imagine, for instance, if NPR had begun as follows: "Today the Congressional Human Rights Caucus heard *allegations* from Kuwaitis and Americans who *purportedly* fled Kuwait after the August 2 invasion. The *speakers* told of atrocities they *claim* they saw committed there by Iraqi soldiers. We caution our listeners that their stories, while graphic, *are also unverified*." With just a few changes, NPR could have distanced itself from the HRC claims and reduced the authority of the discourse. Such changes would have been entirely consistent with journalistic conventions and entirely appropriate given the fact that the HRC hearings were organized by a public relations firm. Instead, NPR endows the HRC speakers with authority, rendering their voices more believable and shareable (Urban 1996, 24)—more likely to be repeated by listeners who might give the story additional "semiotic mobility" (Blommaert 2005, 69).

As the NPR report continues, it only further ascribes credibility to HRC discourse. In fact, Adams introduces Nayirah as follows: "This is Nayirah. She and her mother were visiting family in Kuwait when the Iraqis invaded. Two weeks after the invasion, Nayirah volunteered at a hospital in Kuwait City." Here Nayirah's claims are not even attributed to her and are instead converted into unmodalized facts. Immediately following this introduction, NPR plays an audio clip of Nayirah's speech. This is a basic transcription of this clip, excluding the audible signs of grief (sniffs, sobs, tremulousness, etc.) listeners heard: "While I was there, I saw the Iraqi soldiers come into the hospital with guns. They took the babies out of the incubators, took the incubators, and left the children to die on the cold floor. It was horrifying. I am glad I am fifteen, old enough to remember Kuwait before Saddam Hussein destroyed it and young enough to rebuild it. Thank you." As expected, NPR chooses to replay those portions of Nayirah's testimony where her voice is extremely wobbly and her language is marked by parallelistic constructions. Indeed, NPR splices together the central action of Nayirah's incubator narrative (analyzed in excerpt 3.2) and the conclusion of her testimony ("I am glad I am fifteen . . ."). Originally, these two stretches of discourse were separated by one and a half minutes (see appendix D), but because they are both strikingly emotional, NPR sees fit to combine them in one recontextualized sound bite.

And so it was that Nayirah's performance of the incubator story was not just referred to but replayed on two of the most widely consumed news programs in America. In fact, the video clip of Nayirah's story reached an estimated television audience of 35 million people (Rowse 1992, 28). These people never learned that her performance was staged by a public relations firm—indeed, that the clip they were watching was likely *produced* by a public relations firm. Instead, the journalists recontextualized and reframed Nayirah's performance in ways that presumed the credibility of the hearing, the reliability of the witness, the emotionality of the discourse, and the truth of the "atrocity."

Douglas Walton (1995, 775) suggests that the incubator story succeeded because of its appeal to pity. As he explains, the incubator story provided people with a "morally compelling" reason for war, "an icon that everyone immediately reacts to as outraging basic human instincts to protect vulnerable children." The outrageous content of Nayirah's narrative certainly contributed to its circulation, since journalists are known to prefer melodramatic crisis stories highlighting an ongoing emergency (Gans 1979). But the persuasive power of Nayirah's performance was likely more important than the content of her assertions. The stage for her performance; Nayirah's own physical characteristics, language, and emotions; and the Free Kuwait campaign all contributed to the story's portability. Thus, it was easy for journalists to decontextualize Nayirah's words and equally easy for them to regard (and report) Nayirah's false allegation as a factual description.

This analysis suggests that to understand contemporary call-to-arms propaganda, we should not only investigate argument structures but also scrutinize aspects of staging, micro-rhetorical style, and multimodal performative semiotics. All of these factors contribute to whether a stretch of discourse will achieve "semiotic mobility" (Blommaert 2005, 69), whether it will be recognized as shareable and worthy of recontextualization. When atrocity rhetoric is well choreographed and well delivered, it can induce national media coverage and provoke a visceral sense that war is necessary.

4. Keeping War Fever Alive:
The Circulation of the Incubator Story

Most major U.S. wars over the past
century have been sold to the public
on dubious claims if not outright lies, yet
professional journalism has generally
failed to warn the public.
— Robert McChesney, 2004

It is often suggested that Nayirah's testimony was a defining moment in the campaign for war in Iraq and turned the tide in favor of violence.[1] As Walton (1995, 779) remarks, "Opinion was divided at the time, in the senate debate, and Nayirah's testimony was the kind of tie-breaker needed to swing the weight of presumption in favor of taking action." But it is a mistake to assume that Nayirah's performance alone was the "tie-breaker." Her story might have made a splash, but that splash could not endure forever. In fact, the Senate would not vote on the Iraq question until January, months after Nayirah's speech. Meanwhile, journalists would necessarily move on, reporting more current events. They might even report stories refuting the incubator allegation, weakening and possibly killing it. To have a lasting impact, then, the incubator story would need more than just Nayirah. It would need to be kept alive by others—continually repeated, reperformed, and repropelled into the American consciousness.

If we look closely at the life of the incubator story, we find that Nayirah was not even the first to recount the tale. The story preceded her performance at the Human Rights Caucus and continued to make waves long after. In this chapter, I explore how the narrative managed such a long intertextual life during the campaign for war.[2] I ask: Who were the agents and what were the sociopolitical factors that gave this story "semiotic mobility" (Blommaert 2005, 69)? What discursive features continued to make the story a good candidate for decontextualization and recontextualization in the news? And why didn't this story die a terrible death? That is, why wasn't the story subject to "compromising transformation" (Bauman and Briggs 1990, 77); why wasn't it promptly and permanently discredited?

To trace its intertextual trajectory, I investigate many public texts in which the incubator story appeared, both before and after Nayirah's performance. These texts include press conferences, news reports, congressional ceremonies, political speeches, and more. (See appendix C for an account of data and methods.) At each turn, I examine how the story was readjusted and reenacted, often in ways that enhanced its portability and helped ensure future uptake.

One crucial factor in the story's success is that journalists lacked direct access to Kuwait and had to rely on word-of-mouth reports about what was happening there. Under such circumstances, powerful actors had a tremendous advantage. Their semiotic performances exhibited the qualities most desired by journalists (Bauman and Briggs 1990, 77): exclusive (insider) information, institutional credibility, and melodramatic speech. Thus, elites managed to propagate the story and induced the press to favorably recontextualize the narrative on a mass scale. Meanwhile, those who called the incubator story into question were not perceived to have authoritative voices, making their discourse less shareable in the culture of mainstream journalism (Urban 1996, 24). Their rebuttals were either ignored or allowed only limited mobility—relegated to the periphery where they could not function as "effective and memorable texts" (Bauman and Briggs 1990, 74).

Opening Salvo

Many Americans learned about the incubator story on September 5, 1990, when it appeared in a public letter addressed to the Secretary-General of the United Nations. The letter, written by Kuwaiti representative Mohammed Abulhasan (1990), notifies the United Nations about alleged atrocities carried out by Iraq's occupying forces. Abulhasan, who claims to be "informed by impeccable sources in Kuwait's health institutions," offers a list of Iraq's crimes, including this (the second item on the catalog): "2. The incubators in maternity hospitals used for children suffering from retarded growth (premature children) have been removed, causing the death of all the children who were under treatment." On September 6, 1990, the Associated Press (AP) recounted Abulhasan's letter, producing a brief article that was later picked up by major U.S. newspapers. The AP quotes Abulhasan's letter this way: "'The incubators in maternity hospitals used for . . . premature children have been removed, causing the death of all the children who were under treatment,' his [Abulhasan's] letter said" (Associated Press 1990a).

The fact that the incubator story was reported at all is important. Not every statement from Abulhasan's letter was recontextualized in the news. So why was this one? First, as in Nayirah's telling, the content of the narrative contributes to its reportability.

Abulhasan helps create emotional drama through lexical choices that indicate misery ("suffering") and words that maximize the extent of the fatalities ("causing the death of *all* the children").[3] More importantly, Abulhasan's stated title in the letter ("Permanent Representative of Kuwait to the United Nations") indexes his authority and endows his voice with the capacity to travel in media spaces where such institutional affiliations are "desired qualities" (Bauman and Briggs 1990, 77). Meanwhile, Abulhasan's claim to have "impeccable sources" within Kuwait indexes another desired quality in the press: exclusivity. Iraq had refused to allow reporters into Kuwait and even threatened to "cut off the legs of any person" who entered without permission (Boustany 1990). Any news purportedly from within was thus quite valuable to journalists. Finally, Abulhasan induced recontextualization by endowing elements of his letter with "prepared-for detachability" (Bauman and Briggs 1990, 74). By enumerating and indenting the list of Iraq's crimes, Abulhasan effectively entextualizes that list and enhances its visual salience. This strategy appears to have worked: the AP story sequentially repeats each item in Abulhasan's catalog, while ignoring much of the rest of his prose.

Abulhasan's letter to the United Nations, then, represents a successful beginning for the incubator tale. Even so, we must recognize the limitations of his performance. His claim to institutional authority was compelling enough for the AP to run its story, but it was not enough for most major presses to print an unsubstantiated charge. Moreover, a written letter—even with a well-designed layout—lends itself primarily to print journalism. There were no visuals to enhance the story, no dramatic sound bites to propel it into television news. A letter from an ambassador can only travel so far. For the incubator story to become propaganda, it needed additional performances—more sensational ones by people with an even greater claim to the truth.

Reliable Insiders

To attain a "media afterlife" (Lempert and Silverstein 2012, 39), the propaganda had to be recited again—this time by someone with more proximity to the alleged event in occupied Kuwait. On September 7, 1990, an article appearing in the *Los Angeles Times* provided the first such insider account. The report features the stories of American women who had just escaped from Kuwait, many of whom, it is said, "burst into tears when asked . . . about the husbands they left behind." The charge that "Iraqi troops were pulling premature babies from hospital incubators" is placed prominently in the lede, and the elaborated story is later attributed to two women using pseudonyms: "A woman who identified herself as 'Cindy' from San Francisco said about 1,300 Americans were in hiding in occupied Kuwait. . . . She and another woman, who identified herself as 'Rudi,' said Iraqi troops took premature babies out of incubators in Kuwait. 'Iraqis are beating people, bombing and shooting. They are taking all hospital equipment, babies out of incubators. Life-support systems are turned off. . . . They are even removing traffic lights,' Cindy said" (Reuters 1990). Normally, ordinary American citizens such as "Cindy" and "Rudi" would have a difficult time getting a journalist's attention (Bennett, Lawrence, and Livingston 2007). But when citizens can plausibly claim firsthand knowledge of an international crisis, the perceived importance of their words is elevated, and their words become more "shareable" (Urban 1996, 24). Add to this the fact that the citizens are tearful women—American women who have just escaped rough treatment in an exotic land, leaving their poor husbands behind—and you have all the makings of a news spectacle (complete with familiar gender and Orientalist stereotypes).

Even so, it is remarkable that the *Los Angeles Times* chose to print an unverified allegation from essentially anonymous sources. According to MacArthur (1992, 54), even mediocre reporters understand that they "must never fail to get full names (correctly spelled)" when taking eyewitness testimony about a crime. Apparently, this story was just too colorful to pass up, and so "iron-clad rules" of journalism were cast aside (55).[4] Of course, the fact that the story had already been told by the Kuwaiti ambassador may have enhanced its reportability in this case. These women were not introducing the tale; they were corroborating reports first publicized by Abulhasan. Through a kind of "intertextual ethos," then, Abulhasan's credibility may have carried over to the newly released Americans (Oddo 2014a).

"Cindy" and "Rudi," however, were not the only apparent insiders to extend the life of the narrative. Another September 7 story about the released hostages appeared on the NPR program *All Things Considered*. Again, a woman using a pseudonymous name—this time, "Ruthie"—claims that Iraqi soldiers are "taking infants out of incubators and taking the incubators" (Gjelten 1990). The alleged action is in the present progressive tense ("are taking"), which indexes the "temporal proximity" of the event (Cap 2006) and positions "Ruthie" as someone close to affairs happening right now in Kuwait. Of course, as in the *Los Angeles Times* story, it is never explained whether "Ruthie" is relaying a direct observation or a secondhand account. But it doesn't really matter. The credibility of the story is a function of her closeness to the events in question. "Ruthie" was *there*, in occupied Kuwait, so her report is assumed to be real.

Two days later, on NPR's *Weekend Edition Sunday*, the incubator story is attributed to yet another informant with an inside scoop. This time, a doctor in Saudi Arabia claims to have received the atrocity report directly from hospital staff in Kuwait: "'Time is running out,' said . . . a pediatrician. . . . In a ward for premature infants, soldiers had turned off the oxygen on incubators, she said, and packed the equipment for shipment to Iraq. Dr. Fawzi al-Said said the report came to her by the hospital attendants, who had buried the dead infants" (Amos 1990). To her credit, reporter Deborah Amos notes that the pediatrician recounting this story is a member of "People for a Free Kuwait," a group, it is explained, that consists mostly of exiled Kuwaiti leaders pushing for military intervention.[5] Thus, NPR hints to auditors that this doctor has an interest in publicizing Iraq's purportedly heinous crimes. But this only makes the report more baffling. Why air an unverified allegation from a potentially biased source? Again, the answer may hinge on indexical references to proximity. Yes, Dr. al-Said might stand to gain from sharing the incubator story, but she is also an exiled Kuwaiti with an exiled-Kuwaiti-sounding name. She can credibly claim to be from *there*, where the action is occurring. Moreover, unlike the politician Abulhasan, Dr. al-Said is a pediatrician who presumably has a more direct line to Kuwaiti maternity wards. Her "report" (note that it is not called a "rumor") supposedly came from hospital attendants still in Kuwait. Thus, al-Said is apparently connected to real insiders. For NPR, this represented a scoop. Keep in mind that they had no access to Kuwait, and their audience, who didn't even have access to Kuwaiti exiles, was even farther from the epicenter. Under the circumstances, they were willing to listen to anyone with a claim to the inner circle. Again, we see that "indexical reference to desired qualities" (Bauman and Briggs 1990, 74)—in this case, the desired qualities of proximity and exclusivity—endow discourse with value and enhance the odds it will be decontextualized and recontextualized.

Pushing Back

The incubator story was doubtless enjoying intertextual life when, on September 10, 1990, Glenn Frankel of the *Washington Post* publicly challenged the narrative. Frankel's skepticism is clear from the title of his article: "Iraq, Kuwait Waging an Old-Fashioned War of Propaganda." And his report immediately raises doubts about the tale: "Call it the story of the 22 babies. What it illustrates is the difficulty of separating fact from fiction in the Persian Gulf crisis, and the way both the governments of Kuwait and Iraq and some of their allies have sought to manipulate public opinion to aid their cause" (Frankel 1990). Frankel downgrades the story's believability, in part, by referring to it as a "story," a noun associated with fictional narratives as much as factual ones. Similarly, when Frankel says the story "illustrates the difficulty of separating fact from fiction," he implies that both alternatives (fact *and* fiction) are possible and hints that those behind the story are capable of lying. The veracity of the story is further eroded by the fact that efforts to ascertain the truth have been met with "difficulty." And, of course, Frankel states unequivocally that both Kuwait and Iraq "have sought to manipulate public opinion," signaling a negative judgment of Iraqis and Kuwaitis and explicitly raising concerns about the credibility of the storytellers.

But Frankel does not stop there. He further weakens the incubator story by tracing its origins, pushing it back "upstream" where its status as fact is reduced (Latour 1987, 25). According to his report, "The Kuwaiti baby story originated with a letter from a senior Kuwaiti public health official that was smuggled out of the country by a European diplomat late last month, according to Hudah Bahar, an architect who received the letter here in London. It was supplemented by information gathered from fleeing Kuwaitis and other sources by Fawzia Sayegh, a Kuwaiti pediatrician living here" (Frankel 1990). The incubator charge, Frankel reports, originated in a letter by an unnamed public health official in Kuwait, a letter smuggled out by an unnamed European diplomat. This origin story for the letter is attributed to yet another source, Hudah Bahar, an architect in London. Why a sensitive letter from a European diplomat would be entrusted to a London architect is unclear. But even more troubling is the chain of hearsay reports. To sum up, Hudah Bahar *says* that a European diplomat *says* that he smuggled an unseen letter from a health official that *says* that Iraqi soldiers removed babies from their incubators. By acknowledging this series of contingent reports, Frankel underscores that the incubator story is indeed difficult to label as fact or fiction. Each attribution represents a "compromising transformation" (Bauman and Briggs 1990, 77) and a challenge to the propaganda's legitimacy.

Toward the end of his article, Frankel (1990) comments that "in the old-fashioned propaganda war being waged between Iraq and Kuwait, the suffering of children is an emotive and potentially powerful weapon." Here, Frankel again discredits the story through negative framing, metaphorically implying that atrocity stories pose a threat: he presupposes that a "propaganda war" is being waged and warns the audience that a tale like the incubator narrative might be "weaponized." Unlike previous reporters, Frankel tells his readers that "no one could independently confirm the [incubator] accusations." And, as if to substantiate this claim, he quotes a British official who remarks that "we simply have no way to gather evidence one way or the other. We simply don't know the truth" (Frankel 1990). Here, then, are some rather forceful denials ("no one," "no way," "we simply *don't* know") of the certainty of the incubator story that directly confront any suggestion the account is verified.

One might think Frankel's article would sound the death knell for the incubator tale. He reveals how the story depends on a chain of hearsay; he vigorously denies that the story can be confirmed; and he even discredits it as part of an ongoing "propaganda war." Moreover, Frankel was writing for one of the most reputable newspapers in the country, the *Washington Post*. And yet the incubator story was not killed—not by a long shot. For one thing, Frankel fell short of declaring the allegation false and even left open the possibility that the story might turn out to be a "fact." For another thing, Frankel's article, which appeared on page A18, was hardly eye catching and, thus, was less likely to be recalled and recontextualized. Indeed, a day after Frankel's article was printed, a more prominently placed article (page A8) in the *Post* repeated the incubator allegation (Leff 1990). Thus, Frankel was competing with other journalists at his own newspaper, not to mention the other news providers that repeated the tale in September 1990.

If Frankel's article wasn't a death knell, though, it was at least a warning shot—one that was surely noticed by H&K's research team. The last thing it wanted was a reporter asking intelligent questions and pushing the story back toward its dubious roots. If the incubator allegations were to survive, H&K would need more than hearsay reports from unnamed sources. It would need "real" eyewitnesses to step forward and tell the world what they saw. As observed in the previous chapter, Nayirah provided such insider testimony. She was not the only one.

The U.N. Spectacle

Following its triumph at the Human Rights Caucus in October, the Free Kuwait campaign had a surefire formula for gaining publicity: orchestrate a spectacle at an official venue, line up "eyewitnesses," and coach them to convincingly describe the killing of babies. Accordingly, for the next major telling of the story on November 27, 1990, the campaign chose a site that was sure to draw enormous media scrutiny: the U.N. Security Council. Just two days later, the United Nations would decide whether to authorize military force against Iraq. This performance of the incubator tale, then, would not only garner the attention of the corporate press but might even impact the international vote on war.

With the help of U.S. ambassador Thomas Pickering, who presided over the U.N. session, the Kuwaiti government (along with H&K) staged another lurid presentation of human rights abuses (U.N. Security Council 1990). The walls of the chamber were plastered with giant color photographs of Kuwaiti victims, and the council was packed with television sets so that Kuwaiti representatives could show videotapes "documenting" Iraqi atrocities. After each video, the council heard directly from Kuwaiti "witnesses," accusers who had secretly benefited from H&K training and had sworn no oaths.[6] After a video about the deterioration of medical care in Kuwait, the council heard from a middle-aged man identified as "Dr. Issah Ibrahim," who claimed to be a surgeon at a Kuwaiti hospital. The man's real name was Dr. Ibrahim Bahbahani. He was not a surgeon but an orthodontist. And he didn't work at a Kuwaiti hospital; he worked for the Kuwaiti government as a senior officer of the Red Crescent Society (Abu-Hamad 1992, 6). Still, Dr. Bahbahani described the horrors he witnessed in the "operating room," including the amputation of a teenage girl's leg and the disfigurement of another teen's face. But the most dramatic story told by "Dr. Ibrahim" concerned the death of premature babies.

Like Nayirah, Bahbahani tells a personal experience narrative (Labov 1972). In the orientation, he explains how the hospital morgue filled so quickly that staff had to begin burying the dead "in a single grave." Then, after a 5.3 second pause, he continues (as seen in excerpt 4.1).

Like Nayirah, Bahbahani looks the part. His clothing is suitable both for the U.N. event and his alleged profession: formal attire, complete with a "Free Kuwait" pin on his lapel. His rather enormous glasses may index his "non-Western" identity, as do his skin color and facial structure, which are consistent with stereotypical "Middle

Excerpt 4.1

Time	Frame	Soundtrack*
662–66		The hardest thing was (1.4) burying (1.7) the babies.
667–70		(3.3)
671–77		Under my supervision (1.2) one hundred twenty newborn babies (1.0)
678–83		were bur- were were buried the second week of the invasion. (1.0)

Time	Frame	Soundtrack*
684–93		I myself buried forty newborn babies that had been taken from their incubators by the soldiers.

Easterners." Moreover, Dr. Bahbahani sounds like someone from Kuwait. He speaks with a conspicuous Arabic accent, saying, for example, "nairse" [nɛərs] instead of "nurse" [nɜːrs] and "medeecahl" [mediːkɑːl] instead of "medical" [medɪkʊl]. He also speaks in what is popularly called "broken English," making a number of grammatical errors that index he is a non-native speaker. For instance, he frequently drops articles (e.g., "We had to bury many of people") and occasionally violates rules for pluralization (e.g., "The Iraqis sent into the streets childrens under eighteen"). These nonstandard features make Bahbahani less eloquent than Nayirah but, perhaps, also make him seem more believable as an "ordinary Kuwaiti."

Bahbahani also renders his narrative salient and decontextualizable. Like Nayirah, he uses long and dramatic pauses to hold attention and build narrative suspense. The lengthy 5.3-second pause just before he launches into the story helps audiences to understand this moment as a turning point in his discourse. Meanwhile, the many pauses between words in his narrative add drama. It takes Bahbahani roughly 7 seconds to say, "The hardest thing was . . . burying . . . the babies." Here, the halting nature of his speech perhaps indicates the difficulty of reporting such an awful activity. Then, as if to let this dramatic news sink in, he waits another 3.3 seconds before uttering another word.

Bahbahani also punctuates his narrative with linguistic evaluation (Labov 1972, 370–93), thus enhancing its drama and reportability. For example, in frames 662–66, he uses the superlative "hardest" to maximize the distress he felt as he supposedly buried newborns. Meanwhile, in the central narrative clause, the reflexive pronoun ("I *myself*") represents an evaluative pronouncement, a personal guarantee that the assertion is warrantable (Martin and White 2005, 128). That is, Bahbahani attempts to vouch for the reality of the event by adamantly emphasizing his personal participation in it.

Finally, the doctor increases the newsworthiness of his tale by inflating the number of babies killed. Before the U.N. hearing, the reported figure was typically between 12 and 15. But Bahbahani says he oversaw the burial of *120 babies*. This extraordinary number suggests that Iraqis didn't steal incubators in an isolated incident but continually removed them in a systematic campaign. Importantly, the new figure also makes Bahbahani's story more reportable. If he had merely repeated Nayirah's story of events in a single maternity ward, the doctor would have been rehearsing old news. By increasing the number of babies killed and centering the narrative on the burial of newborns, the doctor upgrades the incubator story and makes it once again new and newsworthy—and more likely to be recontextualized.

Indeed, prominent news institutions noticed Bahbahani's testimony, including all three major networks. I have chosen to analyze only the NBC News report, where the U.N. hearing was the top story. As shown in excerpt 4.2, NBC correspondent John Dancy frames Bahbahani's speech favorably.

Dancy positively evaluates Kuwaiti discourse by referring to the collection of allegations as a "powerful case" for "military action" (frames 29–39). He also helpfully transforms the claim that Bahbahani is a "surgeon" into a fact. Meanwhile, the broadcast highlights emotional distress through carefully selected visuals. As Dancy reports that the Kuwaiti escapees "told of Iraqi rape and murder," the visual frame shows a Kuwaiti woman weeping and being consoled. Viewers are thus led to regard the hearing as credible and moving—a real cause for war.

Interestingly, NBC chose to replay only the last sentence of Bahbahani's incubator narrative. Perhaps this was because, in this sentence, the doctor emphasized his personal investment in the reported action ("I myself"). Or perhaps it was because this was the only utterance in which the doctor specified that the buried newborns "had been taken from their incubators." But it is also likely that only the final sentence was replayed because the doctor diminished the reportability of his earlier assertions. Specifically, when Bahbahani made the newsworthy claim that "120 newborn babies were buried," he repeatedly stuttered over the word "buried" (see frames 678–83 of excerpt 4.2). Such "errors" associated with spontaneous speech may render a piece of discourse less repeatable in news reports (Cramer 2013, 192).

Aside from the TV networks, five major newswires and newspapers also uncritically reported Bahbahani's incubator tale. If these outlets had bothered to look into the matter, they might have discovered, as Middle East Watch did just three days after the U.N. hearing, that there were holes in Bahbahani's account. He had not only falsified his name and lied about being a surgeon but had also failed to report that he had no idea how the babies he supposedly buried had died (Abu-Hamad 1992, 6).[7] Apparently, the U.N. Security Council was also taken in. Two days after its hearing, the council voted to authorize military force against Iraq and gave Saddam Hussein until January 15 to withdraw his troops.

Excerpt 4.2

Time	Frame	Soundtrack*
29–39		The Kuwaitis who say only military action can save their country from Iraq made a <u>powerful</u> case and made it in the very <u>room</u> where the vote will be taken on Thursday. The Security Council chamber.
40–42		Kuwaiti escapees told of Iraqi <u>rape</u> and murder
43–44		as Security Council members listened.
45–58		A surgeon at a Kuwaiti hospital. [**Bahbahani:**] I myself buried forty newborn babies that had been taken from their incubators by the soldiers.

The President's Outrage

Insiders were not the only ones to narrate the incubator story. An important outsider—with enormous symbolic capital (Bourdieu 1991)—frequently rehearsed the tale, commanding the attention of the mainstream press. President George H. W. Bush recited the story *eight* times in public addresses, so often that we can identify generic regularities in his performances. Table 2 enumerates obligatory and non-obligatory components of Bush's incubator speeches and shows how each component is realized linguistically. In appendix E, I provide a supplementary analysis of all eight speeches.

The obligatory components of Bush's incubator performance include a recitation of atrocities, an expression of moral judgment and emotional distress, and a suggestion that military action is imminent. First, the *recitation of multiple atrocities* implies recurring violence and justifies Bush's provocative claim that Iraq is "systematically dismantling" Kuwait. By portraying an atrocity crisis in Kuwait, Bush provides indexical cues to journalists that his discourse is shareable in their culture, endowed with "desired qualities" like drama and emergency (Bauman and Briggs 1990, 77). Also, by reciting many atrocity stories, Bush helps ensure that the incubator story will not be scrutinized. Journalists might examine the incubator story if it were cited as the only evidence of Iraq's evil, but when presented with other stories, it becomes more difficult to challenge and more likely to be reported uncritically. Finally, the recitation of atrocities creates rhetorical momentum, allowing Bush to emphasize the incubator story as the "icing on the cake" when it comes to Iraqi crimes. Bush recites the incubator story last in five of his eight speeches, making it the final insult and the clearest motivation for war. By emphasizing the story this way, he also makes it more memorable and, thus, more detachable and repeatable.

Importantly, as shown in table 2, the move to attribute the atrocity story to a source is a non-obligatory element of Bush's performances. In his first telling of the story on October 9, Bush (1990b) attributes the atrocity story to the emir of Kuwait, indicating that it is a sourced assertion (not a fact), and even uses a speech act noun ("tales") commonly associated with fiction. Indeed, he declares uncertainty about the reliability of the atrocity stories ("I don't know how many of these tales can be authenticated"). But, after this press conference, Bush very rarely attributes the incubator story to the emir, and he never again questions whether the tale can be "authenticated." On October 16, Bush (1990d) sources the atrocity allegations not to individuals but to anonymous "firsthand reports," making them seem credible. By October 23, he stops sourcing the allegations altogether, presenting the incubator story in unmodalized assertions (Bush 1990e, 1990f). Thus, audiences are positioned to regard the narrative as categorically true and potentially worthy of being shared again.

Bush's use of *emotional and evaluative language* is also crucial, because it allows him to crystallize the point of the story: the Iraqis are exhibiting extraordinary cruelty. For example, directly after recounting the incubator story on October 23, Bush

Table 2 Generic components of incubator allegation in speeches by George H. W. Bush

Component	Typical realization	Example
Attribution (non-obligatory)	• Reporting clause • Speech-act noun • Hearsay adverb	• "he reflected" (1990b) • "tales" (1990c) • "reportedly" (1990d)
Recitation of atrocities	Two or more consecutive clauses featuring an aggressor-violation-victim pattern (Oddo 2014b). The aggressor is usually implied but sometimes specified as "Iraqi troops" or "Saddam." The violation—encoded either as a verb or nominalized process—construes a deadly assault. The victim is specified either as "Kuwait" or as vulnerable people within Kuwait (kids, babies, dialysis patients).	"In one hospital, dialysis patients were ripped from their machines and the machines shipped from Kuwait to Baghdad. Iraq soldiers pulled the plug on incubators supporting 22 premature babies. All 22 died. The hospital employees were shot and the plundered machines were shipped off to Baghdad" (1990g).
Expression of moral judgment/ emotional distress	Implication of negative affect, sometimes insecurity and unhappiness, but more often intense displeasure and disgust. Negative emotion is coupled with strongly negative judgments of Iraqi behavior. These are inscribed lexically (e.g. "brutality") or invoked through moralized comparisons to Hitler (Martin and White 2005).	"We've all heard of **atrocities** [judgment] in Kuwait that would **make the strongest among us weep** [affect]. It **turns your stomach** [affect] when you listen to the tales of those that have escaped the **brutality** [judgment] of Saddam, the **invader** [judgment]" (1990i).
Suggestion military action is imminent	Future-tense clauses that directly or indirectly promise remedial action. This remedial action is underspecified but is understood to be military action. Often Bush uses some version of "This will not stand" as his summative comment. Sometimes, he explicitly construes America as an actor that will prevent wrongdoing (e.g., 1990c).	"And so, the bottom line for us is that Iraqi aggression will not be allowed to stand. Saddam Hussein will be held accountable. And the legitimate government of Kuwait will be restored" (1990d).

(1990f) concludes: "And that's what we're dealing with. We're dealing with **Hitler revisited**, a **totalitarianism** and a **brutality** that is <u>naked</u> and <u>unprecedented</u> in modern times." Following Martin and White (2005), I have bolded the negative judgments of Iraq's **propriety** and have underlined the negative judgments of Iraq's <u>normality</u>. Together, these signal that Iraq is *abnormally* evil—its crimes are "unprecedented" even in the age of the Nazis. Of course, this is the kind of rousing language that makes Bush's discourse dramatic and memorable (who could forget a phrase like "Hitler revisited"?) and practically ensures that his speech will be recontextualized by reporters.

The final obligatory component of Bush's performance is a *promise for remedial action*. Bush routinely concludes with some version of the following pledge: "This will not stand." Essentially, this is an epistemic guarantee that Iraqi atrocities will not be permitted to continue, and it strongly implies that the president will use force to halt Iraqi aggression. (Often the president makes this explicit.) But what interests me most about this promise is its rhetorical timing. In every case, the "this will not stand" trope closely follows the recitation of atrocities. The implication could not be any clearer: the atrocities (especially the incubator atrocities) demand a military response. Thus, we see that the incubator story is not simply something Bush haphazardly alludes to. It is strategically linked to the promise of military action and serves as the argumentative ground for war.

The standardized features of Bush's performance are significant. Indeed, by repeating the same material in speech after speech, Bush helps to entextualize it, distinguishing the atrocity segment from the rest of his discourse. Moreover, the extreme comparisons ("Hitler revisited"), intense evaluative language ("evil," "shocking"), and memorable refrains ("this will not stand") all index to journalists that the incubator story is potentially detachable. However, to induce recontextualization in the press, Bush also relied on indexical reference to his own authority. As soon as he is introduced as "President of the United States" and begins speaking from behind a presidential podium, Bush indexes his institutional office, signaling to journalists that his discourse is valuable and reusable.

Indeed, built-in norms of journalism practically require reporters to print whatever the president says, even if what he says is ludicrously untrue. As one journalist told Daniel Hallin, a statement from the president is considered a "quotable fact," something to be repeated without interpretation. Thus, "if the president says, 'black is white,' you write, 'The president said black is white'" (Hallin 1986, 71). Needless to say, this convention virtually guaranteed that Bush's incubator story would be reported without challenge. As shown in table 3, all but one of Bush's performances of the incubator story were repeated in the mainstream press.

Interestingly, journalists routinely repeated every obligatory element of Bush's generic performance and arranged those elements in the same order as Bush had.[8] The stories begin with the president's recitation of atrocities and follow with his promise for remedial action. And in no report do the journalists present a source that refutes the president's incubator claims. Throughout October and November

Table 3 Journalistic recontextualizations of Bush's incubator allegation

Speech	TV replay	Transcription	Quotation	Indirect report
1990b, October 9		AP (Oct. 9)	*LA Times* (Oct. 10)	
1990c, October 15	*MacNeil/Lehrer NewsHour* (Oct. 15)		*NY Times* (Oct. 16)	AP (Oct. 15 & 16); UPI (Oct. 15 &16); *LA Times* (Oct. 16); *USA Today* (Oct. 16)
1990d, October 16				AP (Oct. 16)
1990e, October 23			Reuters (Oct. 23)	*Washington Times* (Oct. 24)
1990f, October 23				
1990g, October 28				*Washington Post* (Oct. 29)
1990h, November 1			*USA Today* (Nov. 2)	
1990i, November 22	Broadcast live on all networks	*NY Times* (Nov. 23)		

1990, then, the incubator story was not only kept alive by President Bush but safeguarded from criticism by the press.

Independent Confirmation

Like journalists, human rights organizations have a professional interest in researching and exposing atrocities. This fact was not lost on Hill & Knowlton, which deliberately fed the incubator story to one of the most venerable human rights organizations in the world, Amnesty International (Manheim 1994, 140). To its great discredit, Amnesty confirmed the incubator charge, yielding even more media coverage. A human rights giant was effectively transformed into an (unwitting) propaganda tool.

Of course, Amnesty didn't need to publicize the incubator atrocity. In fact, another rights organization called Middle East Watch refused to do so, suspecting a public relations ploy (MacArthur 1992, 61–62). Why, then, did Amnesty take the bait? Perhaps something sinister was going on. Francis Boyle (2002), who worked for the human rights group at the time, has questioned Amnesty's entire December 19 report on Iraq's abuses in Kuwait. Boyle says he repeatedly attempted to pull the incubator story from Amnesty's report but was ignored by executives in London. He came to believe that Amnesty had been infiltrated by a spy: "My conclusion was that a high-level official of Amnesty International at that time, whom I will not name, was a British intelligence agent. . . . So certainly when I am dealing with people who want to work with Amnesty in London, I just tell them, 'Look, just understand, they're penetrated by intelligence agents, U.K., maybe U.S., I don't know, but you certainly can't trust them'" (Boyle 2002). Historians should investigate Boyle's claim of interference by an undercover saboteur. Arguably, though, Amnesty would have been attracted to the incubator story anyway. What interests me is how Amnesty recontextualized the story, potentially enhancing its authority and "semiotic mobility" (Blommaert 2005, 69).

Several rhetorical features render Amnesty's recontextualization of the story both credible and reportable in the press. First, Amnesty attributed information to its sources in ways that indexed legitimacy. For example, Amnesty International (1990b, 56) quotes "a Red Crescent doctor," a "doctor working at al-'Addan Hospital," and a "Kuwaiti doctor working at al-Razi Hospital." The quoted informants are kept anonymous, making them impossible to challenge, and they are identified as "doctors" at specific hospitals, assigning them insider status. In fact, the anonymous doctors had no direct knowledge of what had happened to hospitalized babies. For example, the doctor working at al-Razi could not have known firsthand about incubator thefts, since al-Razi is an orthopedic hospital with no maternity ward (Abu-Hamad 1992, 6).[9] Very few Westerners could be expected to know this; for them, hospital affiliation likely served as an index of legitimacy. Amnesty also uses reporting phrases that suggest the reliability of the informants. These phrases misleadingly index sworn oaths ("testimony"), direct knowledge ("knew of"), and firsthand observation and description ("eyewitness account," "reported"). Amnesty might have used phrases to index lack of proof or illegitimacy ("claim," "allegation," "heard," "rumored"), but such words would make their own report less valuable and less worthy of recontextualization.

Next, Amnesty enhances the reportability of the story by endowing it with qualities most valued by journalists: newness, drama, and crisis. For example, new details are given about mass burials. The "Red Crescent doctor" is quoted as saying that he "personally" took part in the burial of 72 premature infants (Amnesty International 1990b, 56). According to this doctor, "a total of 312 babies died" when "Iraqi soldiers took them out of the incubators" (56). Note the figure given for the number of dead infants: 312. This figure is new and dramatic; it is also preposterous. Prior to Iraq's invasion, there were only about two hundred incubators in all of Kuwait, and many of these were "warming beds" (Abu-Hamad 1992, 7–8). Even if every incubator had been occupied by infants and stolen by Iraqi soldiers, that would still leave over 100 babies who could not have died as described. Implausible as it may be, however, a figure of 312 dead babies is also highly reportable—and, as shown below, Amnesty was keen on having such dramatic numbers recontextualized in the press.

Finally, Amnesty rendered the incubator story repeatable by linking different versions of it and thereby creating the sense that it had been independently "confirmed" by multiple parties. For instance, just after quoting the mass burial story of the "Red Crescent doctor," Amnesty attributes a similar account of mass burial to the "doctor working at al-'Addan," who "reported that 36 premature babies were buried in one day alone in August." The second report from al-'Addan seems to substantiate the first. Next, Amnesty alleges that a "15-year-old Kuwaiti girl" (the unnamed informant is Nayirah) provided an "eyewitness account of *such deaths at al-'Addan*" (Amnesty International 1990b, 56; my emphasis). Here, the deictic noun phrase ("such deaths at al-'Addan") refers back to the speech attributed to the doctor from the same hospital. In other words, readers are to understand that the fifteen-year-old girl confirmed the doctor's account of the deaths.[10]

Thus, different versions of the incubator story are tied together so that they appear to corroborate one another. Perhaps readers could dismiss one doctor's claims that huge numbers of premature babies were removed from incubators and buried. But now multiple doctors—and a teenage "eyewitness"—are saying essentially the same thing. As Latour (1987, 33) argues, persuasion is often "a question of *numbers*"— the more sources are stacked together, the harder it is for the reader to dismiss the "mounting" accounts of abuse.

However, Amnesty also provided indexical cues that made the incubator story *less* reportable. For instance, it consistently attributed the story to sources, thereby indicating its status as an alleged narrative. Moreover, the stories of the incubator atrocity are not prominently featured in Amnesty's report, appearing for the first time on page 56 of the 82-page document. Only a meticulous journalist could be expected to read so deeply into the manuscript—and even then, she might choose to ignore the incubator charge or focus on another one.

In fact, Amnesty's account of the incubator story probably would have been ignored if the organization had not also issued a critical press release. As Ridolfo and DeVoss (2009) argue, press releases are always designed with rhetorical velocity in mind: they are made to be reused by third parties in the media. True to form, Amnesty's press release rendered the incubator tale much more salient, entextualizable, and recontextualizable. Indeed, it did not go on for 56 pages before unleashing news of dead babies. Instead, the second paragraph reads, "In its first comprehensive report on human rights violations in Kuwait since the invasion on August 2, Amnesty International details how Iraqi forces have tortured and killed many hundreds of victims, taken several thousand prisoners and left more than 300 premature babies to die after looting incubators from at least three of Kuwait City's main hospitals" (Amnesty International 1990a). Here, Amnesty's report is positively evaluated with words suggesting thoroughness ("comprehensive," "details"). More importantly, the incubator allegations—previously attributed to sources in the report—have here been converted into a statement of fact: "Iraqi forces have . . . left more than 300 premature babies to die."[11]

A few paragraphs later, the press release explains how Amnesty "confirmed" the atrocity: "The organization said it has collected compelling evidence supporting earlier reports of the killing of premature babies by Iraqi soldiers. . . . The organization's investigation team interviewed several doctors and nurses who worked in the hospitals where the babies died. All had seen the dead bodies and one doctor had even helped to bury 72 of them in a cemetery near the hospital. In some hospitals, unofficial records were kept of the number of people who had been killed, including the babies" (Amnesty International 1990a). Essentially, unverified claims have here been branded as "compelling evidence." Moreover, this "evidence" is represented as "supporting earlier reports of the killing of premature babies." In other words, the press release suggests that the new "evidence" in Amnesty's report is somehow different from and superior to "earlier reports," when, in fact, the new evidence is often just the same earlier reports (e.g., Nayirah's account) presented in a new format. Amnesty's researchers are also given an official and legitimizing title ("the investigation team"), and it is reported that they "interviewed several doctors and nurses who worked in the hospitals where the babies died." Crucially, the notion that "the babies died" is presupposed as a fact—not a claim made by Amnesty's informants.[12] The press release also maximizes the number of people ("all") who claim to have "seen the dead bodies," while in the actual report, two of the informants relate what *others told them* about dead babies, not what they themselves witnessed. Finally, the press release describes "unofficial records" of "the number of people killed, including the babies," implying tangible evidence of the incubator atrocity.[13]

Thus, the press release recontextualizes Amnesty's report in ways that enhance its credibility and factuality, indexing that the research was more painstaking than it was, and transforming sourced allegations into categorical facts. These changes are important because journalists who covered Amnesty's report didn't really cover the report itself. They covered the "updated" press release. For example, the Associated Press story on the subject paraphrases the news release: "The Iraqis left more than 300 premature babies to die after stealing their incubators from Kuwait City hospitals, the report said. Amnesty said its investigators interviewed several doctors and nurses and that all saw bodies of the babies. One doctor helped bury 72 bodies, the report said" (West 1990). Again, the sources who originally claimed to have seen the incubator atrocity have disappeared. Instead, the notion that "Iraqis left more than 300 premature babies to die" is attributed exclusively to Amnesty's impersonal and seemingly authoritative report.[14]

Thus, the ever-efficient journalists enhanced the authority of Amnesty's claims by basing their stories exclusively on the confident press release and ignoring the original 82-page document (and all its sourced allegations). Moreover, Amnesty representatives themselves took to the airwaves to boost the warrantability of their claims. On the very day the report was released, Amnesty's deputy executive director Curt Goering appeared on NPR's *All Things Considered*. Reporter Noah Adams (1990b) introduces his interview with Goering this way: "A new report from Amnesty International offers details of atrocities committed inside Kuwait by the Iraqi occupying forces. . . . Kurt Goering of Amnesty International explains how his group gathered information to confirm the accounts it heard about, reports that could have been invented or exaggerated to serve political ends." Using a modal qualifier, Adams explicitly raises the possibility that reports of atrocities "*could* have been invented or exaggerated to serve political ends." However, he suggests this opportunity for spin and propaganda has been neutralized by Amnesty's research. Indeed, Goering supposedly "explains how his group gathered information to confirm the accounts." Notice how the reporting verb ("explains") endorses Goering as an authoritative speaker who will impart knowledge (Martin and White 2005, 126). More importantly, Adams categorically represents Amnesty as a group that performed legitimate research processes of data collection ("gathered information") and verification ("to confirm the accounts")—processes that presumably rule out the publication of fabricated claims.

Moments later, Adams directly asks Goering whether the incubator stories are true:

ADAMS: Did you find, indeed, that many of the stories we heard—including testimony about babies being taken out of incubators in hospitals there, left on the cold floor to die—were those stories true?
GOERING: We now have sufficient information that—and we've been able to confirm that to our satisfaction—that this type of thing has, in fact, happened.

We have spoken with and have received detailed information from doctors who themselves saw what was happening with the babies being taken from the incubators and doctors who, in fact, participated in burying dozens of these babies and other doctors who provided lists of names of babies who were born prematurely and who were in these incubators. (Adams 1990b)

Goering's convoluted response to a yes-or-no question is perhaps telling. Instead of baldly asserting the incubator stories are true, he positively evaluates the quantity of data his group collected ("we now have *sufficient* information"), hedges about the universality of his group's findings ("to *our* satisfaction" does not mean to *everyone's* satisfaction), and insists upon his assertion, indicating an awareness that others hold a countering view ("this type of thing has, *in fact*, happened"). Still, Goering's response is unmistakably affirmative: he confirms the truth of the incubator stories. In doing so, he again positively evaluates his evidence ("*detailed* information") and removes attributional phrases from the original Amnesty document (Doctor A "reported," Doctor B "told of," etc.). For example, Goering doesn't report that doctors *claim* to have seen atrocities but that "*they themselves saw* . . . the babies being taken from the incubators" and that "*they, in fact, participated* in burying dozens of these babies." What was formerly reported speech now appears as taken-for-granted reality.

Citing Amnesty's Report in the Political Debate over War

Amnesty International, then, ran its own public relations campaign—a campaign that sought to affirm the organization's research credentials and expose atrocities compelling enough for national news. In so doing, the group not only kept the incubator story alive but enhanced its authority, rendering it more invulnerable to criticism, more impervious to "compromising transformation" in later users' hands (Bauman and Briggs 1990, 77). Indeed, Amnesty's version of the story was recontextualized again and again by U.S. politicians. For instance, President Bush—who had suddenly become very interested in human rights violations—cited Amnesty's report in an interview with David Frost as proof that Iraq's behavior was "primeval." Bush also kept a copy of the report on his desk, showing it to foreign dignitaries and journalists, as he urged war in the Gulf (Aruri 1991, 313–14).

Following Bush's lead, U.S. lawmakers repeatedly cited the report during their prewar debate. Not surprisingly, Amnesty's reputation for accuracy was exploited by the pro-war faction on Capitol Hill. For instance, Senator John Breaux (1991) extols the human rights group: "Amnesty International, a very well-respected international organization, has documented the types of torture that the Iraqi Army perpetrated on the people of Kuwait." Breaux not only describes Amnesty with intensely positive evaluation ("*very* well-respected") but represents the group as one that has "documented" (and not merely asserted) Iraqi atrocities. Similarly, Representative Dan Burton (1991) characterizes Amnesty's report as a collection of "facts."

The report was deemed so authoritative that, on January 11, 1991, the entire document—and the appended press release—were added to the congressional record in both the House and Senate. Thus, during his statement, Senator John McCain (1991) was able to quote directly from the report. Though McCain deemed some of the material "too degrading to read" in public, he carefully recited the incubator allegations word for word. Meanwhile, in the House, Representative Curt Weldon (1991) also read from the document, supplementing direct quotations with his own fanciful details. For example, after reading about the man who claimed to have buried seventy-two premature infants, Weldon remarks: "This is a sworn statement of a Red Crescent doctor." Of course, the doctor's statement was *not* sworn, not even close. Others simply presented the incubator allegations as fact, without even bothering to cite Amnesty International or anyone else. For example, Representative Jack Fields (1991) baldly declared that Saddam Hussein "took incubators out of hospitals in Kuwait and let little babies die." Thus, Fields concluded, it was "fair to make analogies to Adolf Hitler."

Clearly, the incubator atrocity now had the ring of truth, and emboldened hawks on Capitol Hill took full advantage. No one knows what impact these recitations of the incubator story had on the congressional vote. The war resolution passed easily in the House. But in the Senate, where the incubator story was mentioned seven times, debate was intense. Ultimately, the Senate authorized war against Iraq, passing the resolution by just five votes (MacArthur 1992, 70). Perhaps the incubator atrocity—freshly inscribed with the imprimatur of Amnesty International—had provided just enough impetus.

Resistance and Reification

On January 17, 1991, Alexander Cockburn wrote an article for the *Los Angeles Times* in which he finally exposed the incubator story as a lie. Cockburn (1991) shoots holes in Amnesty's report (ridiculing its figure of 312 dead babies), and he condemns the "deluge of propaganda" used to manipulate the American public. His article is scathing, but it appeared too late to make any difference: the bombing of Iraq had begun a day earlier. After Cockburn, others would continue to discredit the story. In April 1991, Amnesty International (1991, 1) issued an embarrassing retraction of its earlier report, having found, after visiting Kuwait, that there was "no reliable evidence" of the incubator atrocity. Later, John MacArthur (1992) of *Harper's Magazine* exposed the scope of Hill & Knowlton's propaganda campaign by revealing, among other things, the true identity of Nayirah. And Aziz Abu-Hamad of Middle East Watch (1992) issued a report on the incubator tale, pointing out inconsistencies across stories and proving, beyond a reasonable doubt, that the event never occurred.

But even before these revelations, indeed long before the bombing started, others had stepped forward to refute the incubator allegation. An American doctor named Mohammed Said (1992) says he traveled to Kuwait in early September 1990, interviewed doctors who denied the allegation, and took videos of the incubators, which remained intact in Kuwaiti hospitals. Dr. Said apparently held press conferences in Amman, Jordan, and Washington, D.C., where he showed his videos to hundreds of reporters and proclaimed that there was no truth to the incubator charge. Although major news organizations like CNN and ABC were reportedly on hand, no one from the national media ran his story. The best Dr. Said could get was local news coverage in his hometown of Seattle, Washington. Later, Dr. Said says, he contacted the office of Representative Tom Lantos to request that he be allowed to give a statement at the Human Rights Caucus, so he could set the record straight. But, again, he received no reply. Dr. Said says he even contacted Amnesty International to share his story, but no one there was interested either.

Others who refuted the incubator story were more fortunate and managed, at least, to get their statements printed in the press. Iraqi officials, for instance, occasionally rebutted the incubator charges in American news. But these refutations received relatively little coverage. Often, when Iraqis appeared in stories, those stories focused on the atrocities Iraq had supposedly committed. Some Iraqi official might be given a sentence or two—perhaps near the end of the report—to counter the allegations of abuse (e.g., "A spokesman for the Iraqi Embassy in London said Tuesday, 'We deny all these fabrications.'" [Tuohy 1990]). But the rest of the article would be about the suffering of the Kuwaitis, the theft, the torture, and the murder. Even when Iraqi rebuttals were detailed, as they sometimes were in early October 1990, few Americans believed them. Indeed, who could trust the Iraqis, who had just invaded a sovereign country and who were repeatedly being characterized as "butchers" and "animals" by the U.S. political elite?

In fact, only a few credible sources appeared in the press to dismiss the incubator allegation. *USA Today* reported on October 22, 1990, "Kuwaiti doctors, speaking to reporters in the presence of Iraqi press officials, denied allegations . . . that babies were taken from incubators and left to die" (Jolidon 1990). But notice that these unnamed doctors are "in the presence of Iraqi press officials" and presumably under their control. Later, on December 12, 1990, the *Washington Post* reported statements from Dr. Gisli Sigurdsson, head of intensive care at the Mubarak Kabir hospital, who recently escaped from Kuwait. The *Post* writes Sigurdsson "denied that babies had been pulled out of their incubators at his hospital" (Priest 1990). But this doctor's denial pertains only to his hospital. What about all the other hospitals? And what about all the other hospital workers who had already come forward: Dr. Fawzia Sayegh, Nayirah al-Sabah, Dr. Ali al-Huwail, Dr. "Issa Ibrahim." Surely the Icelandic doctor was not refuting all of these genuine Kuwaitis!

Besides, just one week after Sigurdsson was quoted in the *Post*, Amnesty International issued its report on Iraqi atrocities and a flood of new articles reaffirming the incubator tale was unleashed. By early January, Sigurdsson was but a distant memory, but the campaign to promote the incubator story was not yet done. With the help of CFK marketing, author Jean Sasson unveiled a new book specifying Iraqi atrocities, *The Rape of Kuwait*. Included, of course, was the news that "babies had been torn from incubators and thrown to die upon the cold floors" (Sasson 1991, 60). Though hastily published paperbacks rarely receive such treatment, *The Rape of Kuwait* was advertised in major newspapers and featured on forty-three television talk shows (Lee and Lancaster 1991). After a favorable review in the *Wall Street Journal*, the book became a bestseller (Rowse 1991).

Thus, there was always a resounding answer to anyone who rejected the incubator allegations. Dissenters might attract news coverage momentarily. But even when they did, they were either too untrustworthy to be believed (e.g., the Iraqis) or they received such limited exposure that they were overlooked. In other words, their voices lacked the "capacity for semiotic mobility" (Blommaert 2005, 69). They were unable, on a continual basis, to induce favorable recontextualizations in the press. Meanwhile, more powerful voices were able to generate the "conditions for a desired uptake" (68). They could create rhetorical events deemed recontextualizable and authoritative—presidential speeches, congressional hearings, U.N. inquiries, human rights reports, new bestsellers. Such events are always "shareable" in the corporate media (Urban 1996, 24), while dissenting voices seem unworthy of being heard.

When it comes to propaganda, what matters most is not the truth of an assertion but the strength of the actors behind it. In this case, powerful actors provided indexical references to their authority that rendered their discourse more interesting to journalists, more shareable, and more recontextualizable. Thus, the incubator myth appeared again and again in the press, as long as the president and other dignitaries kept repeating it. Indeed, this chapter shows that widespread repetition is not just the goal of deliberate propagandists but their primary strategy. The more something is repeated, the more it is remembered; the more it is remembered, the more it can be repeated again.

In a perfect world, perhaps, journalists would have delayed reporting the incubator allegation until they had checked hospital and cemetery records; examined maternity wards; inspected burial sites for mass graves; interviewed doctors and staff at maternity wards; and spoken to cemetery personnel who had performed burials. They would have directly questioned those alleging the atrocity story; recorded their names; asked if their allegations were based on observation or hearsay; determined what hospitals they worked at, who their coworkers were, how many incubators were stolen, how many babies were killed; challenged them with counterclaims from other witnesses; and confronted them about their own contradictory statements.

All this requires labor. The journalists would have had to, in Latour's (1987) words, push the narrative back "upstream" to the context of its production—a rather demanding project. How much easier it was to just report what the president said; he was the president, after all, and his press conference was right in Washington. How much easier it was to air a clip of Nayirah's testimony, especially when she was so moving and the CFK had gone through all the trouble of providing news video. Occupied Kuwait was far away and off limits. But the incubator story was right in front of them, hanging low on the tree, and looking very juicy. And so, the story traveled along, down the stream, and into public consciousness.

If journalists had difficulty pushing back against the incubator story, then ordinary citizens were even more powerless. First, who would want to challenge a narrative being repeated by seemingly credible eyewitnesses, journalists, authors, lawmakers, a human rights organization, and the president of the United States? And assuming people cared to defy such reputable figures, who had the resources (and the courage) to trace the story back to occupied Kuwait? Finally, even if one discovered the truth, how could that person hope to gain attention in the media marketplace? Dr. Said claimed to know the incubator allegations were false in September 1990, but he didn't have enough influence to testify at the Human Rights Caucus, he didn't have the technology to produce ready-for-TV news clips, and he didn't have a presidential pulpit that could automatically turn his words into national headlines.

The lesson from the incubator story, then, is a simple one: Elites are often best equipped to make their propaganda travel. Those with millions of dollars and the right political connections may have all the resources they need to make a lie more potent than the truth.

Infiltrating Network News

5. Message Force Multipliers:
Rewarding Recontextualization

Members of this group [of analysts] have
echoed administration talking points,
sometimes even when they suspected the
information was false or inflated.

          —David Barstow, 2008

I have shown how deliberate propagandists can induce a favorable uptake of their messages by using semiotic cues to render their discourse detachable and worthy of recontextualization. I have earlier argued that deliberate propagandists need not use purely discursive means to induce a favorable recontextualization of their claims. If they have the resources, they can also offer symbolic or material rewards, effectively compensating people who repeat desired meanings. In this chapter, I take up this issue and investigate how the U.S. government incentivized TV news analysts to replicate official talking points. At the same time, I consider how other institutions—including news corporations—may have rewarded analysts who relayed the government's point of view. I suggest that these inducements, often hidden from the public, are both manipulative and contrary to the ideals of a freestanding press, as they potentially transform news analysis into state (or corporate) propaganda.

In this chapter and the next one, I focus on TV news analysts before the 2003 Iraq War, specifically the period between September 11, 2001 (a date roughly coinciding with the first serious plans for war) and March 19, 2003 (hours before aerial bombing commenced in Baghdad).[1] I concentrate on the "big three" broadcast networks in U.S. media—ABC, NBC, and CBS—since most Americans at this time received their news from these sources (Raine, Fox, and Fallows 2003).[2] During the period, two distinct groups of analysts were featured prominently: (1) *weapons analysts*, especially former U.N. inspectors, who commented on Iraqi disarmament; and

(2) *military analysts* who regularly communicated with the Pentagon and typically commented on war preparations.[3]

I consulted various sources to understand the relationships between these news analysts, journalists, corporations, and governments. For instance, I sought out biographical records for each analyst and identified associations with government and the defense industry. I researched investigative reports about the relationship between the Pentagon and military analysts and examined documents released by the Pentagon concerning its talking points operation. I also made Freedom of Information Act (FOIA) requests to obtain records of interaction between government agencies and weapons analysts. Finally, to further understand the sociopolitical context, I interviewed two former weapons inspectors who worked as news analysts during the prewar period: Dr. David Kay and Ambassador Richard Butler.

I find that news analysts frequently had political and financial allegiances, which raise questions about the integrity and objectivity of their reporting. These analysts often received perks from government officials and special encouragement to repeat desired claims. These included private meetings with officials, appeals to shared ideological goals, and, most importantly, the promise of access to the government's inner circle. Meanwhile, news institutions rewarded analysts for this access: contributors were typically paid based on their ability to find an audience with government elites. Thus, analysts faced a double bind: to secure payment or airtime from news corporations, they had to maintain access; to maintain access, they were sometimes nudged by government officials to repeat government claims. Complicating matters further, several analysts held key positions with defense corporations and neoconservative political organizations, giving them further incentive to recontextualize pro-war (and pro-government) messages. Ultimately, this chapter reveals how governments may influence the circulation of discourse by strategically exploiting weaknesses in corporate journalism and even infiltrating the press to spread its propaganda.

The Curious Position of News Analysts

The status quo in mainstream American journalism is far from desirable, as even the best journalists are largely dependent on "official" sources (Bennett 2012; Domke 2004; Herman and Chomsky 2002; Zaller and Chiu 1996). Still, the American press at least has the potential to act as an independent watchdog, and when the circumstances are right, good journalists can and do challenge government claims (Bennett, Lawrence, and Livingston 2007; Entman 2004). Moreover, even if American journalists routinely depend on elite sources, they are typically not government puppets. Most mainstream journalists believe in strict independence from political parties and moneyed interests. Thus, in its "Code of Ethics," the Society of Professional Journalists (2014) declares that reporters should:

- Avoid conflicts of interest, real or perceived. Disclose unavoidable conflicts.
- Refuse gifts, favors, fees, free travel and special treatment, and avoid political and other outside activities that may compromise integrity or impartiality, or may damage credibility.
- Be wary of sources offering information for favors or money; do not pay for access to news. Identify content provided by outside sources, whether paid or not.
- Deny favored treatment to advertisers, donors or any other special interests, and resist internal and external pressure to influence coverage.

Journalists, then, are expected to resist undue influence from outside forces and reject advancing their own interests.

But journalists are not the only ones who present news. We must also consider the status of what Tugend (2003) calls "quasi-journalists," specifically analysts, who regularly appear on television and radio but who are not formally trained as reporters. What role do these news providers have in contemporary journalism, and just how independent are they?

News analysts don't have the same responsibilities as traditional journalists. Journalists are required to present only the "facts," without evaluating events or drawing conclusions. Analysts, meanwhile, clarify and interpret these facts, dissecting and explaining events in ways that, ideally, deepen public understanding (Albaek 2011). As recognized authorities, then, analysts are licensed to offer opinions—something journalists are not supposed to do. However, unlike partisan editorialists, news analysts are also expected be "objective"; that is, their interpretations should derive from technical expertise, not political conviction. Thus, networks regard analysts as impartial "authorities who can offer information or explanations of events that are untainted by bias" (Steele 1995, 801). They are "perceived as having neutral, factual knowledge" and are expected to be detached from the conflicts they discuss (Albaek 2011, 338).

One might assume, then, that news analysts are also required to avoid conflicts of interest and disclose political or financial commitments that might compromise the integrity of their work. But, since they are *quasi*-journalists, analysts are not necessarily held to the same ethical standards as trained reporters (Barstow 2008). In fact, analysts often have ideological allegiances and financial interests that diminish their credibility (Lee and Solomon 1990; Soley 1992; Steele 1995; Tugend 2003). Moreover, though analysts are frequently presented as expert authorities, their technical knowledge may not be as profound as advertised. As Steele (1995) reports, news producers don't necessarily want experts with terrific scholarly resumes; they don't much care if analysts are well read in their fields or if they publish primary research. In fact, what producers really want are analysts who have "real world" experience (David Kay, personal communication with the author, May 7, 2014)—that is, experience that gives them access to the big players in Washington. Ultimately, one's knowledge is less important than one's ability to network (Steele 1995).

Producers also want analysts who are articulate, colorful, and telegenic—those who can entertain. Networks may even prefer analysts who offer provocative interpretations, regardless of whether the interpretations are supported by facts. And since the analysts are often paid, they may have an incentive to give producers what they want. That is, analysts may exaggerate or embellish in order to get airtime, or, having accepted the "expert" brand, they may feel obligated to discuss subjects they don't understand (Tugend 2003).

Analysts, then, occupy a unique space in the world of contemporary journalism. They are typically connected to the newsmakers in Washington and often provide access and insight into political operations otherwise difficult to penetrate. This access to Washington insiders is precisely what makes them attractive to journalists, and yet it is also what makes them susceptible to undue political influence. Analysts with close ties to officials are more likely to offer favorable interpretations of government. Yet their ties to government—so valued by journalists—are also rendered invisible to news consumers. If my study is any indication, analysts typically appear on screen for eight to ten seconds, hardly long enough for viewers to learn their names, let alone assess their credentials. And during their brief sound bites, they are presented as independent experts, unbeholden to the political establishment.

At the same time, analysts' contributions may be unduly influenced by journalists. Journalists often compose their news stories before they contact analysts and may use analysts to provide "compensatory legitimacy—to confirm the conclusions that they themselves have already reached" (Albaek 2011, 338).[4] Indeed, journalists may keep contacting analysts until they obtain quotations fitting their preconceived frames (Wien 2001), or they may strategically select and recontextualize an analyst's sound bite to ensure it fits with the tenor of the news drama they've constructed.

Ultimately, analysts occupy two worlds simultaneously. They are part of the journalistic community, though they have little control over news editing and fewer obligations to integrity and independence. They are part of the partisan political community, though they hold no government office and are presented as neutral. Their unique position may provide viewers with rare perspective and penetrating insights, but as shown below, it may also be a recipe for conflicts of interest and propaganda.

Incentivizing Military Analysts

News executives may believe their analysts are "neutral authorities" (Steele 1995, 801). However, even if we accept the questionable assumption that neutrality is possible and desirable, there is little evidence to support the conclusion that analysts are disinterested. Indeed, the analysts in this study were often embedded with the political establishment and invested in corporations with a clear interest in war. In addition, some had questionable moral authority or little "cognitive authority" with regard to the events they discussed (Wilson 1983). In appendix F, I list the analysts in this project, specify the newscasts they appeared in, and identify the "real world" experience that likely made them attractive to news producers. In appendix G, I highlight political and financial incentives that might induce these analysts to recontextualize pro-war and pro-government claims.

In many cases, the conflicts of interest are transparent and disturbing. For example, all military analysts in this study participated in a massive Pentagon program designed to spread administration propaganda. As first reported by *New York Times* journalist David Barstow (2008), this program was initiated even before September 11, 2001, as the Pentagon sought "key influentials" who could be depended upon to express favorable viewpoints in media.[5] In 2002, as the Bush administration committed to war in Iraq, the Pentagon decided to recruit news analysts to win over a skeptical public. Victoria Clarke, the public relations executive overseeing the program, reasoned that military analysts particularly would help the Pentagon achieve "information dominance" by saturating the media with pro-war voices that seemed "authoritative and utterly independent" (Barstow 2008).

With help from the White House, the Pentagon assembled a network of about seventy-five military analysts, granted the retired officers unfettered access to top officials, and armed them with key themes and talking points about the "threat from Iraq" (see figure 3). Chosen analysts received a number of symbolic rewards, inducements to recontextualize government claims. As Barstow (2008) explains, they were treated to a "powerfully seductive environment," including uniformed escorts to Donald Rumsfeld's private meeting room, conference tables decked with fine china and embossed name cards, exclusive access to a host of government PowerPoints, requests for advice and consultation, calls for patriotism and service, and friendly thank-you notes from secretary Rumsfeld himself. The special treatment came with only one condition: the military analysts were told not to directly quote their government sources or in any way discuss their interactions with the Pentagon. With this injunction, they took to the air, becoming, in the words of Barstow (2008), a "media Trojan horse."

Meanwhile, the Pentagon hired a private firm, Omnitec Solutions, to monitor the analysts' media appearances. Military analysts who expressed unfavorable opinions were sometimes pressured to get in line or even ousted from the program. Thus, the government also provided material disincentives by punishing those who failed to recontextualize their discourse favorably. However, internal documents show that Pentagon officials were mostly elated with the operation's results. According to Barstow (2008), Pentagon staff "marveled at the way the analysts seamlessly incorporated

- **Hostile Regimes, Terrorists and WMD (threat must be eliminated)**
  - Saddam Hussein stands at the nexus of hostile regimes, terrorist groups and weapons of mass destruction.
  - The Iraq regime is determined to acquire weapons of mass destruction – to blackmail and terrorize the world; and to realize Saddam Hussein's ambitions of regional domination.
  - The United States is acting to defend itself, its friends, and its allies against the threat posed by these weapons in the hands of a dictator like Saddam Hussein.

- **We know that Saddam has weapons of mass destruction. Unaccounted for are:**
  - More than 3,000 tons of chemicals used for weapons.
  - More than 30,000 special munitions for chemical and biological agent delivery.
  - 26,500 artillery rockets used for delivering nerve gas.
  - 5,000 artillery shells filled with mustard gas.

- **We know that Saddam is willing to use WMD.**
  - He used chemical weapons in the Iran-Iraq war.

Figure 3 Excerpt of Pentagon talking points shared with military analysts (U.S. Department of Defense 2003e)

material from talking points and briefings as if it was their own." Indeed, the military analysts were so reliable that Pentagon officials privately referred to them as "surrogates" and "message force multipliers."

Complicating matters, military analysts often had ideological and financial interests that encouraged a pro-war viewpoint—interests also never disclosed to the public. Many analysts had served in the first Persian Gulf War and believed it had been prematurely terminated. Thus, they looked at a new war in Iraq as a way to "finish the job" started in 1991. In fact, the two most prominent military analysts in my study, retired Generals Barry McCaffrey and Wayne Downing of NBC News, had not only participated in the Gulf War but had since then openly advocated for another military confrontation with Iraq. Both men were members of the Project for a New American Century and each worked on the advisory board for the Committee for the Liberation of Iraq. These were neoconservative advocacy groups with ties to the Bush administration and whose stated mission was to overthrow Saddam. Downing was even a lobbyist and advisor for the Iraqi National Congress, a CIA-funded group that cooked up false evidence on Iraq's WMD to strengthen the case for an invasion.

In addition, several military analysts were affiliated with defense corporations that stood to profit from war. Downing, for example, was a board member and stockholder in Science Applications International Corporation (SAIC) and Metal Storm Limited, companies that secured millions of dollars in contracts before and during the war in Iraq. Meanwhile, McCaffrey served on the board of directors for at least four different defense corporations that also made a fortune in the war. Several other military analysts used their position in the Pentagon to curry favor with defense corporations throughout the conflict. According to Barstow (2008), access to the Department of Defense was a major "business advantage." Thus, military analysts were rewarded for recontextualizing pro-war claims, both symbolically and financially, not only by the U.S. government but also by pro-war political organizations and the defense industry.

Incentivizing Weapons Analysts

Barstow's (2008) *New York Times* exposé focused on former military officers. However, my research suggests that weapons analysts, particularly former U.N. weapons inspectors, were even more important in marketing the war to the public. I cannot say whether these weapons analysts were also part of a formal government program aimed at achieving media dominance.[6] However, I have discovered that the U.S. government had its sights on several of them. Indeed, some weapons analysts apparently also attended private meetings where they listened as officials sought to generate a desired uptake of the government view on Iraq (Blommaert 2005, 68).

One weapons analyst who was targeted by the Bush administration was Ambassador Richard Butler, an Australian diplomat. From 1997 to 1999, Butler had served as chairman of the United Nations Special Commission (UNSCOM), the body charged with performing weapons inspections after the first Gulf War. As the Bush administration began campaigning for war in 2002 and 2003, he became one of the top public figures to comment on the conflict, testifying before Congress and appearing as a news contributor on all three broadcast networks.

At a meeting of the Senate Foreign Relations Committee on July 31, 2002, Butler stated publicly how a government official sought to persuade him that Iraq was hiding dangerous weapons. A "very distinguished member of the administration," he said, had twenty-four hours earlier argued to him that Iraq was burying some of its weapons and secretly moving others around in mobile factories. "I think [such arguments] can be overstated, quite frankly," Butler continued, "and I'm a bit concerned about the stridency with which some of those things are said, almost as if to justify a coming invasion" (Butler 2002). I asked Butler if government officials had tried to influence him on other occasions specifically because of his position as a news analyst, that is, whether they had tried to induce him to recontextualize their claims. He told me it would be very naïve for me to think otherwise, given the Bush administration's "mendacity" and "dishonesty." It was "such a crooked business," he said (Richard Butler, personal communication with the author, June 11, 2014).

David Kay, who had worked as a nuclear weapons inspector following the first Gulf War, also contributed to news programs before the 2003 invasion. Indeed, Kay was perhaps the most visible analyst in the prewar period; he was quoted in print stories, featured as an op-ed writer, and recruited to appear on multiple cable and broadcast news programs, especially NBC News, with which he signed an exclusive contract in 2002. In an interview with me, Kay denied that U.S. officials had ever sought him out specifically because of his position as a news analyst. But government records clearly show that the U.S. was keen on exploiting his media profile. In fact, according to a January 2003 State Department memo obtained by FOIA request, the U.S. government arranged for Kay to go on Egyptian Television (ETV) and promote U.S. talking points about the need for war with Iraq. The memo says that Kay was one of several "U.S. interlocutors" who participated as a guest in ETV programs in which "the U.S. point of view is always put forth" (U.S. Department of State 2003).

But the government's relationship with Kay was apparently not limited to promoting "the U.S. point of view" overseas. During the prewar period, Kay says, he worked closely with government and military officials to discuss Iraq's alleged weapons program. In fact, Kay told me, he attended multiple private meetings arranged by Deputy Secretary of Defense Paul Wolfowitz. Assuming that Kay's statements are reliable, these meetings were mainly held to prepare the United States Central Command (CENTCOM) to deal with Iraq's weapons once U.S. troops took over the country.[7] However, Kay says the meetings held at the National Defense University also allowed government officials to "volunteer their view of what the Iraqi programs were like." He told me he was shown briefings and PowerPoints that summarized the government's case on Iraq's chemical, biological, and nuclear weapons. Presumably, the government was aware of his news credentials and was providing him with readily decontextualizable information.

And Kay claims he was not the only one. He says the meetings, which grew more frequent in the months before the war, attracted between twelve and sixty attendees, including not only current government and military officials but also think tank intellectuals, retired military officers, and other former weapons inspectors who contributed news analysis. Kay vaguely recalled that former inspectors Charles Duelfer and Tim McCarthy also attended the gatherings. Like Kay, these men frequently appeared on news programs, expressing certainty about Saddam Hussein's WMD. But the networks never disclosed that these analysts apparently had a working relationship with the U.S. government.

Thus, it seems the Bush administration promoted its case for war privately with some of the most powerful talking heads in American news media, thereby creating "favourable conditions for a desired uptake" of their claims (Blommaert 2005, 68). But often it was the other way around, as weapons analysts initiated contact with government insiders. Kay told me he ran into government officials several times a month at congressional hearings and think tank presentations, where he asked them informally about Iraq's weapons and the progress of disarmament. And he regularly contacted high-level intelligence analysts and administration officials. For example,

Kay said he often spoke to the CIA's lead analyst on Iraq's nuclear weapons program, a former member of the 1991 inspections team. This analyst now apparently tried to convince Kay that Iraq was pursuing an atom bomb. In addition, Kay sometimes paid visits to Robert G. Joseph, a member of the National Security Council (NSC) whom Kay had known for twenty years. Reportedly, Joseph was instrumental in formulating the 2003 State of the Union address and compelling speech writers to include the false assertion that Iraq had sought large quantities of uranium from Africa (Risen and Sanger 2003). Thus, it seems that some of Kay's longtime friends and chief informants were willing to publicize disputed claims about Iraq.

In any case, it appears that weapons analysts were "independent" in a rather limited sense of the word. Many depended on government sources, whether they sought out government officials or officials contacted them. And, if what Kay told me is accurate, some even worked with government officials in private to help prepare for post-invasion contingencies, even as the government publicly suggested that it hoped to avoid war. In my view, such relationships with government officials represent a de facto inducement to recontextualize government claims. That is, officials rewarded analysts with access, thereby encouraging a positive uptake of government discourse and rendering that discourse more available for media recitation.

Government officials also appear to have targeted analysts based on their perceived readiness to support administration viewpoints. Put another way, officials knew that their discourse would be "valued" and "desired" by several weapons analysts (Bauman and Briggs 1990, 77) because these analysts, like their military counterparts, were at least partly in step with the administration's ideology. When shown on screen, even analysts who were sometimes critical of the Bush administration generally supported the case for war. Richard Butler, for example, was no lackey for the Bush administration. He argued that if America and Great Britain went to war in Iraq without U.N. authorization, "it would be the equivalent of taking the law into their own hands, a bit like a posse, a lynch mob" (NBC 2003, Jan. 14). However, Butler only opposed war without U.N. approval; he supported Bush's general argument for war, and his supportive comments (not his critical ones) were much more likely to be broadcast. In fact, news producers more than once showed Butler repeating Bush's declarations that Iraq both had weapons of mass destruction and was producing more.[8] And, after Colin Powell's infamous speech at the United Nations, Butler strongly implied that the United Nations ought to authorize war to disarm Saddam Hussein.[9]

If Butler's criticisms of the United States were muted, other analysts were unerringly supportive of government discourse. Indeed, even analysts with questionable authority could find airtime if they toed the U.S. line. For example, Khidir Hamza was allowed to contribute to NBC News even though he had a history of fabricating stories about Iraq's weapons program (Collier 2002; Hersh 2003). So egregious were his lies that the International Atomic Energy Agency even warned American journalists he had "no credibility at all" (Massing 2004). But Hamza was friendly with the Iraqi National Congress and its sponsors in the U.S. government (Mayer 2004). So, he was promoted on U.S. news programs, where he consistently recontextualized alarmist claims about Iraq.

Perhaps the analyst who most fully subscribed to the administration's hawkish philosophy was David Kay. In the late 1990s, Kay wrote op-eds in which he warned readers about Iraq's supposed arsenal of weapons. And he twice, in 1998 and again in 2002, appeared before Congress to call for the overthrow of Saddam Hussein's government. Regime change, he said, was the only way to fully neutralize Iraq's WMD threat. During this time, Kay might well have had a financial incentive to recontextualize such pro-war talking points. In fact, he was senior corporate vice president and company stockholder at SAIC, the same defense giant that had Wayne Downing on its board of directors and that was awarded millions of dollars in no-bid contracts before the Iraq War. Kay would hold his senior position at SAIC until October 2002, around which time, he says, he signed an exclusive contract with NBC and sold all of his company stock to avoid any semblance of a conflict of interest.[10] However, apparently before he left SAIC, Kay was already working as a part-time contributor at NBC News, where, for example, he asserted in early September 2002 that Iraq was actively pursuing and perhaps very close to building a nuclear weapon. His affiliations—past or present—with SAIC were never discussed on the air.

Assessing Conflicts of Interest and Expert Knowledge

Despite the above evidence, news networks maintain that conflicts of interest could not have been a problem in the prewar period because they always carefully monitor their analysts and permit only disinterested figures on their broadcasts. For example, NBC News issued this statement in 2008: "We have clear policies in place to assure that the people who appear on our air have been appropriately vetted and that nothing in their profile would lead to even a perception of a conflict of interest" (quoted in Barstow 2008). However, according to Barstow (2008), news executives at NBC often failed to ask about analysts' business interests. And they were only "dimly aware" of analysts' interactions with government insiders, with "little grasp" of how frequently analysts convened with officials or what they talked about. In fact, in 2003, when Elena Nachmanoff, vice president of talent development at NBC News, was first asked about military analysts' relationships with defense industries, she declared that defense contracts "are not our interest" (quoted in Benaim, Motaparthy, and Kumar 2003). This statement is ironic given that NBC's then owner, General Electric Company, was itself a major defense contractor that profited enormously in the Iraq War (Solomon 2005; Webb 2008).

Of course, it could be argued that just because analysts interact with government officials or invest in defense corporations, it does not follow that they will make pro-war and pro-government claims. In fact, some news producers say analysts' political and financial affiliations have nothing to do with their on-air statements. Again, Nachmanoff's 2003 comments about military analysts are instructive. "We are employing them for their military expertise," she said, "not their political views" (quoted in Benaim, Motaparthy, and Kumar 2003). However, NBC's military analysts did not confine themselves to discussions of technical combat operations. For example, less than a month after the 9/11 attacks, Barry McCaffrey appeared on *NBC Nightly News* arguing that the War on Terror had to be expanded. As he put it, "Before we are done, we will have to confront the pariah state Iraq, which has brutalized its own population, threatened its neighbors, and continues to actively support international terrorism" (NBC 2001, Oct. 10). Certainly, McCaffrey was not analyzing the mechanics of war. He was arguing that America needed to fight a new war, a political claim if there ever was one.

Others also reject that analysts' relationships with government led to biased interpretations. Former NBC anchor Brian Williams, for example, said that, in spite of any interactions with the Pentagon, the top military analysts on his network always retained their independence and remained "tough, honest critics" (quoted in Greenwald 2008). However, military analysts themselves often noted that "tough, honest criticism" was difficult to achieve when participating in the Pentagon program. For example, former U.S. Army lieutenant colonel Robert Maginnis reported that, though he was disappointed by the lack of hard evidence on Iraq's WMD, he felt "manipulated" into conveying certainty about Iraq's weapons on the air (Barstow 2008). Even analysts who disliked the administration said they found it difficult to offer negative interpretations of the military. Indeed, there were acute social disincentives for any ex-officer who offered an unfavorable recontextualization of military statements. As former army general and ABC news analyst William Nash told the *New York Times*, "It is very hard for me to criticize the United States Army. It is my life" (Barstow 2008).

David Kay explained to me that the "very close relationship" between ex-military officers and current officers could easily lead to unintentional censorship: "What you've got to understand about the military analysts is there is this culture. The people who are serving are people who, by and large, worked for you or worked with you. . . . I mean they knew [one another] in frequent postings. And so, it was a two-way street. [The analysts] called for information, and the [Pentagon] guys called back and said, 'You got it wrong,' or, 'You're causing me and you problems by saying that.' And it was not so much intentionally trying to manipulate. It was the way that military culture operates." Interestingly, while Kay recognized the pitfalls of ex-military officers working closely with current officers, he failed to see how his own proximity to government insiders might threaten objectivity. He insisted he never felt pressured to adhere to the government's point of view. But he also revealed to me that he, like Lieutenant Colonel Maginnis, was privately dissatisfied with government intelligence on Iraq's WMD. Kay says that in the meetings at the National Defense University, he "expressed unhappiness" because "the evidence that the intelligence community was giving [CENTCOM] was pretty thin gruel and old warmed up stuff that most of us had seen from the '90s about the Iraqi program." To be sure, when Kay was on the air, he never referred to the U.S. intelligence on Iraq's weapons as "thin gruel." Indeed, on the air, he found the U.S. case against Iraq "very compelling."[11] Perhaps Kay neglected to reveal his doubts about U.S. intelligence in deference to government sources.

Nevertheless, some maintain we must accept conflicts of interest so news producers can hire qualified experts. Kay himself presented this argument to me, saying that people with ties to government and defense often make the most knowledgeable news analysts. And, he warned, "If you end up with people who have no background and no conflict of interest, you've got the conflict of interest of ignorance." Kay is surely correct that news contributors should have relevant background knowledge about subjects they discuss on air. However, he seems to assume that such background knowledge can only or primarily be found in people with conflicting interests, people with clear incentives to recontextualize pro-war claims. But this is surely not true. In the prewar period, for example, there were many people—disconnected from U.S. government and the defense industry—who could have spoken credibly about the status of Iraq's weapons and the prospects of violence: academics with knowledge of Iraq, former U.N. officials from outside the United States, and members of the International Atomic Energy Agency (IAEA). Indeed, those who lacked access to Washington officials may have been in a better position to critically evaluate U.S. government claims.

But even if we put aside the issue of conflicting interests, there is still the issue of relevant expertise. Analysts were sometimes featured on the air discussing things they did not know much about. For example, NBC military analyst Montgomery Meigs was called upon to discuss ties between Osama bin Laden and Iraq. Meigs had served as commanding general of the U.S. Army in Europe, not as a specialist on Middle Eastern terrorism. But this did not stop him from making categorical (and baseless) assertions about the relationship between Iraq and al-Qaeda: "It's informal, it shifts, it changes, and it works when they have converging interests" (NBC 2003, Feb. 12).

And even in cases where analysts had relevant background experience, the depth of their experience might have been insufficient. David Kay, for instance, was frequently introduced on the news as "former U.N. weapons inspector" or "former nuclear inspector"—often just before he criticized the current inspection regime for its inability to find weapons in Iraq. In 2002, IAEA spokesperson Melissa Fleming charged that Kay had little authority to speak on the subject because of his limited practical experience. "Mr. Kay," she said on ABC, "was an inspector for all of six weeks in 1991. Our inspectors were in Iraq for eight years" (Sawyer 2002). Kay was not necessarily an expert in nuclear technology either. As Dr. Gordon Prather, a physicist who held several government posts, would later write, "David Kay is not a scientist. His PhD is in Foreign Affairs or some such. . . . Please don't get me confused with that guy" (quoted in Seal 2003). In fact, Kay has a PhD in international and public affairs from Columbia University. However, he took courses in physics while he pursued his degree and worked for the IAEA as deputy head of the Iraq Action Team. Thus, relative to the average person, Kay is a bona fide authority on nuclear weapons. But, as Prather's comments suggest, a physicist specializing in nuclear technology might seriously question Kay's expertise.

To be clear, I am not suggesting that people like McCaffrey, Meigs, and Kay had no right to present news analysis. Indeed, they had unique experiences and valuable perspectives (see appendix F). What I am suggesting, however, is that news consumers had a right to know more about these men: the precise nature of their expertise and how that expertise was judged by others in their fields, their political associations and ideological leanings, their private interactions with government officials, and their investments in and relationships with defense corporations. Of course, television news producers would probably not disclose all this information. Jam-packed newscasts hardly allow enough time for a full discussion of each analyst's credentials. Furthermore, if journalists were to bring up an analyst's conflicts of interest or gaps in knowledge, it would likely reduce the credibility of the news network. As Kay explained to me, the whole point of hiring analysts is to "give credibility to the network" by showcasing people who have "actually done something" in the real world. There is simply no incentive for journalists to call into question an analyst's experience, especially when that experience draws them closer to the government sources that journalists crave most (Bennett 2012; Hallin 1986). Thus, news institutions themselves are incentivized not only to recruit analysts who may favorably recontextualize pro-war claims but to withhold information about these analysts, creating "favourable conditions for a desired uptake" of their on-air discourse (Blommaert 2005, 68). The public may be entitled to know who exactly is interpreting the news for them, but serving this public interest is not the top priority of the mainstream press.

I recognize that some news analysts may have advanced government claims without any inducement, but we should not discount the sophisticated effort to recruit "surrogates." As Barstow (2008) revealed, the Department of Defense pulled out all the stops to attract military analysts, welcoming them into the inner circle and stroking their egos. And, as my own research indicates, several weapons analysts were also given special treatment, invited to private meetings, and made part of an official Washington "team." Most importantly, the government provided analysts with privileged information: key themes, talking points, and PowerPoint slides. This information was desirable precisely because it was restricted—off limits to ordinary journalists and, therefore, valuable in the commercial news market.

As demonstrated in Herman and Chomsky's (2002) work, some propaganda spreads partly as a consequence of routines in news business. News analysts are more likely to get airtime (and pay) if they can obtain insider information. And government officials who understand this incentive can selectively grant access to such information, providing entrance only to analysts who are sympathetic to the government's cause or supplying analysts only with "favorable" information, however misleading it might be. Other inducements and disincentives—appeals to friendship and loyalty, the realization of shared political goals, financial gain or the promise of business opportunities, and veiled threats if one goes "off message"—only increase the likelihood that government propaganda will travel through the news media without challenge.

Granted, not all analysts were keen to do the government's bidding. Some were not privy to government information and, therefore, couldn't recite it on air. And even among analysts closest to government sources, not all were susceptible to apparent inducements. After all, not all analysts in this study shared the government's ideology and political aspirations; not all of them had financial ties to the defense industry. Nevertheless, very few analysts adopted an adversarial stance toward the government and its claims.

In any case, the government is hardly responsible for what becomes of analyst discourse once it has made its way into the news studio. As shown below, producers and journalists ultimately regulate how analyst talk is taken up and whether that talk will be regarded as legitimate expertise.

6. Enacting and Entextualizing the Voice of the Expert

By giving . . . purveyors of the preferred
view a great deal of exposure, the media
confer status and make them the obvious
candidates for opinion and analysis.
—Edward Herman
and Noam Chomsky, 2002

Discourse is more likely to propagate—to become successful propaganda—when it is articulated by someone with a powerful voice. But what is a voice, and how does a voice become powerful? As noted, "voice" can be defined as the "capacity for semiotic mobility" (Blommaert 2005, 69), the capacity to be understood favorably even as your discourse moves from place to place. People with powerful voices, then, find that they can generate a desired uptake of their words no matter the context. But this is not the only way to define "voice." As Bakhtin argues (1981, 1984), "voice" can also be defined as a "typifiable speaking person[a]," a "characterological figure . . . indexed by speech" (Agha 2005, 39–40). Conceived this way, voice is akin to ethos: your discourse signals your character, showing the kind of speaker you are. If your speech indicates you are, say, a doctor or a scholar—the kind of person to be believed—then your voice is powerful.

These two senses of "voice"—voice-as-mobility and voice-as-character—are related. First, insofar as a characterological voice is recognizable, distinguishable from others, it is also potentially repeatable and capable of semiotic mobility. As Agha (2003, 243) explains, a characterological voice is "detachable from the current animator," the person presently speaking, and usable in "subsequent moments of circulation." And when a characterological voice comes to index positive values, it is more likely to generate a positive uptake. Indeed, a positively regarded character-voice is more worthy of movement, including repetition and propagation. For example, people who want to sound knowledgeable may try to recontextualize an "expert voice," mimicking or repeating the kinds of things that experts typically say.

In this chapter, I focus on the "voice of the expert" as it was construed before the 2003 Iraq War. I return to the twenty-two military and weapons analysts on broadcast TV news introduced in the previous chapter and examine their on-air contributions during the prewar period (126 appearances over 101 broadcasts).[1] Many factors allowed these analysts to enact an expert voice, one that was detachable and reusable in public discourse. First, news networks safeguarded analysts' credibility by suppressing their conflicts of interest and knowledge deficiencies. Furthermore, the networks characterized analysts as neutral and reliable, indexing their expertise by introducing them with legitimizing vocabulary, surrounding them with dignifying visuals, and ascribing to them interactive roles that signaled their authority. Consequently, viewers were not only denied crucial information about analysts but potentially manipulated into feeling that analysts had greater knowledge than was really the case.

After showing how analysts' authority was established, I explore the kinds of content that characterized their expert voice. Since news narratives generally reflected the government's framing of Iraq, analysts were most likely to get airtime for assertions favorable to the Bush administration. In fact, I find, the networks consistently aired analyst commentary reiterating the themes of the White House. The expert voice, then, typically discredited the Iraqi leadership, questioned the effectiveness of weapons inspections, and promoted the use of military force. To talk like an expert was to justify war.

The Semiotic Production of Expertise

The networks did not tell viewers when analysts received talking points from government officials or when they held positions at defense corporations. Thus, "manipulative silence" helped safeguard the analysts' credibility and prepared the way for a positive uptake of their discourse (Huckin 2002, 2010). But the fact that news producers failed to disclose (or even investigate) their analysts' conflicts of interests is only part of the story. News programs also performed semiotic labor to portray analysts as experts. This semiotic work is important, since, for most news consumers, an analyst's credibility does not come ready made; few of us are familiar with analysts before we see them on TV. Instead, the analyst's expert voice or ethos must be enacted in and through discourse (Aristotle 2007). This discourse does not come exclusively from analysts themselves, who, after all, only have a few seconds to speak on air. Instead, correspondents and news producers often index the characterological figure of the expert, supplying multimodal discourse that effectively shapes a positive ethos for news contributors (Oddo 2014a).

Advertising

One way of enacting an analyst's expert persona is through promotional advertising. During the prewar period, NBC ran a television ad with the following voice-over: "Showdown Iraq, and only NBC News has the experts. General Norman Schwarzkopf,[2] allied commander during the Gulf War. General Barry McCaffrey, he was the most decorated four-star general in the Army. General Wayne Downing, former special operations commander and White House adviser. Ambassador Richard Butler and former U.N. weapons inspector David Kay. Nobody has seen Iraq like they have. The experts. The best information from America's most watched news organization, NBC News." NBC provides limited information about these analysts, briefly describing only their "real world" positions in combat, weapons inspections, and politics. Each is assigned a title or honorific ("General," "Ambassador," "U.N. weapons inspector") that serves a legitimizing function (Van Leeuwen 2007, 2008). And NBC uses intensely positive evaluations, including superlatives that suggest the intrinsic value of the analysts' discourse ("best information"), their unique accolades ("most decorated"), and their unparalleled ability to provide insights on Iraq ("nobody has seen Iraq like they have"). Notably, NBC twice refers to its analysts as "the experts," a phrase that specifies their uniqueness ("the" as opposed to "some"), while maximizing their intellectual capacity ("experts").

As shown in figure 4, this phrase was hard to miss, as it was printed across the screen in bold, military stenciling that further indexes the authority and masculinity

Figure 4 "The Experts" ad from NBC News. From left to right: Ambassador Richard Butler, General Wayne Downing, Dr. David Kay, General Barry McCaffrey, and General Norman Schwarzkopf

of the depicted men (Machin 2007, 93–104). Even the way the analysts are posed signals that they are a serious and imposing group: the formality of their clothing, their stern expressions, and their virtual distance from viewers who are not only far away from the analysts but separated from them by a barrier—"The Experts" logo (Kress and Van Leeuwen 1996; Machin 2007). Together, these signs help to inscribe certain biographical identities with valued qualities: real world experience, expertise, and authority. Simultaneously, they help entextualize the expert voice by signaling that the discourse of these experts is to be regarded as distinct from, and perhaps more valuable than, surrounding reports on network news.

On-Screen Titles

Such ads conspicuously function to convince the public that analysts are remarkable human beings with expert knowledge. But news networks also promote analysts in more subtle ways. In my corpus, for example, analysts were almost always assigned some on-screen label when they appeared on air. Without fail, the on-screen label *nominated* the speakers by specifying their first and last name (Van Leeuwen 2008, 40–41). But typically, the onscreen title also functioned to *categorize* the speakers by specifying their activities and social identity (42). Predictably, the most common categorizations were those specifying the speaker by former occupation. Analysts were designated as former inspectors (e.g., "Former U.N. Weapons Inspector") 58 percent of the time and as retired military officers (e.g., "United States Army, Ret.") 29 percent of the time. In 37 percent of the cases, analysts were also categorized according to their position with the network (e.g., "NBC News Analyst"), though this title was reserved only for those who had long-term contracts, such as David Kay and Barry McCaffrey.[3]

These titles may seem trivial, but they do important ideological work. The fact that the analysts are assigned on-screen titles at all indexes their relative authority. And when analysts are branded with the right title, it enhances their ethos. For example, labeling someone as a retired general in the "United States Army" will likely legitimize that speaker, since those who serve in the U.S. Army are typically valorized in American culture (Snyder 1999). Similarly, a label associating the analyst with the U.N. weapons inspectorate may index to American viewers that the analyst is committed to the goals of this institution, namely peaceful disarmament. Of course, analysts in this study could just as accurately have been labeled according to their political views (e.g., "Conservative"), their positions in think tanks and advocacy groups (e.g., "Lobbyist, Committee for the Liberation of Iraq"), or their work at defense corporations (e.g., "Defense Industry Official"). But these affiliations are deemed irrelevant or suppressed through manipulative silence (Huckin 2002). Even the title "news analyst" is not without characterological implications. As I argue elsewhere (Oddo 2014a), this term emphasizes that the speaker has journalistic authority (news) and does sophisticated intellectual work (analysis). Again, the on-screen titles help typify and differentiate the voice of the expert analyst, associating this voice with respectable real-world experience and professional credentials.

Spoken Introductions

Analysts were identified exclusively through on-screen titles in about 41 percent of their appearances. But more often, correspondents further identified analysts in brief, legitimizing introductions that were spoken aloud. Interestingly, when introduced by reporters, the analysts were rarely specified according to their proper names (n=31). But they were almost always categorized (n=91), typically as former inspectors (n=38) and retired military officers (n=14) but also as news consultants (n=10) or "experts" (n=11). However, the analysts were not always specified as *individuals* (e.g., "A former inspector says . . ."). In fact, correspondents were almost as likely to introduce individual analysts through plural nouns. In Van Leeuwen's (1996, 2008) terms, analysts were *genericized* so they appeared to be an entire class of people, *collectivized* so they appeared to be a monolithic group, or *aggregated* so they appeared to be a portion of some group. In rare cases, analysts were even *objectivated* so they appeared to represent a massive impersonal entity, such as "the United States." Table 4 illustrates these possibilities.

What interests me about these ways of personifying analysts is that, frequently, the analysts are presumed to be speaking not just for themselves but for large numbers of people. One former military official's opinion is presumed to reflect the opinion of all "officials," or one weapons analyst's opinion is presumed to reflect the opinions of "many former inspectors." To be sure, the correspondents never provide evidence that

Table 4 Ways of representing news analysts in spoken introductions

Form of representation	Description	Examples
Individualization (n=42)	Speaker is specified as a singular individual, not a pluralized group.	"*Former chief U.N. weapons inspector Richard Butler* said today he expects the Iraqis to try all kinds of games with the inspectors despite the tough resolution." (ABC 2002, Nov. 10)
Genericization (n=9)	Speaker is represented as a generic "class," as opposed to a specific, identifiable individual or group. Genericization is marked by the plural, without an article or a premodifier.	"*Experts* say the U.S. will likely assemble a coalition of allies." (CBS 2002, Oct. 17)
Collectivization (n=12)	Speaker is represented as a monolithic but specific group. Marked by a pluralized noun with a premodifying adjective.	"*Arms experts* say Iraq has the most to gain if the scientists speak." (NBC 2003, Jan. 25)
Aggregation (n=12)	Speaker is represented as a quantity or percentage of some group. Some reckoning of number, whether precise or imprecise, premodifies the plural noun.	"*Many former arms inspectors* think Saddam is playing for time and trying to create confusion." (NBC 2002, Dec. 7)
Objectivation (n=2)	Speaker is represented by means of reference to an associated place or thing.	"*The U.S.* says the burden is still on Iraq to prove it is complying." (NBC 2003, Jan. 6)

other speakers share the opinions of the presented analyst. Instead, they subtly enhance the persuasive force of an individual analyst's assertion by sourcing it to a plurality of "experts."

Such introductions literally help typify the expert voice, suggesting that it is generally shared by legitimate speakers of the same type: other experts or other vetted professionals. Meanwhile, reporting verbs in these introductions also do characterological work, indexing the analysts' attitudes toward their own speech. About two-thirds of the time, analysts' speech acts were construed with verbs indexing their neutrality and detachment—verbs such as "say" and "state." Thus, the expert voice is shown to be nonpartisan; analysts don't "advocate" or "oppose" or "urge," they neutrally impart things (see appendix H for more details about speech act verbs). Finally, and most basically, the introductions entextualize a "voicing contrast" (Agha 2005, 42) that distinguishes the reported voice of the analyst from the reporting voice of the correspondent. That is, the expert discourse of the analyst (e.g., "Saddam is playing for time . . .") is separated from the framing discourse of the reporter (e.g., "Many arms inspectors think . . ."). The contrast is important since it helps render expert discourse detachable. The correspondents signal not only that the expert voice is valuable (authoritative, widely shared, neutral, etc.) but also portable and repeatable. Viewers can easily locate expert speech and perhaps ascribe to themselves a bit of "expertise" by repeating it.

Background Scenery

News producers also subtly endorsed analysts by framing them against legitimizing scenery. Such scenery is easy to overlook, but background settings can signal important connotations, inducing viewers to attribute ideas and values to figures depicted in the foreground (Machin 2007; Van Leeuwen 2005). Table 5 shows five backgrounds discerned in this study.

Sometimes analysts are pictured in generic offices that signal their corporate professionalism, or they are placed in busy newsrooms that connote the speed and technology of contemporary reporting. However, the most common background associated with the analysts is a literate workspace, typically a library or office crammed with books. The obvious implication of this background is that the analyst is highly literate and presumably studies texts for purposes of scholarship. In reality, analysts rarely publish work in peer-reviewed venues (Steele 1995). Indeed, it is rare for producers to hire academics, since they, like trained journalists, lack "real world" experience and political connections (Kay, personal interview). However, it may be beneficial to insinuate that analysts are engaged in something like academic research. Granted, analysts may have been filmed in their actual offices, in front of books they actually read. But there are signs of artifice. In fact, I discovered different analysts sometimes sat before the same "personal" library. Figures 5A and 5B show one instance of this. David Kay (whose name is spelled incorrectly on screen) appears

Table 5 Backgrounds and related connotations

Background	Example	Connotations
Literate workstation (44%)		Suggests knowledge and expertise by associating the speaker with literacy. Typical background elements include a library of books, computers, and maps. Libraries are also sometimes decorated with American flags.
Generic office (18%)		Suggests professionalism by associating the speaker with a corporate environment. Standard elements include typical furnishings of a corporate office: ferns, lamps, landscape paintings on the walls.
News studio (17%)		Suggests journalistic credentials by associating the speaker with a newsroom environment. Typical background includes rows of television screens and news studio personnel busy at work on computers.
Neutral (14%)	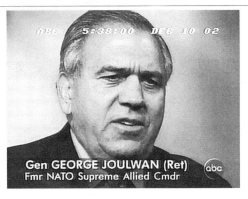	The background is essentially rendered absent, as it is articulated only as a monochromatic "wall" or is entirely cast in shadow. Since the background is too underspecified to provide details about the speaker, I call it neutral.

Table 5 Backgrounds and related connotations (continued)

Background	Example	Connotations
Cityscape (44%)		Indicates the city where the speaker is located (e.g., Washington, D.C.) and suggests the speaker's proximity to and intimacy with important sites of political activity. Typically realized by outdoor vistas, including skylines or specific buildings (e.g., U.N. headquarters).

before the same bookcase as Barry McCaffrey. (Look closely at the books on the top shelf, to the left of each gentleman's head, and toward the right, just above each gentleman's shoulder.)

Such staging indicates how consciously news producers use aspects of visual design to produce their analysts' expert persona. Of course, the background scenery also further entextualizes analyst discourse, providing a clear visual contrast between expert speech and the speech of other news contributors.

Communicative Roles

News networks also helped shape analysts' ethos by assigning them authoritative positions in the unfolding news discourse. In other words, the characterological figure of the expert is also a by-product of the communicative roles that analysts adopted in broadcasts (Johnstone 2008, 139). Table 6 describes the discursive roles that analysts fulfilled and the multimodal signals indexing them.

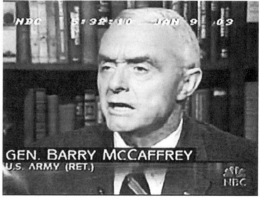

Figures 5a, b Analysts appear before identical libraries

Table 6 Discursive roles fulfilled by news analysts

Discursive Role	Description
Instructor (*n*=23)	The analyst's role is to instruct the audience (and the journalist). The role is indexed multimodally— for example, the analyst uses a pointer to identify and explain items on a map; the analyst is seated before a document he examines and explicates; the speaker is asked knowledge-based questions by the reporter or appears on -screen to supply the "final answer" to a question posed for the viewer.
Adjudicator (*n*=24)	The speaker's role is to refute an incorrect or false assertion; sometimes there is a contrived dialogue in which one source's assertion is immediately denied by the (expert) analyst. Often, a token of counterexpectancy ("but") or denial ("not") indicates that the analyst's discourse represents a counterpoint to some other person's (less legitimate) claim.
Substantiator (*n*=60)	The analyst substantiates, corroborates, or elaborates on a previous report or assertion. The analyst essentially reiterates and expands upon the evaluative and ideational content of earlier discourse.
Commenter (*n*=124)	The analyst comments on a reported event or process, offering an explicit evaluation or opinion. Evaluations are marked by attitudinal discourse (Martin and White 2005), while opinions are marked by first-person subjective stance (e.g., "I believe," "in my opinion") or modals indicating tentativeness (e.g., "it seems," "maybe"). This role could co-occur with other roles.

Perhaps the first thing to notice is that the role of "debater" is conspicuously absent from the list. Analysts in this study were not brought on to argue with one another—for example, to represent the "conservative," "liberal," and "middle-ground" perspectives in a moderated discussion. The newscasts sought a more reductive kind of dialogicality that precluded analysts from live disputation with others (Fairclough 2003). Indeed, analysts almost always appeared by themselves, typically in pretaped sound bites. Thus, viewers were not permitted to weigh the analysts' arguments against other credible positions. For example, experts on military strategy and aggressive disarmament tactics were not put into dialogue with experts on conflict prevention and resolution, international law, human rights, crisis medicine, and disaster relief.

Instead, viewers were invited to regard analysts as somewhat outside of and above back-and-forth contests in the political arena. Almost always, analysts played the role of official commenter, participating in newscasts as credentialed persons who could float above the fray to offer authoritative opinions and evaluations. The closest they came to debate with other interlocutors was when they were called upon to referee others' assertions—judging another speaker's utterance as true or untrue, correct or incorrect. For example, an analyst might appear on screen directly after an assertion by an Iraqi official specifically to render that assertion invalid. Excerpt 6.1 shows a clip from NBC in which weapons analyst Charles Duelfer fulfills the role of adjudicator:

In the first shot (frames 23–29), Iraq's deputy prime minister, Tariq Aziz, asserts his country produced no biological weapons. Immediately, reporter Andrea Mitchell jumps in to refute Aziz's claim, attributing a firm denial ("Not true") to Charles Duelfer, whom she introduces as someone who "led inspections teams to Iraq." As

Time	Frame	Soundtrack*
23–29		**Tariq Aziz:** We produced biological items but they were not weaponized.
30–33		**Andrea Mitchell:** Not true says Charles Duelfer who led inspection teams to Iraq.
34–43		**Charles Duelfer:** I myself have spent an evening in 1995 listening to them describe how they weaponized biological agent.

Mitchell speaks, Duelfer literally sits in judgment of Aziz (frames 30–33), watching the Iraqi speaker on television from an elevated position. In the next shot, Duelfer is further certified as an authority figure, as his impressive credentials are flashed on screen ("Former Deputy U.N. Inspections Chief"). By the time he makes his assertion, directly refuting Aziz's claim, viewers have already been positioned to trust his word is final.

At other times, analysts were presented such that they appeared to fulfill the role of instructor, educating journalists and audience members alike. This could be achieved simply by posing an open question to the viewer and then presenting an analyst sound bite that supplied the answer. Here, for example, Lisa Myers positions NBC military analyst Wayne Downing to instruct viewers about how nervous they should be regarding Iraqi spies:

> MYERS: So how worried should we be about Iraqi agents?
> DOWNING: The Iraqi agents are probably not as capable nor as creative as al-Qaeda. They don't have that fire in the belly. They don't have that willingness to give their life for Saddam Hussein. But having said, that we cannot ignore them. (NBC 2003, Mar. 6)

Often, however, the role of instructor was indexed via even more elaborate props. Analysts might be seated before an Iraqi arms declaration and asked to elucidate it for the audience, as David Kay was on NBC (figure 6).

Or they might be given instructional tools such as pointers and maps. In figure 7, for example, NBC military analyst Montgomery Meigs uses a smart-screen map to trace where Saddam Hussein might flood Iraqi river systems in the coming war. (On the left, another TV screen displays a waving American flag.)

When analysts weren't playing the role of instructor, they fulfilled the discourse role of substantiator, confirming "facts" or assertions previously cited by reporters. In the following report, weapons analyst Charles Duelfer corroborates the preceding claim made by CBS reporter Mark Phillips:

Figure 6 David Kay examines the Iraqi Arms Declaration (NBC 2002, Dec. 9)

Figure 7 Montgomery Meigs uses a smart map (NBC 2003, Mar. 19)

PHILLIPS: After a three-and-a-half-year gap, with sites spread around the country, it could be even harder [for inspectors to find weapons in Iraq] this time.

DUELFER: It's going to be very difficult for the new team, not the least of which is because we have given them —when we were operating in Iraq, we gave them a lot of practice in hiding things. (CBS 2002, Sep. 17)

In this case, both reporter and analyst use nearly synonymous attitudinal discourse. Specifically, they both employ intensified negative appraisals ("even hard*er*," "*very* difficult") of new weapons inspections in Iraq. In fact, Duelfer not only corroborates Phillips's attitude but further substantiates the claim that inspectors will have a hard time. Phillips suggests that inspectors will face challenges for two specific reasons: they have been absent from Iraq for three years, and Iraq contains many potential weapons sites. In his clip, Duelfer adds yet another reason: Iraq has had a lot of practice hiding weapons during previous inspections. Duelfer also adds more certainty to Phillips's earlier assertion. Phillips is tentative about the likelihood that inspectors will have a difficult time, as indicated by his "low probability" modal auxiliary ("*could* be even harder"). But Duelfer suggests greater conviction about the future, saying categorically "it is going to be very difficult." Thus, analysts were embedded in newscasts such that they not only restated journalists' reports but strengthened those reports with additional arguments and enhanced certainty.

Of course, when analysts are brought on to substantiate correspondents' reports, it indexes their presumed expertise. The analysts appear to offer the authoritative final word on the subject. What viewers may not realize is that analysts may be corroborating accounts that actually originated with them. David Kay told me that, upon interviewing him, reporter Andrea Mitchell would commonly use his most germane comments in her own on-air reports, apparently without attribution. Then, to fill space, she would simply drop in "fifteen seconds of the most inane, stupid comment" that Kay had made. As he explained, "It was stupid in the sense that it confirmed what the on-air personality, using what you had said in the interview as information, had just asserted." Often what Kay had viewed as a "sensible analytical discussion" of a problem was reduced by news producers to a "very, very stupid and superficial assessment."

If Kay's remarks are any indication, news institutions may not always care if analysts make penetrating insights—as long as they can be used to fill ten- to fifteen-second holes in a segment. This merely underscores why news producers labor to construe their analysts' expert personae. From the producers' point of view, what the analysts say matters less than who they are, and who they are can be enacted discursively—through promotions, introductions, background scenery, and the interactive roles analysts inhabit.

The Experts Make the Case for War

I don't mean to suggest that what analysts say is unimportant to news producers. Indeed, as Kay's comments reveal, an analyst's discourse might become the basis for a correspondent's report. This was probably most common with the military analysts, who, according to Elena Nachmanoff of NBC, often played an "influential role behind the scenes, briefing executive producers and holding seminars for staffers that provide[d] 'texture for both on-air pieces and background'" (quoted in Benaim, Motaparthy, and Kumar 2003). The analysts then shaped what news producers put on the air. But news producers also shaped the analysts' expert voice by posing questions, promoting certain responses, and selectively recontextualizing fragments of taped interviews in their newscasts.

Internal Pressure to Be Sensationally Pro-war

One way that networks shaped the analysts' on-air voice was by indirectly encouraging sensational and hyperbolic assertions. Analysts reported to me that they weren't openly pressured to exaggerate, but they nevertheless recognized that networks preferred melodramatic sound bites. For example, Richard Butler explained that, as he grew accustomed to the news business, he recognized that the more he said in pretaped interviews, the more likely it was the networks would seize upon a comment that could be "readily sensationalized." As he put it, you had to be "as tight as a drum," repeating only a few carefully worded key points.

Of course, analysts who understood journalists' fondness for punchy language might (unintentionally) give them what they wanted. And, in fact, some circumstantial evidence suggests that the voice of the analyst was more hearable (that is, more likely to be aired) on news broadcasts when it contained extreme and colorful lexis. In the vast majority of their on-air appearances (approximately 89 percent), analysts used language with a high degree of force. That is, the analysts tended to "turn up the volume" of their discourse to maximize its intensity (Martin and White 2005, 37). On ABC, for example, George Joulwan intensified his opinion that U.S. troops could fight Iraq without any outside assistance—conveying maximal <u>certainty</u>, employing **categorical assertions**, and *repeating a key phrase*: "<u>Certainly</u>, we *can do it alone*. The risk, in my opinion, goes up, but we *can do it*. **We have the wherewithal** to *do it alone*. **We have forces in the region** that *can do it alone*" (ABC 2003, Jan. 23).

In another instance, NBC analyst David Kay intensified his attitudes about Iraq and the dangerousness of its weapons. After inspectors discovered *empty* warheads that Iraq could theoretically use to carry chemical weapons, Kay said the following: "At the very least, you have them guilty of not declaring and keeping in a forward-deployed bunker chemical warfare delivery agents" (NBC 2003, Jan. 16). Here, Kay's chosen negative judgment of Iraq ("guilty") is up-scaled compared to other possible expressions ("responsible," "at fault"). And he construes a modalized process (e.g., warheads *could* deliver chemical weapons) into an elemental attribute of the warheads ("chemical warfare delivery agents"). Clearly, Kay's language seems intended to heighten the sense that Iraq is threatening. And his intensified adverbial phrase ("at the very least") suggests Iraq might be "guilty" of additional wrongdoing.

Another way that networks shaped the on-air voice of their analysts was by fostering a general climate in which pro-war assertions were welcomed and antiwar positions were suppressed (Bennett, Lawrence, and Livingston 2007; Oddo 2014a). Most on-air sources supported military action in Iraq (Fairness in Accuracy and Reporting 2003), and those who suggested alternatives to war were often ignored or criticized. Richard Butler told me, for instance, that before the war there was "absolutely" pressure to avoid contradicting the Bush administration. As noted in the previous chapter, Butler had suggested in January 2003 that, if the United States and Great Britain acted without U.N. approval, it would be equivalent to a "lynch mob" fighting in Iraq (NBC 2003, Jan. 14). Not long after this, he says, he was "told quite bluntly" by NBC that such comments were "not acceptable." Once the fighting began in Iraq, he says, it became "one's patriotic duty to support [the troops]," and it was simply "not permissible to say those people shouldn't be there."

Similarly, David Albright said that when he worked as a news contributor during the fall of 2002, he felt compelled to make assertions supporting a pro-war frame. "I felt a lot of pressure to stick to the subject," he told author Michael Massing in 2004, "which was Iraq's bad behavior." Albright recalled one occasion on a cable news program in which he endorsed continued inspections in Iraq and suggested delaying the rush to war. During the break, Albright said, the host "got really mad and chastised me" (quoted in Massing 2004). Albright believes that rather than critically examining rationales for war, journalists were taking their cues from the Bush administration.

My own analysis tends to confirm this charge. The networks frequently adopted news frames endorsing an invasion. For example, both NBC and CBS chose visual graphics encouraging audiences to view Iraq as a target for violence and to regard potential war as an exciting showdown with Saddam Hussein (Oddo 2014a, 2014b). Meanwhile, verbal reports across all networks typically focused on apparently pro-war themes, including:

- the Bush administration's case for violence in Iraq ($n=19$);
- U.S. war preparations and planning ($n=30$); and
- doubts about Iraqi sincerity and the capabilities of weapons inspectors ($n=36$).[4]

Sometimes the focus of the news story seemed to be the demonization of Iraq's leader. On October 15, 2002, for instance, an NBC segment offers "chilling answers" to the question "What's going on in the mind of Saddam Hussein?" An image of Saddam is slowly decolorized to enhance its creepiness, as Andrea Mitchell explains how reputable officials view Saddam as "a complete psychopath: sadistic, sociopathic, egocentric, ruthless beyond any measure."

Other news stories celebrated the power of the U.S. military. On September 27, 2002, for example, NBC ran a segment showcasing the new Longbow Apache helicopter, dubbed by reporter Don Teague as "a new weapon for a new war." Seated in the cockpit of the helicopter, Teague raves, "A single Longbow Apache can wreak havoc on the battlefield. From this seat, one pilot can destroy dozens of enemy targets, things like radar installations, artillery pieces, and tanks." Teague goes on to explain that the army has certified several of these attack helicopters combat-ready, "the pilots and aircraft prepared for service in Iraq."

As these examples suggest, reporters during the prewar period had a propensity for echoing government propaganda (Domke 2004). Thus, analysts were probably best able to get airtime for their assertions when those assertions reflected Washington's views on war (Bennett, Lawrence, and Livingston 2007, 39). In other words, journalists were more likely to perceive an analyst's voice as reportable and recontextualizable not only when it was forceful and vivid but when it advanced a pro-administration frame. Indeed, if one interactive role of analysts was to substantiate the positions of journalists, then there was incentive for analysts to articulate a pro-war stance.

Key Themes Expressed by News Analysts

Thus far, I have shown that news producers helped characterize the personae of their analysts, construing a distinct expert voice associated with knowledge, experience, and authority. Meanwhile, journalists provided cues to analysts as to what kind of content would be desirable on the news, potentially suggesting what was sayable on the air. What remains to be seen is what the analysts actually said during the prewar period. What kinds of statements and value positions typified the expert voice? To answer this question, I offer a critical intertextual analysis of on-air statements, identifying key themes (or overarching meanings) that recurred across all the analyst's assertions (Thibault 1991). Table 7 specifies these themes, classifying them according to the political questions they touch upon. (See appendix I for more details).

Results indicate that the news analysts consistently generated assertions supporting the Bush administration and its attitudes about Iraq. Indeed, as detailed in appendix J, the themes most evident in news analyst discourse are also discernible in the Bush administration's prewar talking points. The voice of the on-air expert characteristically repeated the claims of the presidency.

Of course, to speak of one expert voice is a bit misleading. The two kinds of analysts—weapons and military—claimed and produced different kinds of expertise, though both typically recited administration propaganda. One function of weapons analysts was to suggest that Iraq was legally obligated to disarm—and would face consequences if it failed to comply with U.N. Resolution 1441. For example, on CBS's November 11, 2002, newscast, David Albright explained, "Noncooperation is a material breach in this climate, and that can be one of many things: denying access to a site, getting caught in a lie." Importantly, Albright identifies only the ways Iraq can violate legal requirements, listing different forms of noncooperation that would result in "material breach." In so doing, Albright endows Iraq's potential wrongdoing with rhetorical presence (Perelman and Olbrechts-Tyteca 1969, 117) while suppressing ways Iraq might cooperate with inspectors. Thus, analysts were called upon to rearticulate the demands of the U.N. Security Council and imagine how Iraq might fail to address those demands.

In fact, the most commonly repeated theme among analysts was to suggest that Iraq was a deceptive regime that continued to conceal its WMD and aimed to produce additional munitions. As shown in table 7, weapons analysts were primarily responsible for articulating this theme, as they commented frequently on the status of Iraq's weapons and the prospects of the disarmament process. Often weapons analysts personally recounted Iraq's past efforts at foiling inspections. For example, on October 3, 2002, Charles Duelfer spoke on ABC about his attempt to inspect Iraq's presidential palaces in 1998: "You couldn't find a piece of paper anywhere in these places. They had done an excellent job of sanitizing these locations before we arrived." The implication, of course, is that Iraq had gotten rid of compromising materials. In essence, Duelfer suggests that his inability to find evidence of WMD ("couldn't find a piece of paper anywhere") was a sign that incriminating evidence had been removed. Such personal knowledge of past Iraqi deception was grounds for current suspicions. Thus, Duelfer speculated in the same program, Iraq could be hiding weapons in these presidential palaces now: "They're large areas, and they could contain any number of things, not just records, but actually weapons themselves."

Table 7 Kinds of themes evinced in news analyst discourse

Question	General answer	Theme	Weapons analysts	Military analysts	Total
Should Iraq verify disarmament?					
	Yes				**17**
		Iraq must fully and immediately disarm.	11	1	12
		Iraq must cooperate; we cannot hope to find a "smoking gun."	4	1	5
Does Iraq hide and produce WMD?					
	Yes				**83**
		Iraq lies to retain WMD.	60	5	65
		Iraq seeks and produces WMD.	18	0	18
	Maybe				**2**
		It is unclear if Iraq has WMD.	2	0	2
Can inspections work?					
	No				**33**
		Inspections almost certainly will fail.	24	0	24
		The U.N. is not fully committed or credible.	9	0	9
	Yes				**11**
		Inspectors can pressure Iraq / turn up weapons.	11	0	11
	Maybe				**7**
		Inspectors must establish authority.	7	0	7
Is war necessary and legitimate?					
	Yes				**54**
		Violence appears justified.	7	6	13
		War with Iraq is extremely likely or inevitable.	0	9	9
		U.S. credibility and case for war is strong.	8	1	9
		Iraq threatens world security.	5	4	9
		Saddam Hussein is morally depraved and subhuman.	5	4	9
		Iraq conducts terrorism / aids terrorists.	2	3	5
	Maybe				**4**
		Bush administration must make a case for war.	4	0	4
	No				**1**
		U.S. credibility and motives are questionable.	1	0	1
What will war be like?					
	Challenging				**27**
		Warfare will be unpleasant or dangerous.	4	9	13
		Warfare will involve certain technical operations / tactics.	0	10	10
		The U.S. military will face some logistical challenges.	0	4	4
	U.S. will win handily				**21**
		U.S. troops are fully prepared to fight and win.	0	17	17
		The Iraqi military is not prepared / cannot win against the U.S. military.	0	2	2
		The war will be over quickly.	0	2	2

In the above example, Duelfer raises the possibility that weapons exist in Iraq (and perhaps even hints this is likely), but he also modalizes his assertion by saying the palaces *could* contain weapons, while leaving open the possibility they might not. It was not unusual for analysts to offer such uncertain speculation that nevertheless raised doubts about Iraq. However, weapons analysts also offered a voice of certainty when stating unequivocally that Iraq possessed weapons, lied about their existence, and would continue to hide them during the new inspections regime. For example, Richard Butler appeared on NBC News in September 2002 to rebut Iraq's statements: "Iraq has said, 'We have no weapons of mass destruction whatsoever.' I'm going to say to you plainly: that is not true. The issue is, will they be able to conceal that or not?" (NBC 2002, Sep. 17). Butler categorically denies the veracity of Iraq's past assertions ("not true") and presupposes that Iraq will attempt to conceal its weapons in the future.[5]

Weapons inspectors were also asked to discuss the challenges facing the new inspectors, often with the suggestion that the inspectors had little hope of succeeding. David Kay, for example, frequently offered negative judgments about the ability of the inspectors to carry out their mission. On November 25, 2002, Kay commented on NBC, "I think the inspections as they've started now are not adequate to disclose the Iraqi concealment program or their weapons of mass destruction, or really in any meaningful way to confront the Iraqis." Here, Kay presupposes both Iraq's deceptiveness and the existence of WMD ("the Iraqi concealment program," "their weapons of mass destruction"), while explicitly negating the capacity of the inspectors to uncover wrongdoing ("not adequate") or substantially confront the Iraqi leadership in Baghdad ("not adequate . . . in any meaningful way").

This is not to say that weapons analysts always supported Bush administration propaganda. For example, Richard Butler questioned the legitimacy (and perhaps the legality) of a unilateral war (NBC 2003, Jan. 14), and David Albright suggested that war was not urgent and recommended inspections be given more time (NBC 2002, Sep. 24). However, news producers almost never aired these kinds of assertions. And analysts such as Butler and Albright, who may have had reservations about the war, were much more likely to be featured describing Iraq's methods of deception or reminding viewers that any Iraqi lie could trigger violence.

In fact, taken together, the themes most often expressed by weapons analysts constitute an argumentative syllogism. As shown in table 8, the premises that weapons analysts regularly articulated lead to the conclusion that war in Iraq is necessary.

Table 8 Syllogism suggesting war with Iraq

Premise:	Iraq must fully and immediately disarm to avoid material breach.
Premise:	Iraq is not disarming but is lying, cheating, and concealing WMD.
Premise:	Weapons inspections are failing to uncover WMD.
Conclusion:	Thus, war is likely the only way to disarm Iraq.

Of course, analysts could openly suggest war was necessary. Recall, for example, Barry McCaffrey's declaration that, before finishing the War on Terror, "we will have to confront the pariah state Iraq" (NBC 2001, Oct. 10). More often, though, both weapons analysts and military analysts suggested the necessity of war more obliquely, by implying that war was inevitable or virtually inescapable (e.g., "The order that came out from the Defense Department, moving the thirty-five thousand troops, I think it's a clear indication that we're in the countdown mode for a ground attack." [Bernard Trainor on NBC 2003, Jan. 11]); by offering positive evaluations of Bush administration officials making the case for war (e.g., "I think [Colin Powell] made a powerful case" [David Kay on NBC 2003, Feb. 5a]); or by presenting extremely negative evaluations of Iraq, its leadership, or its ties to terrorism (e.g., "[Saddam's] twisted; he's mentally twisted. He gained enormous pleasure from inflicting pain on people" [Khidir Hamza on NBC 2002, Oct. 15]).

As indicated in table 7, weapons inspectors implicitly justified war on the grounds that Iraq was hiding WMD, but military experts generally took a different angle. They suggested war was legitimate on grounds of feasibility, emphasizing American military power and the ease with which the United States could conquer Iraq. Often, they commented on the strength of American weaponry. For example, on ABC, General George Joulwan described America's unmanned surveillance planes: "You can see tank formations. You can see enemy aircraft batteries. You can see missile sites. High-resolution, extremely accurate, real-time video" (ABC 2002, Dec. 23). Here, Joulwan endorses American military equipment through strongly positive valuations ("high-resolution, extremely accurate") and lexical repetition emphasizing what the equipment enables troops to accomplish ("you can see").

The military voice was also typified by confident predictions of U.S. operations, again indicating the supremacy of American armed forces. Barry McCaffrey, for instance, envisioned urban warfare on NBC (2003, Jan. 13): "We'll enter places like Baghdad at high speed and go to vital areas and seize them using tanks, two-thousand-pound air-delivered bombs, and enormous levels of violence. And we'll do it all in the dark." McCaffrey uses the plural pronoun "we," indexing his (and perhaps the viewers') identification with American troops. He then categorically predicts successful U.S. military operations ("we'll . . . go to vital areas and seize them") and offers a proliferation of means by which we will seize important sites ("tanks," "bombs," "violence"), often premodifying head nouns with descriptors indicating strength ("*two-thousand-pound air-delivered* bombs," "*enormous levels* of violence"). Finally, as if to awe the viewer, McCaffrey adds the news that "we'll do it all in the dark." The phrase "we'll do it all" maximizes the quantity of predicted successes, while the prepositional circumstance ("in the dark") likely counters the viewer's expectation that such fighting would require daylight, further suggesting the unparalleled power of the U.S. military.

Certainly, military analysts also suggested war would be unpleasant and dangerous, and they sometimes described setbacks that could adversely affect troops. But even then, the analysts typically reaffirmed that U.S. troops would carry out their mission. For example, in early March 2003, Turkey refused to allow American troops on its soil, requiring the army to relocate personnel and equipment. General McCaffrey commented on NBC (2003, Mar. 2): "That equipment will now have to transit through the Suez and get in position to offload in Kuwait. I'm sure they could do that in less than three weeks, but this is a huge logistical challenge to the United States Navy and Army to reposition." McCaffrey clearly suggests relocating equipment presents a problem, even up-scaling the magnitude of the challenge facing soldiers ("*huge* logistical challenge"). But he also expresses maximal confidence ("I'm sure") about the capacity of U.S. troops to meet this challenge ("they could do that").

Rearticulating and Reinforcing Government Propaganda

Overall, then, the expert voice supplied by military and weapons analysts articulated propaganda themes favored by the Bush administration. In some cases, analysts even appeared to repeat talking points shown to them by government officials. For example, as displayed in the extract below, one of the talking points documents shared with military analysts concerned the likelihood that Iraq would flood its dams.

- **During its war with Iran in 1983, Iraq breached dams and flooded waterways to block Iranian troop advances in the south.**
- These acts prove Saddam is not above wasting a scarce resource (water) as a tool of warfare.
- Today, innocent Iraqis could again be victimized should Saddam choose to use flooding in his military campaign.
- Iraq has nine major flood control and hydro-electric power dams.
  - Five are associated with the Tigris River and four with the Euphrates River.
  - Two of the dams associated with the Tigris are in Kurdish-controlled northeast Iraq.
  - The Euphrates River dams are key water sources to Baghdad and southern cities.
- **Destroying key dams in Iraq would affect at least 3.5 million residents outside the Baghdad area.**
- In addition to affecting millions, destroying the Tigris River dams would damage or destroy much of Iraq's wheat and barley crops and transportation and electrical utilities.[6]

The document explains that Iraq has major flood control along the Tigris and Euphrates Rivers and warns that "innocent Iraqis could again be victimized should

Saddam choose to use flooding in his military campaign." The same month these talking points were published, Montgomery Meigs appeared on NBC News and, while tracing the Tigris and Euphrates rivers on a smart map (see figure 7 above), explained to viewers that "by flooding these river systems," Saddam could pose a "real danger . . . to the people that live there." Notice that both the talking points and Meigs's report articulate the same generic meaning: Saddam could flood his rivers and endanger innocent people.

However, news experts did not merely rearticulate administration propaganda; they also inspired it. Indeed, administration officials sometimes recontextualized language generated by the analysts. Recall that, in several news appearances, Richard Butler stated categorically that Iraq had weapons of mass destruction (e.g., NBC 2002, Sep. 17). Incidentally, Butler told me this was a mistake. He said he had spoken "too sharply about unaccounted-for materials in Iraq" and apologized for having done so: "I'm sorry about that. I wouldn't say that today. I regret that." Unfortunately, Butler's misstatements may have convinced millions of television viewers. But that's not the whole of the story. For, in an intertextual world, Butler's expert voice could be recontextualized and revived by political elites.

In fact, on December 5, 2002, White House press secretary Ari Fleischer seized upon Butler's words during a briefing with reporters. A journalist asked Fleischer if he had "anything that constitutes proof" Iraq was lying when it denied having WMD. In response, Fleischer presented Butler's 2002 testimony before the Senate: "Let me cite for you something I think you will find constructive," he said. "This is a statement by Richard Butler, formerly of the United Nations. Quote—this is Richard Butler speaking: 'It is essential to recognize that the claim made by Saddam's representative that Iraq has no weapons of mass destruction is false. Everyone concerned, from Iraq's neighbors, to the U.N. Security Council, to the secretary of the U.N., with whom Iraq is currently negotiating on this issue, everyone simply, Mr. Chairman, is being lied to.'" After quoting Butler at length, Fleischer offered that the public should consider whom to trust: "President Bush has said Iraq has weapons of mass destruction. Tony Blair has said Iraq has weapons of mass destruction. Donald Rumsfeld has said Iraq has weapons of mass destruction. Richard Butler has said they do. The United Nations has said they do. The experts have said they do. Iraq says they don't. You can choose who you want to believe" (Fleischer 2002). Indeed, "the experts," as Fleischer referred to them, had been quite believable—certainly much more believable than Iraq. Former inspectors and military officers had made a convincing case for war, both in public statements and in regular appearances on the evening news. In lieu of evidence, the Bush administration was happy to cite their work.

A powerful voice isn't something that belongs to a speaker: it is something enacted one communicative event at a time. In this case, the characterological figure of the news analyst was jointly enacted by anchors, correspondents, set designers, wardrobe staff, caption generators, and the analysts themselves. It was developed by many people who selected bits and pieces of analyst talk, framed that talk with ethos-enhancing signs, and ensured that the content of the talk would reflect administration themes.

Thus, the expert voice became distinct and detachable from surrounding discourse—recognizable across texts and repeatable by anyone wishing to claim expert knowledge, that is, anyone wishing to sound like an expert. Granted, not all news consumers would accept analysts' talk as legitimate. But news institutions had certainly worked to induce a favorable uptake. Following Agha (2003, 266), we might say they had provided a "model of exemplary speech to very large audiences, thus homogenizing the conditions for subsequent response behaviors and role alignments. . . . However particular audiences may [have] respond[ed], more and more of them [were] responding to the same thing." In other words, the news institutions had *propagated* the expert voice, recontextualizing it on a mass scale and priming audiences to regard it as worthy of repetition. Whether audiences repeated the themes of analyst talk is a matter for further study, but cues that they should align with "the experts" were present in the news.

Not only were news consumers denied crucial information about analysts' financial commitments, political ties, and private arrangements with officials, but they were also exposed to misleading claims about Iraq's alleged possession of WMD and its supposed ties to terrorists. News producers were most likely to air analyst talk if it repeated government propaganda, even as they characterized this pro-government talk as disinterested expertise. Ultimately, then, this chapter suggests how governments and news institutions can work symbiotically to ensure, first, that propaganåda is circulated and, second, that it is interpreted favorably. They depend on each other and fulfill each other's needs. The needs of the citizenry, meanwhile, may be overlooked.

7. The Evolution of a Talking Point

Two things you'll almost certainly never
hear from a TV pundit: "I don't know"
and "I have no opinion about that."
                              —Paul Farhi, 2016

Propaganda is, by definition, public. If discourse is confined to private spaces, it cannot be recontextualized on a mass scale; it cannot become successful propaganda. However, propaganda sometimes originates in private contexts—for instance, secret intelligence claims may be cited for massive public audiences. It can be instructive to examine similarities and differences between private intelligence and the public propaganda derived from it. Such comparisons can reveal how deliberate propagandists (re)fashion discourse to ensure favorable recontextualization in media. Through processes of "focalization" (Hodges 2008b, 493), for example, officials may highlight favorable aspects of intelligence reports that they hope will be replicated by the press. Meanwhile, through processes of "erasure" (Irvine and Gal 2000, 38), they may ignore or de-emphasize aspects that detract from a "preferred reading" (Hodges 2008b, 493). Focalization and erasure are just two ways propagandists seek to "control how their discourse will be entextualized and recontextualized" (Bauman and Briggs 1990, 78). But even when officials use these strategies, their discourse is still subject to change, as journalists ultimately decide whether and how to include it in their reports.

As seen in the previous chapter, news analysts before the Iraq War often rearticulated government talking points. Here, I consider how one such talking point came to exist in the first place, examining the discursive life of a key claim in the Bush administration's case for war. The claim was that Iraq had tried to import aluminum tubes specifically designed for a gas centrifuge. To President Bush, these tubes were evidence that Iraq was reconstituting its nuclear weapons program. I study the intertextual chain of discourse surrounding the tubes, following its trajectory from classified intelligence reports to public speeches and news analysis. (See appendix K for details.) A major concern is how speakers and writers use engagement resources (Martin and White 2005) to open up or close down space for alternative viewpoints. In Martin and White's (2005) terms, some locutions are "dialogically expansive," allowing for rival points of view. Other locutions, however, are "dialogically contractive," suppressing the expression of alternative positions.

Tellingly, in this study, classified intelligence reports were dialogically expansive, in that they entertained alternative views about the tubes, including the view that they were designed for conventional rockets (not nuclear weapons). However, public information was dialogically contractive and often presented only the administration's claim that the tubes were intended for a nuclear device. This suggests that expansive resources—such as hedges and references to counterclaims—were deemed unfavorable and removable from administration propaganda. Insofar as the administration's claim about the tubes was disputed, it could not travel effectively in the press. To become propaganda, signs of dispute had to be silenced (Huckin 2002, 2010), while signs of consensus had to be emphasized and focalized. The case study illustrates how deliberate propagandists ensure that preferred meanings gain mobility in public spaces. In an amazing display of contemporary propaganda, the Bush administration transformed internal debates into a categorical talking point, publicized the talking point in an orchestrated media campaign, and watched as it was corroborated by nominally independent news analysts.

The Classified Debate

In early 2001, U.S. intelligence obtained documents showing that Iraq was seeking about sixty thousand aluminum tubes. Analysts at the CIA reasoned that the tubes were intended as rotors in a gas centrifuge, since they were made from a high-strength aluminum alloy (7075-T6 aluminum) that could withstand the rapid spinning needed to enrich uranium (Isikoff and Corn 2006, 37). On April 10, 2001, the CIA forwarded this assessment to President Bush and other officials in a highly classified intelligence brief, the starting point for this analysis. (As a convention, I **bold** Martin and White's [2005] engagement terminology).

The brief's key conclusion is that the tubes "have little use other than for a uranium enrichment program." Here, even as the CIA projects certainty that the tubes are used for uranium enrichment, it nevertheless indexes the possibility that the tubes have non-nuclear applications. After all, asserting that the tubes have "little use other than" nuclear weapons still admits the slim ("little") possibility the tubes could be used for some other purpose, though this possibility is **countered** and suppressed ("other than"). In fact, the first CIA report even acknowledges that the tubes are seemingly inappropriate for nuclear weapons. It states, "Using aluminum tubes in a centrifuge effort would be inefficient and a step backward from the specialty steel machines Iraq was poised to mass-produce at the onset of the Gulf War." Here, the CIA **entertains** ("would be") negative attitudes about the tubes' applicability in a centrifuge ("inefficient," "step backward"), subtly suggesting an alternative view: the tubes are not well suited for a nuclear device. However, as if to fend off this implication, the CIA immediately **counters** that Iraq made use of obsolete machinery when trying to build a nuclear bomb in the past: "Iraq successfully used outdated enrichment technologies, such as its electromagnetic isotope separation effort, before the war." In terms of attitudinal discourse, the CIA says Iraq demonstrated positive capacity in its pre-Gulf War efforts to enrich uranium ("Iraq *successfully* used"), despite the fact that it was employing negatively valued enrichment technologies ("outdated"). Thus, as shown in table 9, the CIA entertains potential opposition to its assessment of the tubes, only to reaffirm its position.

In fact, this a classic argumentative move whereby a competing claim is introduced precisely so it can be countered. Such argumentative discourse is indexical of a context "pregnant with responses and objections" (Bakhtin 1981, 281). That is, the CIA is signaling that its assertions are arguable—that they are capable of being contradicted by others in the intertextual universe.

And, in fact, the CIA's assertions were quickly challenged by analysts from the Department of Energy (DOE), the intelligence community's foremost specialists in nuclear technology. One day after the CIA's initial report, the DOE responded:

Based on the reported specifications, the tubes could be used to manufacture gas centrifuge rotor cylinders for uranium enrichment. However, our analysis indicates that the specified tube diameter, which is half that of the centrifuge machine Iraq successfully tested in 1990, is only marginally large enough for practical centrifuge applications, and other specifications are not consistent with a gas centrifuge end use. Moreover, the quantity being sought suggests preparations for large scale production of centrifuge machines, for which we have not seen related procurement efforts—and the

Table 9 Rebutting a counterargument

Potential counterargument

Premise:	Iraq would not want to use inefficient materials and take a step backward.
Premise:	The tubes are inefficient and a step backward for Iraq's nuclear program.
Conclusion:	Thus, it is unlikely that the tubes are intended for a gas centrifuge.

Favored argument

Premise:	Iraq successfully used outdated technologies to enrich uranium in the past.
Premise:	Iraq would presumably use outdated technologies, such as the tubes, again.
Conclusion:	Thus, it is likely that the tubes, though outdated, are intended for a gas centrifuge.

tubes' specifications suggest a centrifuge design quite different from any Iraq is known to have. Thus, we assess that this procurement activity more likely supports a different application. . . . For example, the tube specifications and quantity appear to be generally consistent with their use as launch tubes for man-held anti-armor rockets or as tactical rocket casings. Also, the manner in which the procurement is being handled (multiple procurement agents, quotes obtained from multiple suppliers in diverse locations, and price haggling) seems to better match our expectations for a conventional Iraqi military buy than a major purchase for a clandestine weapons-of-mass destruction program.

Once again, we find the classic argumentative move, wherein an opposing thesis is **entertained** as a modalized possibility ("the tubes *could* be used to manufacture gas centrifuge rotor cylinders") only to be countered with the favored thesis. In this case, the DOE explicitly **counters** with the adverb "however" and **denies** the CIA claim ("*not* consistent with a gas centrifuge end use"). In addition, the DOE provides three data-based reasons why the tubes are unlikely for nuclear weapons: (1) "the tube diameter is . . . only marginally large enough for practical centrifuge applications"; (2) "the quantity being sought suggests preparations for large scale production . . . for which we have not seen related procurement efforts"; (3) "the tubes' specifications suggest a centrifuge design quite different from any Iraq is known to have." Finally, the DOE offers its own thesis—the tubes are more likely designed for conventional rockets—and provides two data-based reasons in favor of this interpretation: (1) "the tube specifications and quantity appear to be generally consistent with their use as launch tubes for . . . rockets"; (2) "the manner in which the procurement is being handled . . . seems to better match our expectations for a conventional Iraqi military buy." About a month later, the DOE added yet another reason in favor of this interpretation: "Iraq [had] purchased similar aluminum tubes previously to manufacture . . . a multiple rocket launcher." Like the CIA, the DOE does not categorically state the tubes are designed for conventional rockets. Indeed, many evidentials **entertain** other possibilities: the tubes "appear to be generally consistent" with rocket production, and procurement "seems to" match a conventional rocket. Thus, their discourse, too, indexes an argumentative environment in which opposing claims are entertained, countered, and refuted, while favored claims are supported by carefully hedged reasons.

In June 2001, the CIA managed to intercept a shipment of the tubes before they arrived in Iraq, so intelligence officials could analyze them directly (Isikoff and Corn 2006, 39). Still, the top-secret dispute between the CIA and DOE raged on. The CIA (and others) continued to argue the tubes were most likely intended for nuclear weapons, while DOE experts (and others) continued to insist the tubes were more likely suited for conventional rockets.[1] As the debate intensified, the arguments on each side grew more detailed and technical. On July 2, 2001, for example, the CIA pointed out that the thickness of the tubes exceeded requirements for conventional rockets and further asserted that the dimensions of the tubes "match those of a publicly available gas centrifuge design from the 1950s, known as the Zippe centrifuge." A report from the Defense Intelligence Agency concurred that the tubes were "very similar" to Zippe's design, even listing their precise dimensions: "an outer diameter of 74.2–81.9-mm, an inner diameter of 68.6–76.3-mm, a wall thickness of 2.8-mm, a length of 279.4–381-mm and a tolerance of 0.1-mm."

On August 17, the DOE responded that the tubes were also "too thick for favorable use" in a nuclear weapon, since they "exceed[ed] the nominal 1-mm thickness" of known aluminum rotors. And on December 1, the DOE refuted the CIA's contention that the tubes "matched" the Zippe centrifuge, pointing out that the tubes Iraq sought were roughly three times thicker and longer than those called for in the Zippe design.[2] The DOE went on to note that if Iraq chose to pursue a nuclear weapon using these tubes, it would face major manufacturing obstacles. To get enough highly enriched uranium (HEU) for just one nuclear weapon, Iraq would need to operate "more than 12,000–16,000 centrifuges," a task for which they had neither the machinery nor the operational experience. "In short," the DOE concluded, "we judge it unlikely that *anyone* could deploy an enrichment facility capable of producing weapons significant quantities of HEU based on these tubes" (my emphasis).

Thus, the leading authority on nuclear weapons argued forcefully against the interpretation that the tubes were intended for gas centrifuges. However, without additional evidence, the DOE could not completely rule out the CIA's counterclaim. It was, after all, theoretically possible that the tubes could be adapted for a nuclear weapon. Consequently, DOE experts consistently signaled the plausibility of the CIA's case when suggesting, for example, that "a gas centrifuge application is credible but unlikely" and offering that a rocket application is merely the "more likely" scenario. Similarly, the CIA could not discount the possibility that the DOE was correct. Thus, CIA reports acknowledged that the tubes "could be used as rocket bodies for multiple rocket launchers," while maintaining that this view was "less likely." Ultimately, each side in the contest recognized the other, citing the opposing argument and suggesting its merits through positive evaluation (e.g., "credible") or **entertaining** its potentiality through modalized verbs phrases (e.g., "could be"). However, each side also maintained that their own claims were more probable, projecting qualified certainty through resources of modality paired with comparative premodifiers (e.g., "more likely"). In Fairclough's (2003) terms, both sides produced discourse accentuating dialogue and difference, entertaining rival views while stressing disagreement.[3]

Initiating the Propaganda Campaign

The intelligence debate, however, did not take place in a vacuum. It was being monitored closely by members of the Bush administration. Indeed, even before they knew what the tubes were for, officials began discussing how to use them to discredit Baghdad. As early as June 29, 2001, a memo to Colin Powell suggests "publicizing the interdiction [of the tubes] to our advantage," noting the importance of "getting the right story out" (U.S. Department of State 2001). By this point, the administration had indicated to intelligence officials that it desired reports painting a negative picture of Iraq (Goodman 2006). CIA director George Tenet was happy to oblige. Reports claiming that the tubes were likely intended for Iraq's nuclear program were sent directly "to high-level policymakers and were not made available to intelligence analysts from other agencies" (S. Rep. No. 108–301 (2004), at 90–91). Nevertheless, by 2001, key administration officials—President Bush, Dick Cheney, Donald Rumsfeld, Colin Powell, and Condoleezza Rice—knew of the internal debate surrounding the tubes.[4] However, having all but decided on an invasion, they seized upon the CIA's interpretation, while ignoring the DOE's view that the tubes were ill-suited for uranium enrichment (Barstow, Broad, and Gerth 2004).

By late summer 2002, the administration was ready to campaign for war—and had finally settled on "the right story" about the tubes. The White House leaked its version of events to the *New York Times*. On Sunday, September 8, 2002, a front-page article by Michael Gordon and Judith Miller appeared with the headline "U.S. Says Hussein Intensifies Quest for A-Bomb Parts." The lede reads: "More than a decade after Saddam Hussein agreed to give up weapons of mass destruction, Iraq has stepped up its quest for nuclear weapons and has embarked on a worldwide hunt for materials to make an atomic bomb, Bush administration officials said today. In the last 14 months, Iraq has sought to buy thousands of specially designed aluminum tubes, which American officials believe were intended as components of centrifuges to enrich uranium." Of course, the placement of the story on page A1 signals its importance and indexes that it is comparatively more repeatable or reusable than other stories in the paper. Meanwhile, both the headline and lede, the most salient parts of the story, showcase the presupposition that Iraq is on a "quest" for nuclear weapons. As if to corroborate this, the lede also attributes to "American officials" the assertion that Iraq's aluminum tubes are "intended as components of centrifuges to enrich uranium." However, references to the DOE argument—that the tubes were likely intended for rockets—are absent. Indeed, the authors never acknowledge any dissent, providing an entirely one-sided picture of the tubes debate. Furthermore, as the *Times* describes the tubes, it excludes almost all the technical details in the intelligence reports. There is no mention of the Zippe design and no indication of the tubes' precise measurements. Instead, the article reports that, according to officials, the "the diameter, thickness and other technical specifications of the aluminum tubes had persuaded American intelligence experts that they were meant for Iraq's nuclear program" (Gordon and Miller 2002). Thus, evidence supporting the tubes' nuclear application is left underspecified. To believe the claim, readers had to rely on the apparent conviction of "American intelligence experts," here represented as a monolithic group.

Once discourse about the aluminum tubes reaches the public, then, differences of opinion are erased and only one interpretation is offered—saliently and with minimal supporting data. Instead of vigorous debate, one finds a "bracketing of difference" (Fairclough 2003, 42), as the *Times* signals a consensus requiring no argumentative justification. Still, the *Times*'s report at least indexes that alternative interpretations of the tubes are possible. The view that the tubes are intended for centrifuges is attributed to officials, using a verb suggesting tentativeness ("American officials believe"). And, while "officials" are to be regarded as legitimate sources, the writers of the article do not explicitly claim solidarity with them. In Martin and White's (2005, 115) terms, the article "simply conveys the views of others," **acknowledging** their voices without necessarily supporting them. Thus, while the nuclear application is focalized—featured prominently and presented without challenge—it is not endorsed by the news writers or represented as a categorical fact.

But now that their leak had been featured in America's top newspaper, administration insiders could declare even more confidently that Iraq was reconstituting its nuclear program. The same morning the *Times* broke its story, leading officials hit the Sunday talk shows to cite the authoritative *Times* article. On NBC's *Meet the Press*, for example, Dick Cheney (2002) said the "story in the *New York Times* this morning" revealed that Saddam Hussein "has been seeking to acquire . . . the kinds of tubes that are necessary to build a centrifuge." Based on this evidence, Cheney declared, "we do know, with absolute certainty, that [Saddam] is using his procurement system to acquire the equipment he needs in order to enrich uranium to build a nuclear weapon." Similarly, on Fox, Colin Powell stated "as we saw in reporting just this morning, [Saddam] is still trying to acquire, for example, some of the specialized aluminum tubing one needs to develop centrifuges that would give you an enrichment capability," adding, there was "no question that . . . he is striving get even more" weapons (Snow 2002). Finally, on CNN, Condoleezza Rice was most emphatic, declaring "we do know that [Saddam] is actively pursuing a nuclear weapon," since he has sought shipments of "aluminum tubes . . . that are only really suited for nuclear weapons programs" (Blitzer 2002).

The consistency with which these officials describe the tubes suggests a choreographed propaganda operation. Undoubtedly, each had been briefed and provided with decontextualizable talking points, similar to those shown below.

Nuclear Weapons

- Saddam has kept together cadres of nuclear scientists, and has a design for a nuclear bomb. As far as we know, Iraq lacks fissile material, but is seeking the means to enrich uranium.

- Procurement efforts include high specification aluminum tubes for gas centrifuges used to enrich uranium, a production plant for magnets suitable in centrifuge work, and machines suitable for balancing centrifuge rotors.[5]

When Cheney, Powell, and Rice recontextualize claims about the aluminum tubes, they add new degrees of certainty. Interestingly, they no longer cite the intelligence community but instead attribute the tubes claims to the *Times*, suggesting publication in the newspaper is an index of validity. For example, Powell **endorses** the *Times*'s reporting ("as we saw in reporting just this morning"), suggesting that the evidence has already been observed by all of us ("we saw") and perhaps indicating that the recency of the report gives it validity in the here and now ("just this morning"). Meanwhile, after noting the *Times* report, Cheney (2002) similarly says "it's now public that, in fact, [Saddam] has been seeking to acquire" nuclear weapons. Again, the recent publication ("now public") is presented as a sign of evidential force, while the **pronouncement** ("in fact") further indicates the warrantability of the proposition.

Of course, these officials also erase alternative views about the tubes, manipulatively silencing all signals of contingency and dispute (Huckin 2002, 2010). Indeed, unlike the CIA, these officials do not entertain the idea that the tubes "could be used for rockets"—even though they were well aware of this possibility. And they do not qualify their own view of tubes as simply a "more likely" hypothesis. Instead, they describe the "specialized aluminum tubing **one needs** to develop centrifuges" or the kind of tubes "**necessary** to build a centrifuge," misleadingly suggesting through **deontic modals** that anyone trying to build a nuclear bomb *needs* to use such aluminum tubing, when this was not the case. Similarly, officials declare the tubes are "**only** suited for nuclear weapons," providing no evidence for this claim yet **countering** and silencing any alternative viewpoint. Simultaneously, they maximize certainty that Iraq is pursuing a nuclear bomb, insisting upon the warrantability of their assertions through a series of **pronouncements**: "we do know with absolute certainty," "there can be no question," "we do know" (see Martin and White 2005, 127). This confident language is a far cry from the hedged assessments in intelligence reports and also from the *Times* article, which had not represented the tubes' suitability for centrifuges as a categorical fact but as something "American officials believe."

Corroboration from a News Expert

Once the tubes story had broken in the *Times*, television news providers quickly recontextualized it again. For example, a day after the *Times* story, NBC (2002, Sep. 9) devoted a segment to describing the status of Iraq's WMD. Excerpt 7.1 shows a portion of Andrea Mitchell's report.

Excerpt 7.1 NBC (2002, Sep. 9)

Time	Frame	Soundtrack*
15–29		**Andrea Mitchell:** Saddam Hussein giving a pep talk to his nuclear scientists earlier this year. But he may be up to a lot more than cheerleading, U.S. intelligence officials say. They've blocked several shipments of
30–37	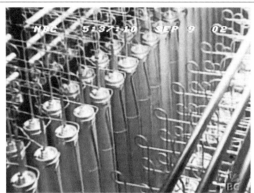	aluminum tubes heading toward Iraq, the kind of tubes only used in a centrifuge to make nuclear fuel.
38–49		**David Kay:** This is not like we're producing three or four. It is multiple orders, going into the thousands of tubes. This looks like a classic import for a gas centrifuge program.

On NBC, the transformation is nearly complete. What had once been a hotly contested and highly qualified claim—that the tubes might be used as rotors in a gas centrifuge—is now recontextualized as something like a fact. Mitchell does not source the tubes claim to the *Times* article or even to administration officials on the talk shows. Instead, she reports that the tubes are the kind "**only** used in a centrifuge to make nuclear fuel," thereby **countering** and warding off any other possible interpretation. Meanwhile, the visual shot displays metal cylinders—presumably the aluminum tubes—enhancing the sense that the evidence against Iraq is concrete.

Then, news analyst David Kay enters the picture. He is described on screen as a "Fmr. Nuclear Weapons Inspector," a title indicating his capacity to speak credibly about nuclear technology. So introduced, Kay promptly implies Iraq has an expansive nuclear weapons program. He first **denies** Iraq has sought a small number of aluminum tubes ("it's *not* like we're producing three or four") and then dramatically up-scales the quantity of tubes, implying a major effort on the part of Iraq to acquire centrifuge material ("it is *multiple* orders, going into the *thousands* of tubes"). Ironically, experts at the DOE regarded these vast numbers as evidence that the tubes were *not* intended for nuclear weapons, since Iraq didn't have the machinery needed for such a large-scale manufacturing effort. But Kay, apparently unaware of this argument, suggests the tubes are ideal for nuclear weapons production. He states, "This looks like a classic import for a gas centrifuge program." Kay's evidential phrase ("looks like") suggests a degree of doubt on his part, but the premodifier used to describe Iraq's import ("classic") indicates not that the aluminum tubes are potentially viable in a nuclear weapon but that they are, in fact, the industry standard for a gas centrifuge program.

I asked Kay how he came to this conclusion. He said that he had made the mistake of over-relying on secondary source material. Specifically, he said he had depended on Gordon and Miller's article in the *New York Times*, believing that "what they were saying [about the tubes] made a lot of sense."[6] But, as noted, Gordon and Miller provided few details about the aluminum tubes and nothing at all about their precise dimensions. So, if Kay was indeed relying on the *Times* article, it is difficult to see what evidence convinced him the tubes were designed for nuclear weapons. Indeed, how could Kay conclude this was a "*classic* import for a gas centrifuge" based on such limited data?

Curious about this, I also asked Kay if anyone from the U.S. government had tried to convince him the tubes were intended for nuclear weapons. He could not recall with certainty, but he explained that he often talked to the CIA's lead analyst on Iraq's nuclear program and reasoned that he "almost certainly would have" discussed the tubes with him. Thus, Kay also may have based his on-air commentary on information he received directly from the CIA. In any case, it is clear that Kay did not have sufficient knowledge to provide meaningful news analysis. Indeed, he was not analyzing data at all. Either he was reciting allegations made by anonymous sources in the *New York Times*, or he was repeating an apparently one-sided account offered to him by a CIA informant. Furthermore, Kay's suggestion that Iraq had made a "classic import" for a nuclear weapon is more forceful, more hyperbolic than either the *Times* article or the CIA's classified reports.[7] He was not simply rearticulating the CIA's view; he was enhancing it.

Squelching Public Debate

At the time, Kay says, he was unaware that different intelligence agencies had conflicting opinions about the tubes. But another news analyst, David Albright, knew about the internal debate. Albright, a physicist and former weapons inspector, ran a Washington think tank called the Institute for Science and International Security. Back in 2001, he received a phone call from a concerned scientist at the International Atomic Energy Agency (IAEA), the world's authority on nuclear weapons. This scientist had recently listened to a CIA presentation arguing that Iraq's aluminum tubes were meant for a gas centrifuge. He thought the CIA's interpretation was wrong, so he reached out to Albright to discover what was happening in the intelligence community (Isikoff and Corn 2006, 37). In turn, Albright began contacting experts at the Department of Energy who told him about the intelligence split over the tubes.

In fact, before the *New York Times* ran its story on September 8, 2002, Judith Miller tried to reach Albright for comment, but he had been out of town. When he saw that the *Times* article failed to account for the DOE's assessment, Albright called Miller back and alerted her to the debate in the intelligence community (Albright 2003, 17). Partly in response, Miller agreed to run an additional story. In the meantime, President Bush continued to whip up support for war in Iraq. In a September 12 address before the United Nations, Bush (2002b) repeated the misleading and categorical charge that the tubes were "used to enrich uranium for a nuclear weapon" and warned that Iraq might have such a weapon "within a year." The president had finally transformed disputed intelligence into an unmodalized fact about Iraq's nuclear ambitions. Albright hoped the new *Times* article would set the record straight. But when the article finally appeared on September 13, it did little to challenge Bush's public claims.

The new *Times* story by Judith Miller and Michael Gordon was relegated to page A13, and its headline suggested nothing about an intelligence debate: "Baghdad's Arsenal; White House Lists Iraq Steps to Build Banned Weapons." The follow-up article, then, was designed to be less decontextualizable and repeatable—and titled such that anyone wishing to repeat its claims would be induced to focus on Iraq's supposed "arsenal" of weapons. Granted, the article does finally acknowledge that "some experts" disputed the tubes' applicability for a gas centrifuge. But note how the imprecise quantifier "some" down-scales the number of dissenters. Indeed, the new article remains heavily slanted toward the CIA's position. Miller and Gordon never quote any DOE experts and instead overwhelmingly cite assertions from unnamed administration officials. These officials refer to the argument that the tubes are intended for rockets as the "minority view," one not shared by "more senior" analysts. They further say "it was the intelligence agencies' unanimous view that the . . . tubes . . . are used to make . . . centrifuges," adding that "the best technical experts and nuclear scientists at laboratories like Oak Ridge supported the C.I.A. assessment" (Miller and Gordon 2002).

The report was wildly inaccurate. There was no "unanimous view" among the intelligence agencies. And contrary to the *Times* story, the "best technical experts" and the "most senior" analysts at DOE's Oak Ridge National Laboratory believed the tubes were intended for conventional rockets, not nuclear bombs. Again, the *Times* had focalized CIA claims (vaguely attributed to "officials") while manipulatively silencing the DOE's objections (Huckin 2002, 2010). Albright was stunned. He had provided Miller with information about a major intelligence dispute, but voices of dissent had been ignored and smoothed over as the article sought to project a consensus.

Meanwhile, the DOE was concerned about challenging the CIA when Bush was so clearly relying on CIA intelligence to argue for war. On September 13, the same day the *Times* ran its follow-up story on the tubes, the DOE "sent a directive forbidding employees from discussing the subject with reporters" (Barstow, Broad, and Gerth 2004). DOE employees got the message. A top scientist at Oak Ridge worried that "he would give up his whole career if he went public" with a dissenting view (quoted in Isikoff and Corn 2006, 61). Another DOE analyst complained to Albright that the Bush administration can "release whatever they like, and they expect us to be silent" (Albright 2003, 17). One way the administration controlled entextualization and recontextualization practices, then, was to alert people that they would be punished for opposing the official line.

Dissent on the Margins

Still, Albright was determined to publicize the intelligence dispute. Based on conversations with the DOE's nuclear experts, he decided to write a research report about the tubes issue and completed a draft within a week of the first *New York Times* article (Albright 2003). Albright (2002) asserted that the intelligence community was "deeply divided about the purpose of the tubing," noting that dissenters had been told to keep quiet. He presented evidence on each side of the controversy, finally giving a fair hearing to the DOE's assessment of the tubes and providing key details about the tubes' thickness, coating, and their suitability for a Zippe design. Albright also reaffirmed uncertainty about the tubes through hedges, caveats, and modal qualifiers. For example, in describing the CIA's case, Albright (2002) wrote: "**Before** an aluminum tube of the type . . . **could** be used in a centrifuge, it **would** be **necessary** to modify it by cutting it in half and reducing its wall thickness to less than one millimeter. This task **can** be accomplished by cutting the tube and shaving aluminum off the wall until the required thickness is obtained. Accomplishing this task is complicated, but within Iraq's capabilities both in terms of available machine tools and expertise." Albright creates uncertainty about the CIA's case in several ways. He uses a conditional clause structure, in which one premise ("an aluminum tube . . . could be used in a centrifuge") is represented as dependent on an as-of-yet unmet condition ("it would [first] be necessary to modify it"). He also **entertains** dialogic alternatives to the CIA claim, modalizing the probability the tubes are adaptable for nuclear weaponry ("*could* be used," "*can* be accomplished") and highlighting the contingency of the CIA case ("*would* be *necessary*"). Finally, he employs evaluative vocabulary that signals the difficulty of cutting the tubes down to size ("complicated").

Like the DOE, Albright did not rule out the CIA's assessment, but he did make clear that the tubes had non-nuclear applications. "By themselves," Albright (2002) concluded, "these attempted procurements are not evidence that Iraq is in possession of or close to possessing nuclear weapons. They also do not provide evidence that Iraq has an operating centrifuge plant or when such a plant could be operational." Thus, Albright **denied** the administration's claims that the tubes were an unequivocal indication of Iraq's nuclear ambitions ("*not* evidence," "*not* provide evidence"). And he converted what had become a "factual" talking point back into a debate.

But Albright's report—a draft from a little-known Washington think tank—was hardly in the public eye. To compete with administration propaganda, he would need to draw major media attention—no easy task. Indeed, he could not approach the *New York Times*, which, in his view, had "made a decision to ice out the critics" (quoted in Massing 2004). And the television networks for which he sometimes worked were apparently no better. For example, NBC, which had given David Kay a forum to suggest the tubes were intended for a gas centrifuge, never showed Albright rebutting Kay's conclusion. Still, with his connections to media and government, Albright managed to find a reporter willing to publicize his findings. On September 19, 2002, the *Washington Post* ran an article by Joby Warrick (2002) that described Albright's work and the intelligence dispute about the tubes. It was the first widely available report to truly contradict the administration's claims. However, Warrick's article was buried on page 18, where it was unlikely to find an audience or induce future recontextualization. In fact, the *Post*'s editors believed that Warrick only filed the story because he "had been scooped by the *Times* on the importance of the tubes," and they were unwilling to prominently display his work (Isikoff and Corn 2006, 62). Thus, the political economy of the press—particularly, the imperative to compete for market share—helped ensure Albright's voice was marginalized (Herman and Chomsky 2002). The *Post* apparently buried the story simply because they believed a rival newspaper had a competitive advantage.

Meanwhile, on its inner pages, the *Times* continued to say Iraq was close to building a nuclear weapon and still provided neoconservatives a platform to argue for war. A day before Warrick's story appeared in the *Post*, Judith Miller penned another story, which quoted former Iraqi scientist and sometimes news analyst, Khidir Hamza, who claimed that Iraq was "within two to three years of mass producing centrifuges to enrich uranium for a bomb" (Miller 2002). Likewise, President

Bush continued to reiterate the tubes talking point. For months, in major speeches, he repeated the "fact" that Iraq was pursuing aluminum tubes "used to enrich uranium for a nuclear weapon" (Bush 2002b) or attributed to "our intelligence sources" the view that the tubes were "suitable for nuclear weapons production" (Bush 2003). Indeed, even when Bush sourced the nuclear tube claim, he smoothed over debate by attributing it to "our intelligence sources," as if all such sources were of one mind. Warrick's article and similar reports were more accurate and comprehensive, but as Unger (2007, 254) explains, "no one paid attention" to such accounts, scattered as they were in newspapers around the country. "Once the conventional wisdom had been forged," says Unger, "mere facts did not suffice to change things."

Ultimately, after the 2003 invasion of Iraq, David Kay was handpicked by the Bush administration to lead the Iraq Survey Group (ISG), which was charged with finding Iraq's supposed caches of weapons. To his credit, Kay reported what the evidence indicated: Iraq had no stockpiles of WMD. The aluminum tubes, Kay found, were not meant for a centrifuge program but were intended for artillery rockets.[8] The experts at the Department of Energy had finally been proven right. But it was far too late to make a difference. The war was already raging.

The Bush administration's propaganda strategy was both simple and extremely manipulative. Officials realized that a disputed claim about the tubes could not travel effectively in the media, so they simply eliminated signs of dispute. Once again, we see how much propaganda relies on manipulative silence, the deliberate omission of pertinent information (Huckin 2002, 2010). However, erasure was only part of the administration's strategy. Also important were the practices whereby officials submitted their preferred reading to the press and disincentivized the expression of alternative views.

Thus, officials effectively controlled public discourse by manipulating intelligence and orchestrating a propaganda campaign to market the invasion. The administration worked in partnership with corporate media, as journalists focalized hawkish claims in their headlines, minimized space for alternative views, and recited the government's talking points. Here, manipulation was not only a feature of propaganda but a technique for spreading it. By suppressing alternative views, the administration and the press made their preferred view most portable, most capable of being recontextualized on a mass scale.

The Art of the Slogan

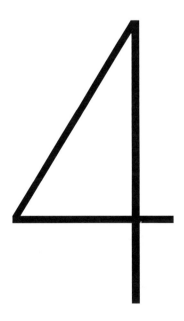

8. "Support Our Troops" as Portable Text and Cultural Tradition

Once the war against Saddam begins, we expect every American to support our military, and if they can't do that, to shut up.

—Bill O'Reilly, 2003

People in the United States are quite familiar with the slogan "Support Our Troops" (SOT). They can encounter it almost anywhere—from T-shirts and bumper stickers, to public service announcements and political speeches. (I was once asked to "Support Our Troops" before a killer whale show at SeaWorld.) The SOT slogan is recontextualized widely, including in settings ostensibly having nothing to do with U.S. troops, and it is manipulative, as it potentially pressures people to silence dissent and support military policies. The question, as always, is what has allowed this discourse to gain currency, to be replicated so extensively as propaganda.

Noam Chomsky (2002, 25–26) offers one possible answer when he suggests that "Support Our Troops" succeeds because it is meaningless:

> It doesn't mean anything. That's the point. The point of public relations slogans like "Support our troops" is that they don't mean anything. They mean as much as whether you support the people in Iowa. . . . That's the whole point of good propaganda. You want to create a slogan that nobody's going to be against, and everybody's going to be for. Nobody knows what it means, because it doesn't mean anything. Its crucial value is that it diverts attention from a question that does mean something: Do you support our policy?

Similarly, Steven Salaita (2013) argues that the slogan is "most effective" because it "lacks the burdens of substance and specificity. It says something apparently apolitical while patrolling for heresy to an inelastic logic. It's only concrete function is to situate users into normative spaces."

Chomsky (2002) and Salaita (2013) suggest that the uncontroversial (and underspecified) meaning of the slogan belies its purpose: to integrate citizens into normative roles and suppress unorthodox talk. In this chapter and the next one, I wish to build on this insight, exploring what allows the SOT slogan to function as effective propaganda. Specifically, I examine what has allowed the slogan to become a "coherent, effective, and memorable text" (Bauman and Briggs 1990, 74), a text worthy of recontextualization.

I first investigate the verbal artistry of the slogan, including the linguistic properties that make it memorable and decontextualizable. However, my main focus is to explain why the slogan is deemed "shareable" in so many quarters of American life, why it "make[s] for better culture" (Urban 1996, 24). To address this issue, I examine the slogan's roots and show how it has become "indexically anchored" to prior speech contexts and larger messages (Hodges 2014, 359). That is, I situate this propaganda in its sociohistorical and intertextual context by chronicling the rise of "Support Our Troops," as it was first uttered in the Vietnam era and later circulated during the Persian Gulf War. Simultaneously, I trace the emergence of "pro-troops" narratives, prevailing stories about soldiers that the slogan inevitably indexes.

I argue that, as a short and discrete text, the slogan has formal properties that make it more amenable to repetition—and, thus, more capable of traveling. However, the slogan's readiness for mobility is just one factor making it suitable as propaganda. Even more important is the history of the slogan and the "residue of prior contexts" that have attached to it (362). Indeed, the slogan is wrapped in a web of cultural significance, including deeply held myths about American wars. "Support Our Troops" reflects and reifies these larger wartime narratives in which substantive policy questions are averted, troops and their mission are venerated, and dissent against war is portrayed as a nearly treasonous offense.

Verbal Artistry and Repeatability

Good slogans are typically designed with care. Indeed, slogans are artistic creations: they must be crafted to comply with formal conventions (such as conciseness and internal rhythm) and to achieve rhetorical objectives (such as memorability, repeatability, and, of course, positive identification with a candidate, policy, or brand). Thus, to understand what makes the SOT slogan so effective, we might begin by analyzing aspects of linguistic design: phonetics, lexicogrammar, and semantics.

Perhaps the first thing to notice about the SOT slogan is the way it sounds. As a number of researchers have suggested, acoustic patterns can help make a slogan memorable and catchy (Miller and Toman 2014; Nemickiene 2013; Reece, Vanden Bergh, and Li 1994), and "Support Our Troops" certainly substantiates this claim.

First, the slogan has a regular rhythm, alternating between unstressed and stressed syllables in a pair of iambs:

sŭppórt ŏur tróops

In addition, the slogan exhibits a high degree of consonance, with the /s/, /p/, /t/, and /r/ sounds all recurring. In fact, the slogan exhibits balanced consonance, a kind of phonemic chiasmus where the arrangement of consonant sounds in the first word is inverted in the last word:

- initial consonant sounds in **supp**ort: /s/ /p/ . . . final consonant sounds in troo**ps**: /p/ /s/
- final consonant sounds in suppo**rt**: /r/ /t/ . . . initial consonant sounds in **tr**oops: /t/ /r/

The internal rhythm and balance of sounds may seem trivial, but they have import-ant rhetorical consequences. For one thing, the poetry of the slogan contributes to a sense of pleasure, which, as Lanham (2007, 57) explains, "makes part of the success" of any message. Just compare "Support Our Troops" with the synonymous expres-sion "back our troops." The latter may have roughly the same meaning, but it doesn't have the same ring. It lacks the rhythm and symmetric consonance of "Support Our Troops" and, thus, fails to produce the same sense of beauty. In fact, the pleasure-inducing sound of "Support Our Troops" may help foster positive associations with the military campaigns to which the slogan is applied.

The patterned sounds of the slogan also contribute to its memorability and por-tability. As Reece, Vanden Bergh, and Li (1994) note, rhythm and repetition of sound elements can help people recall a slogan and associated products. Indeed, the inter-nal sound dynamics of "Support Our Troops" may help people recognize it as a dis-crete text with identifiable "borders." Specifically, the inversion of consonant sounds seems to give the slogan a clear beginning and end. This is important since once a snippet of discourse appears to be a self-contained unit, it is more readily decontex-tualized and recontextualized (Bauman and Briggs 1990). That is, it is more likely to be repeated verbatim in new discursive contexts. The fact that the slogan is also brief—totaling only three words—adds to its portability. The concise expression can be inscribed on nearly any platform, even objects as small as lapel pins. Thus, the formal characteristics of the slogan are part of the reason why it propagates. A short, rhythmic expression such as "Support Our Troops" is much more likely to be remem-bered and reproduced than a lengthy, arrhythmic expression like "back the men and women of the United States military."

Aside from its acoustic properties, "Support Our Troops" also has lexicogram-matical qualities that increase its replicability. First, though the slogan sometimes takes the form of a declarative statement (e.g., "We support our troops"), it more often appears in the imperative mood, as a command: "Support our troops!" The imperative is a way of demanding obedience, and when speakers employ this mood, they expect hearers to immediately undertake a desired action. Thus, part of the power of the SOT slogan is that its grammatical mood exerts social pressure. The command may even index an asymmetry of power between speaker and addressee, implying the authority of the speaker and the relative inferiority of the audience. What is unique about the SOT command, however, is that it is not typically spoken by a real person but posted on signs, bumper stickers, and window decals. Thus, the "authority figure" behind the SOT command is often invisible. The injunction may appear to emerge from the community as a whole, increasing the pressure to conform.

The ideational meaning of the SOT slogan is difficult to pin down, and that is precisely what makes it so repeatable. For example, the material process "support" might mean (1) to sustain someone's spirits during a difficult trial or crisis, (2) to supply someone with necessities, or (3) to advocate someone's cause or objectives. In a wartime context, any of these meanings is possible, and those enjoined to "Support Our Troops" can fittingly respond by wishing for soldiers' health and safety, sending letters and care packages, or promoting their wartime mission and all its material and ideological consequences. This helps to explain why the slogan has such broad appeal. Advocates of a military intervention can claim to "Support Our Troops" by unconditionally backing wartime policy, while antiwar critics can make the same claim by expressing sympathy for the troops as they deal with the perils of war. In short, the slogan works because it is polysemous and capable of appealing to a diverse range of audiences.

Of course, "support," however defined, is a moralized process. That is, as long as the represented beneficiaries are not plainly evil (e.g., "terrorists"), then "offering support" to those beneficiaries will be regarded as positive and prosocial behavior. In this case, the represented beneficiaries, "our troops," are very likely to be regarded as good and worthy of aid. For one thing, the personal possessive pronoun "our" indicates the troops are part of the in-group to which both speaker and addressee belong. The pronoun enacts an "aura of 'common ground' and 'partnership'" between speaker, addressee, and the troops (Cap 2013, 54), who are all part of the same social-ideological team. Even when the personal pronoun is replaced by a definite article ("*the* troops"), there is a sense that both speaker and hearer share common knowledge, that both are intimately familiar with the same context. Thus, the language of the slogan helps to foster a sense of "Us," a sense that speaker and addressee agree on key premises, identify with each other, and bear mutual responsibility for the troops.

Interestingly, the slogan does not seem to derive its persuasive power from the specialized authority of the speaker, and this makes it somewhat different from other forms of propaganda. For example, an atrocity story becomes more credible and repeatable if the narrator is able to adopt the ethos of a journalist or eyewitness. A talking point becomes more credible and repeatable if the speaker can adopt the ethos of a political insider or expert analyst. But a slogan such as "Support Our Troops" does not require that the speaker project any cognitive or administrative authority. Indeed, the power of the slogan has little to do with a speaker's strategic self-presentation and more to do with the speaker's transsituational identity.[1] As long as the speaker is "American" and can make a legitimate claim to "our" troops, then that person is free to repeat the slogan. As I show in the next chapter, people may even repeat the slogan as a way of constituting an American identity.

Finally, much of the slogan's impact derives from the use of the noun "troops," the represented object of our "support." Of course, the word "troops" indexes many positive values in American society, a point I return to in subsequent sections. But, even if we put these indexical associations aside, the word "troops" has additional qualities that make it ideal for use in a slogan. First, "troops" is roughly synonymous with "soldiers." As such, its primary function is to focus attention on the participants in the war, rather than, for example, the reasons why they are fighting (Chomsky 2002). As Stahl (2009, 549) writes, "The term anchors the soldier at the center of war discourse, calling civic attention away from the point of policy's deliberation and toward its point of execution." Whereas questions of policy may invite controversy, the prospect of supporting our soldiers usually invites widespread agreement. Thus, a slogan like "Support Our Troops" is more repeatable precisely because it focuses on supporting the participants—not the politics—of war.

The grammatical number of the word "troops" may also contribute to the slogan's replicability. "Troops" is pluralized, inviting audiences to regard soldiers not as specific individuals but as a monolithic collective (Van Leeuwen 2008). (Even in singular form, the word "troop" can refer to a unit of soldiers, rather than an individual one.) Thus, the "troops" are very likely to be envisaged as a "singular organism." In reality, of course, "the troops" are a highly differentiated group consisting of individuals with diverse histories, classes, races, and ideologies (Salaita 2013). But the plural "troops" draws attention away from this vast diversity and compels audiences to regard all soldiers as having a uniform character. As Stahl (2009, 549) explains, the word works to "fuse lower-rank soldiers together with the leadership into one consubstantial entity of singular purpose"; it "erases the individual soldier . . . and offers a composite image of the military." Of course, when individual soldiers are assimilated into a "homogenous, consensual group" (Van Leeuwen 2008, 38), it is easier to offer that group unqualified support. The pluralization itself makes the slogan more shareable.

Ultimately, then, the "Support Our Troops" slogan works through semantic underspecification. It does not identify the form of support we must offer, nor does it identify which troops are in need of our backing. This lack of specificity is crucial not only because it permits different audience members to comply with the command in different ways, but because it allows the slogan itself to be reused in any military conflict. Other wartime slogans, such as "Free Kuwait," "Attack Iraq," or "Get bin Laden," specify participants and locations and, thus, are limited in their repeatability. But the SOT slogan "makes sense" in any wartime scenario, whether in Vietnam, Iraq, or elsewhere. In this regard, "Support Our Troops" is like traditional advertising slogans. As Reece, Vanden Bergh, and Li (1994, 41) explain, a key function of corporate slogans "is to summarize the brand's message and to provide continuity from one advertising execution to another." Thus, the "I'm lovin' it" slogan, which never specifies what "it" is, can be used by McDonald's to compel brand loyalty across multiple advertisements, whether they are marketing the Big Mac or the Jalapeño Double. In the same way, "Support Our Troops" can be used by U.S. leaders to compel patriotic loyalty across multiple military interventions, whether they are marketing Operation Desert Storm or the War on Terror.

The SOT slogan, then, has important phonemic and lexicogrammatical qualities that enhance its memorability and repeatability. However, to better understand what makes this slogan "shareable" (Urban 1996, 24), we must go beyond its superficial linguistic qualities. After all, effective political slogans are not just catchy units of language but sometimes also potent ideographs, which "represent in condensed form the normative, collective commitments" of the entire culture (Condit and Lucaites 1993, xii).[2] The SOT slogan needs to be examined in a broader intertextual context, with an eye toward unpacking the "network of historical meaning" that gives it shape (Kaufer and Carley 1993, 202). In the next sections, I take a discourse-historical approach (Reisigl and Wodak 2009; Richardson and Wodak 2009), tracing the origins of the SOT slogan and explaining, as far as possible, its special resonance in American culture.

The Genesis of "Support Our Troops" in the Vietnam Era

As Hodges (2014, 358–59) explains, political slogans work through processes of indexicality, as short phrases are indexically linked to larger stretches of discourse. Initially, a slogan may be juxtaposed with a campaign message, literally uttered alongside a larger narrative. "As the slogan travels forward into subsequent contexts," Hodges says, "it points backwards toward the prior contexts in which that narrative was told, thereby reinforcing the indexical ties." Eventually, the slogan is "indexically anchored" to the broader message, such that the message need not be repeated in full (359). The slogan alone serves as an "economical reminder" of the larger point (358), carrying forth "the residue of prior contexts" in which it was uttered (362).

Indexicality explains how the SOT slogan has become associated with larger narratives about war, soldiers, and civic responsibility. Specifically, as Stahl observes, the slogan is connected to two larger rhetorical tropes.[3] The first trope, *deflection*, legitimizes war by redefining it as a struggle to protect soldiers, rather than a struggle to achieve political goals (Stahl 2009, 536). With this trope, the point of war is exclusively to safeguard heroic troops from danger. The second trope, *dissociation*, defines the role of wartime citizens, portraying good citizens as supportive of the troops and their mission, while coding public dissent as an attack on the soldier's body (548). Accordingly, those who protest war endanger soldiers and fail as citizens.

We can examine how these larger themes came to be associated with the SOT slogan by investigating historical narratives about troops and protesters. Emerging during the Vietnam era, many such narratives were directly juxtaposed with the SOT slogan or variations of it, providing an indexical link between the slogan and larger ideas about appropriate wartime conduct. Other narratives, though, emerged later to provide argumentative grounds for future troop support. Speakers who told these narratives did not necessarily utter the words "Support Our Troops," since there was no longer any war in which soldiers were fighting. Nevertheless, they generated myths about soldiers and war that were consistently referenced by those who used the slogan later on, during the Gulf War and the War on Terror. To understand, we must trace the slogan back to its origins in the latter half of the Vietnam conflict.[4]

Lyndon Baines Johnson was the first American president to say "Support Our Troops." In fact, Johnson used the phrase in several speeches in 1966 and 1967—just as the anti-Vietnam War movement was growing more powerful (Small 2002). Protests erupted nationwide, both spontaneously and as prearranged mass gatherings featuring religious leaders such as Daniel Berrigan and Martin Luther King Jr. (DeBenedetti and Chatfield 1990; Small 2002). Young people increasingly resisted the draft, while soldiers increasingly deserted or joined the antiwar movement upon returning home (Zinn 2003, 492–97).

As revealed in the *Pentagon Papers*, Johnson and colleagues worried about the backlash against the war. As early as 1965, the CIA director John McGone expressed concern about "pressure to stop the bombing . . . from various elements of the American public" (quoted in Zinn 2003, 499). In 1966, John McNaughton, the assistant secretary of defense, fretted about a "counterproductive wave of revulsion abroad and at home" and, in 1967, he became "deeply concerned about the breadth and intensity of public unrest and dissatisfaction with the war . . . especially with young people, the underprivileged, the intelligentsia and the women" (499).

Thus, the first presidential call to "Support Our Troops" was indexically linked to a context of broad antiwar sentiment. Indeed, Johnson's use of the slogan was a strategic response to this sentiment—a propaganda tool aimed at deflecting attention from the increasingly suspect rationale for violence and toward soldiers who allegedly needed backing. For example, in January 1967, Johnson wrote a letter to Congress that requested more funding for military operations in Vietnam. In it, he never mentions why the fighting is necessary or what policy objectives will be gained. Instead, he repeatedly refers to soldiers and explicitly links funding the campaign with supporting the soldiers' cause:

I know that you will want to continue your firm support of the nearly 500,000 American fighting men who are bravely defending the cause of freedom in Southeast Asia. . . . We should in the Congress and the Executive Branch match the magnificent morale of these men with the means they require to carry out their mission. Last year, we pledged to the Nation that we would give our fighting men what they must have, every gun and every dollar and every decision, whatever the cost or whatever the challenge. We must demonstrate our continuing support of these young Americans so that we may prove to them—half a world away—that our determination is no less than theirs. . . . The Congress and the country will support our troops who bear the burden of combat by providing the funds they need to do the job. (Johnson 1967)

Here, the SOT phrase is juxtaposed with language characterizing American soldiers as heroic. Johnson uses explicitly positive evaluations of the troops ("bravely," "magnificent morale," "determination"), and he construes material actions that suggest their self-sacrifice ("bear the burden of combat") and their desire to achieve a positively moralized purpose ("defending the cause of freedom"). This portrayal of soldiers with "magnificent morale" and complete devotion to "the cause" in Vietnam is highly dubious. In fact, "estimates of the number of soldiers serving in Vietnam who directly engaged in dissent and disobedience range from 20 to 37 percent, figures unprecedented in U.S. military history" (Coy, Woehrle, and Maney 2008, 168 n. 5). But Johnson's SOT propaganda can only work if the troops themselves are represented as fully committed to the mission and morally beyond reproach.

Notably, Johnson represents funding for the war not as a way of achieving policy goals but as a way of fulfilling the soldiers' requirements. The soldiers are twice represented as agents who need more funding and supplies ("the means *they require*," "the funds *they need*"). Thus, the slogan is also juxtaposed with the idea that the troops lack necessities and are vulnerable unless we help. Of course, increasing funding for a war arguably threatens soldiers, since it prolongs violence and exposes them to continuing danger. But, for Johnson, funding the war is represented as a way of proving one's support for and solidarity with the troops. He uses verbs implying that funding is either a demonstration of enduring help ("we must *demonstrate* our continuing support") or a demonstration of equal resolve in a mutual cause ("we may *prove* to them . . . our determination is no less than theirs"). From its earliest uses in presidential discourse, then, the SOT phrase has functioned to justify the continuation and escalation of war. Particularly when faced with popular resistance, presidents since Johnson have sought to legitimize ongoing war by coding it as a way of fulfilling soldiers' needs and helping them execute their mission.

But Johnson's SOT legacy goes beyond his public speeches and correspondence. He also instructed future administrations on how to use surrogates to circulate pro-troops propaganda. For example, the Johnson administration created the National Committee for Peace with Freedom in Vietnam, a front group led by former presidents Harry S. Truman and Dwight D. Eisenhower, as well as other officials, entrepreneurs, educators, and religious figures (DeBenedetti and Chatfield 1990, 177). The key was to make it appear that these opinion leaders were acting independently from the administration. Thus, John Roche, the White House aide responsible for assembling the group, assured President Johnson, "I will leave no tracks" (Small 2002, 66). The Johnson administration also helped pioneer the strategy of countering antiwar protests with supposedly grassroots protests in favor of the war. For example, in response to the antiwar movement's Spring Mobilization in 1967, the White House helped organize demonstrations and a letter-writing campaign titled "Support Our Boys in Vietnam." This strategy met with some success. In New York City, one "Support Our Boys in Vietnam" parade drew seventy thousand participants (Small 2002, 66). Thus, SOT rhetoric was also juxtaposed with "patriotic" movements allegedly springing up from the masses. Again, the slogan was designed to index "good citizenship" that might counter the "reckless citizenship" of the peace protesters.

Indeed, while helping to popularize the SOT slogan and its variations, the Johnson administration simultaneously launched a campaign to discredit the antiwar movement by representing demonstrators as communists and declaring that protest encouraged the enemy (DeBenedetti and Chatfield 1990, 177). Pro-troops rhetoric often contrasted war dissenters with American GIs, portraying the dissenters as selfish and irresponsible (unlike the heroic troops) and suggesting that they placed soldiers at greater risk. For example, one ad promoting the "Support Our Boys in Vietnam" parade placed images of unkempt antiwar demonstrators side by side with images of dead American soldiers (Small 2002, 66). This dissociation of protester and soldier was also evident in verbal propaganda. A group called the Support Our Servicemen Committee urged Congress to penalize dissenters who gave "aid and comfort" to the enemy (DeBenedetti and Chatfield 1990, 178). Later, General William Westmoreland and Commander U.S. Grant Sharp each claimed that antiwar protests encouraged the Viet Cong and damaged the position of U.S. forces in Southeast Asia (DeBenedetti and Chatfield 1990, 177). And Johnson (1966) himself sharply criticized "men who exercise so well the right of dissent, but let others fight to protect them."

This type of propaganda only intensified under President Richard Nixon, who "embarked on further strategies to portray the soldier and the protester as natural political enemies" (Stahl 2009, 551). When Nixon took office, though, he faced a problem in constructing the now familiar dissociation between demonstrators and troops: thousands of soldiers had joined the peace movement (Lembcke 1998, 52). Vietnam Veterans Against the War (VVAW), for example, reportedly claimed twenty thousand members by 1971 (Appy 2004, 395). Taking a page from the Johnson administration, the Nixon White House formed its own front group called Vietnam

Veterans for a Just Peace that created "the appearance of a large grass roots silent majority of veterans in support of Nixon's policies" (Stahl 2009, 551). John O'Neill, who headed Nixon's front group, often publicly debated John Kerry, spokesperson for VVAW. These debates encouraged the perception that most veterans—the "good" veterans—supported the war, though, in reality, the opposite was probably true (Stahl 2009, 551; Lembcke 1998, 53).[5]

Meanwhile, leaders in the Republican establishment continued to insist that protesters were morally depraved and fundamentally opposed to the decorous troops. Vice President Spiro Agnew described the antiwar movement as "an effete corps of impudent snobs who characterize themselves as intellectuals" (quoted in Lembcke 1998, 50). California governor Ronald Reagan claimed that the peace movement "lent comfort and aid" to the enemy, and he complained that "some American [soldiers] will die tonight because of activity in our streets" (quoted in Perlstein 2008, 431). Nixon (1969) himself claimed to have observed demonstrators carrying a sign reading, "Lose in Vietnam, Bring the Boys Home." He warned that if this "vocal minority . . . prevails over reason . . . this Nation has no future as a free society." Later, two days before the Kent State shooting of May 4, 1970, Nixon famously contrasted derelict protesters with dutiful soldiers: "You see these bums, you know, blowing up college campuses today . . . storming around about this issue. . . . Then out there we have kids who are just doing their duty. They stand tall and they are proud . . . They are going to do fine and we have to stand in back of them" (quoted in Beamish, Molotch, and Flacks 1995, 352). Again, the troops whom we are obligated to support ("we have to stand in back of them") are described through positive evaluations ("doing their duty," "stand tall," "proud"), while the antiwar movement is described in negative terms ("bums," "blowing up college campuses," "storming around").

For its part, the mainstream American press also helped portray the growing antiwar movement as fringe, juvenile, and dangerous to heroic soldiers. When covering the peace protests, journalists commonly labeled demonstrators with derisive terms such as "beatniks" and "peaceniks," often focusing on the most outrageous (most stereotypically "scruffy-looking") elements while ignoring the ordinary people who better represented the movement (DeBenedetti and Chatfield; Small 2002, 66). In addition, reporters often questioned the value of antiwar demonstrations and repeated that protesters were encouraging the Viet Cong. For example, a *Time* magazine article covering a massive antiwar demonstration of 250,000 people remarked that the protest was "about as damaging [to the administration] as a blow from daffodils," and concluded that protesters were surely "delighting Ho Chi Minh" (quoted in Small 2002, 65).

Despite this propaganda, the peace movement—and the many veterans who joined its ranks—were not against the troops. Granted, college activists often objected to the presence of the Reserve Officers' Training Corps (ROTC) and occasionally vandalized ROTC buildings. But this was not typical, and, of course, opposition to ROTC programs on college campuses did not necessarily mean students opposed the troops themselves. In fact, there is scant evidence that the peace movement adopted an "antitroop" position. In a thorough study of newspapers covering the movement between 1965 and 1971, Beamish, Molotch, and Flacks (1995) found that protesters quoted in the news virtually never targeted the troops with negative criticism. In fact, though they criticized the leadership, protesters generally had positive things to say about the troops (if they talked about the troops at all). Nevertheless, in 56 percent of the articles, protesters were still portrayed as "antitroop," largely because the newspapers disproportionately quoted officials who described the peace movement as hostile to GIs.

Ultimately, as Stahl (2009) argues, elite propaganda in the Vietnam era downplayed questions about the legitimacy of war policy while focusing attention on heroic troops and their presumed need for protection. Simultaneously, this propaganda painted the antiwar movement as being opposed to the troops and consubstantial with the enemy. Crucially, the SOT slogan was juxtaposed with this propaganda and eventually came to index it. Indeed, the slogan still carries with it the "residue" of elite narratives about the good soldiers who need our help and the bad protesters who endanger them (Hodges 2014, 362). Remarkably, these narratives did little to dampen the peace campaign. In fact, most of the public soon joined protesters in calling for troop withdrawal, and in 1973, Nixon suspended offensive military action in Vietnam. He would later admit that "the antiwar movement caused him to drop plans for an intensification of the war" (Zinn 2003, 501).

Vietnam Syndrome and the Stabbed-in-the-Back Narrative

The experience in Vietnam left many Americans with a distaste for organized violence. This distaste was so widespread that the political establishment even gave it a name, "Vietnam Syndrome," a term that was meant to convey citizens' antipathy for war, distrust of political leadership, and unwillingness to support an interventionist foreign policy. In effect, a reasonable public position—reluctance to go to war—was metaphorically represented as a disease that needed a cure. In any case, throughout the rest of the 1970s, the United States avoided overt military interventions (even if it still engaged in covert operations), and use of the SOT phrase declined.

Still, the government was determined to overcome Vietnam Syndrome, and it accomplished this, in part, by mythologizing the Vietnam conflict itself. To antiwar activists, Vietnam had been a criminal assault on a sovereign nation—pointless bloodshed finally halted by an outraged public. But the establishment cultivated a different narrative: Vietnam was a just war that had been lost due to a lack of domestic commitment. *New York Times* journalist C. L. Sulzberger (1971) captured this sentiment quite early on: "We lost the war in the Mississippi valley, not the Mekong valley. Successive American governments were never able to muster the necessary mass support at home." Authorities not only blamed the Vietnam failure on lack of "support at home" but also sought "to contrive a sentimentalized version of the American military experience and an idealized image of the American soldier" (Bacevich 2005, 97). Accordingly, soldiers who served in Vietnam were portrayed as tragic figures—heroes who, in spite of their determination, were "stabbed in the back" by irresolute leaders, media critics, and, especially, antiwar protesters (Stahl 2009, 553; Lembcke 1998, 118). The story was a powerful one, and no one told it better than Ronald Reagan.

Indeed, from the beginning of his presidency, Reagan took every opportunity to honor American soldiers and to correct alleged injustices done to them during the Vietnam conflict. In 1981, for example, he explained that soldiers who served in Southeast Asia "came home without a victory" because they had "been denied permission to win." The soldiers, he continued,

> were greeted by <u>no parades</u>, <u>no bands</u>, <u>no waving of the flag</u> they had so **nobly served**. There's been <u>no "thank you"</u> for their **sacrifice**. There's been <u>no effort to honor and, thus, give pride to the families</u> of more than 57,000 young men who **gave their lives** in that faraway war. (Reagan 1981)

Above, I have **bolded** the positive evaluations of the soldiers, and <u>underlined</u> all the negated rewards that, it is implied, should have been bestowed upon the troops. During his presidency, Reagan vowed, U.S. soldiers would not be betrayed again. Troops would benefit from huge increases in military spending, and perhaps more importantly, they would finally receive the praise they deserved. To anyone in the military, "Reagan granted the status of patriot, idealist, and hero; of citizens, he asked only that they affirm that designation." Thus, Reagan managed to establish "support *for* 'the troops'—as opposed to actual service *with* them—as the new standard of civic responsibility" (Bacevich 2005, 108).

In this context, calls to give soldiers support came to be juxtaposed with a larger narrative of betrayal. As Stahl (2009) explains, the charge that the troops had been "stabbed in the back" was directed at multiple targets, including the news media. Disillusioned officers argued that "critical coverage of the war effort had been an important factor in bringing about the U.S. defeat" (Thompson 1991, 47). And this view was largely shared by the political leadership. Lyndon Johnson (1971, 384), for example, complained in his memoirs of the "emotional and exaggerated reporting of the Tet offensive" and claimed that "lurid and depressing accounts" misled the public into believing that U.S. troops had suffered a major defeat. Similarly, in his memoirs, Richard Nixon (1978, 350) criticized the mainstream press for contributing to the impression that the country was "fighting in military and moral quicksand. . . . More than ever before, television showed the terrible human suffering and sacrifice of war

. . . The result was a serious demoralization of the home front, raising the question of whether America would ever again be able to fight an enemy abroad with unity and strength of purpose at home." For his part, President Reagan alleged that reporters had worked to serve the interests of the enemy. "The media had decided that the war was wrong," Reagan said. "Had that been done in World War II, in behalf of the enemy that was killing American military men, I think there would have been a revolution in America" (quoted in Associated Press 1982).

Had slanted and demoralizing news reports undermined the troops and aided the enemy? According to Carpenter (1995, 155), the idea that the media lost the war "is one of the most tenacious but inaccurate aspects of the stab-in-the-back myth." In fact, Hallin (1986) finds that the mainstream press was generally supportive of the war and reluctant to criticize either American officials or soldiers in combat. Early in the conflict, journalists echoed government leaders and recited official descriptions of the escalating violence. Even as the public dissented, news coverage still tended to reflect Washington orthodoxy that the war was necessary, honorable, winnable, and so on. The coverage did not become skeptical until journalists' sources—government and military officials—began openly criticizing Vietnam policy. And even in this later "adversarial" period, Hallin finds, journalists "continued often to be a source of power to an administration which knew how to use them to manage the news" (207). He concludes, "There is no evidence that the military considered the press a source of significant damage to [its] operations" (211). Nevertheless, the notion that the media had undercut the Vietnam War effort—and let down American GIs—remains potent to this day.

The press, however, was not the only group accused of betraying the troops. "Stabbed-in-the-back" propaganda was also levied against the civilian government itself. Near the end of the Vietnam War, the Nixon administration had fostered the myth that thousands of American soldiers were being held captive by the Viet Cong. The official number of prisoners of war (POWs) was actually closer to fifty (Franklin 2000). According to Stahl, the "impression that Vietnam still held thousands of live servicemen breathed new life into the war effort and aided the [Nixon] administration in prolonging military operations well into the 1970s amid massive public disillusionment." Once again, political leaders had justified war on the grounds of protecting vulnerable soldiers (i.e., "supporting our troops") and not on the grounds of achieving meaningful policy objectives (Stahl 2009, 537). But even after the war ended and all POWs returned home, the myth of American soldiers in enemy captivity lingered. By the 1980s, some suspected that the government had left American soldiers behind out of neglect (553).

The myth of abandoned soldiers had a massive "cultural fallout," readily observable in post-Vietnam war films (Stahl 2009, 537). For example, 1980s films—such as *Rambo: First Blood Part II* and the *Missing in Action* franchise—featured "hypermasculine American bodies performing inhuman feats of rescue," super-soldiers liberating the neglected captives in Vietnam (538). Aside from glorifying the power of the American soldier, these films helped reinforce the narrative that the troops had been sabotaged and deserted. However, instead of blaming government leaders for the crisis, the films pointed the finger at protesters who had allegedly thwarted the military mission and scorned GIs. "Under these terms," Stahl (2009, 554) writes, "war resistance became the equivalent of a de facto attack on the soldier body, not simply a failure to 'finish the job' but actively throwing the embattled U.S. soldier to the wolves."

The war dissenter's apparent willingness to assail soldiers is perhaps epitomized in those oft repeated stories about protesters spitting on returning Vietnam veterans. These stories, which still proliferate today (Sirota 2012), first started to gain widespread currency in the 1980s, as the image of the spitting protester was circulated in mass media. For example, in the film *First Blood*, the character of John Rambo offers this soliloquy: "It wasn't my war. You asked me, I didn't ask you. And I did what I had to do to win. But somebody wouldn't let us win. Then I come back to the world, and I see all those maggots at the airport. Protesting me. Spitting. Calling me baby killer. . . . Who are they to protest me? Huh?" (Kotcheff 1982). In his scholarly investigation, however, Jerry Lembcke (1998, 82) finds "no basis for the widespread belief that the alleged spitting incidents actually occurred." Indeed, like other researchers, Lembcke finds scant evidence to suggest the peace movement was "antitroop."

But the narrative of the spitting protester fit in with the "stabbed-in-the-back" story Reagan had helped popularize. Indeed, Reagan, more than anyone else, "deserves the credit for conjuring up the myths that nurture and sustain present-day American militarism" (Bacevich 2005, 99). He helped cement in the American imagination the idea that soldiers—the very people who embody heroism and selflessness—had been betrayed by their fellow citizens: irresolute leaders, craven journalists, and, especially, treacherous antiwar protesters. In so doing, he helped encourage a national sense of obligation—a sense that the country now owed the troops its support and that anything less than enthusiastic support was both an insult and a threat to them. At the same time, Reagan learned how to make military intervention once again palatable to ordinary Americans, "by tighter control of information, by avoiding a draft, and by engaging in short, swift wars over weak opponents [e.g., Grenada], which didn't give the public time to develop an anti-war movement" (Zinn 2006).

The Gulf War and the Obligation to Support Our Troops

Reagan's lessons "were not lost on other astute politicians who profited from his example" (Bacevich 2005, 99). For instance, President George H. W. Bush (1991a) kept the "stabbed-in-the-back" narrative viable at the start of the Persian Gulf War and explicitly juxtaposed this larger narrative with an appeal to give troops support. "This will not be another Vietnam," the president reassured the public, vowing that

American soldiers would never again "be sent out to do a job with one hand tied behind their back." In contrast to the Vietnam conflict, Bush said, the troops in the Persian Gulf "will continue to have the support they need to get the job done, get it done quickly. . . . And that support is not just military, but moral—measured in the support our servicemen and women receive from every one of us here at home. When the brave men and women of Desert Storm return home, they will return to the love and respect of a grateful nation." Here, the president declares that the entire country will unify behind the troops, who are as usual described in explicitly positive terms ("brave"). Like Johnson, Bush represents "support" as something the troops themselves "need to get the job done," so they won't be working "with one hand tied behind their back." The obvious implication is that failing to show support is akin to sabotaging the troops, depriving them of their "necessities," and forcing them to fight with something like a physical disadvantage. Interestingly, Bush's verb phrase "our Armed Forces . . . *will continue to have* the support" presupposes that troops are already supported, while predicting that this support will stretch into the foreseeable future. Indeed, Bush declares that a maximal number of citizens ("*every one of us here at home*") will provide support that is explicitly "moral" and even specifies the kinds of positive affect we will feel for the troops once they return from battle ("love," "respect," "grateful").

The president reasserts the familiar rhetorical tropes of deflection and dissociation, limiting the country's focus to the troops standing in harm's way while implying dissent is tantamount to betrayal. But notice that, unlike Johnson and Nixon, Bush does not wait for public disapproval to grow before deploying these strategies. Instead, he delivers the tropes just as the battle begins, when support for the war is at its highest (Mueller 1994, 70). Thus, Bush seeks to neutralize the antiwar movement when it is already weak and makes an early attempt to persuade the public that future dissent should be regarded as anti-American and antitroop. In addition, Bush continued Reagan's tradition of showering the troops with lavish praise. Days into the war, in his State of the Union address, he remarked:

> There is no one more **devoted**, more **committed** to the hard work of freedom than every soldier and sailor, every marine, airman, and coastguardsman, every man and woman now serving in the Persian Gulf. You see—what a wonderful, fitting tribute to them. Each of them has **volunteered, volunteered** to provide for this nation's defense, and now they **bravely** struggle to earn for America, for the world, and for future generations a just and lasting peace. Our commitment to them must be equal to their **commitment** to their country. They are truly **America's finest**. (Bush 1991b)

Above, I have bolded every explicitly positive judgment of the troops (Martin and White 2005) and have underlined all positively moralized purposes and goals ascribed to them (Van Leeuwen 2008). Note how often Bush "turns up the volume" on these positive evaluations, through up-scaled quantifications ("*no one*," "*every* soldier," "*every* marine"), repetition ("volunteered," "volunteered"), and superlative adjectives ("America's *finest*"). Of course, these strongly positive remarks are coupled with yet another call to show support, as Bush, echoing Johnson, reminds his audience that "our commitment to them must be equal to their commitment to their country."

By all accounts, this pro-troops propaganda largely resonated with the American public and news media. Before Desert Storm commenced on January 18, 1991, national debate over whether to wage war had been contentious. But the debate quickly evaporated when the president announced the start of the war and exhorted the country to rally around the flag and support the soldiers. The Senate, which had passed a war resolution by just five votes, now unanimously adopted "a resolution expressing support for U.S. military forces and for President George Bush's leadership" (Koenig 1991). A day later, the House passed an identical resolution by a count of 399 to 6 (Dahl 1991). A similar flood of patriotism erupted in cities across the country. Millions of people began reciting the "Support Our Troops" slogan. Indeed, ordinary citizens rushed to express their solidarity with American soldiers, often by displaying supportive merchandise such as T-shirts, posters, and, especially, yellow ribbons, which were wrapped around trees, incorporated into news logos, and even draped over bridges and town squares (Larsen 1994). Meanwhile, mainstream journalism transitioned from covering debate over war to covering troop support. In the weeks before Desert Storm, network news reports had focused on the controversy surrounding a potential invasion. However, once war began, the networks highlighted pro-war exhibitions and controversy stories were supplanted with accounts of the yellow ribbon phenomenon (LaMay 1991a, 1991b).

The dominance of pro-troops propaganda significantly constrained the antiwar movement. As Beamish, Molotch, and Flacks report, Gulf War opponents "themselves accepted, sometimes enthusiastically, the need to express support for the troops." In fact, Gulf War opponents even recited the "stabbed-in-the-back narrative," openly expressing their desire to compensate for "the sins of Vietnam-era activists" (Beamish, Molotch, and Flacks 1995, 345). As one antiwar demonstrator explained to the *Los Angeles Times* in November 1990, Vietnam protesters "wound up condemning our troops," whereas today's protesters "wholeheartedly support the 210,000 GI's in the gulf." Another antiwar activist commented during Desert Storm that he would now "become nearly a jingo patriot" in support of the soldiers "to make amends for an injustice committed against Vietnam veterans" (quoted in Beamish, Molotch, and Flacks 1995, 345). Mainstream journalists who covered the antiwar movement were often uninterested in its arguments and focused instead on the lengths to which protesters went to demonstrate their support for soldiers. Peace activists lucky enough to get airtime often had to squander it, confirming their support for the troops rather than discussing their substantive criticisms of the war (345).

The Gulf War, like the wars in Grenada and Panama, was so brief that the peace movement never impacted its course. Antiwar activists were vocal, but SOT propaganda dominated the landscape. When the soldiers finally returned home, they were greeted with lofty praise, exultant parades, and more yellow ribbons (Quintanilla 1991; Heilbronn 1994). President Bush (1991c) was ecstatic: "The specter of Vietnam," he announced triumphantly, "has been buried forever in the desert sands of the Arabian Peninsula." Vietnam Syndrome had finally been kicked. And the American public had learned that, during war, everyone is obliged to support the troops, regardless of their opinions about the fighting.

Pro-troops Dominance in the Era of Perpetual Militarization

As historian Andrew Bacevich writes, "The decade following victory in the Gulf became a period of unprecedented American military activism." Small-scale interventions were launched in Somalia, Haiti, Rwanda, Bosnia, Afghanistan, Sudan, and Iraq (again). The Pentagon publicly embraced a doctrine of "full-spectrum dominance," literally announcing its intention to achieve worldwide hegemonic control. Leaders from both parties adhered to this policy, which would thrust "the United States into a condition approximating perpetual war" (Bacevich 2010, 16). And yet, the escalating militarism was largely ignored by American journalists. Between 1990 and 2010, major American newspapers produced zero articles including the words "full-spectrum dominance," compared to 852 articles including the words "Support Our Troops."[6]

Similarly, American war films ignored the militarization of U.S. foreign policy and avoided examining the justifications for intervention. Instead, these films focused overwhelmingly on the perseverance of heroic soldiers in brutal combat conditions. As Stahl (2009) explains, the rescue narrative popularized in the 1980s was updated to offer a more "realistic" portrait of war. Instead of superhuman hulks, soldiers were now portrayed as normal people who were vulnerable to the physical and psychological perils of battle. In these films, soldiers endure unspeakable brutality, yet their suffering appears justified insofar as it serves to protect endangered comrades. Thus, films such as *Saving Private Ryan* and *Black Hawk Down* have an "antiwar aesthetic," as they graphically depict carnage and reveal the soldiers' personal trauma. Yet they still have a "pro-war effect," not because the war achieves some favorable policy objective but because its mission is to rescue the heroic troops (Stahl 2009, 538–39; Klien 2005, 428). These films celebrate "the camaraderie, sacrifice, and heroism of the fighting soldier" and invite audiences to conflate support of the troops with support of American military policy (Klien 2005, 428). This may explain why both films "received full production support from the Pentagon's

Hollywood Liaison Office." Paradoxically, war is legitimized on the grounds that it protects soldiers; the only ones who can save the troops from harm are other heroic troops. Of course, this "emerging narrative of war" deflects attention from the real reasons why we fight, "marginalizing questions of policy and narrowing the frame to the immediate concerns of the battlefield" (Stahl 2009, 539).

By this point, then, the "Support Our Troops" slogan was "indexically anchored" to dominant cultural narratives (Hodges 2014, 359): narratives portraying the anti-war movement as reckless, narratives portraying the troops as heroic and dedicated, stabbed-in-the-back narratives where troops are betrayed by bad citizens and irresolute leaders, and rescue narratives where the troops' only mission is to protect one another from the horrors of war. Such narratives were sometimes exploited by U.S. political leaders, who seemed happy to keep the focus on "the troops" as they deployed them in war after war. As shown in table 10, since the early 1990s, each American president has used the SOT slogan to help legitimize military interventions.[7] But no one used the SOT slogan more than George W. Bush.

Table 10 U.S. presidential discourse featuring the "Support Our Troops" slogan

President	Uses of the slogan
George H. W. Bush	1
Bill Clinton	14
George W. Bush	152
Barack Obama	22

It may be tempting to conclude from this data that G. W. Bush was somewhat aberrant as a president, given his predisposition to use the slogan more than his counterparts. But remember, even when other presidents did not necessarily use the exact phrase "Support Our Troops," they may have suggested the same meaning in other ways. More importantly, Bush's increased use of the slogan is probably less a consequence of his own idiosyncrasies and more a consequence of his launching the biggest American military campaign since Vietnam. Indeed, one would expect to find the slogan used more when hundreds of thousands of troops have been called upon to fight in a protracted military campaign. And one would expect the slogan to persist as that campaign grew more intractable and unpopular. Bush's War on Terror fulfilled these conditions.

In fact, when Bush launched the War on Terror following the 9/11 attacks, there was an immediate upsurge in SOT propaganda, just as there had been a decade earlier during Desert Storm. Early in the war, Bush (2001b) explicitly called upon all Americans to "support our troops in the field," as this would "help in our fight" against terrorism. But even before this, citizens were already holding impromptu gatherings to express solidarity with soldiers, recontextualizing the slogan again and again. "I think it's important for the older people to show the younger people that we support our troops that have to go overseas," said a citizen at a vigil in Missouri (Jarman 2001). We must "do all we can to support our troops," said another at a patriotic Halloween parade in York, Pennsylvania (Krebs 2001). In Littleton, Massachusetts, citizens organized a "Support Our Troops" rally (*Lowell [MA] Sun* 2001); in New Jersey, school children wrote "Support Our Troops" letters to commemorate Veterans Day (Mayk 2001). Even peace demonstrations in Atlanta and Berkley made sure to accommodate advocates of the war—as long as they were holding posters with the words "Support Our Troops" (*Atlanta Journal-Constitution* 2001; Cannon 2001). As one Nebraska newspaper instructed readers in its headline: "Oppose War? Support Our Troops Anyway" (*Lincoln [NE] Journal Star* 2001).

However, SOT propaganda intensified when President Bush announced his intentions to invade Iraq. Even before the war, conservative commentators warned the peace movement against disloyalty. "Once the war against Saddam begins, we expect every American to support our military, and if they can't do that, to shut up," said Bill O'Reilly (quoted in Hart 2003). Pat Buchanan (2003) reiterated this sentiment on the eve of war: "We've had a good debate for eight months on this conflict . . . but now it seems when the war comes, the debate ends." He added, "The right thing to do for patriots when American lives are at risk and Americans are dying is to unite behind the troops until victory is won." When the war began, citizens responded with an immediate outpouring of SOT sloganeering. In the first weeks of fighting, thousands of "Support Our Troops" rallies popped up around the country (Jehl 2003).

Such early SOT discourse may have been designed to forestall development of the antiwar movement, but as in the Vietnam era, war opponents became more and more numerous as the conflict dragged on. As the original rationale for fighting collapsed, sectarian violence increased, the torture abuse scandal at Abu Ghraib came to light, and the death tolls reached hundreds of thousands, the antiwar movement grew stronger. And, predictably, the president and his administration ratcheted up the SOT talk.

In fact, two-thirds of President Bush's uses of the "Support Our Troops" slogan occurred between 2004 and 2006—just as public opposition to the war made a dramatic climb (Pew Research Center 2008). Often, Bush recontextualized the slogan to deflect attention from the lack of WMD in Iraq and focus instead on the need to show common cause with soldiers in combat. For example, Bush (2004a) publicly endorsed Operation Support Our Troops, a citizen-led organization devoted to "demonstrat[ing] to members of the Armed Forces and their Commander in Chief that they are supported and deeply appreciated" (Operation Support Our Troops 2005). On the campaign trail against Democratic presidential nominee John Kerry,

Bush also suggested that defunding the war was a betrayal of endangered soldiers. Kerry had voted to authorize the war in 2002 but later opposed funding it in what he described as a "protest vote." Bush (2004b) condemned the Democrat for rejecting "funding to support our troops. . . . When American troops are in harm's way and defending our country, they deserve better than to have a candidate for President use them as a protest vote."

The call to "Support Our Troops" also permeated other aspects of Bush administration discourse. The slogan was included "on a variety of publicly available White House documents . . . including budget requests that encouraged Congress to approve ad-hoc funding for the war" (Leitz 2011, 240). In fact, in 2004, if you had searched Google for the phrase "support our troops," you would have discovered that the U.S. Department of Defense owned the rights to the first-listed website. This site, called "America Supports You, Our Military Men and Women," gave citizens a chance to "thank, celebrate, and encourage the soldiers" fighting around the world (Coy, Woehrle, and Maney 2008, 164). As I suggest in the next chapter, Bush's repeated calls to "Support Our Troops" likely helped him extend the Iraq War, even as the public turned against it.

For his part, Barack Obama used the slogan less often and somewhat differently. For example, Obama (2013b) defined "support" for the troops not just as enthusiasm for military operations but as care for disabled veterans: "We're also doing more to support our troops and our veterans who are suffering from things like traumatic brain disorder—or traumatic brain injury or PTSD, posttraumatic stress disorder. Today, we lose 22 veterans a day to suicide—22. We've got to do a better job than that, of preventing these all too often silent tragedies. That's why we've poured an enormous amount of resources into high-quality care and better treatment for our troops." In this context, "support" is again coded as a way of saving endangered soldiers. Interestingly, though, the salvation occurs not on the battlefield but on the home front, as "support" is defined in terms of positively valued medical attention ("*high-quality* care," "*better* treatment"). Obama also made the novel suggestion that "support for the troops" can involve cutting military expenditures. For example, Obama (2009) suggested that "every dollar of waste in our defense budget is a dollar we can't spend to support our troops." To be clear, Obama consistently increased the overall defense budget, but his rhetoric about cutting waste to support soldiers is a departure from previous administrations.

Despite these differences, however, Obama also recontextualized the SOT slogan in traditional ways, following his predecessors in explicitly defining troop support as a continuation of military operations. In 2013, for example, Obama proved once more that, when a military campaign is unpopular, the SOT slogan can be an effective rallying cry. With public support for the war in Afghanistan waning, Obama (2013a) declared: "In the Afghan war theater, we must—and will—continue to support our troops until the transition is complete at the end of 2014. And that means we will continue to take strikes against high value al Qaeda targets, but also against forces that are massing to support attacks on coalition forces." Here, Obama could not be more explicit in signaling the "desired uptake" of his words (Blommaert 2005, 68). He instructs listeners on how to interpret the phrase "support our troops," explaining what "that means," namely that "we will continue to take strikes" against enemy forces. Indeed, as Obama tells his audience, supporting the troops (via airstrikes) is not only a deontic obligation (something "we must" do) but a virtual epistemic guarantee (something we "will continue" in fulfillment of our American identity and in keeping with the goals of the War on Terror).

Thus, though different presidents have used the slogan at different rates, in recent history, all have found it a useful tool of pro-war propaganda, as they have repeatedly associated the slogan with calls to maintain and extend military intervention.[8] At the same time, these presidents have reinforced the slogan's indexical ties to larger themes dating back to Vietnam, especially the themes that war is a time to think about soldiers, not policy; that soldiers want and need wars to continue; and that to oppose war is to frustrate and offend the troops.

To understand why "Support Our Troops" resonates in America, one must look not only at the artful design of the slogan itself but also at the web of cultural meaning that shapes how people use and understand it. Indeed, in its wider intertextual context, the slogan is not just a command but a response to a perceived injustice: the alleged betrayal of soldiers during the Vietnam era. Thus, the slogan has come to index an acceptable role for wartime citizens, requiring that civilians confirm their allegiance to American GIs and guard against dangerous war opponents. At the same time, the slogan draws power from its juxtaposition with dominant texts in American culture, namely the political and media discourse in which soldiers are so mythologized that they appear to embody all things positive: they are heroes who sacrifice for one another and for their country. Thus, despite the torture scandal at Abu Ghraib, widespread homophobia, and the plague of sexual assaults in the U.S. military, "the troops" remain a nearly unimpeachable group that inherently deserves public support.

From this long cultural history, then, the SOT slogan has emerged as a kind of pro-war bludgeon, a persuasive tool that has special utility after the fighting has started and in the face of public dissent. American presidents from Johnson to Obama have used this propaganda to stifle protest and legitimize violence. In the next chapter, I look more closely at how the slogan has been used strategically by such political leaders. However, I also turn my attention to the slogan's most important champions: the American people themselves.

9. "Support Our Troops" as Vertical and Horizontal Propaganda

"Support the troops" is the most overused
platitude in the United States, but still the
most effective for anybody who seeks
interpersonal or economic ingratiation.
—Steven Salaita, 2013

Elite actors have an advantage in spreading propaganda, since they have access to mass media and can enact a powerful voice capable of "semiotic mobility" (Blommaert 2005, 69). But elitcs are not the only ones to keep propaganda alive. Ordinary people also recite propaganda, especially readily available slogans such as "Support Our Troops." To understand contemporary propaganda, then, we should consider how it is recontextualized by different groups, how it travels along different trajectories.

Two such trajectories are described by Ellul (1965, 81–83), who distinguishes between vertical and horizontal propaganda. *Vertical propaganda* travels in a top-down direction from leaders to the masses. Such propaganda tends to be calculated as elites exhort ordinary people to act immediately. Alternatively, *horizontal propaganda* is made among the masses, traveling across groups of people who are, in principle, equals. Instead of exhorting people to action, horizontal propaganda might aim instead at sociological integration, slowly creating an atmosphere that compels individuals to conform with societal norms. Ellul sometimes refers to this as "pre-propaganda," since it prepares people for action at a later time by suggesting useful myths that make action possible.

In this chapter, I investigate how the "Support Our Troops" slogan functions as both vertical and horizontal propaganda, blurring lines between the two categories. First, I examine two cases of vertical propaganda in which the slogan is used by politicians addressing the general public. In these argumentative contexts, the slogan functions both to compel support for war and to demarcate social identities. Next, I examine how vertical and horizontal movements complement each other, as propaganda is marketed to the public from the top down and circulated horizontally by ordinary citizens. Specifically, I consider the commodification of the SOT slogan and investigate how it is recontextualized in advertisements and public displays of merchandise. Again, I find SOT commodities have the dual function of urging certain behaviors while integrating people into normative social roles.

Finally, I focus more exclusively on horizontal propaganda and analyze how the slogan has been recontextualized by ordinary people on Twitter. Here, average citizens have greater creative control over discourse and may even choose to recontextualize the slogan negatively. Nevertheless, most Twitter users recite slogan orthodoxy, thereby justifying troop support through popular myths about soldiers and freedom. Simultaneously, sloganeers on Twitter "police" one another, disciplining nonconformists and rewarding the faithful. This data shows clearly how the public may propagandize itself.

"Support Our Troops" in Presidential Arguments

I have shown that the SOT slogan is indexically tied to larger stories about U.S. soldiers and wartime citizenship, as it calls to mind residual meanings accrued in prior contexts. However, for the slogan to propagate effectively, it must "be recontextualized in a manner that maintains fidelity" to past uses, "continually renew[ing] its association" with favored narratives (Hodges 2014, 359). Politicians help encourage faithful recitation of the slogan, modeling how it should be used and perhaps inducing others into following their example (358). This is the essence of vertical propaganda, which is designed and performed by elites to influence the masses. Here, I study two cases of such propaganda, examining first how George W. Bush used the SOT slogan in his 2007 State of the Union address.

Bush's 2007 State of the Union

The State of the Union (SOU) address, delivered yearly to a joint session of Congress, allows presidents to report on the country and propose legislation. Short on policy details, the speech is nevertheless marked by great pomp and ceremony, as it reaffirms American values and celebrates national identity (Campbell and Jamieson 2008, 139). It is also one of the few instances when presidents address the other branches of the federal government, giving Congress the opportunity to register support for, or opposition to, the executive's legislative agenda.

Since the SOU became a televised event in the 1950s, members of Congress have sought to display alignment and disalignment with the president through multimodal signs. Seating is separated along party lines, with Democrats on the left and Republicans on the right. And the speech is continuously interrupted by partisan applause. When the president makes a controversial recommendation, roughly half the room rises and claps, while the other half sits in silent protest. But when the president makes uncontroversial statements, the entire room stands and applauds in the spirit of bipartisan consensus.

By the time of President Bush's (2007) SOU, one key issue was Iraq. The country was fragmented by violence (Bacevich 2010, 179), and Americans had soured on both the president and his mission. In the 2006 midterm elections, voters overwhelmingly supported Democratic candidates, largely on the premise that they would end the Iraq War (Nagourney and Thee 2006). For the first time in twelve years, Democrats controlled both houses of Congress, and with the president's approval rating at only 28 percent, they seemed poised to stop the occupation. However, Bush and the Republicans had no intention of withdrawing from Iraq. Instead, days before the SOU, the president unveiled a counterinsurgency (COIN) strategy that included sending in twenty thousand more troops to stabilize the country. The "surge" strategy, as it was called, was unpopular at the time of the speech, as 66 percent of the public opposed Bush's call for additional soldiers (Roberts 2007a). The SOU, then, gave the president another chance to sell the surge to the American electorate—while giving the Democratic majority a chance to display its opposition to his plans.

In his speech, Bush claimed that "the security of [the United States hung] in the balance," as all factions in the Iraqi civil war had "the same wicked purposes," including the desire "to kill Americans, to kill democracy in the Middle East, and gain the weapons to kill on an even more horrific scale." America had to create a free Iraq, Bush said, "for the sake of our own security." After rehearsing his COIN plan, he then addressed the congressional audience: "Many in this chamber understand that America must not fail in Iraq, because you understand that the consequences of failure would be grievous and far-reaching." Indeed, he concluded, "Nothing is more important at this moment in our history than for America to succeed in the Middle East, to succeed in Iraq, and to spare the American people from this danger."

Thus, Bush distinguished between "failure," that is, withdrawal from Iraq and its "grievous and far-reaching" consequences, and "success," that is, his surge strategy and its entailments of security and democracy. With this binary established, he addressed Congress for a second time, insisting that he valued all opinions. "I have spoken with many of you in person," he said, "I respect you and the arguments you've made." He continued as shown in excerpt 9.1.[1]

The excerpt is interesting in terms of addressivity, the way the speech points to and hails different addressees (Bakhtin 1986, 95; Lempert and Silverstein 2012, 110). As noted, Bush directly addresses his local audience, members of Congress, as indicated both by the second-person pronoun ("you") and by the president's gaze, which is directed at legislators in the crowd rather than television viewers. Bush signals that these local addressees are divided on the surge. His initial claim that "we went into [the war] largely united in our assumptions and in our convictions" suggests that a

Excerpt 9.1

Time	Frame		Soundtrack*
36:47–37:06			We went into this largely united (0.7) in our assumptions and in our convictions. (1.5) And whatever you voted for you did not vote for failure. (1.6) Our country is pursuing a new strategy in Iraq and I ask you to give it a chance to work (0.8) and I ask you to support our troops in the field and those on their way.
37:07–37:31	  		*[whistling and applause ↓]* (25.2)

period of unity has ended, that Congress is no longer as united. Specifically, Bush implies, some members of the audience have altered their assumptions and convictions, losing sight of core principles that initially guided their actions. However, Bush's use of the pronoun ("we") suggests that, though legislators may be divided, they are still part of a larger American unity. Thus, Bush construes an audience already bound together (part of a "we") and suggests that this audience may yet discover greater togetherness by recalling and regaining the unity and conviction of its past.

Continuing to address members of congress, Bush refers to past votes. He even includes those who voted against the Iraq War, saying, "Whatever you voted for, you did not vote for failure." Again, Bush seeks unity in a divided audience, implying that regardless of how legislators voted, they all wanted "success" in Iraq. Of course, the president also suggests "failure" is a possibility, and since all members of Congress wish to avoid "failure," they should support the surge.

Having reinforced the success-failure binary, Bush then makes a direct appeal for the surge plan. "Our country is pursuing a new strategy in Iraq," he declares, "and I ask you to give it a chance to work." Bush might have said, "I am pursuing a new strategy in Iraq," making himself the responsible agent for the surge. Instead, he makes "our country" the agent, suggesting that those opposing the strategy also oppose the will of the entire nation. Bush also chooses the present progressive verb form ("is pursuing"), which subtly suggests that the surge strategy is not a proposal to be considered but an ongoing activity one can either encourage or obstruct. The president does not ask legislators to "vote for" his surge strategy but to "give it a chance to work," the obvious implication being that those who oppose the strategy unfairly deprive the country of an opportunity for success.

But the president does not stop there. After pausing for eight-tenths of a second to inhale audibly, Bush follows his appeal to "give [the surge] a chance" with another plea: "And I ask you to support our troops in the field and those on their way." The brief pause here is important. Typically, when Bush wants to come to a "full stop," he pauses for about one-and-a-half seconds. When he pauses to inhale for only an eighth of a second, however, the effect is something like a comma; that is, Bush indicates his intention to speak again. In the context of the SOU, this means the audience should hold its applause and wait for the president to signal an opportune time to clap. Had Bush come to a "full stop" after asking Congress to give his surge a chance, probably only half the audience would have burst into applause, and television viewers would have seen the Democratic majority sitting in protest. Instead, Bush quickly links his appeal to support the surge strategy with his appeal to "support our troops in the field and those on their way." Now, if the Democrats sit in protest, they would appear to be opposing "our troops"—an unthinkable act. Thus, like Pavlov's dogs, Democrats and Republicans alike rise and clap exuberantly when they hear the magic words "support our troops." Meanwhile, the president's "superaddressees" (Bakhtin 1986, 126)—those watching at home—are treated to an apparent display of bipartisan support for the surge. Even House Speaker Nancy Pelosi, who vowed to end the war (Egelko 2006), is seen clapping in support, just above Bush's shoulder. Indeed, the camera pans to show the whole chamber erupting with applause, a standing ovation that lasts nearly thirty seconds.

This display may explain why many Americans reacted positively to the president's SOU. According to one poll, 52 percent of viewers now favored sending more troops to Iraq—a major reversal (Roberts 2007b). Following the speech, congressional Democrats also had a change of heart about ending the war. Hemmed in by the president's propaganda, House Democrats managed to propose only a nonbinding resolution that conveyed disapproval for the surge—and explicitly reaffirmed their support for the troops in Iraq. Even this superficial resolution, which could never become law, failed to pass the Senate. Of course, the Democrats might have ended the war simply by blocking funding for the surge. But again, they could not bring themselves to oppose the president—or our troops—during wartime. "Having tendered their ritual denunciations," writes Bacevich (2010, 184), they "routinely voted the money needed to ensure the war's continuation."

Thus, Bush effectively recontextualized the SOT slogan and pressured audiences into compliance with his war policy. On the one hand, such propaganda moves from one elite institution to another, as the chief executive compels the legislature into accepting that a vote against the surge is tantamount to a vote against our troops. Simultaneously, this propaganda moves vertically from the government to the public. Of course, spectators at home are also subjected to the president's manipulative rhetoric, which positions withdrawal as "failure" and the surge as a way to "support" soldiers. But they are also influenced by the display of unity in the House chamber, where seemingly all parties support the new military mission. These optics subtly increase the pressure on public audiences to conform, not only with the apparently unanimous decision to extend the war but also with the prevailing notion that the troops require fervent and automatic support.

John McCain's "Troop Funding" Ad

Politicians recontextualize the SOT slogan not just to secure obedience for war policies but to proclaim and enact appropriate wartime identities. This is seen in John McCain's "Troop Funding," a thirty-second ad that aired before the 2008 presidential election. The ad is another example of vertical propaganda, where an elite agent urges public action—in this case, voting.

As Lempert and Silverstein (2012, 49) argue, campaign ads aim to associate each candidate with an appropriate brand. The brand a candidate advances should "generate . . . a sense of trust and reliability," while the negative brand applied to an opponent should generate an aura of suspicion. In America, candidates often brand their opponents negatively, especially when trailing in the polls (Lau, Sigelman, and Brown Rovner 2007; Damore 2002). So, it is unsurprising that John McCain used negative branding in his "Troop Funding" commercial. At the time, in July 2008, the Republican candidate trailed Democrat Barack Obama by a significant margin (Hart and Newhouse 2008). Excerpt 9.2 shows a multimodal transcript of McCain's (2008) ad.

In the first ten seconds of this ad, several multimodal resources combine to create an aura of suspicion and anxiety around Barack Obama. As Obama appears on screen, the viewer hears sinister music: a haunting melody featuring tubular bells reminiscent of the theme from *The Exorcist*. Obama is pictured from a low vertical angle, perhaps suggesting a menacing power over the viewer (Kress and Van Leeuwen 2006, 146). Framed against a featureless blue background, he smiles broadly as he holds a microphone. Thus, the viewer is led to regard him as a political speechmaker—an affable stage performer perhaps, but not a serious political leader.

This impression is enhanced verbally as a male voice recites charges against the Democratic nominee. Each charge is attributed on screen to a news institution, which suggests independent verification in the press; however, all accusations were later shown to be misleading (Jackson 2008). The charges employ negation, highlighting what Obama has *not* done: "Barack Obama *never* held a single Senate hearing on Afghanistan; he *hasn't* been to Iraq in years; he voted *against* funding our troops." Such negation introduces an affirmative position, only to reject it (Martin and White 2005, 118). Here, the speaker introduces and rejects claims that Obama has done due diligence on questions of foreign policy ("held hearings," "traveled to Iraq") and has shown commitment to the military ("funding our troops"). Indeed, the negations aim to correct any of the audience's misconceptions about Obama and his record.

Of course, the implication is that Obama should have performed the positive actions—a "real" commander in chief would have done so. This is especially clear in the last charge, where Obama is said to have "voted against funding our troops."[2] Note that the funding Obama opposed is not for some misguided objective (e.g., "the occupation of Iraq") but for people the viewer is supposed to cherish ("our troops"). The betrayal of "our" side is enhanced through imagery. In frames 6–10, the uniformed soldier symbolizes the "troops" whom Obama has allegedly failed to fund. The soldier is positioned in the same space where maps of Afghanistan and Iraq had been, and he appears to "look back" at Obama, signaling that he is in a war zone far from the presidential candidate who deprived him of resources.

The speaker completes the character attack by declaring that Obama's shameful positions "helped him win his nomination." The implication is not only that Obama adopted positions merely to win office but that the Democratic Party rewarded his bad leadership. The speaker concludes, "Now Obama is changing to help himself

Time	Frame	Soundtrack*
1–5		Announcer: Barack Obama never held a single Senate hearing on Afghanistan. [*sinister music: tubular bells ↓*]
6–10		He hasn't been to Iraq in years. He voted against funding our troops.
11–15		Positions that helped him win his nomination. Now Obama is
15–18		changing to help himself become president. [*shift to inspirational music: flourish of cymbals, then orchestral violins and horns ↓*]

Time	Frame	Soundtrack*
19–21		John McCain has always supported our troops and the surge that's working. ["church" bell rings]
6–10	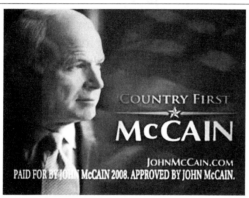	McCain. Country first. [trumpets ↓] **McCain:** I'm John McCain and I approve this message.

become president." Again, the ad highlights Obama's selfishness (he acts "to help himself"), while suggesting through the present progressive verb ("is changing") that Obama is altering his true identity simply to win. As if these claims were insufficient, the ad also prints negative judgments of Obama on screen, questioning his veracity and resolve ("DISINGENUOUS," "THE CANDIDATE OF CHANGE MY MIND").[3]

With this, the ad shifts toward John McCain and his allegedly superior moral character. The shift is marked by a pronounced change in music, as the sinister melody is abruptly ended by a flourish of cymbals and replaced by an inspirational tune (similar to the theme from *Back to the Future*), featuring violins and horns. Subsequent images of McCain also differ from those of Obama. Always presented with the American flag, an unsmiling McCain offers a detached and contemplative gaze. Unlike Obama, who grins and holds a microphone (like a TV gameshow host, the ad would suggest), McCain stands behind a podium, looking serious and presidential.

The speaker announces, "John McCain has always supported our troops and the surge that's working." The implied contrast with Obama is now obvious. The present perfect verb phrase "has always supported" suggests McCain's consistency. While Obama "is changing himself," McCain "always" holds his position. Of course, McCain supports the very troops whom Obama neglected to fund: *our* troops. Thus, the Republican is identified with "our" deictic center, our people and values (Chilton 2003; Cap 2013). The speaker suggests that supporting our troops is not just a matter of funding, however, by pointing out that McCain has also "always supported . . . the surge that is working." Here the ad evaluates Bush's COIN plan positively ("working") and implies that Obama, who opposed this plan, used poor judgment.[4] At the same time, it reinforces the idea that troop support is linked to supporting military policy.

Granted, Obama won the presidency, but McCain consistently out-polled him on the question of who would be a superior commander in chief (Saad 2008; Siddique 2008). Thus, McCain apparently succeeded in exploiting SOT propaganda to brand Obama as irresolute and disloyal and to characterize himself as a strong and reliable wartime leader. Again, the slogan is recontextualized not only to urge immediate action but to enact an identity for ideal leaders—those who always stand with the troops and permit them to "surge" ahead.

Commodification in Merchandise and Advertisements

Politicians have frequently urged troop support, but the chief propagators of the SOT slogan have been and continue to be members of the American public. During the Gulf War in 1990, it was ordinary citizens who posted "Support Our Troops" on their homes, cars, and clothing. And ever since, U.S. citizens have spread the propaganda horizontally, most often by purchasing and displaying pro-troops merchandise. If we are to understand why the SOT slogan has proliferated, then, we must consider American habits of consumption in the era of "commodity capitalism" (Breazeale 1994, 31).

As Fairclough (1992, 207) explains, commodification occurs when language and other semiotic practices "come . . . to be organized and conceptualized in terms of commodity production, distribution, and consumption." That is, commodification is the process whereby discourse is subjected to "economic calculation" and "designed for success on markets" (Fairclough 1999, 77).

Since Desert Storm, the commodification of "Support Our Troops" has been rampant, as the slogan has literally been inscribed on materials one can buy and sell. This is partly because the slogan has accrued cultural value, emerging as a way to register loyalty to soldiers and discipline protesters. However, the slogan would not have become a saleable commodity without changes in the routines of American production and consumption. Specifically, during the Vietnam War—just as calls to "Support Our Troops" proliferated—manufacturers began producing merchandise reflecting popular culture, and consumers (especially young ones) began buying this merchandise to assert their identities.

For example, posters and bumper stickers, which were once used to advertise other goods, became commodities in their own right—platforms for displaying youth identity, including ironic and countercultural slogans (Sontag 1970; Cushing 2009; Baker 2011; Endersby and Towle 1996). Likewise, T-shirts, which were considered underwear in the 1950s, became a way to proclaim one's attitudes and identity during the Vietnam era (Katz 1992, 25). As products were increasingly "semioticised" (Fairclough 1999, 77), they began to exhibit all kinds of discourse, including political statements, corporate brand names, and popular catchphrases (Breazeale 1994, 32).

Thus, by the time of the Gulf War, the appeal to "Support Our Troops" had acquired not only cultural value but the potential for commodification, as the economic infrastructure stood ready to incorporate it into a host of material goods (Breazeale 1994, 32–33). Since 9/11, the commodification of the slogan has only intensified as SOT products have grown more numerous and diverse. Today, you can purchase the slogan not only on traditional "identity signifiers," such as T-shirts, pins, and posters, but also on miscellaneous domestic products, such as placemats, hand towels, garden gnomes, and dog tag necklaces.

The widespread commodification and display of SOT propaganda has important rhetorical consequences. First, with the slogan "artifactualized" in products, it can now "be encountered . . . by mass audiences" (Agha 2003, 270). Companies making SOT merchandise create top-down propaganda to advertise their goods. These advertisements alone reach millions of people, some of whom are induced to purchase and recontextualize "supportive" merchandise in their own communities. Those who display SOT products spread the propaganda horizontally, reaching additional audiences. For example, Case (1992, 107) estimates that each bumper sticker "is likely to be seen tens or even hundreds of thousands of times by members of the general public." Thus, even those who don't purchase the SOT slogan nevertheless consume it "in the sense of being surrounded and confronted by its signs" (Breazeale 1994, 34).

Public displays of merchandise are also more likely to catch on. When citizens purchase and exhibit SOT merchandise, they not only signal their own political stance but enjoin others to follow their example. Any time a sign with the slogan is displayed, the SOT command is rearticulated, and the pressure for conformity is enhanced. Sign readers can demonstrate compliance with the command by publicly exhibiting more "patriotic" merchandise. Again, the goal of this horizontal propaganda is not necessarily to do something for the troops but to communicate values and standards of good behavior, inducing people to embrace societal norms.

Finally, when incorporated in merchandise and advertisements, the slogan is aestheticized—dressed in different styles of typography, infused with colors, and surrounded with visual symbols. In such multimodal environments, the potential meanings of the slogan expand and multiply (Lemke 1998). To illustrate these phenomena, I analyze a few artifacts and advertisements from the first Gulf War and the War on Terror.[5]

"Support Our Troops" Commodities in Desert Storm

Figure 8 shows a "Support Our Troops" poster (24″ × 36″) produced in 1991 by Funky Enterprises. The command "Support Our Troops" is on top, while the prepositional phrase "in The Gulf" is at the bottom. Presumably, the troops "in The Gulf" are those serving in Operation Desert Storm. The text is printed in bold white letters with a red drop shadow, placed against a blue background. Thus, the poster recontextualizes the colors of the American flag, indexing that "our" troops are American and suggesting that one can claim an American identity by offering support.

The most salient image is the yellow ribbon, which is tied in a bow at the center and appears to wrap around the poster horizontally. The image is reminiscent of yellow ribbons wrapped around trees before and during the war. Of course, the poster's words direct viewers to interpret the ribbon as a show of support for our troops. However, the ribbon also has its own intertextual history and brings its own set of indexical associations, helping to define what "support" means. In 1979, explains folklorist Gerald Parsons (1991), yellow ribbons were displayed to draw attention to American hostages being held prisoner in Iran. This custom was revived during Iraq's occupation of Kuwait, when some three thousand Americans were taken hostage by Iraqi soldiers. Though the hostages were quickly returned, hundreds of

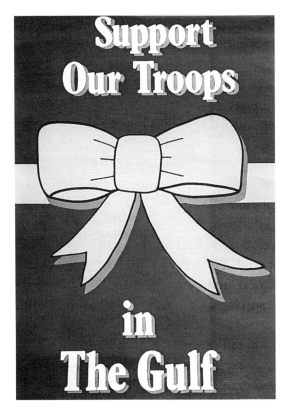

Figure 8 Yellow ribbon poster from the Gulf War (1991)

thousands of American soldiers effectively "took their place." Thus, Americans increasingly came to link the yellow ribbons not with hostages but with troops (Santino 1992, 26).

The yellow ribbon on the poster, then, helps define "support" as a kind of devotion to absent soldiers. As Stahl (2009, 545) explains, the ribbon is a "feminine" symbol, which suggests that the citizen's role in wartime is akin to a domesticated wife who faithfully waits for her husband's return. Meanwhile, the troops are framed as akin to captives in a faraway land, heroes who must endure suffering until the war ends and they are finally "released." Notice that, in this framework, "civic deliberation is simply irrelevant" (547). Americans are not to question why the troops are at war, nor are they to seek an end to the combat that holds the troops captive. Instead, the decision to release the troops from their duty lies with someone else, and citizens are required only to remain faithful and await a happy reunion.

Figure 9 displays a 1991 T-shirt sold for $15 by clothing maker Joe Kaufenberg. One dollar from each sale was devoted to purchasing personal radios for the troops (Fashion Staff 1991), but Kaufenberg reported substantial profits as his company sold more than two hundred thousand T-shirts during the Persian Gulf conflict (Harris and Meyer 1991).

The T-shirt has more design elements than the poster, but its themes are similar. For example, the words "SUPPORT OUR TROOPS" are inscribed in an arch-shape at the top in bold yellow letters. And at the bottom, on a very salient yellow ribbon, are the words "OPERATION: DESERT STORM." Thus, the T-shirt again links troop support with the image of the yellow ribbon. However, this ribbon is assigned more "masculine" characteristics, not only because it is superimposed over the martial symbol of the shield but also because the words "DESERT STORM" are inscribed in military stenciling (Machin 2007, 93–104).

Interestingly, the T-shirt recontextualizes the official emblem of the United Nations, a world map encased in a wreath of olive branches. This image appears several times, most strikingly behind the eagle, where the map is also encircled by the national flags of U.N. Security Council members. The U.N. emblems suggest the international legitimacy of the mission against Iraq, a mission authorized by the Security Council and presumably consistent with the United Nations' stated goal of peace. Perhaps the U.N. emblems were also included to suppress the idea of America as the "world's police," emphasizing instead a joint effort for security.

The largest figure on the T-shirt is the bald eagle, flying with outstretched wings and clutching a red, white, and blue shield. Of course, the eagle is symbolic of the United States, which appears to take the lead in the international effort for war. (Note how the eagle appears in the foreground, "in front" of other world nations.) In fact, the image of the eagle is borrowed from the "Great Seal of the United States," America's official coat of arms. Figure 10 shows the Great Seal, whose design was officially adopted in 1782.

Figure 9 Support Our Troops T-shirt (1991)

According to tradition, the eagle in the Great Seal represents America taking its place among the other nations of the world, represented by the stars (U.S. Department of State, Bureau of Public Affairs 2003). The eagle looks toward an olive branch held in one of its talons, symbolizing a preference for peace, but also holds a bundle of arrows in the other talon, symbolizing readiness for war. In its beak, it carries a scroll with the Latin motto *E Pluribus Unum* (from the many, one).

The T-shirt, then, seeks to link the Desert Storm mission with the historical mission of the United States as reflected in the Great Seal. But while the shirt suggests that America is remaining faithful to its noble calling, it also transforms the Great Seal's iconography to fit the present moment. The *E Pluribus Unum* motto is replaced with a popular wartime slogan, "UNITED WE STAND." Meanwhile, the eagle on the T-shirt is both more detailed and more menacing. Its red eye peers out fiercely at the

Figure 10 The Great Seal of the United States

viewer as it opens its beak to reveal an angular red tongue. One might say the entire image has a "hyper-masculine biker sensibility" reminiscent of tattoo designs (Breazeale 1994, 32). Also, while the eagle still holds an olive branch in one talon, the arrows in its other talon are unusual. Instead of feathered arrows, there are three red vectors pointing to the yellow banner and the words "OPERATION: DESERT STORM." Thus, the T-shirt literally points away from peace and toward a military mission in Iraq. The T-shirt, then, not only imagines the United States as the world's indispensable leader but also as a "manly" nation that is intimidating and bellicose. In this context, the injunction to "SUPPORT OUR TROOPS" is also an injunction to get behind America as it leads a furious charge for war.

"Support Our Troops" Commodities in the War on Terror

During the War on Terror, SOT commodities showcased similar themes: yellow ribbons suggesting fidelity to troops, references to American identity, and recontextualizations of military discourse and symbolism. Indeed, all these themes are evident in the magnet in figure 11, which I found on a car bumper near Pittsburgh, Pennsylvania. The oval-shaped magnet is about five inches long and reads: "SUPPORT OUR TROOPS." Here, the most salient word, "OUR," is both inscribed with an image of

Figure 11 Support Our Troops vehicle magnet

the U.S. flag, explicitly linking "us" to America, and adorned with a yellow ribbon "tied" around the second vertical upright in the letter "U." Meanwhile, the words "SUPPORT" and "TROOPS" are stenciled in military-style lettering and colored so as to mimic camouflage worn by soldiers. These stylistic touches may be an attempt to enact solidarity with the military, identifying with "their" colors and typography in "our" message of support. Following 9/11, variations of such ribbon magnets were enormously popular (Garofoli 2005). In fact, in a study of over eight thousand cars in nearly fifty American cities, Lilley et al. (2008) found that about a thousand (12.3 percent) displayed war-related ribbons.

The image in figure 12 also exhibits familiar themes but offers a more confrontational and disciplinary stance. The decal is from a yellow truck I photographed near Detroit, Michigan, part of a fleet from the Central Transport freight company owned by Manuel Moroun, one of the richest people in America (*Forbes* n.d.). Since the Iraq War, all Central Transport trucks have carried some version of this SOT image.

The square-shaped decal lies on the bottom right of the truck's rear panel. Its most salient image is a traditional U.S. flag whose red, white, and blue colors complement those of the verbal message: red and blue lettering against a white background. The symbolic connotations to America hardly deserve comment. Above the flag, in the top left corner of the square, we find the words "*My* USA." This grammatical subject is followed on the next line by its predicate ("Supports Our Troops") and a subordinate clause ("Whenever *We* Go . . ."). Below the flag are the words "No Aid or Comfort To the Enemy," followed in the bottom right corner by the exclamation, "*No*

Figure 12 Decal on Central Transport truck

Way!" Interestingly, most of the personal pronouns on the sign are italicized, indicating an intense desire to identify with certain in-groups. For example, "*My* USA" emphasizes the first-person singular pronoun, perhaps suggesting that the author wishes to separate himself from those citizens with questionable claims to "Americanness."[6] The author also emphasizes the first-person plural pronoun in "Whenever *We* Go," suggesting that he identifies with the troops so strongly that he imagines going with them to war. Interestingly, the subordinate conjunction ("whenever") is also inherently intense (compare to "when"), allowing the author to stress that troops should be supported each and every time there is a war.

After stressing this pro-troop/pro-war identity, the author defines and negates a counteridentity. With the lines "No Aid or Comfort To the Enemy, *No Way!*," the author implies that anything less than fervent support of the troops is anti-American and advantageous to an unnamed foe. Of course, the author dissociates himself from this counteridentity, emphatically denying its legitimacy ("No Aid . . . *No Way!*"). Thus, in this case, SOT propaganda delineates the appropriate role of wartime citizens, offering a clear distinction between true Americans who show unqualified support and faux Americans who merely encourage the enemy.

Figure 13 Support Our Troops bumper sticker

Figure 13 shows another bumper sticker (about four inches long) from a car near Pittsburgh. Once again, the slogan is juxtaposed with an image of the U.S. flag, reinforcing the familiar notion that troop support affirms American identity. What interests me more, however, is the artist's portrayal of the troops as shadows marching in front of the flag. The silhouetted troops wear combat gear and helmets as they carry rifles and backpacks. Yet the silhouette abstracts away from other details, erasing markers of personal identity, as well as any indicators of time and location. These soldiers could be anywhere, fighting against anyone, for any reason—yet the viewer is still instructed to offer them unqualified support. As Stahl (2009, 551) explains, the silhouette has become a stock image for representing soldiers, one that helps promote the view that war is a remote, decontextualized phenomenon. We are encouraged to sympathize with the abstract collection of soldiers as they embody "stamina and survival," yet the war itself remains a "distant object of uncritical consumption."

"Support Our Troops" Advertising

The meaning of the SOT slogan changes each time it is recontextualized and redisplayed by an ordinary person. Each commodity surrounds the slogan with a different array of multimodal signs, and each individual presents the slogan in different circumstances. So an SOT slogan on a T-shirt in 1991 suggests different meanings than the same slogan on a bumper sticker in 2016. And yet, as the slogan has been commodified, it has retained its indexical ties to larger cultural narratives, linking troop support with "Americanness" and encouraging viewers to adopt an appropriate

Figure 14 Masthead for FlagsOnCars website

wartime posture. These commodities—spread horizontally by ordinary people—are not the only signs performing such ideological work. Commodities inscribed with the slogan are prefigured by advertisements encouraging purchase. Indeed, the SOT ad is a major form of vertical propaganda that further recontextualizes the slogan and extends its intertextual life.

Following the Gulf War—and especially in the post 9/11 era—American companies increasingly began to market themselves and their products as "pro-troop" (Elliot 1991; Heilbronn 1994; Garofoli 2005). FlagsOnCars is just one online company fully devoted to selling "supportive" goods. Indeed, as shown in figure 14, this self-proclaimed "patriotic superstore" presents a webpage displaying SOT merchandise.[7] On the left of the masthead, the Statue of Liberty is set against a backdrop of exploding Fourth of July fireworks and a waving U.S. flag—images that celebrate America. To the right, one finds the troops, who are separated from these icons of America but who cast their gaze back toward them, suggesting their distance from "home" and their longing to return as they observe and defend American values.[8] All the troops are represented as male, and all are dressed in combat gear. Thus, the visual suggests the troops are a sympathetic group, far from home and standing in harm's way.

This image is complemented by the verbal introduction to the "Support Our Troops" page:

> We at FlagsOnCars are proud to Support Our Troops and to help others do the same by providing a range of high-quality "Support Our Troops" products. Our military personnel give of themselves day in and day out, without holidays, without question and are always prepared to make the ultimate sacrifice on our behalf. For this reason, they deserve our ongoing support no matter where they're serving, no matter our politics. From "Support Our Troops" pins and bumper magnets to flags and keychains, our selection of items is designed to allow you to show your support in a way that's compatible with your lifestyle. (FlagsOnCars n.d.)

As always, we find strong positive judgments of "our military personnel," including appraisals of propriety ("give of themselves," "make the ultimate sacrifice") and tenacity ("day in and day out," "without holidays," "always prepared"). In particular, the prepositional phrase "without holidays" reinforces the meaning of the visual, suggesting the soldier's distance from festivities on the home front. The troops' selfless determination is then explicitly cited as the reason why we must offer them support ("*For this reason*, they deserve our ongoing support"). Such support is defined in purely economic terms, as the sellers announce that both they and their customers can help soldiers "by providing a range of high-quality 'Support Our Troops' products." Thus, FlagsOnCars suggests that buying and selling goods provides a tangible benefit to troops, even though, unlike other sellers, it doesn't seem to earmark any proceeds for soldiers.

Also noteworthy is how FlagsOnCars construes an identity for site visitors. The frequent use of the pronoun "our" assumes a bond between buyer and seller, establishing the buyer's relationship to the troops. Specifically, buyers are identified as "co-owners" or "co-sponsors" of the troops (e.g., "our military personnel"), but also as beneficiaries of their sacrifice (the troops "make the ultimate sacrifice *on our behalf*"). The sellers also envision an audience that may not be convinced of the universal need to support soldiers. The assertion that "troops deserve our ongoing support" is immediately followed with explicit denials that there are exceptions to this rule: "*no* matter where they're serving, *no* matter our politics." Here, the sellers imply that members of the audience may be politically opposed to specific wars but expressly deny that this should prevent them from offering support (i.e., buying products). Remarkably, the sellers also imply an audience who may not believe SOT merchandise is harmonious with their identities. Thus, they directly reassure the audience that their selection of products will "allow you to show your support *in a way that's compatible with your lifestyle.*" Again, the implication is that SOT products are apolitical; they can fit your "lifestyle" regardless of your feelings about war and peace.

The final ad I consider aired on the Fox TV network on July 26, 2013, during an episode of *The Following* (Fox Broadcasting Company 2013). Excerpt 9.3 displays a multimodal transcript. The ad is epideictic, intended to reinforce values rather than exhort the audience. Specifically, the ad promotes the value of expressing gratitude for the troops. In fact, each celebrity repeats the words "thank you" at the ad's conclusion, and even before this finale, two Fox celebrities have already expressed thanks: Naya Rivera asserts, "We . . . are grateful for your protection and bravery," and Jane Lynch employs <u>intensified quantifications</u> to deny we can adequately express the extent of our thankfulness: "We can <u>never</u> say or do enough to express *all* our gratitude." The implication is that the troops are owed gratitude, that past gratitude has been insufficient.

On its face, the ad is addressed directly to the troops, as celebrities gaze into the camera and repeatedly employ the pronouns "you" and "your." The addressed troops are again imagined to be far away, as indicated by the appeal to "come home soon," as well as the affective process "we *miss* you." As in the FlagsOnCars ad, the troops are associated with positively moralized attributes and behaviors: "you've been there

Excerpt 9.3

Time	Frame	Soundtrack*
0–2		You've been there for us and we'll be there for you. [inspirational music: violins and cymbals ↓]
2–4		You're America's best and we will stand by you and your family.
5–6		We owe our freedom to you.
7–9		We miss you and are grateful for your protection and bravery.

Time	Frame	Soundtrack*
10		Come home safely.
11–15		We can never say or do enough to express all our gratitude for all that you do.
16–21		But we want you to know that (0.6) we're thinking about you and your families (0.3) and that we're behind you every step of the way.
169		Thank you. ↓ ["thank you" is repeated by four more celebrities] [ad ends with flourish of violins and cymbals]

for us," "you're America's best," "protection and bravery." In fact, contentious assertions about the troops are projected as universal truths. For example, Kevin Bacon categorically proclaims that "we owe our freedom to [the troops]," when, arguably, many American freedoms have been won in nonmilitary contexts by ordinary citizens. In any case, the point of the ad is not just to recognize the troops' heroism but to adopt an appropriate attitude toward them. Thus, the ad frequently signals our continuing consideration for troops ("we're thinking about you") and our commitment to stand in solidarity with them ("we'll be there for you," "we'll stand by you and your family," "we're with you every step of the way").

However, the ad's primary audience is not the troops overseas, who are rather unlikely to be watching a Friday night rerun of *The Following*. The more likely viewers are typical Americans, subsumed in the pronouns "we" and "our." Thus, while one of its aims is surely to thank soldiers for their service, the ad's chief purpose is to establish communion with the general public, to promote the Fox lineup, and to associate the network with a respectable pro-troops identity. The ad prominently and continuously displays the clause "FOX SUPPORTS OUR TROOPS," as opposed to "We Support Our Troops" or simply "Support Our Troops." By placing itself in the subject position, the network can claim credit and responsibility for a prosocial act. At the same time, the network displays each celebrity's name and the title of the Fox program on which they appear, as twinkling stars scud serenely across the screen, as if to reaffirm the "star" status of each actor. Of course, stirring music plays throughout, signaling the positivity of the message. Thus, viewers are encouraged to identify with Fox and its values, to learn the names of Fox's celebrities and hit TV shows, and to associate the Fox brand with the propriety of supporting our troops.

The irony of ads like this is they exploit the troops for purposes of crass self-promotion, even as they claim to be venerating soldiers for their sacrifice. Perhaps more importantly, such ads indicate the degree to which SOT propaganda has been naturalized in the United States. To be sure, these ads make political statements that an antiwar critic might regard as debatable ("we owe our freedom to you") or implicitly supportive of American military actions ("we're behind you every step of the way"). Yet the ads project themselves as if what they are saying is entirely apolitical and taken for granted. Ultimately, such commodified discourse encourages Americans to ignore debates about war and peace while perpetuating the notion that the troops require only our emotional support.

"Support Our Troops" on Twitter

To better understand mundane SOT propaganda, I examined the slogan as it was recontextualized on Twitter, a social media platform with millions of registered users. Twitter users develop networks by "following" one another. Users can follow as many profiles as they want; however, relationships need not be reciprocal: "If member A chooses to follow member B, this does not entail that member B will automatically gain access to member A's profile information" (Page 2012, 183). As Page (2012) explains, some famous Twitter users have huge followings, while others may gain "micro-celebrity" status by cultivating devotees. Nevertheless, most Twitter users are ordinary people with relatively few followers (Stadd 2013). This means Twitter is also a key site for horizontal propaganda, as most discourse is shared among people who are basically equals (Ellul 1965, 81–83).

Twitter users communicate via "tweets," publicly visible posts that, until 2017, could be no longer than 140 characters. Typically, one's tweets are only seen by one's followers, who can choose to pass them on, or "retweet" them, with or without commentary. As Page (2012, 184) observes, Twitter users rely on a number of conventions to keep track of their discourse. The prefix "@" is used to signal another member's username;[9] the abbreviation "RT" indicates a message has been retweeted; and a hashtag prefix (#) is used to "make a term searchable and therefore visible to others interested in tweets written about the same topic." Popular hashtags may even become "trending topics," thus extending their visibility throughout Twitter.

For this study, I analyzed 18,014 tweets posted by at least 9,981 unique users from March 2007 through December 2009, with each tweet containing some version of the phrase "Support Our Troops."[10] My findings indicate not only that ordinary people recontextualized "Support Our Troops" on a mass scale but also that they commonly (re)used the slogan to promote social integration—assimilating themselves and their followers into a pro-military, pro-American, and pro-war community. Indeed, this propaganda relied heavily on what Huckin (2016, 1320) calls the "collective presuppositions . . . of the entire community," as thousands of people recycled prevailing myths about troops, freedom, and proper civil conduct during times of war.

As shown in table 11, I identified four basic kinds of SOT tweets: (1) links to external sites with information on how to support the troops, (2) advertisements for supportive merchandise, (3) requests for material donations, and (4) sociopolitical appeals that provide reasons for (or against) troop support.[11] The first three categories take the slogan's sentiment for granted, implying an audience who already supports the troops but who may need more information on how to perform this support (whether through shopping or contributing material goods). Indeed, tweets in these categories typically provide no reasons for supporting the troops, thus indicating the degree to which troop support has become a cultural presupposition. Tweets in the first three categories were also less likely to come from ordinary users and more likely to come from private organizations, such as charities, nonprofits, and corporations.

Tweets in these first three categories were interesting, but they were far less common than sociopolitical (SP) appeals, which accounted for more than 75 percent of the data. Prototypically, SP appeals came from ordinary people who called on followers to support the troops and provided reasons for doing so. In SP appeals, "support" was typically defined as discursive, not material: followers were urged to express

Table 11 General types of "Support Our Troops" tweets

Type	Description	Example
How-to link (*n*=673)	Provides a link to an external site, identifying the site as a resource with one or more "ways to support" the troops.	"101 Ways To Support Our Troops (PDF) [link]" 8/16/2009 7:01:54 PM
Advertisement (*n*=1,486)	Sells a product or promotes a for-profit service, sometimes with the assurance that some proceeds will go to the troops. Typically, advertisements link to product descriptions in an online marketplace.	"Support Our Troops Mouse Pad – [link]" 12/6/2009 11:24:20 AM
Material donation appeal (*n*=2,001)	Calls on followers to support troops through material donations. Appeals for money or raw goods with functional uses (e.g., socks, cell phones, etc.), not for correspondence or moral support.	"Help support our troops by contributing your used cell phones this weekend. See article for drop-off points. [link]" 11/19/2009 5:29:18 PM
Sociopolitical appeal (*n*=13,732)	Makes a sociopolitical appeal to support the troops (or not), providing justifications. Sociopolitical appeals may legitimize or delegitimize the slogan and its adherents, reciting the phrase faithfully or adversely.	"Today is #militarymon #MilitarayMonday ! Support our troops who fight for us in other countries defending our country!" 8/3/2009 1:37:14 PM
Other (*n*=122)	Mentions the slogan but does so for an unclear, unrelated, or apolitical purpose; for example, a request for clarification.	". . . I dunno either but I'll ask too. RT: @[username] What does #SOT mean? ~ I'm guessing support our troops?" 9/7/2009 10:41:18 PM

gratitude or moral support for the troops (through cards or emails), or they were simply invited to join a supportive campaign. As I discuss below, however, not all SP appeals recited the slogan faithfully. Some recontextualized it in oppositional ways, such as reworking the slogan for new ends or delegitimizing it and its adherents. Still others sought to regulate use of the slogan by defining proper ways to support the troops and patrolling the boundaries of the in-group community.

I examine these sociopolitical appeals more closely, since they are the most important source of ordinary propaganda in the corpus. Table 12 describes categories of SP appeals, citing how often they appeared.[12]

The most common SP appeal was the *general appeal*, typically a generic command or statement expressing troop support. Often these appeals recited the slogan and nothing else, as in the example in table 12, or they offered a personal declaration of support as in tweet 9.1:

9.1 I support our troops. (9/3/2008 11:06:45 PM)

Other tweets in this category, such as tweet 9.2, attempted to use mass repetition to make the "Support Our Troops" hashtag a "trending topic":

Table 12 Sociopolitical appeals in "Support Our Troops" tweets

Type	Common subtypes	Description	Example
General appeal (n=4,887)	Bare command Invitation Declaration	Offers a generic invitation to "support our troops" or an unelaborated declaration of support.	"Support our troops" 9/24/2009 8:27:04 PM
Rational appeal (n=4,431)	Hero appeal Need appeal Personal appeal Victory appeal	Justifies supporting the troops, explicitly or implicitly.	"Support our troops cuz they are supporting you" 12/7/2009 4:52:02 PM
Integration appeal (n=3,919)	Discipline appeal Model appeal Universal appeal	Regulates the SOT community, rewarding insiders, disciplining outsiders, and judging (un)acceptable attitudes.	"@[username] Starbucks doesn't support our troops. Shame on them." 12/3/2009 1:01:30 PM
Counterappeal (n=495)	Humor/irony Concede + counter Critical reframing	Offers a counterhegemonic appropriation of the slogan, whether serious or facetious.	"Support our troops: Bring them ALL home NOW!" 5/25/2009 1:07:30 PM

9.2 #SupportOurTroops #SupportOurTroops #SupportOurTroops #SupportOurTroops #SupportOurTroops #SupportOurTroops #Support OurTroops trending topic (12/19/2009 9:13:23 PM)

The general appeal category also included specific invitations, including summonses to participate in supportive events. For example, tweets in this category often included hashtags for "Military Monday" or "Red Friday," weekly events in which people show appreciation for soldiers. On Red Fridays, for instance, members of the SOT community wear red "because the troops bleed red."

Sometimes, ordinary users directed general appeals at celebrities, asking them to participate in #militarymon and #RedFriday.[13] Usually, though, generic calls for participation were exchanged among the "masses" and supportive displays were executed in virtual space. For example, tweet 9.3 shows a promotion for a "twibbon" campaign, inviting followers to add a virtual SOT ribbon to their profile pictures. There were hundreds of such "twibbon" invitations in the corpus, each one issued by an ordinary user and subsequently "supported" by dozens of (and sometimes more than a thousand) followers.

9.23 Support Support Our Troops, add a #twibbon to your avatar now!— [link] (11/19/2009 3:50:17 PM)

After the general appeal, the next most dominant type was the *rational appeal*, which directly or indirectly justified supporting our troops. That is, users who make rational appeals give reasons why troops should be supported, perhaps implying that they believe some followers still need to be persuaded. The most common, and often most subtle, kind of rational appeal is the need appeal, which occurred over 2,500 times in the corpus. This appeal suggests the troops need support because of something they currently *lack*: physical safety, as implied by "in harm's way" (tweet 9.4); encouragement and social contact, as implied by the request for "morale boosting email" (tweet 9.5); gratitude, as the call to "always say Thank You" suggests that gratitude is always insufficient (tweet 9.6); or simply the knowledge that they are supported, as in "let them know you're standing behind them," which implies they don't already know this (tweet 9.7). As the examples show, the need appeal is a call for verbal or moral support, not for raw materials such as socks or radios.

> 9.4 RT @[username]: just want to say again for #milmon ~ please remember all our troops in harm's way ~ #SOT @supportourtroops (10/20/2009 12:15:41 AM)
>
> 9.5 You can volunteer to serve in a small way. Help us support our troops through morale boosting email and letters. #eMOM (1/20/2009 1:34:30 PM)
>
> 9.6 @[username] True dat! We need to support our troops, and always say "Thank You!" when vets pass by during parades . . . (12/2/2008 4:43:36 PM)
>
> 9.7 Support our troops—let them know you're standing behind them. OurVoicesUnited [link] (12/3/2009 7:01:38 PM)

Often, the need appeal mentioned the "holiday season" (twect 9.8). In fact, "holiday season" was the seventh most common two-word phrase in the corpus (*n*=544), and specific national holidays were mentioned hundreds of times more.

> 9.8 PLEASE RT click on support our troops.they need us to remember them in our holiday season.our brothers and sisters. [link] (12/24/2009 9:12:41 AM)

In fact, use of the slogan peaked in July and November, right around the patriotic holidays of Independence Day and Veterans Day and the family holidays of Thanksgiving and Christmas. Such holiday tweets help naturalize an appropriate domestic attitude, identifying holidays as a special time to remember troops who are implicitly depicted as distant and forgotten.

Very interesting need appeals were tweeted in early December 2009, as President Obama announced he would send thirty thousand more troops to fight in the now unpopular Afghanistan War. During a primetime speech on December 1, Obama never used the SOT slogan, but he often referenced the troops and their bravery, using "Heroic Troops" rhetoric to rally the public and gain consent for his surge (Oddo 2014b, 527). This rhetoric appears to have worked on several Twitter users, who "live-tweeted" Obama's address. Tweets 9.9 through 9.11 show that Obama's announcement of a surge inspired a "Support Our Troops" response in the Twitterverse. Indeed, some users expressly juxtapose the slogan with the troop increase, suggesting the increase is a cause for renewed support (tweets 9.10 and 9.11). Others simply declare their support for the troops during Obama's speech (tweet 9.9), a "conditioned reflex" to the presidential call for war (Ellul 1965, 31).

> 9.9 I am sitting here, watching Obama's address to the nation; SUPPORT OUR TROOPS! (12/1/2009 8:34:36 PM)
>
> 9.10 President Obama Announces add'l 30K troops to Afghanistan. Support our Troops! [link] (12/1/2009 9:01:30 PM)
>
> 9.11 Local military wife: Support our troops: In light of President Obama's decision to send 30,000 additional troops . . . [link] (12/1/2009 11:48:47 PM)

The reasoning in these tweets appears to be some version of the following: when the president announces he's sending troops to battle, the troops need our support. However, some Twitter users reasoned differently and suggested that sending troops to battle *is* troop support. This was clearest in many tweets delivered while Obama was still deliberating about what to do in Afghanistan. For example, the author of tweet 9.12 addresses the proposed troop surge, before Obama's final decision. Here, the author links troop support with support for General Stanley McChrystal, who, at the time, was recommending a surge of up to eighty-five thousand soldiers. McChrystal is referred to as "OUR General," indicating intense solidarity with military leadership, and the author suggests that accepting McChrystal's proposed strategy amounts to giving him "what he needs." Thus, sending troops to war is depicted as the fulfillment of soldiers' needs, a way to help generals and soldiers succeed in their mission.

> 9.12 RT @[username1] @[username2]: #SOG So, Support OUR General, Support OUR Troops, tell your politicians, your party to send McChrystal what he needs . . . (10/24/2009 9:32:29 PM)

Another noteworthy rational appeal is the hero appeal (*n*=1,056), which suggests that the troops need support because of who they are and what they do. The hero appeal differs from the need appeal in that support is justified based on qualities or accomplishments the troops have attained, not qualities they lack. Often the appeal is implied when users list positive attributes of the troops, such as "brave," "valor," and "courage" (tweets 9.13 and 9.14).

9.13 SUPPORT OUR TROOPS OUR BRAVE MEN & WOMEN OF THE ARMED FORCES! GOD BLESS AMERICA! (5/21/2009 12:25:47 AM)

9.14 The valor & courage of R young women & men in the #militaryR a shining example 2 all of the world! #SOT SUPPORT OUR TROOPS (10/5/2009 9:10:44 PM)

More commonly, as in tweets 9.15 through 9.18, the hero appeal is based on what the troops do (or have done) for "us."

9.15 In Iraq and can only say one thing . . . Support our Troops! these people are going through a lot for us. PS I love Sandstroms! (7/13/2009 3:57:33 PM)

9.16 RT @[username]: #MilitaryMon As Our Troops risk all and sacrifice much to bring us Peace, We Support Our Troops, and demonstrateOur Gratitude #SOT (10/19/2009 1:16:01 PM)

9.17 Support our troops, your freedom depends on them. (11/20/2009 10:23:35 AM)

9.18 they fight 2 keep us free #supportourtroops (12/30/2009 12:24:22 PM)

In these examples, the troops are represented not only as sacrificing (e.g., "going through a lot") on our behalf but as producing positive outcomes for us, such as peace and, especially, freedom. Indeed, the notion that the troops provide freedom was recited over eight hundred times in the corpus.

Two other rational appeals deserve mention: the personal appeal (n=393) and the victory appeal (n=93). Personal appeals link troop support to a personal affiliation with the military. Some explain such support on the grounds that the speaker has served (or intimately knows people who still serve) in the armed forces (tweet 9.19). Often, personal appeals appeared to come from family members of soldiers: spouses, siblings, mothers and fathers (tweets 9.20 and 9.21). Such tweets contained first names (e.g., "Joe") and nicknames ("hubby," "little bro"), as well as lexis indicating negative emotion, including expressions of hope and concern about specific troops ("hope your okay," "getting worried"). Several, such as tweet 9.21, were especially heart-wrenching. Though relatively rare in the corpus, these personal appeals show that, for some, troop support is part of an intimate relationship tied up with feelings of anxiety. At the same time, such tweets epitomize the attitude that the SOT slogan typically prescribes for all citizens—intense devotion to vulnerable soldiers rather than political debate about the justifications for war.

9.19 Please support our troops my dad was one, my sister is one and soon my little brother will be one . . . (6/3/2009 2:01:55 AM)

9.20 support our troops @[username]: Lil' bro' I miss u and hope your okay
    . . . (6/18/2009 9:33:01 AM)

9.21 gettin worried about my sweetie n IRAQ havent heard frm him since
    easter :(. .SUPPORT OUR TROOPS!!! (4/29/2009 1:19:06 PM)

In some ways, the victory appeal is the opposite of the personal appeal, since it often references wartime missions rather than individual troops. More specifically, the victory appeal equates troop support with military triumph, defeating the enemy, and supporting the cause for war. Often, victory appeals suggest that citizen-led "support" (which usually remains ill-defined) helps soldiers achieve battlefield victory (tweet 9.22).

9.22 RT @[username]: #MilitaryMon Each Citizen that does something to
    Support Our Troops, has helped to win this war. (7/20/2009 1:51:56 PM)

In other cases, though, "support" is more clearly associated with defeating a dangerous enemy (tweet 9.23) or, much more rarely, achieving a just cause. Indeed, tweet 9.24 was one of the only tweets in the corpus that explicitly tied troop support to a stated political goal for war, underscoring how much the slogan has become untethered to external justifications for violence.

9.23 I will continue to support our troops and advocate a victory strategy
    against terrorism, Islamic fascism, and totalitarianism. (5/25/2009
    9:42:06 PM)

9.24 Liberate Iraq / Support Our Troops (3/7/2009 2:12:05 PM)

Overall, rational appeals recycled dominant ideas, including the ideas that heroic soldiers are the primary guarantors of liberty, that troops are generally underappreciated, that moral support achieves military victory, and that the troops themselves need and desire additional war. To enforce adherence to these ideas, though, Twitter users relied on appeals of a different kind, namely *integration appeals*. These appeals tended to regulate the SOT community, rewarding insiders and chastising outsiders.

One common subtype was the discipline appeal (*n*=1,739), which criticized individuals for failing to support troops, for insufficiently supporting them, or for supporting them in the wrong ways. Sometimes disciplinary flak came in the form of slogans, such as "If you can't stand behind our troops, feel free to stand in front of them." This slogan—tweeted 136 times in the corpus—suggests those who don't support the troops ought to be subjected to violence, either from enemies on the front lines or the troops themselves. However, discipline could also be more targeted, such as calls for opposition to antiwar protests (tweet 9.25) or direct criticism sent to another user (tweet 9.26). In such cases, evaluative vocabulary makes clear that those who allegedly don't support our troops are deviant or incompetent ("nuts," "dense," "misinformed").

> 9.25 oct17 codepink & more protesting nationwide find 1near U & counter protest the nuts & support our troops [link] RT #glennbeck (10/7/2009 12:07:27 AM)
>
> 9.26 @[username] Why do you think we shouldn't SUPPORT our troops? Are you dense or just misinformed? (12/14/2009 12:31:07 PM)

More often, though, discipline appeals were directed at businesses or politicians, especially President Obama, who was criticized hundreds of times (e.g., tweets 9.27 through 9.29).

> 9.27 #DearSanta I want a president who will support our troops! @white house #tcot #tweetcongress @gopleader (11/19/2009 8:26:49 PM)
>
> 9.28 Obama "Dithers" as our American Heros take casualities in Afghanistan! Support our troops or pull them out Obama! He is Not a Leader! ABO! (10/23/2009 12:11:30 AM)
>
> 9.29 Mr. Obama: Make a decision to support our troops or get them home . . . NOW! This is a disgrace. (11/22/2009 11:32:31 AM)

Not surprisingly, such tweets often came from users who self-identified as conservative (the hashtag "#tcot" in tweet 9.29 stands for "top conservatives on Twitter"). Many disciplinary appeals directed at Obama, such as the ones in tweets 9.28 and 9.29, referenced that he had not yet decided on whether to approve the proposed troop surge in Afghanistan. As shown in tweet 9.28, the time that Obama took to make a decision was often coded as "dithering" while troops suffered losses on the battlefield. More interestingly, in more than a hundred of these tweets (including tweet 9.29), the call to "Support Our Troops" was contrasted (via the conjunction "or") with an appeal to "bring them home." The obvious implication is that the president has only two choices: (1) "supporting our troops," which means sending in reinforcements to save endangered soldiers, or (2) bringing the troops home to take them out of harm's way. Interestingly, the preferred way to support the troops is to prolong the war or, as these users would have it, to provide troops with sufficient numbers to carry out the mission. Meanwhile, bringing the troops home is not considered a way to support them, presumably since "pull[ing] them out" would end their mission prematurely.

The counterpart to the discipline appeal was the model appeal (n=1,740), which praised individuals or organizations for showing proper support for the troops and thereby "modeling" appropriate behavior. This appeal could be as simple as thanking someone for supporting our troops and thereby implying troop support is deserving of social recognition. Other model appeals came in the form of "Follow Friday" tweets. As Page (2012, 189) explains, Follow Friday is a "weekly practice whereby Twitter members promote to their follower list the user names of other members that are deemed worthy of interest." Being nominated in such a list is "considered a token of esteem within the linguistic economy of Twitter," a form of recognition that can enhance one's status. Tweet 9.30 shows how, in this corpus, nominations for Follow Friday depended on whether users supported the troops, making "proper behavior" a precondition for social acknowledgment.

> 9.30 #FollowFriday those who Support Our Troops! #SOT @[username1] @[username2] @[username3] @[username4] @[username5] @[user name6] @[username7] @[username8] (7/31/2009 9:19:59 PM)

Model appeals could also be self-serving, as users tried to show off their pro-troops conduct. For example, the purpose of the personal narrative in tweet 9.31 seems to be to demonstrate how a good citizen is "compelled" to treat soldiers.

> 9.31 A lrg contingent of soldiers from the army came into my coffee shop 2day and I felt compelled to buy their beverages #supportourtroops #fb (8/9/2009 3:04:57 PM)

Of course, the model appeal could also be used to credit others for pro-troop performances. For example, tweet 9.32 rather interestingly praises muggers for returning possessions to a victim after they realized he was a soldier. Meanwhile, tweet 9.33 recognizes President Obama for (finally) supporting our troops and approving the surge in Afghanistan.

> 9.32 Shout out to those muggers in Milwaukee who decided to return dudes ish when they saw he was in the Military. Support our Troops! Happy-Vday (11/12/2009 12:01:59 AM)
>
> 9.33 Kudos to Obama for finally making a decision on Afghanistan. Took 2+ months. Support our troops, and you will have our support. (12/4/2009 11:09:27 AM)

Closely related to the model appeal is what I dub the universal appeal (*n*=440), which helps regulate the SOT community by showing that it is permissible for *everyone* to adopt the appropriate attitude. More specifically, the universal appeal suggests all people can and should support the troops, regardless of their views on war. This appeal could be general, as in 9.34, which provides a polite reminder to everyone about the "importance" of supporting our troops. Or it could address specific users, as in 9.35, which explicitly uses deontic modals to show that even opponents of the war are permitted to support the troops ("you *can*"). Finally, the universal appeal could be tied to policy, as in 9.36, which urges people to support the troops even if they don't support Obama's decision to send more soldiers to Afghanistan.

> 9.34 RT @[username]: Please remember how important it is to support our troops no matter how you feel about war. #militarymon #SOT (10/26/2009 3:39:10 PM)
>
> 9.35 RT @[username1] RT @[username2] #spreadlove to those fighting for us overseas. <You can support our troops even if you don't support war. (9/23/2009 (1:14:43 AM)
>
> 9.36 whether or not you agree with the decision, support our troops: [link] (12/1/2009 4:44:03 PM

Integration appeals sought to create a pro-troops orthodoxy, prescribing appropriate behaviors, criticizing nonconformists, and praising social exemplars. Even so, some chose to reappropriate the slogan in counterhegemonic ways. Specifically, users making counterappeals (n=495) critiqued the slogan or simply repurposed it in an unorthodox fashion. A few counterappeals critically reframed the slogan by referring to the Iraq and Afghanistan Wars as "illegal" or "occupations," thereby equating troop support with support for unjust policies. Other counterappeals slammed the slogan itself as a distraction from the ugliness of war (tweet 9.37).

> 9.37 As if a few pretty ribbons that say "support our troops" could make war look one bit better . . . (10/24/2007 7:06:44 PM)

However, most counterappeals were not so critical. Several simply made humorous use of the slogan, redefining it as support for fictional stormtroopers in Star Wars or linking troop support with physical intimacy, as in tweet 9.38, which was awarded the most "favorites" in the corpus.

> 9.38 Don't tell me, sir, that I don't support our troops. I make out with our troops at every available opportunity. (7/28/2009 2:16:00 PM)

Such ironic appeals may have reduced the seriousness of the slogan, but they did not necessarily challenge its wisdom. Meanwhile, appeals such as tweet 9.39 literally countered the slogan with unorthodox meanings. We might call these "concede + counter" pairings, since they concede that troop support is necessary but counter that war is unjustified or undesirable. Closely related were tweets that supplemented the slogan with calls to bring soldiers home (tweet 9.40). Here, unlike in disciplinary appeals, bringing troops home is a way of supporting them, often "the best way."

9.39 i support our troops for all that they do, but i hate war. (12/1/2009 7:55:22 PM)

9.40 the best way to support our troops is to bring them home. (2/24/2009 9:59:21 PM)

Again, counterappeals were not entirely critical of the slogan. Though some appealed to antiwar messages, they still focused on troops, thus reaffirming the necessity of troop support and opposing the war only as a means to protect soldiers. Few criticized the external justifications and legality of the fighting. Thus, even counterappeals often revealed the dominance of SOT logic.

Propaganda only succeeds if many agents recontextualize it and keep it alive. This chapter details the many groups who keep alive "Support Our Troops" propaganda through both vertical and horizontal campaigns. Political contestants exploit the slogan in top-down appeals, establishing their credentials and compelling support for war. Similarly, corporate elites produce SOT merchandise, commodifying the slogan and advertising products in vertical campaigns that reinforce cultural norms. However, the slogan is not simply disseminated by elites; it is recontextualized by ordinary people—faithfully, continually, and on a massive scale. These average citizens circulate the slogan and its associated ideas horizontally, displaying it on their cars and clothing, or recontextualizing it more creatively on social media.

Ultimately, the slogan plays an interesting and pivotal role in American wartime propaganda. On the one hand, recurring calls to "support our troops" function as what Ellul (1965, 30–31) calls "pre-propaganda": continuous messaging that prepares people for action and makes then "mobilizable" at the appropriate moment. The slogan may even induce a "conditioned reflex" of nationalism, reinforcing myths of the heroic soldier and the disloyal dissenter (31). On the other hand, the slogan can also function as "active propaganda," a "propaganda of crisis" that serves as an "incitement to action" (30). After all, the slogan literally commands audiences to do something, and politicians use it to justify participation in war, not just readiness to fight. Thus, the slogan is versatile. It can be used as a gentle reminder, a ribbon campaign that slowly conditions people to adopt appropriate attitudes. Or it can be used like a prod, coercing people to accept specific wartime policies.

One hesitates to say that the "Support Our Troops" slogan will be with us forever. Perhaps its usage will decline as war is increasingly fought remotely via unmanned aircraft. For now, anyway, it remains a powerful propaganda device. As this chapter shows, the slogan is popular even with peace activists, who have sought to reappropriate it for their own purposes ("support our troops: bring them home"). Such uses of the slogan may redefine troop support by elaborating what Coy, Woehrle, and Maney (2008, 183) call a "discourse of betrayal." Accordingly, it is not protesters who betray soldiers, but politicians who imperil them through misguided policies.

Such reappropriations, however, may be ineffective. As Stahl (2009, 559) says, the call to support our troops by "bringing them home" persists in focusing attention on soldiers and their bodies, while failing to address the reasons offered for war. Presumably, peace activists would still oppose the War on Terror, even if American troops were better protected in battle. If the focus remains only on troops' welfare, other (better) reasons to oppose war are lost. Moreover, while the antiwar movement is significant, there is not yet an antiwar discourse to compete with pro-war propaganda. Narratives—spread by elite actors and ordinary people—continue to portray war as a heroic struggle fought by vulnerable (and often shorthanded) troops. Thus, antiwar arguments premised on "protecting the troops" are trumped by more dominant pro-war stories, which suggest we protect endangered GIs not by ending war but by sending in more salvific soldiers.

Perhaps the best way to neutralize the power of the "Support Our Troops" slogan may not be to recontextualize it for antiwar ends. Instead, activists would do better to reframe the conversation altogether and, one day, generate a movement that can broadly influence the culture. Indeed, America may never free itself from perpetual war until a true discourse of peace takes hold of the popular imagination and governs our understanding of political life.

Conclusion
War Propaganda and the Prospects for Resistance

There are occasions when it is right to be
alarmist about propaganda.
                              —Randall Marlin, 2013

This book has articulated a theory of propaganda, examining specific cases of American war propaganda from the last twenty-five years. I have argued that propaganda is best viewed as an intertextual process that employs manipulative discourse and serves antidemocratic ends. And I have investigated the persuasive properties of war propaganda, identifying linguistic, symbolic, and social factors that allow wartime messages to be heard, believed, and recontextualized on a mass scale. In this conclusion, I discuss contributions of this study and consider the implications of my work for academics and ordinary citizens.

I begin by reflecting on the limitations of my methodology and offering directions for future research. Next, I review the book's key claims about propaganda, including specific observations about the propaganda of war. I also consider whether scholars have overstated the problem of propaganda while ignoring the public's capacity to resist its allure. Finally, I offer recommendations on how concerned citizens might respond to propaganda and potentially undermine its influence.

Methodological Limitations and Directions for Future Research

Writing this book, I faced several methodological challenges, including the challenge of integrating different approaches to discourse analysis (DA). I mainly employed methods from systemic-functional linguistics, such as Martin and White's (2005) appraisal framework. But I also found other frameworks useful, for example, Cap's (2006) spatial-temporal-axiological (STA) model. Adding to the complexity, I complemented linguistic analysis with analyses of multimodality (e.g., Baldry and Thibault 2005). These different analytic frameworks sometimes clashed, but they also allowed me to learn more than I would have with just one approach.

Another methodological concern is the reliability of inductive coding categories (such as those used to code news analyst contributions). To help ensure reliability, I used a collaborative coding approach, training a second analyst in my coding schemes and consulting with her about all assigned codes. The idea was to "reach agreement on each code through collaborative discussion rather than independent corroboration" (Smagorinsky 2008, 401). Of course, my codes are tentative and not applicable to other data.

I also faced a more general challenge, namely that propaganda is a macrolevel phenomenon, while my DA training has equipped me to deal with micro-rhetorical features. To address large-scale sociocultural factors, I tried to supplement DA with historical analysis and, where possible, analysis of interview data and government records. The historical analyses are crucial, and yet they are also partial and uneven. For example, the history behind the "Support Our Troops" slogan is important for understanding why this slogan resonates in American culture. However, I could not systematically examine every use of this slogan and had to rely heavily on secondary source materials. Meanwhile, in the chapters on news analysts before the 2003 Iraq War, I had difficulty gaining access to human sources and government documents. Some news analysts were unwilling to talk to me. And the U.S. government systematically denied most of my Freedom of Information Act (FOIA) requests concerning interactions between analysts and government officials. FOIA offices frequently insisted my requests were too broad to be processed. It was only after repeated attempts that my requests were handled at all, only to be delayed such that I am still waiting to hear back.

Aside from these issues, I faced more technical challenges when analyzing large corpora of discourse. Because I am still most comfortable analyzing discourse "by hand," I usually opted to examine short strings of discourse over many texts and long time periods. Thus, I chose to examine only the "incubator narrative" and its many reincarnations in media discourse, only the relatively brief appearances of news analysts on mainstream TV, and only a single talking point and its journey from intelligence reports to public speeches. Though this approach allowed me to closely examine the continual recontextualization of small units of discourse, I was not always able to examine larger patterns of recontextualization—for example, the recontextualization of whole genres and entire arguments for war.

A final limitation of this study is that I was unable to account for much of the propaganda circulated by ordinary people. I addressed some of this propaganda when I examined the "Support Our Troops" slogan on Twitter. But I would have liked to study more how mainstream news propaganda gets recycled by ordinary citizens—how propaganda moves downward from elite circles and then horizontally across society. This remains an interesting direction for future scholarship, particularly as new quantitative research tools allow us to examine how information moves across social networks.

Propaganda Is an Intertextual Process

One of this book's key claims is that propaganda is an intertextual process, a consequence of continual recontextualization. In order for it to spread, a propaganda meaning must be extracted from one text and then "repeated, reaffirmed, and reified" in subsequent texts (Hodges 2008a, 2). This means it is not quite accurate to speak of a single propagandist who intentionally delivers a self-serving message to the masses. Certainly, such deliberate propagandists exist, but they cannot operate alone and must induce other propagandists to recontextualize their messages favorably.

Once one accepts that propaganda is an intertextual and distributed process, a number of important implications follow:

- *Propaganda cannot be defined as "furthering the desired intent of the propagandist."* There is no one propagandist, and so no single intent in a propaganda campaign.
- *Propaganda can be circulated unwittingly.* A victim of propaganda, manipulated by a propaganda message, may unwittingly spread that propaganda to new parties.
- *Propaganda may move vertically, or horizontally, or in both directions at once.* Propaganda can move in a top-down direction from powerful elites to the public, or it can move horizontally among people who are more or less equals. However, vertical propaganda often works in conjunction with horizontal. For example, a politician making a manipulative argument may marvel as that argument travels down to citizens who then regularly recontextualize it in face-to-face interactions or across social media.
- *Propagandists can induce recontextualization using both social and semiotic resources.* Propagandists, whether witting or unwitting, can provide multimodal cues to audiences, signaling which snatches of discourse are detachable and worthy of recontextualization. Semiotic signals of detachability may include explicit metadiscourse or performative poetics. Deliberate propagandists may also just repeat a message continually over time, making it more memorable and reusable. However, there are more social ways to induce recontextualization, such as peer pressure or the provision of material (dis)incentives. Elites may also induce recontextualization simply because they can enact for themselves a powerful voice, capable of "semiotic mobility" (Blommaert 2005, 69).
- *Propaganda is most likely to spread if the intertextual process is initiated by those with access to mass media.* Theoretically, propaganda can be spread by anyone,

but elite agents with access to, or influence over, channels of mass communication have an advantage, since they can generally trust that their propaganda meanings will be instantaneously mass-recontextualized throughout the private media system. Indeed, this book confirms that government actors have vast power to influence mainstream news by reliably inducing journalists to repeat their discourse favorably and on a mass scale.

Propaganda Is Manipulative and Antidemocratic

According to my definition, propaganda is also manipulative and antidemocratic. As a general rule, propaganda manipulates people by suggesting a binary between "Us" and "Them," presenting *our* side in positive terms, while accentuating *their* negative features (Van Dijk 2006). This book confirms that war propaganda is almost always characterized by this strategy of positive self-presentation and negative other-presentation (Hodges 2013; Van Dijk 2007). Human biology may prepare us to associate out-groups with a threat to survival (Hart 2010). But manipulative propaganda exploits inborn cognitive mechanisms, coercing fear and anger even when the threat is minor, remote, or nonexistent.

Discursive manipulation can take other forms as well: lying, distortion, doublespeak, misleading implication, and textual silence (Huckin 2002, 2010). These kinds of manipulation are so common in American war propaganda that Campbell and Jamieson (2008, 242–52) even identify "strategic misrepresentation" as an essential characteristic of presidential war rhetoric. Such misrepresentation is obvious in the case studies in this book, from the false incubator story to the misleading talking points before the 2003 Iraq War. Perhaps the most pernicious form of manipulation, though, is the widespread manipulation of dialogic space, whereby certain voices and ways of seeing the world are suppressed and excluded from mainstream discourse. In the aluminum tubes case, for example, people were prevented from making fully informed democratic choices, as certain viewpoints were kept out of the mainstream. Similarly, during the Persian Gulf War and the start of the Afghanistan War, "Support Our Troops" rhetoric was so dominant that antiwar criticism became nearly unspeakable. When entire topics are rendered silent (Huckin 2010, 421), when relevant perspectives are subdued and erased, democracy suffers.

Indeed, as I define it, propaganda is necessarily antidemocratic: it harms the Many and serves the Few. Specifically, propaganda tends to promote (or reify unfair) power relations and social inequality. One can see this, too, in the cases of propaganda analyzed in this book. There is little evidence that this war propaganda produced positive outcomes or enhanced Americans' safety. But a good deal of evidence indicates that the wars called into being by propaganda intensified anti-American hatred and provoked more violence (Cockburn 2014). At the same time, these wars caused unimaginable suffering for people in the Middle East. Thus, I argue, the Many have not benefited appreciably from this propaganda justifying war. But the Few certainly did: The executive branch expanded its power, waging undeclared wars and creating secret programs of mass surveillance. And globally, the United States followed the path of empire, arguably violating international law and ignoring mandates of the U.N. Charter. In my view, the only citizens who have clearly benefited from the war propaganda are those who already exercise undue influence in political life: corporate stockholders from the defense and intelligence industries, think tank intellectuals, and purveyors of news-entertainment.

Propaganda Anxiety

Of course, some would say I am overstating the problem. Joseph (2006, 116), for example, suggests that many scholars are suffering from "anxiety about propaganda, especially that generated by governments." In his view, much critical scholarship of propaganda is elitist: "No one ever expresses anxiety that *they themselves* are having their minds controlled from without. . . . But they are certain that the vast majority of human beings are not so enlightened, and are therefore the pawns of the oligarchy" (126). If propaganda were as powerful as these scholars believed, says Joseph, we would find whole populations "becoming homogenised in their political views . . . consistently in favour of the ruling parties." Yet despite the fact that "we are surrounded by propaganda," he observes, "people's politics are . . . deeply divided" (132). The truth is "ordinary people do not simply accept what those in power tell them, but question it, are sceptical about it, resist it, appropriate it and tweak it in order to suit their own ends" (126).

In a democracy, Joseph continues, "the government has the responsibility to explain and justify its policies and actions, and it must use the media to do this" (133). The degree to which the government is "propagandizing" will always be debatable. Regardless, he says, the government will never have total influence. We need not worry, as long as "choices . . . are actually available to those in the population who *resist* the government's message" (134).

I agree with much of Joseph's (2006) critique of "propaganda anxiety." I reject the view that only "the masses" are susceptible to propaganda, whereas scholars are too enlightened to be taken in by it. In fact, I know I have been the victim of propaganda, believing (and sharing) some widely circulated manipulative claim, only to learn later that it was groundless. Furthermore, I reject that ordinary people are simply "pawns of the oligarchy," and I wholeheartedly agree that people may question, undermine, or otherwise recontextualize government discourse for their own ends.

However, I think Joseph (2006) underestimates how much propaganda can mislead people and prevent them from meaningful participation in democracy. Yes, in a democratic society, "there will always be a hard core of political opposition," as

Joseph observes (134).[1] Yet despite this resistance and the diversity of opinion in America, we have observed moments when huge segments of the population were misled into accepting demonstrably false ideas.

How is it that, before the Iraq War, large majorities of Americans came to believe that Iraq had weapons of mass destruction and Saddam Hussein had links to al-Qaeda? How is it that these majorities persisted in such belief, even after evidence had disproven the claims? When vast majorities retain false beliefs—against available evidence—we must look to propaganda as a key problem in democratic life. Furthermore, when Americans collectively agree on policies the rest of the world reject, we must also consider whether propaganda has resulted in a crisis of democracy. Again, how is it that, in the wake of the 9/11 attacks, Americans almost universally supported war against terrorism, when most of the rest of the world's population favored a policy of multilateral policing? Yes, many Americans wanted revenge, but they might have considered solutions other than bombing Afghanistan had U.S. media discourse abstained from "all-out war hysteria and militarism" (Kellner 2004a, 49).

Of course, people are not always so homogenized in their opinions, and over time, such uniformity does tend to dissolve, especially when (and if) democratic debate resumes. Eventually, most Americans came to reject the false justifications for war in Iraq, with most now coming to see that war as a mistake. And remarkably, Americans are now evenly split on whether it was a mistake to wage war in Afghanistan in 2001 (Newport 2014). But these significant changes in opinion coincided with changes in the media landscape. Support for war did not decrease until the prevailing propaganda was finally challenged by dissenting voices in the mainstream press. Before the fighting—arguably when it mattered most—war propaganda largely dominated the media, and American public opinion largely followed it. Again, none of this is to suggest that people are a mindless herd at the mercy of a scheming government. But when the public is more than once moved to accept war on false premises and with little meaningful debate, perhaps some "propaganda anxiety" is in order.

I also have problems with Joseph's (2006, 133) depiction of democratic society wherein the government must use the media to "explain and justify its policies and actions." It's not that I object to this depiction per se. Indeed, a democratic government should provide reasons for its policies. But it is not as if this is the government's only responsibility. It is not as if the government is just supposed to come up with policies and defend them against critics. A democratic government also has a responsibility to be responsive to the people—arguably, including the people in countries being attacked by that government. Indeed, people are supposed to be sovereign; the government is supposed to draft the polices that the people demand. If the people's only role is to visit the voting booth and occasionally opine about government decisions in polls, then it isn't much of a democracy. It's more like "managerial control" over the electorate (Wolin 2008, 189). A democracy requires informed debate, popular participation in decision-making, and, above all, a government that doesn't just sell its policies but responds to the hopes and needs of the governed.

American society appears very far from this ideal. Political life is hardly characterized by "shared power, civic involvement, and egalitarianism" (242). Instead, it is characterized by asymmetrical power, civic disengagement, and staggering inequality in social, political, and economic affairs. When the government is beholden to corporate wealth, occupied by the demands of empire, embroiled in nearly perpetual war, and increasingly untethered to its own constitution, then it is not enough to simply ask that it "explain and justify its policies." Instead, it is time to ask for change, to demand that the government alter its course and live up to its democratic promise.

As long as propaganda dominates public discourse, any project for social change is weakened, if not incapacitated. Again, the run-up to the Iraq War is a case in point. Before 2002, Americans were not clamoring for a confrontation with Saddam. But during the Bush administration's media campaign, war suddenly became an "issue" for the public. Over many months, mainstream debate was flooded with elite voices denouncing Iraq and advocating militarism. Still, as Joseph (2006) would predict, skeptical citizens resisted government claims and offered credible counterarguments. Indeed, many people opposed this war, protesting around the world. And yet, in the United States, protests and dissenting voices received little exposure, as channels of mass communication were still dominated by pro-war propaganda. The result, in my view, was an unjust invasion of a sovereign country, carried out with majority approval from the American people. Propaganda won, and popular debate was deliberately misdirected to serve the interests of power.

At times, Joseph (2006) seems to suggest that as long as people are free to dissent, propaganda is no cause for anxiety. After all, elites cannot control the entire population and never will. They cannot, as Sproule (1989, 236) memorably put it, "infuse their messages into a passive or irrational public." But, as the Iraq War demonstrates, propaganda can still work sufficiently well, such that discourses benefitting the powerful dominate, at least temporarily, while counterdiscourses are neutralized or suppressed. In the end, Joseph (2006, 134) is right to conclude that what matters are the "choices . . . available to those in the population who *resist*." But, realistically, what are those choices? What are the prospects for effective resistance in the age of propaganda?

Resisting Propaganda

For practitioners of critical discourse studies (CDS), resistance has typically taken the form of scholarship. CDS aims to intervene in social problems by analyzing language and other symbolic forms, thereby "demystifying" how discourse enacts and sustains unfair power arrangements. Most CDS scholars intervene on behalf of marginalized groups and see their academic inquiries as forms of social action that work against dominant discourses and an unfair status quo. In fact, CDS analyses continue a long tradition of what we might call anti-propaganda scholarship, dating back to the 1930s (Sproule 1989).

I am happy to be part of this tradition. I think scholars of rhetoric and discourse should examine propaganda, using techniques of language analysis to develop critical literacy (Oddo and Dunmire 2016). However, I think CDS practitioners need to recognize the limits of scholarly critique. Those suffering as a consequence of propaganda are probably not helped much by publications from well-intentioned academics. Indeed, those who are truly suffering probably never read this scholarship, while elite institutions, so often the target of CDS critique, likely couldn't care less. If CDS scholarship is an intervention against injustice, it is an intervention of a limited kind—one that reaches a narrow audience of like-minded researchers.

Ultimately, as Cunningham (2001, 140) writes, "It is not just enough to think about and analyze propaganda, to be aware of it, and to lament its ubiquity. Rather, we need to do something about it." Critical discourse analysis is one avenue of resistance, but in order to truly "do something about [propaganda]," other forms of resistance are needed. In fact, CDS might benefit from returning to its roots in ancient rhetoric, which, after all, was not primarily an analytic enterprise but a productive one. The old rhetorical educators aimed at helping people become decent citizens, teaching them to speak well in public democratic spaces, while always remaining "devoted to the welfare of [humanity] and our common good" (Isocrates 1992, 276–77).[2]

This seems to me to be a project for our time: we should not just analyze and criticize propaganda but design a civic rhetoric that is its opposite, one aimed at the welfare of the Many. In fact, this is what Sproule (1994, 339) recommends: a revitalization of the rhetorical tradition, a restoration of *eloquence*. Such eloquence "incapacitates propaganda," eroding "the power of unsupported conclusions by inculcating an appreciation for reasons" (340). Indeed, unlike propaganda with its base appeals to "hate or fear or self-assertion," eloquence is characterized by reasoned argument and impassioned commitment to "the highest values of the society" (343). One such value, especially in times of conflict, is peacemaking. Somehow, citizens need to embrace a rhetoric that transcends the "black and white tableau of them and us" and engage in "self-critical thought" (Hedges 2003, 10).

As Ivie argues, "Given that the strategy of war propaganda is to dehumanize adversaries so that they can be portrayed as utter enemies, . . . *tactics of resistance are most aptly focused on expressing the unity of humanity*" (2007, 107; emphasis in original). More specifically, Ivie recommends peacemaking dissent, which includes a "double gesture of nonconformity and solidarity." Such dissent involves a "sharp critical thrust against governing opinion or official policy" (109) but avoids "reverse recrimination that demonizes the nation at war and its leadership" (5). Citizens need to treat one another with political friendship and goodwill (170–71), while also acknowledging flawed institutions. At the same time, they must seek to apprehend the "enemy's" perspective and embrace an attitude of reconciliation (184–221).

As Galtung (1993, xi) has argued, the value of peacemaking could also be the foundation of journalism on international conflict. In his view, contemporary journalism often amounts to propaganda, displaying a "perverse fascination with war and violence," while ignoring the voices and activities of peacemakers. Thus, Galtung champions the project of peace journalism, which aims to tell the stories of those seeking nonviolent solutions to conflict. Lynch and Galtung (2010, 12–14) offer a useful comparison between war journalism and peace journalism:

- War journalism is "violence-oriented," focused on two parties in an allegedly winner-take-all battle, obsessed with physical effects of violence, and uninterested in background context (other than who threw the first stone). Meanwhile, peace journalism is "conflict-oriented," sensitive to the goals and issues of various parties, attentive to potential win-win solutions, aware of the invisible effects of violence, and keenly interested in the many background causes of conflict (historical, cultural, psychological, and so on).
- War journalism is "propaganda-oriented." It gives voice to our side of the conflict and ignores theirs; it sees them as the problem and us as the solution; it exposes their untruths while suppressing our lies. Peace journalism is "truth-oriented." It gives voice to all parties; humanizes all parties; and exposes untruths and cover-ups on all sides.
- War journalism is "elite-oriented," focused on diplomats and officials. Peace journalism is "people-oriented," focused on ordinary peacemakers and marginalized voices.
- War journalism is "victory-oriented." It regards peace as military victory plus a ceasefire; conceals peace initiatives; and ignores postwar conditions that lead to additional violence. Peace journalism is "solution-oriented." It regards peace as nonviolence plus creativity; highlights peace initiatives; and addresses reconstruction and reconciliation.

Perhaps if mainstream reporters embraced values of peace journalism, war propaganda would have little influence over public opinion and international violence might be reduced.

Another value that might incapacitate propaganda is what Rauch (1993, 65) calls liberal science, an epistemology defined by "the desire to find error, to find new beliefs which correct the inadequacies of old ones." As Cunningham (2001, 144) remarks, by embracing a "dialectic of open discussion," a community "filters out weak and unsupportable opinions, and confirms others as knowledge—subject always, of course, to later revision." Taking a feminist approach, Foss and Griffin (1995, 4) offer other values that might disable propaganda: "equality, immanent value, and self-determination." They suggest that traditional persuasion is aimed at changing and gaining control over others. While such persuasion is often necessary, they argue, it needs to be complemented with "invitational rhetoric," a "nonadversarial" framework of communication that values listening to other perspectives in order to achieve understanding, not to "win over" an opponent (5).

Taken together, these scholars endorse alternatives to manipulative discourse—alternatives that break free of us-them polarization; that answer fear-mongering and fallacy with evidence and reasoned argument; that replace elitism, coercion, and certitude with equality, dialogue, and skepticism. These proposals strike me as positive. And yet, on their own, they are insufficient. For they mainly seek to correct the discursive dimension of propaganda—Manichean logic, disregard for truth, willful manipulation—without addressing the asymmetrical power structures that enable such discourse to dominate.

A war critic might be as eloquent as Cicero, denouncing violence through reasoned argument and passionate appeals to humanism, empathy, and self-critique. But eloquence is meaningless if no one hears it. If civic rhetoric is not recontextualized on a mass scale, then it cannot compete with propaganda. The eloquent orator might as well be speaking from inside a dumpster. Of course, eloquent war critics might find greater audiences if mainstream reporters embraced values of peace journalism, giving those critics a chance to be heard. But the aims of peace journalism seem incompatible with the political economy of the corporate press. It is simply more economical to gather statements from nearby Washington officials, more profitable to provide entertaining news featuring violent "showdowns" between us and them. Similarly, an epistemology of liberal science cannot work on the unequal playing field of contemporary media. One cannot filter out weak and unsupportable claims, if one is barred from the mainstream debate. Finally, while invitational rhetoric has utility in certain contexts, it is less appropriate when a dominant power is exercising control over popular discourse (Lozano-Reich and Cloud 2009). War makers in the Pentagon are uninterested in open, nonadversarial dialogue with critics. Nor is such dialogue likely in traditional mass media. As Arthos (2013, 585) argues: "The relevance of invitational rhetoric or debate is attenuated the further the rhetorical situation moves away from the town square into the simulacrum of a mass mediated environment."

Goals and Tactics

Of course, we must envision the kinds of discourse that ought to replace propaganda: eloquent dissent, peace journalism, reasoned debate, dialogue. But such alternatives cannot incapacitate propaganda discourse as long as media control is concentrated in the hands of the Few. Ultimately, the success of any anti-propaganda project depends on "public ownership of the airwaves and encouragement of noncommercial broadcasting" (Wolin 2008, 292). One intriguing possibility is to give all adult citizens a $200 news voucher to spend on any nonprofit or noncommercial medium of their choice (McChesney and Nichols 2010). This would help democratize media and potentially allow alternative, nonpropagandistic news sources to compete on more equal footing with corporate behemoths.

However, public control over media is a long-term goal that remains remote in conditions of growing media monopoly. For now, those wishing to upend propaganda must work within existing constraints. As Arthos suggests, there is "potential for counter-hegemonic resistance," but such resistance will require "the cunning of instrumental and strategic communication" (2013, 588–89). First, citizens must have no illusions about the conditions they face: media consolidation and vast corporate control of news, and representative government that tolerates some public pressure but precludes direct democracy and collective self-rule (Ivie 2007, 101–5). In such conditions, "tactics are all that a people have at their disposal" (105). In other words, citizens must "locate cracks in the structure and exploit them, to find temporary points of entry where the social narrative can be altered or transformed" (Arthos 2013, 591).

Cracks do exist. Flawed as it is, the mainstream press publishes stories that challenge those in power. However, these stories are often scattered over time or relegated to the back pages. Citizens must work harder to find them. Meanwhile, alternative news sources are already available on the internet. Many websites feature voices and perspectives absent from mainstream debate, making them an invaluable resource. One tactic of dissent, according to Ivie (2007, 143), is "web watching," the practice of probing alternative media to find "humanizing metaphors" that can challenge the ritual vilifications of war propaganda.

However, to confront propaganda meaningfully, citizens must go beyond the critical consumption of media. They must also become producers of civic rhetoric. For instance, as Jensen (2001, 2016) suggests, citizens might place op-eds in mainstream newspapers and alternative websites. A well-placed editorial, he argues, can present a general audience with marginalized viewpoints, while commentary in alternative platforms can help those who share a political philosophy sharpen their arguments (2016, 269).

Such measures may be inadequate, however, since they are unlikely to sustain public attention and make a lasting impact. Ultimately, those who wish to incapacitate propaganda must think about how to reproduce one of its qualities: inducing the continual recontextualization of favored meanings. But they must do so *without* reproducing propaganda's negative qualities: egregious manipulation (demonizing the "other," deliberate lies) and the promotion of an inegalitarian society. In other words, citizens must compete with propaganda—circulating messages as widely as possible—but in ways that are ethical.

Arthos (2013, 597) suggests how one can balance strategy and ethics when trying to circulate "effective counter-narratives." He argues that, when possible, counter-hegemonic rhetoric should follow norms of "humane and dialogic communication." But the realities of "intractable hegemony" and "institutional violence" require that the disempowered also experiment with unorthodox, provocative forms of communication (596). For example, citizens may employ "guerilla tactics" to induce mass-recontextualization in the media: "whisper campaigns, viral videos, sensationalized PR stunts, [and] confrontations with the majority party leaders" (593). Or they may design grassroots movements that transcend "ritualized conventions of protest" (595), using strategies that are "directly confrontational and interruptive" (594). In fact, some suggest that, given asymmetrical power arrangements, we may need "uncivil" techniques (Lozano-Reich and Cloud 2009) or "reasonable hostility" (Tracy 2010). For ordinary people, nonviolent direct action may be the best rhetorical resource available.

The key question is how to generate a grassroots movement that produces good narratives. By "good narratives," I mean not only prosocial narratives but narratives with prepared-for detachability, narratives that are recontextualizable on a mass scale. Perhaps educators could work on developing such narratives throughout higher education. Universities could promote propaganda courses in programs for journalism, law, political science, peace studies, and rhetoric.[3] Again, the goal of such courses should not simply be raising awareness of propaganda but educating people on how to *replace it* with better alternatives.

Despite such opportunities, there are reasons for pessimism. Many citizens are preoccupied with work and survival. They don't have time to stay informed, let alone participate in protests. Also, "people are flooded with a pacifying array of amusements" (Jensen 2016, 269). They confront what Huckin (2016, 132–33) dubs the propaganda of distraction: the constant barrage of advertising and entertainment that diverts attention from social ills and prevents meaningful political involvement. I think this problem can be overstated, since people surely deserve some amusement and diversion. But I agree that people must also make space for democratic deliberation, taking seriously the responsibilities of citizenship.

Ultimately, a grassroots movement needs to grow into something bigger and more sustainable: a culture in which civic rhetoric and social democracy flourish, a culture in which the discourse of peacemaking supersedes the reigning doctrine of war. There are no simple ways to bring about such change. War propaganda, especially, shows few signs of relenting, as both elite leaders and ordinary people find solace in the seductive messages of fear and hate. Indeed, as Ivie (2007, 9) notes, "Making war difficult is never easy." Still we must try. In an age of perpetual war and propaganda, resistance is the only moral choice.

Appendix A: Studying Discourse in Context

Discourse generally refers to situated text and talk—language in use. I view discourse from a systemic-functional (SF) perspective (Halliday and Matthiessen 2004), which holds that language is not a system of rules but a resource for making meaning. That is, people select among the resources in their linguistic repertoires in order to interact with others, define situations, and achieve goals. Language, though, is just one path of communication; people also use images, gestures, proxemics, and the like. Thus, I take a multimodal view of discourse (Kress and Van Leeuwen 2001, 2006) and try to see how various signs contextualize one another.

I assume that living discourse does not have natural boundaries. Instead, people ascribe boundaries to texts through "entextualization processes" (Silverstein and Urban 1996, 4). For example, when we label something a "conversation," we entextualize discourse by selecting and circumscribing portions of talk from what is in reality an unending flow (Johnstone 2008, 20–21). The notion that language is in a "ceaseless flow of becoming" (Volosinov 1973, 66) is very important to this book, for it "invites us to look beyond the [imagined] boundaries of particular communicative events" and observe how such events are related to others in a larger stream of text and talk (Blommaert 2005, 46–47). Put another way, it invites us to see discourse as intertextual, flowing across and between texts in an endless dialogue.

According to this view, people constantly borrow from the past when they form utterances in the present (Bakhtin 1981, 1986). That is, people constantly recontextualize discourse, extracting elements from prior texts only to relocate and refashion those elements in new contexts (Linell 1998). At the same time, people understand their own discourse is subject to future recontextualization; they anticipate how their own texts may be detached, reused, and reinterpreted by others (Bauman and Briggs 1990; Urban 1996).

To study propaganda intertextually, I use methods of discourse analysis (DA), many of which are outlined in Oddo (2013) and described in other appendixes. Broadly, DA examines structures and functions of language, alongside other kinds of signs (Baldry and Thibault 2005; Johnstone 2008; Blommaert 2005; Kress and Van Leeuwen 2006). A discourse analysis, however, is more than a systematic analysis of text; it is also a study of context.

Context and discourse are interrelated. Context shapes discourse, informing how people produce and interpret language.[1] And discourse, in turn, shapes context, helping define reality and social identities.[2] With this in mind, DA practitioners seek to place discourse in both its local contexts and its broader cultural, historical, and intertextual contexts (Halliday 1985; Kress 1995). To establish an intertextual context, one can examine empirically how language users have borrowed from prior discourse, recycling available meanings (Blommaert 2005, 46). In addition, one can usually discern the cultural and historical factors relevant to discourse participants. Sometimes speakers directly refer to events influencing their discourse. In other cases, researchers make educated guesses about the circumstances affecting someone's speech.

However, a description of context cannot be limited to a speaker's (likely) understanding of circumstances. In fact, what we call "context" is open to debate, since different people interpret circumstances in different ways. Granted, language users can be said to share a culture and history. For example, most people living in the United States identify themselves as "American" and associate this identity with norms and traditions (everything from democratic elections to Super Bowl parties), as well a shared history of important events (e.g., the 9/11 attacks). Of course, large numbers of people can acquire such "common sense" views of identity, culture, and history only if they are socialized in more or less standard ways. For example, every American is made to perform the Pledge of Allegiance in school, expressly asserting loyalty to the United States. And there are countless other institutional mechanisms whereby masses of people are socialized in relatively similar ways (e.g., public education, consumption of mass media).

Thus, some forces seek to centralize and unify society, but other forces work to fracture it. Indeed, dominant norms of society are constantly threatened by the realities of difference (Bakhtin 1981, 1984, 1986; Fairclough 2003; Kress 1995). Everyone has a different social history and a different social status. This is because each of us occupies a different position in the social system, a position structured by factors such as geography, age, class, race, and gender. As a result, we use and experience language differently, often ascribing different meanings to the same events. Such differences in meaning are important, as they indicate that there is no one stable object we can call "the context." Instead, there are competing representations of context—different views of the world, including both the immediate situation and broader sociopolitical and historical events.

The fact that we are socially different—positioned differently within a social system— also means we have different capacities to intervene in history. We are not all equal in terms of our access to resources and our power to influence outcomes. For example, the president has enormous power to both legitimize and initiate war. He has access to channels of mass communication (a "bully pulpit"), and he can count on the press to publicize his call-to-arms messages. He has educated speechwriters, staffers, and, indeed, whole government agencies at his disposal. And as commander in chief, he can mobilize the military and launch wars. By comparison, peace activists have far less power—no bully pulpit, no speechwriters and intelligence agencies, and no constitutional authority to deploy (or withhold) military force.

In this book, I try to account for such asymmetries of power and explain how these asymmetries influence the circulation and perceived legitimacy of discourse. I assume that all speakers and writers have political and ideological interests that generally coincide with their positions in society. Speakers not only create texts that privilege their own views of reality but may also seek to suppress or deny the existence of other views of reality. Deliberate propagandists, especially, are likely to present their own representation of "the context" as self-evident and universally agreed upon, when, in fact, other representations of reality exist and may even be more valid (Kress 1995; Fairclough 2003).

Among other things, a critical discourse analysis should examine how propagandists use language and other symbolic forms to (1) valorize their own views of reality, (2) suppress competing views, and (3) promote unfair social practices. At the same time, analysts recognize that texts are also "sites of contestation and struggle" (Dunmire 2011, 18) and that even propaganda includes traces of other voices and alternative viewpoints (Fairclough 1995, 2003). Insofar as critical discourse analysts expose these alternative voices and meanings, they potentially undermine the power of propaganda and expand the range of democratic debate.

Appendix B: Factors Facilitating Detachability and Recontextualization

Table B.1

Features making recontextualization more likely		Example
Textual Design Factors		
Audiovisual	Visual salience Audio salience	Boldfaced headlines at the top of a page are detachable and recontextualizable
Stylistic	Brevity Poetic devices / figuration Intense lexis Local repetition Reported speech Metadiscursive cues Rhetorical presence	Poetic devices like parallelism are marked as distinct and detachable.
Performative	Shifts in pitch / intonation / timbre Marked elongation, deceleration, pausing Emphatic gestures Emotional shifts	An emotional shift toward "sadness" calls attention to itself, marking the emotive discourse as distinct and detachable.
Generic shift	Shifts in genre Embedded genre	A personal narrative embedded in an argument on climate change stands out as detachable from its discursive surround.
Desirable content (in mainstream journalism)	Negativity / threat / scandal Drama Officialdom Immediacy	Discourse about a president's extramarital affair is "sharable" in the press because it indexes scandal.
"Common sense"	Myths Clichés Master narratives Orthodoxy	"Collective presuppositions" are virtually always recontextualizable (Huckin 2016, 130). Examples include terms like "democracy," as well as sayings like "creating good-paying jobs" and "winning the war on terror."
Contextual Factors		
Legitimacy of speaker	Speaker prestige Cues of authority	Signals of celebrity, political power, intellectual status, etc.

Table B.1 (continued)

Features making recontextualization more likely		Example
	Contextual Factors	
Access to and fluency in genres aimed at recontextualization and publication	Talking points Press releases Press conferences Video news releases Interviews Book proposals Op-ed submissions	Press releases are designed to be repeated in news reports. Thus, participating fluently in the genre of the press release facilitates recontextualization.
Access to technologies allowing for reproduction	TV / radio station Industrial press Internet Industrial clothing manufacture Personal printer Social media account	Owners of a printing press can mass-recontextualize a message and increase chances of favorable uptake.
Power to provide (dis)incentives	Financial incentives Access to the inner circle Flak for going "off message"	If paid in advance, PR firms typically recontextualize one's message.

Appendix C: Data and Methods for Intertextual Analysis of the Incubator Story

I examined accounts of the incubator story that appeared between August 2, 1990 (the day of the Iraqi invasion of Kuwait) and January 17, 1991 (the start of aerial bombing in Operation Desert Storm). The following materials were analyzed:

Transcripts from the public papers of President George H. W. Bush	• Searched for appearances of the incubator story, finding eight addresses.
	• Analyzed video of the president's October 9, 1990, news conference via the C-SPAN archive and video of his October 23, 1990, speech in Burlington, Vermont.
American news sources	• Searched LexisNexis for "incubator" and "Iraq" in newspapers, wire services, news magazines, television, and radio news sources. Search limited to "hard news" stories; irrelevant articles were discarded.
	• Newspaper, wire, and magazine sources: *New York Times*, *Washington Post*, *Washington Times*, *USA Today*, *Los Angeles Times*, Associated Press, United Press International, *Newsweek*, and *U.S. News and World Report*.
	• Television and radio news sources: *NBC Nightly News*, *CBS Evening News*, *ABC World News Tonight*, PBS, *The MacNeil/Lehrer NewsHour*, CNN (*Larry King Live*), National Public Radio. Video broadcasts obtained from the Vanderbilt Television News Archive. NPR transcripts obtained from the NewsBank database.
Congressional records	• Analyzed transcript and video (from the C-SPAN archive) of the Congressional Human Rights Caucus (October 10, 1990). Using the ProQuest database, examined transcripts of congressional sessions that included "incubator" and "Iraq."
United Nations records	• Analyzed copies of letters written to the U.N. Secretary-General about the Iraqi occupation, dated September 2, and September 5, 1990.
	• Analyzed transcript and video (from the C-SPAN archive) of the U.N. Security Council session of November 27, 1990.

Other documents	• Analyzed the December 19, 1990 Amnesty International report on human rights violations in Kuwait.
	• Examined *The Rape of Kuwait* (Sasson 1991).
	• Obtained data from CBC's *To Sell a War* (Docherty 1992), including images of video news releases.

Methods

For each account of the incubator story, I analyzed lexicogrammar (Halliday and Matthiessen 2004) and, where applicable, narrative form and function (Labov 1972). I focused on represented participants, processes, and nominalizations, as well as evaluative vocabulary (Martin and White 2005; Van Leeuwen 2008). I also examined whether and how the story was attributed to sources, noting the reporting verbs and speech act nouns used in attributional phrases.

Texts were analyzed multimodally (Kress and Van Leeuwen 2006). To analyze videos, I adapted Baldry and Thibault's (2005) transcription framework and supplemented their techniques with tools from ELAN (Wittenburg et al. 2006). I also drew on Hepburn's (2004) work to transcribe crying, and Kipp, Neff and Albrecht's (2007) scheme for annotating conversational gestures.

Appendix D: Transcript of Nayirah's Performance at the HRC

Audio Transcription Conventions

Symbol	Description
die on the ↑ cold ↑floor	Upward arrow indicates sharply increased pitch.
we <u>shall</u> repeat it again	Underlined text indicates extra prominent vocal emphasis.
°floor°	Degree signs mark noticeably quieter speech.
(2.1)	Numbers in parentheses measure pauses in seconds and tenths of seconds. Pauses between lines were only measured if they lasted one second or more.
again we (.) ask	Period in parentheses represents micropause.
[*gulp*]	Additional notes are italicized and placed in parentheses.
comma,	Comma marks continuation, i.e., the speaker is not done.
full stop.	Period indicates stopped intonation.
Th- the second week	Hyphens mark a cutoff of the preceding sound.
(hhh)	Aspiration (out-breaths); the more letters, the longer the aspiration.
(.hhh)	Inspiration (in-breaths); proportionally, as above.
(.HIH)	Capital H's in parentheses represent sobs; a period before indicates inhaled sob.
(.shih)	Wet sniff.
~~I am glad I am fifteen~~	Words enclosed by tildes indicate wobbly voice; the more tildes, the more wobbly.
[cameras clicking]	Words in brackets describe other ambient sounds.

Transcript of Nayirah's Performance with Introduction by Tom Porter

REP. PORTER:

1. Our final witness is also using an assumed name
2. and again we (.) ask uh our friends in the media to resp<u>ec</u>t
3. the need to- for her to protect her <u>fam</u>ily.
4. (1.1)
5. And we finally call on Nayirah to testify.
6. (2.9)

NAYIRAH:

7. Mister Chairman and members of the committee
8. my name is Nayirah
9. and I just came out of Kuwait.
10. (6.7) [*adjusts microphone*]
11. My mother and I were in Kuwait on August second for a peaceful summer holiday.
12. (1.2)
13. My older sister had a baby on July twenty-ninth.
14. And we wanted to spend some time in ~Kuwait with her~.
15. (1.9)
16. I only pray that none of my tenth-grade classmates had a summer vacation ~like I did~.
17. (2.7)
18. ~I may have wished sometime that I could be an~~adult~~
19. (1.5)
20. ~~that I could grow up quickly~~.
21. (2.6)
22. (.hhh) ~What I saw happening to the children of Kuwait
23. and to my country has changed my life forever~.
24. (1.1)
25. ~has changed the life of (.) all Kuwaitis (.) young and old~.
26. (1.1)
27. ~~We are <u>chil</u>dren no more~~.
28. (3.5)
29. (.hh) ~~My sister with my five-day old nephew~~(.hh)
30. ~~traveled across the desert to safet- safety.~~
31. (1.3)
32. ~~There is no milk available for the (.) baby in Kuwait~~.
33. (2.6)
34. ~~They barely escaped when their car was stuck in the desert~~
35. desert <u>sand</u> and help came from ~Saudi Arabia~.
36. (2.0)
37. (.hh) ~I stayed behind and wanted to do something for my country~
38. (1.9)
39. ~~Th- the second week after invasion~~
40. ~~I volunteeled- volunteered at the al-'Addan Hospital~~

41. ~with 12 other women~
42. ~who wanted to help as well~.
43. (.shih) ~I was the youngest volunteer~.
44. ~The other women were (.) from twenty to thirty years old~.
45. (1.3)
46. ~While I was there I saw the Iraqi soldiers~ ~~c- come into the hospital with guns.~~
47. (1.0)
48. ~~~They took the babies out of the incubators~~~.
49. (3.4 *between words*) (2.6 *before her wet sniff*)
50. (.shih) ~~~took the incubators and left the children to die on the ↑°cold° ↑°floor°~~~
51. (4.0 *between words*) (2.5 *before her wet sniffs*)
52. (.shih)(.shih) [*gulp*] ~~It was horrifying~~. (.HIH)
53. ~~I could not help but think of my nephew~~ (.shih)
54. ~~who if born premature might have died that day as well~~ (.shih)(.shih)
55. (1.2)
56. (hh.) ~After I left the hospital~ (.shih)
57. ~some of my friends and I distributed flyers condemning the Iraqi invasion~
58. (.shih)~~until we were warned we might be killed if (*gulp*) the Iraqis saw us~~,
59. ~~if the Iraqis saw us~~. (.) (.shih)
60. ~The Iraqis have destroyed everything in Kuwait~. (.shih)
61. ~Th- they stripped the supermarkets of food~,
62. ~the pharmacies of medicine~,
63. ~the factories of medical suprise (.) supplies~,
64. ~~ransacked their houses and tortured neighbors and friends~~. (.shih)
65. [*swallow*] ~I saw and talked to a friend of mine after his torture and release by the Iraqis~.
66. (.shih) (.) ~He is twenty-two ~~but he looked as though he could have been an old man~~.
67. ~~The Iraqis dunked his head into a swimming pool until he almost drowned~~.
68. ~~They pulled out his fingernails and applied electric shocks to s- sensitive private parts of his body~~.
69. [*gulp*]
70. ~He was lucky to survive~.
71. (1.1)
72. (hhh) ~If an Iraqi soldier is found dead in a neighborhood~
73. ~they burn to the ground all the houses in in the general vicinity~,
74. ~and would not let firefighters come ~~until th-~
75. ~until the (.8) only ash and rubble was left~.
76. (.shih) ~The Iraqis were making fun of President Bush and ~~verbally and physically abusing
77. my family and me~~ (.) on our way out of Kuwait~.
78. (.shih) ~~We only did so because life in Kuwait became unbearable~~.(.shih)
79. (1.2)
80. (hhh) ~They have forced us to hide (.) burn or des- destroy any- everything identifying (.shih)

81. our country and our government~.

82. (.shih)~I want to emphasize that Kuwait is our mother and the Emir our father~.

83. ~~We repeated- we repeated this on the roofs of our houses in Kuwait~~

84. ~~until the Iraqis began shooting at us~~.

85. ~~~and we <u>shall</u> repeat it again~~~.

86. (1.0)

87. ~~~I am glad I am fifteen~~~

88. ~~~old enough to remember Kuwait before Saddam Hussein destroyed it~~~

89. ~~~and young enough to rebuild it~~~.

9 o. ~~~Thank °you°~~~. (.shih)

91. (1.6)

92. (.H)

Appendix E: Generic Components of George H. W. Bush's Incubator Allegations

Table E.1

Speech	Attribution	Recitation of atrocities (incubator atrocity in **bold**)	Moral judgment / emotional distress	Suggestion military action is imminent
1990b, October 9	written on by Amnesty International; the tales told us by the Emir; he [the Emir] reflected; tales	People on a dialysis machine cut off, the machine sent to Baghdad; **babies in incubators heaved out of the incubators and the incubators themselves sent to Baghdad.**	very much concerned; brutality; unbelievable; sickening; concerns us enormously;	my patience is wearing very thin [on the sanctions]
1990c, October 15	I met with the Emir of Kuwait. And I heard horrible tales	**Newborn babies thrown out of incubators and the incubators then shipped off to Baghdad.** Dialysis patients ripped from their machines, and those machines then, too, sent off to Baghdad. The story of two young kids passing out leaflets: Iraqi troops rounded up their parents and made them watch while those two kids were shot to death—executed before their eyes.	horrible; Hitler revisited.	But remember, when Hitler's war ended, there were the Nuremberg trials. America will not stand aside. The world will not allow the strong to swallow up the weak.
1990d, October 16	let me just mention some reports, firsthand reports; reportedly	**At a hospital, Iraqi soldiers unplugged the oxygen to incubators supporting 22 premature babies. They all died. And then they shot the hospital employees.** At another hospital, troops reportedly cut off oxygen supporting the 75-year-old mother of a Kuwaiti Cabinet Minister. Iraqi naked aggression. Iraqi naked aggression—taking dialysis machines, taking the patients off them, shipping the machines to Baghdad—systematically dismantling a member of the United Nations, a member of the Arab League.	don't mean to be overly shocking; Iraqi aggression. Iraqi naked aggression; systematically dismantling.	And so, the bottom line for us is that Iraqi aggression will not be allowed to stand. Saddam Hussein will be held accountable. And the legitimate government of Kuwait will be restored.
1990e, October 23	Two young kids, mid-teens, passing out leaflets—Iraqi soldiers came, got their parents out and watched as they killed them. They had people on dialysis machines, and they ripped them off of the machines and sent the dialysis machines to Baghdad. **And they had kids in incubators, and they were thrown out of the incubators so that Kuwait could be systematically dismantled.**	And there's a parallel between what Hitler did to Poland and what Saddam Hussein has done to Kuwait . . . ; systematically dismantled; concerned; aggression.	So, it isn't oil that we're concerned about. It is aggression. And this aggression is not going to stand.

(continued)

Table E.1 (continued)

1990f, October 23		. . . the other day in Kuwait, two young kids were passing out leaflets in opposition. They were taken, their families made to watch, and they were shot to death—15- and 16-year-old. Older people on dialysis machines taken off the machines, and the machines shipped to Baghdad. **Kids in incubators thrown out so that the machinery, the incubators themselves, could be shipped to Baghdad.**	Just as it happened in the past [with Hitler]; Hitler revisited; totalitarianism; brutality; brutal	And that must not stand. We cannot talk about compromise when you have that kind of behavior going on this very minute; this must not stand.
1990g, October 28		In one hospital, dialysis patients were ripped from their machines and the machines shipped from Kuwait to Baghdad. **Iraq soldiers pulled the plug on incubators supporting 22 premature babies. All 22 died. The hospital employees were shot and the plundered machines were shipped off to Baghdad.**	evil; wrong; shocking new horrors; reign of terror; without provocation; without excuse.	But you cannot pull the plug on a nation. The invasion of Kuwait was without provocation. The invasion of Kuwait was without excuse. And the invasion of Kuwait will not stand.
1990h, November 1		Iraq began to brutally and systematically dismantle Kuwait, shipping its medical equipment, its machines, its records, its assets all back to Baghdad; taking machines out of the factories and machinery out of the hospitals, sending it back to Baghdad. They've tried to silence Kuwaiti dissent and courage with firing squads, much as Hitler did when he invaded Poland. They have committed outrageous acts of barbarism. **In one hospital, they pulled 22 premature babies from their incubators, sent the machines back to Baghdad, and all those little ones died.**	brutally and systematically dismantle; much as Hitler did; outrageous acts of barbarism;	The United States and the rest of the world, united in anger and outrage, determined to force Saddam Hussein out of Kuwait . . . And today I am more determined than ever in my life: This aggression will not and must not stand.
1990i, November 22	It turns your stomach when you listen to the <u>tales of those that escaped the brutality of Saddam, the invader.</u>	Mass hangings. **Babies pulled from incubators and scattered like firewood across the floor.** Kids shot for failing to display the photos of Saddam Hussein. And he has unleashed a horror on the people of Kuwait.	atrocities; would make the strongest among us weep; turns your stomach; brutality; Saddam, the invader; horror	Three simple reasons: protecting freedom, protecting our future, protecting innocent lives. And any one is reason enough why Iraq's unprincipled, unprovoked aggression must not go unchallenged. Together they make a compelling case for you to be away from your families on this special Thanksgiving Day. They make a compelling case for your mission.

Appendix F: Featured News Analysts and News Broadcasts

Table F.1 shows weapons and military analysts, citing how often they were featured on the news before the war. I briefly describe each analyst's "real world" experience as of 2002, the experience that networks were likely to highlight.

Table F.1

No.	Analyst name	Abbrev.	"Real world" experience	Appearances
1.	David Kay (weapons)	DK	In 1991, following the Gulf War, Kay served as the U.N.'s chief nuclear weapons inspector in Iraq. He exposed documents on Iraq's nuclear weapons program and famously spent days in a Baghdad parking lot as a hostage of the Iraqi government. Kay was also senior fellow at the Potomac Institute for Policy Studies, an Arlington-based think tank.	33
2.	Richard Butler (weapons)	RB	Butler served diplomatic roles for the Australian government. In 1983, he was appointed Australia's permanent representative on disarmament to the United Nations. From 1992 to 1997, he served as Australian ambassador to the United Nations. From 1997 to 1999, he was executive chairman of the United Nations Special Commission (UNSCOM), charged with disarming Iraq.	14
3.	David Albright (weapons)	DA	A physicist, Albright founded the Institute for Science and International Security. From 1992 to 1997, he served on the International Atomic Energy Agency action team. In 1996, he was a nuclear weapons inspector in Iraq.	10
4.	Charles Duelfer (weapons)	CD	From 1993 to 2000, Duelfer was deputy executive chairman and later acting chairman of UNSCOM. Before this, Duelfer held positions in the U.S. government, especially the State Department under Reagan and George H. W. Bush.	8
5.	Gary Milhollin (weapons)	GM	Milhollin founded the Wisconsin Project on Nuclear Arms Control. He earned a mechanical engineering degree and a JD from Georgetown University.	5
6.	Khidir Hamza (weapons)	KH	Until 1990, Hamza was a scientist in Iraq's nuclear weapons program. He defected to the United States in 1994.	4
7.	Kelly Motz (weapons)	KM	Motz edited *Iraq Watch*, a website devoted to assessing Iraq's WMD capabilities, published by the Wisconsin Project on Nuclear Arms Control.	4
8.	Tim McCarthy (weapons)	TM	McCarthy was an UNSCOM inspector in Iraq from 1994 to 1998. He was also senior analyst at the Monterey Institute for Nonproliferation Studies.	4

Table F.1 (continued)

No.	Analyst name	Abbrev.	"Real world" experience	Appearances
9.	Jonathan Tucker (weapons)	JT	In the early 1990s, Tucker worked on arms control and nonproliferation for the State Department. In 1995, he was a weapons inspector in Iraq and was later a research fellow at the Monterey Institute for Nonproliferation Studies. He earned a degree in biology and a doctorate in nonproliferation studies.	2
10.	Richard Spertzel (weapons)	RS	Spertzel, who had degrees in microbiology, had worked for the U.S. Army Medical Research Institute of Infectious Diseases. He also worked for UNSCOM in the 1990s as senior biologist in Iraq.	2
11.	Scott Ritter (weapons)	SR	After serving in the military, Ritter worked as an intelligence officer for the U.S. Marine Corps. From 1991 to 1998, he worked for UNSCOM in Iraq.	1
12.	Chris Cobb-Smith (weapons)	CCS	After serving in the British military, Cobb-Smith worked for UNSCOM in Iraq.	1
13.	Barry McCaffrey (military)	BM	McCaffrey was a decorated general in the U.S. Army. After many combat tours, he received honors, including three Purple Hearts and two Silver Stars. In the first Gulf War, he commanded the Twenty-Fourth Infantry Division.	12
14.	Wayne Downing (military)	WD	Downing was a general in the U.S. Army, highly decorated for service in many combat tours. He was commanding general of U.S. Special Operations forces and worked for the George W. Bush administration as deputy national security advisor for combating terrorism.	5
15.	George Joulwan (military)	GJ	Joulwan was a highly decorated general with the U.S. Army. In the 1990s, he served as supreme allied commander of NATO forces.	4
16.	Montgomery Meigs (military)	MM	Meigs was commanding general of the U.S. Army Europe in the 1990s and early 2000s.	4
17.	Jack Jacobs (military)	JJ	A colonel in the U.S. Army, Jacobs received the Medal of Honor for service in Vietnam.	4
18.	Ken Allard (military)	KA	Allard, a U.S. Army colonel specializing in operational intelligence, had degrees in international relations and public administration.	4
19.	William Nash (military)	WN	Nash, a major general in the U.S. Army, served in Vietnam, the Gulf War, and Bosnia.	2
20.	Buster Glosson (military)	BG	Glosson was a lieutenant general in the U.S. Air Force. He commanded the Fourteenth Air Division in the first Gulf War.	1
21.	Rick Francona (military)	RF	Francona was a lieutenant colonel in the U.S. Air Force specializing in Middle East intelligence. He served with the National Security Agency, the Defense Intelligence Agency, and the Central Intelligence Agency.	1
22.	Bernard Trainor (military)	BT	Trainor was a lieutenant general in the U.S. Marine Corps. He served in Vietnam and Korea, earning a number of awards.	1
Total weapons				88
Total military				38
Grand total				126

Table F.2 shows the news broadcasts in which weapons and military analysts appeared. Weapons analysts appeared most often during the fall and winter of 2002, as the administration began campaigning for war. However, around mid-February 2003, weapons specialists appeared less frequently, perhaps reflecting newsroom thinking that the case about Iraq's weapons had been decided. Military analysts, meanwhile, appeared more often as war drew closer. In fact, nearly 80 percent of their appearances occurred after December 8, 2002, as war preparations intensified. By March 2003, with war looming, military analysts appeared almost daily.

Table F.2

No.	Date	Analysts	Network
1.	10/10/2001	BM	NBC
2.	10/26/2001	RS	ABC
3.	03/07/2002	DA	NBC
4.	04/22/2002	KM	NBC
5.	04/24/2002	CD	NBC
6.	04/29/2002	CD	CBS
7.	05/09/2002	CD	NBC
8.	07/16/2002	CD	NBC
9.	09/04/2002	GM	ABC
10.	09/09/2002	CD, DK, KM	NBC
11.	09/13/2002	RB	CBS
12.	09/17/2002	RB, DK, DA, KM	NBC
13.	09/17/2002	CD, GM	CBS
14.	09/24/2002	GM, DA	NBC
15.	09/27/2002	KA, BM	NBC
16.	09/29/2002	CCS	NBC
17.	10/03/2002	CD	ABC
18.	10/14/2002	DK, KM	NBC
19.	10/15/2002	KH	NBC
20.	10/16/2002	BM	NBC
21.	10/17/2002	GM	CBS
22.	10/22/2002	DK	NBC
23.	10/28/2002	DK	NBC
24.	10/29/2002	WN	ABC

Table F.2 (continued)

No.	Date	Analysts	Network
25.	11/08/2002	DA	NBC
26.	11/09/2002	JJ	NBC
27.	11/10/2002	RB	ABC
28.	11/11/2002	DA	CBS
29.	11/11/2002	DK	NBC
30.	11/12/2002	CD	CBS
31.	11/14/2002	DA	CBS
32.	11/14/2002	DK	NBC
33.	11/17/2002	DK	NBC
34.	11/18/2002	DK	NBC
35.	11/22/2002	DA	NBC
36.	11/25/2002	DK	NBC
37.	11/25/2002	SR, RS	CBS
38.	11/25/2002	DA	ABC
39.	11/27/2002	DK	NBC
40.	11/30/2002	DK, BM	NBC
41.	12/03/2002	DK	NBC
42.	12/04/2002	JT	NBC
43.	12/06/2002	DK	CBS
44.	12/06/2002	KH	NBC
45.	12/07/2002	DK	NBC
46.	12/08/2002	DK	NBC
47.	12/09/2002	DA, DK	NBC
48.	12/09/2002	TM	ABC
49.	12/10/2002	GJ	ABC
50.	12/16/2002	WD, DK	NBC
51.	12/21/2002	DK	NBC
52.	12/22/2002	WD, DK	NBC
53.	12/23/2002	GJ	ABC
54.	12/24/2002	DA, KH	ABC
55.	12/27/2002	JJ	NBC
56.	12/28/2002	DK	NBC
57.	01/03/2003	WN	NBC

Table F.2

No.	Date	Analysts	Network
58.	01/03/2003	TM	CBS
59.	01/04/2003	DK	NBC
60.	01/06/2003	TM	CBS
61.	01/06/2003	DK	NBC
62.	01/08/2003	DK	NBC
63.	01/09/2003	BM	NBC
64.	01/11/2003	BT	NBC
65.	01/13/2003	BM	NBC
66.	01/14/2003	RB	NBC
67.	01/16/2003	RB, KH, DK	NBC
68.	01/16/2003	GM	ABC
69.	01/18/2003	RB	NBC
70.	01/20/2003	RB	NBC
71.	01/21/2003	BM	NBC
72.	01/23/2003	GJ	ABC
73.	01/23/2003	RB	NBC
74.	01/25/2003	DK	NBC
75.	01/26/2003	DK	NBC
76.	01/27/2003	RB	NBC
77.	02/03/2003	DK	NBC
78.	02/05/2003a	RB, DK, BM	NBC
79.	02/05/2003b	RB	NBC
80.	02/05/2003	JT	ABC
81.	02/08/2003	JJ, DK, JJ	NBC
82.	02/09/2003	RB	NBC
83.	02/10/2003	KA	NBC
84.	02/10/2003	GJ	ABC
85.	02/12/2003	MM	NBC
86.	02/13/2003	RB	NBC
87.	02/15/2003	MM	NBC
88.	02/26/2003	TM	CBS
89.	02/28/2003	DK	NBC
90.	03/01/2003	MM	NBC

Table F.2 (continued)

No.	Date	Analysts	Network
91.	03/02/2003	BM	NBC
92.	03/03/2003	DK, BM	NBC
93.	03/06/2003	WD, RB, WD	NBC
94.	03/08/2003	BM	NBC
95.	03/12/2003	KA	NBC
96.	03/12/2003	BG	CBS
97.	03/13/2003	RF	NBC
98.	03/17/2003	BM	NBC
99.	03/17/2003	WD	NBC
100.	03/18/2003	DK, KA	NBC
101.	03/19/2003	MM	NBC

Appendix G: Incentives for Recontextualizing Pro-war and Pro-government Claims

Table G.1

Analyst	Political commitments and undisclosed government affiliations	Financial conflicts of interest
David Kay	Kay told me he attended government meetings prompted by Paul Wolfowitz (then deputy secretary of defense) and organized by the National Defense University. According to Kay, these meetings intensified in the three months prior to war in Iraq and included former inspectors, think tank analysts, government officials, and military officers. The main purpose was to prepare U.S. Central Command to deal with Iraq's presumed weapons programs after a U.S.-led invasion, but meetings also summarized intelligence on Iraq's WMD. Apparently, Kay was privy to government documents and slideshows that both established the U.S. case for war and projected postinvasion contingencies. According to a January 2003 State Department memo, the U.S. government recruited Kay to go on Egyptian Television (ETV) and promote U.S. talking points about the need to confront Iraq. According to the memo, Kay was one of several "U.S. interlocutors" who participated as a guest in ETV programs. The memo observes that, in these programs, "the U.S. point of view is always put forth." In 2002, Kay supported the reelection campaign of Republican congressman Todd Akin. Kay reportedly spoke to Akin's constituents about the "urgent threat" from Iraq and made a supportive appearance in Saint Louis, using campaign funds to pay for his trip (Quaid 2002; Wittenauer 2002).	From 1993 to October 2002, Kay held shares and worked in senior positions at Science Applications International Corporation (SAIC), an intelligence and defense corporation that secured major contracts in Iraq (Barlett and Steele 2007). Kay told me he was offended by accusations that his role at SAIC had conflicted with his role as a news contributor. He says that before he was contracted to work for NBC, he resigned from SAIC and sold all his company stocks—specifically because he did not want to be perceived as having a conflict of interest. However, Kay was apparently commenting about Iraq in news media before he resigned his post at SAIC—including in September 2002 when the Bush administration launched its public campaign for war. Also, while a stockholder and senior vice president at SAIC, Kay twice testified before congressional committees—on May 21, 1998 and again on September 9, 2002—both times recommending that Saddam be removed from power.
Charles Duelfer	According to David Kay, Duelfer also attended government meetings prompted by Paul Wolfowitz. It is unclear if Duelfer was still working as a news analyst when he allegedly attended these meetings. For details, see the entry for "David Kay" above.	

Analyst	Political commitments and undisclosed government affiliations	Financial conflicts of interest
Khidir Hamza	Hamza was affiliated with the Iraqi National Congress (INC), a CIA-funded group interested in toppling Saddam. The INC boosted the U.S. campaign for war by providing the CIA with faulty intelligence on Iraq's weapons (Isikoff and Corn 2006).	
Tim McCarthy	David Kay recalled, with some uncertainty, that McCarthy also attended government meetings prompted by Paul Wolfowitz. For details, see the entry for "David Kay" above.	
Barry McCaffrey	Member of the Pentagon's military analyst program. Advisory board member of the Committee for the Liberation of Iraq, a neoconservative advocacy group aimed at overthrowing Saddam. Member of the Project for a New American Century, a group that lobbied for increased military spending and regime change in Iraq (Rampton and Stauber 2003).	Board of directors at four defense firms: Metritek, Veritas Capital, Raytheon Aerospace, and Integrated Defense Technologies. All secured multi-million-dollar defense contracts in Iraq (Benaim, Motaparthy, and Kumar 2003).
Wayne Downing	Member of the Pentagon's military analyst program. Advisory board member of the Committee for the Liberation of Iraq, which sought to overthrow Saddam. Lobbyist and advisor for the Iraqi National Congress, a CIA funded Iraqi opposition group interested in toppling Saddam (Isikoff and Corn 2006). Member of the Project for a New American Century, which lobbied for Saddam's removal (Rampton and Stauber 2003).	Board of directors and stockholder for SAIC, the intelligence and defense industry that won major contracts for operations in "soon-to-be occupied Iraq" (Barlett and Steele 2007). Board of Directors for Metal Storm Limited, a ballistics company that secured defense contracts in Iraq (Metal Storm Limited 2006). Lobbied U.S. representatives and the Pentagon for the Spectrum Group on behalf of Robertson Aviation.
George Joulwan	Member of the Pentagon's military analyst program.	Director and stockholder in General Dynamics Corporation, a defense contractor that supplied Stryker armored combat vehicles throughout the Iraq War. Director of Alion Science and Technology Corporation, a defense contractor that secured millions for WMD destruction and hospital construction before and during the Iraq War.
Montgomery Meigs	Member of the Pentagon's military analyst program.	According to the Pentagon, Meigs was affiliated with an unnamed defense contractor before the 2003 Iraq War (U.S. Department of Defense, Inspector General 2011, 54).
Jack Jacobs	Member of the Pentagon's military analyst program.	
Ken Allard	Member of the Pentagon's military analyst program.	

Table G.1

Analyst	Political commitments and undisclosed government affiliations	Financial conflicts of interest
William Nash	Member of the Pentagon's military analyst program.	According to the Pentagon, Nash was affiliated with an unnamed defense contractor before the 2003 Iraq War (U.S. Department of Defense, Inspector General 2011, 54).
Buster Glosson	Member of the Pentagon's military analyst program. Advisory board member of the Committee for the Liberation of Iraq, a neoconservative advocacy group backed by the Bush administration with the mission of overthrowing Saddam. Member of the Project for a New American Century, a neoconservative group that lobbied for increased military spending and regime change in Iraq (Rampton and Stauber 2003).	Director of American Materials & Technologies Corporation, a subsidiary of Cytec Industries that supplies military and defense materials. Vice chairman of the Board at Skysat Communications Network Corp., a company specializing in telecommunications systems.
Rick Francona	Member of the Pentagon's military analyst program.	
Bernard Trainor	Member of the Pentagon's military analyst program.	

Appendix H: Analysis of Speech Act Verbs

Verbal introductions typically took the form of reported speech, construing a speaker (*a former inspector*), speech act (*says*), and speech (*the team will probably return*). Here, I show how correspondents chose to represent analysts' **speech acts** (Calsamiglia and López Ferrero 2003; Hyland 2000; Martin and White 2005). First, I analyzed if speech acts were construed as **research verbs** (*X finds*), **cognitive verbs** (*X thinks*), or **discourse verbs** (*X says*). Discourse verbs were used about 75 percent of the time and cognitive verbs about 25 percent of the time. (Research verbs were used only twice in the corpus.) So correspondents usually sought to portray analysts as "sayers," not "researchers."

Next, I analyzed what the verbs suggested about the *analyst's attitude*: whether the analyst was **positive** about an assertion (*X maintains*), **neutral** (*X says*), **tentative** (*X suggests*), or **critical** (*X refutes*). About 63 percent of the time, speech act verbs indicated the analysts were neutral, while verbs indicated analysts were positive about their assertions about 24 percent of the time. Tentative and critical verbs were rare. Thus, correspondents usually did not convey that analysts felt strongly about claims, portraying them as "neutral" speakers.

Finally, I analyzed how the speech act verbs worked to signal the *correspondent's attitude* toward the analyst's assertion: whether the correspondent **endorsed** the analyst's assertion (*X shows*), **rejected** the analyst's assertion (*X fails to see*), **distanced** herself from the assertion (*X claims*), or remained **neutral** about the assertion (*X says*). I found that correspondents remained neutral about 89 percent of the time, endorsed the analysts about 6 percent of the time, and distanced themselves from the analysts' assertions the rest of the time. Thus, the journalists largely sought to remain "objective" in their reporting verbs, acknowledging that analysts made assertions while endorsing those assertions only rarely.

Appendix I: Recurring Themes in News Analyst Discourse

A theme (or thematic formation) is a generic meaning realized by more specific wordings within and across texts (Thibault 1991). To discern themes, I examined analyst's ideational and evaluative discourse (Halliday and Matthiessen 2004; Martin and White 2005) and assigned inductive codes to overarching meanings that reappeared across newscasts (Oddo 2014b). My coding unit was the analyst's television appearance, including all verbal discourse in a news segment. Themes could be indicated explicitly or implicitly. For example, an analyst could indicate the theme, "violence in Iraq appears justified or necessary," through an explicit assertion (e.g., "at this point, going to war in Iraq is the most reasonable option"); a presupposition (e.g., "some international leaders fail to recognize the *necessity of war in Iraq*"); or a logical inference (e.g., "Iraq's hidden weapons will never be neutralized through diplomacy, inspections, or other peaceful means"). Discourse could be double coded. For instance, the last example sentence ("Iraq's concealed weapons will never be neutralized through diplomacy, inspections, or other peaceful means") indicates both the "violence is likely justified" theme *and* the "Iraq lies to retain WMD" theme (since it presupposes Iraq retains and conceals weapons). Table I.1 describes typical discursive features that indicate each theme and provides examples.

Table I.1

Theme	Typical realization	Example
Iraq must fully and immediately disarm	• Assertions suggesting Iraq must positively show disarmament • Iraq or U.N. as actor in deontically modalized process that encodes dismantling weapons ("these weapons should be destroyed") • Reference to U.N. mandate requiring full disarmament • Implication Saddam should disarm immediately because he will otherwise grow stronger	"I think what [the inspectors] are insisting that Iraqis do is substantial actual progress, something that is showable as opposed to just promises of future cooperation." (DK on NBC 2003, Feb. 8)
Iraq must cooperate; we cannot hope to find a "smoking gun"	• Pairs of clauses where clause 1 negates that inspectors must find or uncover weapons and clause 2 reaffirms that Iraq is obligated to reveal its weapons • Negated modals with regard to finding a "smoking gun"	"[Iraq] must demonstrate that they are cooperating. It's not, it should not be the responsibility of the inspectors to find a smoking gun." (DA on NBC 2002, Sep. 17)

Table I.1 (continued)

Theme	Typical realization	Example
Iraq lies to retain WMD	• Assumption or explicit assertion that Iraq possesses weapons • Iraq as (implied) agent in process or nominalization that encodes concealed possession of weapons and implies wrongdoing ("hide," "conceal," "cheat," "does not cooperate")	"[Saddam Hussein] will continue to try to conceal [weapons], and that's why you're into an inspection process that has a very tough road ahead of it." (DK on NBC 2002, Nov. 11)
Iraq seeks and produces WMD	• Iraq as (implied) agent in process encoding desire ("wants," "seeks") or creation of ("makes," "produces") weapons	"I mean, short of changing the regime and putting in a democratic government, Iraq will seek nuclear weapons." (DA on NBC 2002, Mar. 7)
It is unclear if Iraq has WMD	• Modals indicate epistemic uncertainty about Iraq's WMD • Tokens of counterexpectancy and negations may suggest evidence is limited or deficient ("<u>just one</u> <i>un</i>named source") • Evaluations index lack of evidence	"It's unclear exactly what she was doing in Baghdad, because by then small pox had been eradicated worldwide. So that, if true, and we just have one unnamed source to go on, would be troubling." (JT on NBC 2002, Dec. 4)
Inspections almost certainly will fail	• Negated modals when it comes to weapons inspections ("can't," "won't") • Negative evaluation of weapons inspections / credibility ("ludicrous") • Implication of likely failure because weapons inspectors are said to face major challenges or lack needed resources	"The inspectors are not capable at this point—they don't have helicopters, they're still getting equipment in. They're not going to be conducting serious surprise inspections of the Iraqis." (DK on NBC 2002, Nov. 27)
The UN is not fully committed or credible	• U.N. as agent in processes encoding tolerance for Iraqi wrongdoing • Negated processes or attributes encoding U.N. commitment or unity ("not committed") • Implied negative evaluation of U.N. commitment or unity	"There is a clear gap between what [President Bush] has articulated—that is zero tolerance for any of the old cheat and retreat games of the Iraqis—and the view the [U.N.] Secretary-General has articulated." (DK on NBC 2002, Nov. 14)
Inspectors can pressure Iraq / turn up weapons	• Positive evaluation of inspections • Assertions of modalized possibility / capability regarding inspection • Inspectors as agents in unmodalized processes that encode uncovering or locating weapons ("Inspectors found shells") • Discussion of how inspectors will evaluate weapons they have just discovered	"These shells provide a key. Inspectors can swab them, find out what chemical it was, [and] ask Iraq to now explain all." (RB on NBC 2003, Jan. 16)
Inspectors must establish authority	• Deontically modalized assertion about inspectors need to establish authority or free travel in Iraq ("Inspectors must")	"You [inspectors] also want technological surprise. You want to go in there with tools that the Iraqis don't understand." (DA on NBC 2002, Nov. 22)

Table I.1 (continued)

Theme	Typical realization	Example
Violence appears justified or necessary	• Assertion that "regime change" is the only way to disarm Iraq • Deontically modalized assertion that U.S. must confront Iraq or bring it democracy / progress • Assertion that Iraq is in material breach of U.N. Resolution 1441 (implying war is next logical step) • Deontically modalized assertion or implication that U.N. must adopt a new war resolution • Argument that U.S. must "finish the job" started in the first Gulf War	"I mean short of changing the regime and putting in a democratic government, Iraq will seek nuclear weapons." (DA on NBC 2002, Mar. 7)
War with Iraq is extremely likely or inevitable	• Predictions of war processes or postwar processes that take for granted war is going to happen • Relational processes, attributes, or enthymemes characterizing war as extremely likely or inevitable	"Well, we've put tremendous investment into moving those forces. You don't do that lightly, and the administration has made it very clear that they are going to disarm Iraq and ensure without any equivocation at all that the weapons of mass destruction are gone." (MM on NBC 2003, Feb. 15)
Iraq conducts terrorism / aids terrorists	• Iraq as actor in process that encodes terrorism or supporting terrorists • Relational processes that characterize the "relationship" between Iraq and al-Qaeda	"[Iraqi sleeper cells are] going to try to assassinate key Americans. I think they're going to bomb our interests as they can. They're going to harass us." (WD on NBC 2003, Mar. 6)
U.S. credibility and case for war is strong	• Positive evaluation of U.S. discourse or intelligence about the Iraqi threat • Positive evaluation of U.S. commitment and resolve with regard to disarming Iraq • Assertions that naturalize the ambiguity, or lack, of hard evidence by indicating heightened usuality ("evidence is always ambiguous")	"I think it's a very compelling case, Tom. A compelling case on the key point: Is Iraq continuing to conceal and cheat as the inspectors are trying to carry out their mission? I think there could be no doubt after you listen to the evidence that, in fact, that is the case indeed." (DK on NBC 2003, Feb. 5a)
Saddam Hussein is morally depraved and subhuman	• Intense negative judgments of Saddam Hussein's personal character / propriety • Dehumanizing language used to describe Saddam Hussein	"[Saddam Hussein is] twisted, he's mentally twisted. He gained enormous pleasure from inflicting pain on people." (KH on NBC 2002, Oct. 15)
Iraq threatens world security	• Aggressor-violation-victim pattern (Oddo 2014b), in which Iraq is responsible for violent process affecting innocent victims • Category is not about WMD possession, but the threat of violence	"Yes [Saddam would use chemical or biological weapons]—anywhere, in any form, in any way that will implement his power or get his way." (KH on NBC 2002, Oct. 15)
U.S. credibility and motives are questionable	• Negative evaluation of U.S. motives in Iraq	"If the United States and the United Kingdom decide to go it alone, sadly, I have to say this, that would be equivalent of taking the law into their own hands, a bit like a posse, a lynch mob. . . . I don't know that it would be a good thing for this greatest of all democracies to behave in international law as if it were an autocracy." (RB on NBC 2003, Jan. 14)

Table I.1

Theme	Typical realization	Example
Bush administration must make a case for war	• Deontically modalized assertion suggesting the Bush team must offer additional evidence • Relational processes that negatively characterize the U.S. case as insufficient	"It clearly puts a heavier burden on the Bush administration to publicly explain why it is certain that the Iraqis have weapons of mass destruction and why military action sooner rather than later is called for." (DK on NBC 2003, Jan. 4)
Warfare will involve certain technical operations / tactics	• U.S. troops as agents in future-tense material processes encoding military operations and tactics	"We'll enter places like Baghdad at high speed and go to vital areas and seize them using tanks, two-thousand-pound air-delivered bombs, and enormous levels of violence. And we'll do it all in the dark." (BM on NBC 2003, Jan. 13)
Warfare will be unpleasant or dangerous	• Negative evaluations characterize soldier's experience of warfare ("challenging," "miserable") • Iraq as actor in future-tense process encoding violence aimed at U.S. troops	"[Urban warfare is] a mess. You know it's chaotic. You're vulnerable to enormous numbers of casualties if you don't fight it the right way." (BM on NBC 2002, Sep. 27)
The U.S. military will face some logistical challenges, sometimes as a result of mistakes in U.S. diplomacy	• Relational processes encode conditions for U.S. military action as challenges or setbacks • Setbacks specified in future processes with U.S. troops as actors • Modals of ability indicating troops can overcome challenges or evaluative lexis indicating challenges are surmountable • Negative lexis describing U.S. diplomacy as it relates to negotiations; does not question U.S. policy in Iraq, only how the U.S. has cooperated with allies	"Equipment will now have to transit through the Suez and get in position to offload in Kuwait. I'm sure they could do that in less than three weeks but this is a huge logistical challenge to the United States navy and army to reposition." (BM on NBC 2003, Mar. 2)
U.S. troops are fully prepared to fight and win	• Positive evaluation of U.S. military capabilities (troops, training, preparedness, equipment)—either now or in the future • Material processes construing how others will help U.S. troops	"If you have got any thought at all of going in—particularly fighting in and around Baghdad—the Long Bow gives you a capability that you literally have not had before and you better use it and use it well." (KA on NBC 2002, Sep. 27)
The war will be over quickly	• Relational process predicting limited duration of war against Iraq	"This thing will be locked and cocked and could act in concert with regional allies to conduct an intervention that in my judgment will last twenty-one days." (BM on NBC 2003, Jan. 21)
The Iraqi military is not prepared / cannot win against the U.S. military	• Negative evaluations of Iraqi troop capabilities and preparedness • Predictions in which Iraqi troops are agents who surrender	"Saddam doesn't trust his army, and the army won't fight and die for him as a person. They're going to desert by the thousands, if they are faced with a major attack." (BM on NBC 2002, Oct. 16)

Appendix J: Themes Repeated by Analysts and Administration Officials

Appendix J shows Iraq-related themes evident in both news analyst discourse and the discourse of the Bush administration. To sample administration discourse, I examined documents the Pentagon shared with military analysts before the war: briefings with key themes, talking points, or notable quotes. These documents specify utterances that the administration deemed decontextualizable and repeatable. Indeed, they showcase talking points that administration officials frequently recited in their own public speeches. The evidence indicates that news analysts were rehearsing themes central to the administration's public campaign for war in Iraq.

Theme	Example from Bush administration talking points
Iraq must fully and immediately disarm	"The Iraqi regime must reveal and destroy, under U.N. supervision, all existing weapons of mass destruction." (U.S. Department of Defense [DoD] 2002a)
Iraq must cooperate; we cannot hope to find a "smoking gun"	"The burden of proof is not on the United Nations or on the inspectors to prove that Iraq has weapons of mass destruction, their job is only is [*sic*] confirm evidence of voluntary and total disarmament (Source: Rumsfeld 12.5.02)." (U.S. DoD 2002d)
Iraq lies to retain WMD	"Saddam Hussein has developed a highly advanced system of denial and deception for Iraq's weapons of mass destruction and ballistic missile programs, hiding them from the rest of the world, but specifically to thwart the efforts of renewed U.N. monitoring and inspections programs (Source: White House, DIA)." (U.S DoD 2002d)

Iraq seeks and produces WMD	"The Iraqi regime is actively pursuing weapons of mass destruction, amassing large, clandestine stockpiles of biological and chemical weapons, and has an active program to acquire and develop nuclear weapons." (U.S. DoD 2003b)
Inspections almost certainly will fail	"If a country decides not to cooperate, it is terribly difficult for a U.N. monitoring and inspection team to tackle a country of that size if the government is determined to deny and deceive and lie. (Source: Rumsfeld, 12/5.02)." (U.S DoD 2002d)
The UN is not fully committed or credible	"The President has challenged the U.N. to enforce its resolutions. It is an important moment for the credibility of the United Nations." (U.S. DoD 2002b)
Inspectors can pressure Iraq / turn up weapons	"The new UN inspection mandate provides a means to test whether the Iraqi regime has made a strategic shift and decided to give up its WMD." (U.S. DoD 2002c)
Inspectors must establish authority	"We do continue to believe that it's terribly important for [inspectors] to take people, knowledgeable people—scientists, technicians, people who have been involved in weapons of mass destruction programs—and get them out of their country, with their families, so that they can speak honestly and tell the truth, because the success of the inspectors that inspectors have had in the past is not as finders . . . but by talking to knowledgeable people (Rumsfeld, 1/15/03)." (U.S. DoD 2003a)
Violence appears justified or necessary	"1441 is simple and clear. It calls for full, immediate, unconditional, and voluntary disarmament, beginning with a complete, open, and honest declaration. It gives Iraq one final opportunity to comply. Iraq has not disarmed; its 12,000-page declaration is incomplete and inaccurate; its final opportunity has been squandered." (U.S. DoD 2003c)

War with Iraq is extremely likely or inevitable	"Tomahawk land-cruise missiles launched from ships in the Mediterranean, Red Sea, and Persian Gulf will supplement air-to-ground weapons." (U.S. DoD 2003h)
Iraq conducts terrorism / aids terrorists	"Saddam provides safe haven and training to al-Qaida." (U.S. DoD 2003d)
U.S. credibility and case for war is strong	"Secretary Powell's 90-minute presentation to the UN Security Council proved that Saddam's pattern of denial and deception continues to this day. The presentation . . . documented the lengths to which Saddam is willing to go to deceive the inspectors and the world—in clear violation of UN Security Council Resolution 1441 which compels Iraq to cooperate with disarmament." (U.S. DoD 2003b)
Saddam Hussein is morally depraved and subhuman	"Saddam Hussein has turned Iraq into a prison, a poison factory, and a torture chamber for any who disagree with him. The list of his atrocities are numerous in length and almost too horrendous to recite." (U.S. DoD 2003b)
Iraq threatens world security	"The [Iraqi] regime is one of the most repressive regimes on the face of the earth. They threaten all their people every day. That's how they live in that country, under the threat of government—Secretary Rumsfeld, 3/11/03." (U.S. DoD 2003j)
Warfare will involve certain technical operations / tactics	"The military will use precision-guided bombs and missiles. Through laser and satellite-guided systems these smart munitions pinpoint military targets with incredible accuracy and lethality." (U.S. DoD 2003h)
Warfare will be unpleasant or dangerous	"There are dangers when taking prisoners. Iraqi suicide attackers armed with poison gas or infected with diseases like smallpox may hide among surrendering Army units." (U.S. DoD 2003g)

The U.S. military will face some logistical challenges	"There are several options for basing U.S. and Coalition forces on Turkish soil. Whatever the Turkish Parliament decides, it will not adversely affect the outcome of military action. U.S. and coalition forces will prevail." (U.S. DoD 2003i)
U.S. troops are fully prepared to fight and win	"U.S. military forces are the best equipped, best trained and most capable of any in the world." (U.S. DoD 2003h)
The war will be over quickly	"The [Iraqi] army's size is about 350,000 and the coalition anticipates the army will fold immediately or soon after taking casualties." (U.S. DoD 2003h)
The Iraqi military is not prepared / cannot win against the U.S. military	"Of Iraq's approximately 350 aircraft, an estimated two-thirds are not operational. Their fighter/attack planes, older model Soviet MiG-23's and -25's and French Mirage-F1 jets are no match for coalition counterparts." (U.S. DoD 2003h)

Appendix K: Reports About Aluminum Tubes in Classified Documents and Public Discourse

Appendix K shows reports about high-strength aluminum tubes sought by Iraq. The earlier reports—from April 2001 to early September 2002—are intelligence documents, parts of which have been declassified. On September 8, 2002 and thereafter, claims about the tubes were finally aired in news discourse and public speeches. To analyze all reports, I adapted the scheme outlined in Oddo (2013). I examined engagement (Martin and White 2005), determining how each source recognized alternative voices. I studied argumentation, including technical details and the proofs furnished for claims. As the tubes story was recontextualized, I considered how it was transformed—how linguistic resources were added, deleted, or otherwise altered.

Date	Source
04/10/2001	CIA Senior Executive Intelligence Brief 01–083CH (quoted in S. Rep. No. 108–301 [2004], at 88)
04/11/2001	Daily Intelligence Highlight, *Iraq: High-Strength Aluminum Tube Procurement*, Department of Energy paper (quoted in S. Rep. No. 108–301 [2004], at 89)
05/09/2001	Daily Intelligence Highlight, *Iraq: Aluminum Alloy Tube Purchase*, Department of Energy paper (quoted in S. Rep. No. 108–301 [2004], at 89)
06/14/2001	CIA, Senior Publish When Ready (quoted in S. Rep. No. 108–301 [2004], at 90)
07/02/2001	CIA intelligence assessment (quoted in S. Rep. No. 108–301 [2004], at 90)
08/02/2001	Defense Intelligence Agency internal background paper (quoted in S. Rep. No. 108–301 [2004], at 91)
08/17/2001	Technical Intelligence Note, *Iraq's Gas Centrifuge Program: Is Reconstitution Underway?* (TIN000064), Department of Energy (quoted in S. Rep. No. 108–301 [2004], at 91–92)
11/30/2001	Military Intelligence Digest Supplement, *Iraq: Procuring Possible Nuclear-Related Gas Centrifuge Equipment*, Defense Intelligence Agency
12/2001	*Iraq Seeking Additional Aluminum Tubes*, Department of Energy (quoted in S. Rep. No. 108–301 [2004], at 112–13)
09/2002	*Iraq's Reemerging Nuclear Weapons Program*, Defense Intelligence Agency (quoted in S. Rep. No. 108–301 [2004], at 93)

09/08/2002	"U.S. Says Hussein Intensifies Quest for A-Bomb Parts," *New York Times* (Gordon and Miller 2002)
09/08/2002	*Meet the Press*, interview with Vice President Dick Cheney (2002)
09/08/2002	*Fox News Sunday*, interview with Colin Powell (Snow 2002)
09/08/2002	*CNN Late Edition with Wolf Blitzer*, interview with Condoleezza Rice (Blitzer 2002)
09/09/2002	NBC News
09/12/2002	George W. Bush, address to the United Nations (Bush 2002a)
09/13/2002	"Baghdad's Arsenal; White House Lists Iraq Steps to Build Banned Weapons," *New York Times* (Miller and Gordon 2002)
09/2002	"Aluminum Tubing Is an Indicator of an Iraqi Gas Centrifuge Program: But Is the Tubing Specifically for Centrifuges?," *Institute for Science and International Security* (Albright 2002)
09/19/2002	"Evidence on Iraq Challenged: Experts Question If Tubes Were Meant for Weapons Program," *Washington Post* (Warrick 2002)
10/7/2002	George W. Bush, address in Cincinnati, OH (Bush 2002b)
1/29/2003	George W. Bush, State of the Union address (Bush 2003)

Notes

Introduction

1. Observations are based on a July 3, 2015, search of the *New York Times* database for news about propaganda.

2. King (1963) calls Eugene "Bull" Connor a "racist" (name-calling) (49), quotes Victor Hugo to establish authority (testimonial) (119), and frequently uses "glittering generalities," associating nonviolence with virtue words such as "heroism" (38) and "miracle" (44).

3. Most of my analyses still focus on traditional propaganda campaigns driven by elites. The reason for this is that campaigns for war almost always travel from elites to the public, from the top down, not the other way around. That is, government and press often bear the most responsibility for war propaganda. Nevertheless, this book shows (especially in chapter 9) how ordinary citizens themselves may propagandize.

4. "Critical discourse studies" is commonly abbreviated as CDS, but the field is also referred to as "critical discourse analysis," or CDA.

5. But see Huckin (2016).

6. This claim is based on a January 2015 search of current and back issues of the following journals: *Critical Approaches to Discourse Analysis Across Disciplines*, *Critical Discourse Studies*, *Discourse and Communication*, *Discourse and Society*, *Discourse Studies*, and the *Journal of Language and Politics*. Only ten articles in these journals included "propaganda" in their titles or keywords.

7. I deem discourse to be "harmful" if it is antidemocratic, creating inequitable conditions for the practice of free speech and preventing citizens from making informed decisions.

Chapter 1

1. By "dialogic," I do not mean a cooperative back-and-forth. I mean that propaganda advances when audiences respond to an original message and reuse it in new contexts.

2. The root of "disseminate" suggests a man spreading his semen.

3. "Mass scale" is a relative term, and a mass audience can range from smaller communities (e.g., a university, a town, a state) to larger ones (e.g., an entire country). The more massive the scale of recontextualization, the more successful the propaganda.

4. We must be careful about how we apply the term "unwitting propagandist." I would not label someone an unwitting propagandist just because she produces messages superficially similar to those of some self-serving organization. For example, both American peace activists and Russian state propagandists

produce discourse critical of U.S. militarism. But peace activists are not therefore "useful idiots" of the Russian government. Indeed, accusing dissenters of being "useful idiots" of a foreign power is itself an ugly form of propaganda.

5. A failed attempt at propaganda may nevertheless be interesting to study.

6. I focus on linguistic manipulation, though other semiotic modes are also relevant.

7. Orwell never actually uses the word "doublespeak." The term derives from two other Orwellian words, "Newspeak" and "doublethink."

8. See Marlin (2013, 91–137) and Pratkanis and Aronson (2001) for relevant discussions.

9. The Portuguese caption reads, "MORTE: O uso deste produto leva à morte por câncer de pulmão e enfisema."

Chapter 2

1. Seeking control over oil, the U.S. Central Intelligence Agency (CIA) helped stage the overthrow of Iran's prime minister in 1953, installing the Western-friendly shah (Blum 2004, 65–71).

2. Another hijacked jet was retaken by passengers and crashed into an empty field in Pennsylvania.

3. Congress gave the executive branch so much power that, as I write, the 2001 resolution is still being used as grounds to strike terrorist suspects who took no part in the 9/11 attacks.

4. Resolution 687 also extended devastating economic sanctions on Iraq, causing hundreds of thousands to die. Meanwhile, the United States and the United Kingdom continued to bomb Iraq almost daily over a twelve-year period, without U.N. authorization (Pilger 2000).

Chapter 3

1. By "major news item," I mean a news story that received special prominence either by its placement on the front page of a newspaper or by its inclusion in a heavily watched television broadcast.

2. See appendix C for a discussion of methods and appendix D for the full audio transcript and coding scheme.

3. Tom Porter literally refers to Nayirah as a "witness" and calls on her to "testify." Her position behind the microphone, her body posture, and her gaze all index that she is a witness delivering formal testimony.

4. Surely, people from the Middle East may have light hair, light skin, and so on. My point is that Nayirah's appearance matches persistent Western stereotypes about Middle Eastern women (Abu-Absi 1996).

5. Nayirah has no discernible Arabic accent and speaks error-free "standard" American English, perhaps indexing her access to Western society and education.

6. Nayirah typically looks either at the lawmakers or down at the papers in front of her.

7. Pathos and ethos are often linked, since "stimulating the appropriate emotions . . . is a necessary part of displaying the desired character in a speaker" (Garver 1994, 110).

8. Lantos opts for practiced histrionics: pregnant pauses, followed by emphatic denunciations of Iraq. His political show of outrage is apt, but he does not communicate authentic pathos. Morella is even less convincing, reading aloud from a prepared statement and displaying little "natural" feeling.

9. Nayirah's performance was also aired on CNN's *Larry King Live* and printed in major newspapers.

10. NBC makes one minor change to Nayirah's narrative by cutting the initial clause "while I was there." This cut was likely made because NBC could not easily connect the pronoun "there" with its antecedent, "al-'Addan hospital," a location Nayirah mentioned almost a full minute before telling the incubator story.

Chapter 4

1. See Rowse (1992) and MacArthur (quoted in CBS 1992).

2. I examine the period from August 2, 1990, when Iraqi forces invaded Kuwait, to January 17, 1991, the beginning of Operation Desert Storm.

3. Abulhasan (1990) could have chosen his words even more wisely. For example, he said the premature infants suffered "from retarded growth." In American English, the word "retarded" is collocated with the discourse of intellectual disability; often its use is considered offensive. In choosing this word, Abulhasan likely rendered his letter less quotable. Indeed, the AP (1990a) story carefully elides the phrase "suffering from retarded growth," preferring to quote only the more standard "premature children."

4. The *Times* never tells readers why "Cindy" and "Rudi" use pseudonyms.

5. People for a Free Kuwait is another front group similar to CFK.

6. Five of the seven speakers used false names, and many told false stories (MacArthur 1992, 65; Strong 1992, 13).

7. The doctor later changed his story, reducing the number of babies he personally buried to "around thirty."

8. Only the November 2, 1990, report in *USA Today* fails to include Bush's promise for remedial military action.

9. Meanwhile, the "Red Crescent doctor" was an employee of the Kuwaiti government (Abu-Hamad 1992, 7).

10. Though Amnesty International investigators quoted Nayirah's "testimony" before the HRC, they apparently never interviewed her.

11. The press release twice intensifies quantities ("more than" three hundred babies died at "at least three" hospitals), leading readers to imagine even greater numbers of deaths.

12. Doctors are also said to have "worked in the hospitals *where* the babies died." But not all doctors quoted in the Amnesty report claim to have worked at such hospitals (one worked at a hospital with no maternity floor).

13. These records are not cited in Amnesty's report. Official records tend to disconfirm the story (Abu-Hamad 1992).

14. The Amnesty report was publicized by several major news outlets. Only ABC noted that another human rights organization, Middle East Watch, disputed the incubator charge.

Chapter 5

1. Days after the 9/11 attacks, U.S. officials began urging war against Saddam (Clarke 2004).

2. See Capus (2001–5), Murphy (2000–2005), and Slavin (2000–2004).

3. I only study analysts in the Pentagon's outreach program; other military contributors also appeared at the time.

4. The notion of "compensatory legitimation" originally comes from Weiler (1983).

5. Unless otherwise noted, information about the Pentagon's analyst program is taken from Barstow's (2008) Pulitzer Prize–winning exposé.

6. In an attempt to document interactions between analysts and government, I placed Freedom of Information Act requests with the Pentagon, U.S. Central Command, the CIA, and the State Department. Only the State Department fulfilled my requests.

7. I could not corroborate whether the meetings Kay described took place; no relevant news reports exist, and the U.S. government turned down my FOIA requests for more information. Still, I have no reason to doubt Kay, as circumstantial evidence supports the claim that he met with government officials. For example, in an NBC (2003, Feb. 5a) broadcast before Colin Powell's February 5, 2003, speech at the United Nations, Tom Brokaw said Kay had already "had a kind of a preview" of Powell's address. Presumably, such an exclusive preview of Powell's speech would only be available to someone who had been invited to meet with U.S. officials.

8. Butler repeatedly and categorically made such accusations, in his book *The Greatest Threat: Iraq, Weapons of Mass Destruction, and the Crisis of Global Security* (Butler 2000, 242), in news broadcasts, and when he appeared before the Senate in July 2002. To be fair, some of Iraq's weapons from the past were now unaccounted for. But, since inspectors had left the country in 1998, no one could say with certainty whether Iraq still had these weapons (or if it was producing more).

9. After the speech, Butler said on NBC (2003, Feb. 5b): "[Powell] has made a major challenge to the Security Council, probably the most important challenge it's faced in its history. It will deal with this man and his weapons, or it will fail, and he made that clear." Given the purpose of Powell's speech, the call for the U.N. to "deal with" Saddam seems to suggest that the council ought to sanction war.

10. I was unable to corroborate Kay's assertion that he sold his stock before becoming a full-time consultant at NBC News. Kay could not recall when he terminated his relationship with SAIC but estimated that he sold all his company stock in August or September of 2002, before he became a full-time analyst. The Center for Public Integrity (2006) reports that Kay

did not leave SAIC until October. In newspapers, Kay was still being referred to as "senior vice president" at SAIC in late September (Radler 2002) and even December (Brookings Institution 2002). In an effort to confirm Kay's account that he sold all his stock, my research assistant Les Bennett made a Freedom of Information Act request with the Securities and Exchange Commission (SEC), asking for any records of stock sales involving David Kay. Our thinking was that, as a senior corporate vice president, Kay might be deemed an insider who would, by law, have to disclose any sale of company stock to the SEC. The FOIA search yielded no records of Kay selling SAIC shares at any time during the prewar period. This finding, however, does not necessarily refute Kay's assertion. Possibly he was not deemed an insider, in which case, he would not have been required to report sales of company stock.

11. Kay made this comment on NBC News with regard to Colin Powell's 2003 presentation to the United Nations (NBC 2003, Feb. 5a), the lengthiest presentation on Iraq's alleged weapons put forward by the Bush administration.

Chapter 6

1. I examine the networks' evening newscasts and special reports (e.g., coverage of Colin Powell's U.N. speech), focusing on appearances in which analysts were invited to discuss Iraq, its weapons, or the prospect of war. See appendix F for details.

2. Schwarzkopf was only twice called upon to comment on Iraq before the war. I do not examine his on-air contributions.

3. Less common on-screen titles were still legitimizing. For example, analysts were sometimes referred to as "experts" (e.g., "Weapons Expert") or identified as "literate" professionals (e.g., "Iraq Watch Editor").

4. Other reports described the new inspections team ($n=9$), international debate over war ($n=4$), and Iraqi claims of innocence ($n=2$).

5. This was not the only time Butler expressed certainty about Iraq's WMD on the news. Before Colin Powell's 2003 U.N. speech, Butler stated, "The case against Iraq, I think, is substantially proven. It does have weapons of mass destruction" (NBC 2003, Feb. 5a). And later, after Powell's speech, Butler presupposed Iraq's weapons existed: "[Saddam] hasn't made any decision at all to get rid of these weapons" (NBC 2003, Feb. 5b).

6. "Pentagon Talking Points about Potential Flooding of Iraqi Dams" (U.S. Department of Defense 2003f).

Chapter 7

1. The Defense Intelligence Agency shared the CIA assessment that the tubes were intended for gas centrifuges. Meanwhile, the Bureau of Intelligence and Research rejected this claim and joined the DOE in arguing the tubes were meant for artillery rockets. The IAEA also judged the tubes unsuited for nuclear weapons (Albright 2003).

2. Iraq's tubes had a wall thickness of 3.3 millimeters and a length of 900 millimeters, while the Zippe rotors had a wall thickness of only 1 millimeter and a length of only 332 millimeters. One DOE consultant even called Gernot Zippe, who also rejected the assertion that Iraq's tubes "matched" those bearing his name (Isikoff and Corn 2006, 39–40).

3. Allegedly, CIA reports sent to Bush's cabinet between July 2001 and July 2002 failed to acknowledge dissenting views about the tubes (Isikoff and Corn 2006, 41), but this cannot be corroborated, as these reports remain classified.

4. According to the *New York Times*, the CIA shared with the White House differing opinions about the tubes. By late 2001, President Bush and Condoleezza Rice reportedly knew that DOE experts found the tubes unsuitable for nuclear weapons (Barstow, Broad, and Gerth 2004). Powell and Cheney apparently knew about the dispute by early 2002. In fact, in late 2001, Powell's own intelligence outfit, the State Department's

Bureau of Intelligence and Research, told him it concurred with the DOE: the tubes were not for gas centrifuges (Isikoff and Corn 2006, 40).

5. "Talking Points about Aluminum Tubes" (U.S. Department of Defense 2003b). The document postdates the administration officials' television appearances of September 8, 2002, but it approximates the kind of talking points with which officials were surely provided.

6. Kay said he had also relied on other news reports, aside from the *Times* article, but he is likely mistaken. By September 9, 2002, the *Times* was the only paper reporting about the aluminum tubes. However, as suggested, Kay may have had other sources.

7. Neither the classified CIA reports nor the sources quoted in the *Times* refer to Iraq's attempted import of aluminum tubes as a "classic" indicator of a nuclear weapons program. In fact, the CIA labored to show how the tubes might be adapted for a gas centrifuge, scouring the literature to find the 1950s Zippe prototype.

8. Kay later described the aluminum tubes issue as "an absolute fraud" (Isikof and Corn 2006, 307). He told me the exclusion of the DOE counterclaim was "not only negligent" but "really fraudulent."

Chapter 8

1. Anderson (2007, 97–98) argues that it is important to distinguish between ethos and identity. Ethos entails strategically projecting a discursive character appropriate to a rhetorical situation. Meanwhile, identity is a more permanent aspect of the self, an "essential" and trans-situational characteristic.

2. The concept of the ideograph was first theorized by McGee (1980).

3. Throughout this chapter, I am indebted to Stahl (2009); Beamish, Molotch, and Flacks (1995); Coy, Woehrle, and Maney (2008); and Lembcke (1998).

4. The idea that we must support troops in times of war predates Vietnam. As one reviewer pointed out to me, references to this idea are observable in 1952 newspaper columns about the Korean War. However, during Vietnam, the SOT slogan and its close relatives (e.g., "Support Our Boys in Vietnam") gained national prominence.

5. Nixon also continued Johnson's strategy of matching peace protests with pro-war demonstrations covertly sponsored by the government (Lembcke 1998, 53–54).

6. Results were obtained using the Lexis Nexis database. I searched for instances of each phrase ("full spectrum dominance" and "support our troops") between January 1, 1990, and January 1, 2000, limiting my results to major U.S. papers.

7. Table results were derived from the public papers of the U.S. presidents, collected in the *American Presidency Project*. I searched the database for all uses of "support our troops" and "support the troops" through the end of Obama's presidency.

8. George H. W. Bush and Bill Clinton employed the slogan to justify "humanitarian" missions in Somalia and Bosnia, respectively. Due to space limitations, I cannot analyze their discourse.

Chapter 9

1. See appendix D for the coding scheme.

2. Obama once opposed a war-funding bill but voted to (re)fund the war in Iraq ten other times (Jackson 2008).

3. Obama's waving and smiling may invite a view of him as a fawning politician who panders to curry favor.

4. That the surge was "working" was dubious, as violence in Iraq persisted at appalling levels (Bacevich 2010, 202).

5. I purchased Gulf War merchandise from online sellers. I searched on cars for "War on Terror" artifacts in the summer and fall of 2014, mainly in Pittsburgh, Pennsylvania, but also in other areas (Detroit, Michigan; State College,

Pennsylvania; Buffalo, New York). I tried to photograph these artifacts, but in most cases, original pictures were poor, so I purchased replicas. To find advertisements of SOT merchandise, I relied on newspapers and online searches.

6. For simplicity, I refer to "the author" of the sign, though I don't know who that is. I also make this author a "he." I realize the sign may have been made by someone with another gender identity.

7. To find this website, I searched "support our troops products" on two different search engines: Google and DuckDuckGo. As of May 19, 2015, Google returns the FlagsOnCars website as the fifth result out of roughly 4,790,000 total results. Meanwhile, DuckDuckGo returns the FlagsOnCars site as the first overall result.

8. Interestingly, the troop in the center, who appears to be African American, casts his gaze downward, perhaps indicating a "low" feeling as he contends with the struggles of warfare.

9. To protect privacy, I make usernames anonymous (e.g., @[username1]).

10. The Twitter messages were collected using *Twitter-Search-API-Python* (Dickinson 2016). Though I collected data from 2007 to 2009, the vast majority of the tweets (about 96 percent) come from 2009, probably because Twitter was still relatively unknown before then (Kazeniac 2009).

11. To save space, I replace hyperlinks with the generic "[link]."

12. I assigned each sociopolitical tweet one code; however, tweets often blended traits of multiple categories.

13. The occasional success of such appeals shows that Twitter can be a site for "bottom-up" propaganda, moving from grassroots users to cultural icons and tastemakers who enhance message visibility.

Conclusion

1. In fact, opposition emerges in every society. Even in Orwell's *1984*, there were pockets of resistance, despite conditions of total propaganda and constant surveillance.

2. I use the word "humanity" instead of "man," which appears in the English translation by George Norlin.

3. Exciting initiatives are already being proposed by the Rhetoricians for Peace (Henderson and Braun 2016, 11).

Appendix A

1. Context does not shape discourse directly; we experience context subjectively and cognitively (Van Dijk 2008).

2. According to SF theory, discourse shapes context through three basic "metafunctions": the ideational, which construes reality; the interpersonal, which enacts social relationships; and the textual, which orders information. Context is categorized under three related headings: field, tenor, and mode. "Field" refers to what is happening, the action or event taking place. "Tenor" refers to who is participating, including their social and interactive roles. "Mode" refers to the role that discourse plays in the situation, including overall rhetorical function (persuasive, expository, and so on) and the medium of communication (spoken, written, and so on).

Bibliography

ABC. 2000–2004. *World News Tonight*. Produced by P. A. Slavin. Retrieved from the Vanderbilt Television News Archive, Vanderbilt University. [Television broadcast video.]

Abu-Absi, S. 1996. "Stereotypical Images of Arab Women." *Phi Beta Delta International Review* 6:55–64.

Abu-Hamad, A. 1992. "Kuwait's 'Stolen' Incubators: The Widespread Repercussions of a Murky Incident." *Middle East Watch*, February 6. Retrieved September 14, 2013, from http:// www.hrw.org/reports/pdfs/k/kuwait/kuwait922.pdf.

Abulhasan, M. A. 1990. "Letter Dated 5 September 1990 from the Permanent Representative of Kuwait to the United Nations Addressed to the Secretary-General." September 5. Retrieved September 13, 2013, from http://undocs.org/S/21713.

Ackerman, S. 2014. "41 Men Targeted but 1,147 People Killed: US Drone Strikes—The Facts on the Ground." *Guardian*, November 24. Retrieved March 13, 2018, from https://www .theguardian.com/us-news/2014/nov/24/-sp-us-drone-strikes-kill-1147.

Adams, N., reporter. 1990a. "Alleged Iraqi Atrocities in Kuwait." *All Things Considered*, National Public Radio, produced by P. Breslow, October 10. Retrieved from NewsBank. [Radio broadcast transcript.]

———, reporter. 1990b. "Iraqi Atrocities in Kuwait Reported." *All Things Considered*, National Public Radio, produced by P. Breslow, December 19. Retrieved from NewsBank. [Radio broadcast transcript.]

Agha, A. 2003. "The Social Life of Cultural Value." *Language and Communication* 23 (3–4): 231–73.

———. 2005. "Voice, Footing, Enregisterment." *Journal of Linguistic Anthropology* 15 (1): 38–59.

Albaek, E. 2011. "The Interaction Between Experts and Journalists in News Journalism." *Journalism* 12 (3): 335–48.

Albright, D. 2002. "Aluminum Tubing Is an Indicator of an Iraqi Gas Centrifuge Program: But Is the Tubing Specifically for Centrifuges?" *Institute for Science and International Security*, October 9. Retrieved June 19, 2014, from http://isis-online.org/isis-reports/detail /aluminum-tubing-is-an-indicator-of-an-iraqi-gas-centrifuge-program-but-is-t/9.

———. 2003. "Aluminum Tubes: Separating Fact from Fiction." *Institute for Science and International Security*, December 5. Retrieved July 7, 2014, from http://www.leadingtowar.com /PDFsources_claims_aluminum/2003_12_05_IS IS.pdf.

Amnesty International. 1990a. "Amnesty International Urges End to Torture and Killings in Iraq: Major Report Details Widespread Human Rights Violations." December 18. [Press release.]

———. 1990b. *Iraq/Occupied Kuwait: Human Rights Violations since August 2, 1990*. MDE 14/016/1990. London: Amnesty International. Retrieved March 15, 2018, from https:// www.amnesty.org/en/documents/mde14/016/1990/en/.

———. 1991. "Kuwait: Amnesty International Calls on Emir to Intervene Over Continuing Torture and Killings." April 19. [Press release.]

Amos, D., reporter. 1990. *Weekend Edition Sunday*, National Public Radio, produced by R. Malesky, September 9. Retrieved from NewsBank. [Radio broadcast transcript.]

Anderson, D. 2007. *Identity's Strategy: Rhetorical Selves in Conversion*. Columbia: University of South Carolina Press.

Anderson, T. H. 2011. *Bush's Wars*. New York: Oxford University Press.

Appy, C. G. 2004. *Patriots: The Vietnam War Remembered from All Sides*. New York: Penguin.

Aristotle. 2007. *On Rhetoric: A Theory of Civic Discourse*. Translated by G. A. Kennedy. New York: Oxford University Press.

Arkin, W. M. 1999. "The Difference Was in the Details." *Washington Post*, January 17. Retrieved July 30, 2015, from https://www.washingtonpost.com/wp-srv/inatl/longterm/iraq/analysis.htm.

Arthos, J. 2013. "The Just Use of Propaganda (?): Ethical Criteria for Counter-Hegemonic Communication Strategies." *Western Journal of Communication* 77 (5): 582–603.

Aruri, N. 1991. "Human Rights and the Gulf Crisis: The Verbal Strategy of George Bush." In *Beyond the Storm: A Gulf Crisis Reader*, edited by P. Bennis and M. Moushabeck, 305–24. New York: Olive Branch Press.

Associated Press. 1982. "Reagan Criticizes Media 'Slant' on El Salvador." *Fort Scott (KS) Tribune*, March 15, 7.

———. 1990a. "Kuwait Says Iraq Is Plundering Hospitals, Blood Banks." September 6. Retrieved September 16, 2013, from http://www.apnewsarchive.com/1990/Kuwait-Says-Iraq-is-Plundering-Hospitals-Blood-Banks-With-AM-Gulf-Rdp-Bjt/id-29e63f35012a2b3ff686164dbe5cd02e.

———. 1990b. "Doctor Says He Helped Bury More than 50 Premature Babies." November 10. Retrieved from LexisNexis Academic.

Atlanta Journal-Constitution. 2001. "On the Homefront." September 26, 2C.

Bacevich, A. J. 2001. "A Less than Splendid Little War." *Wilson Quarterly* 25 (1). Retrieved September 26, 2014, from http://wilsonquarterly.com/stories/a-less-than-splendid-little-war/.

———. 2005. *The New American Militarism: How Americans Are Seduced by War*. New York: Oxford University Press.

———. 2010. *Washington Rules: America's Path to Permanent War*. New York: Metropolitan Books.

Baker, W. 2011. "Soapbox for the Automobile: Bumper Sticker History, Identification, and Preservation." *Collections: A Journal for Museum and Archives Professionals* 7 (3): 251–70.

Bakhtin, M. M. 1981. *The Dialogic Imagination: Four Essays*. Edited by M. Holquist. Translated by C. Emerson and M. Holquist. Austin: University of Texas Press.

———. 1984. *Problems of Dostoevsky's Poetics*. Edited and translated by C. Emerson. Minneapolis: University of Minnesota Press.

———. 1986. *Speech Genres and Other Late Essays*. Edited by C. Emerson and M. Holquist. Translated by V. W. McGee. Austin: University of Texas Press.

Baldry, A. P., and P. J. Thibault. 2005. *Multimodal Transcription and Text Analysis: A Multimedia Toolkit and Coursebook*. London: Equinox.

Barlett, D. L., and J. B. Steele. 2007. "Washington's $8 Billion Shadow." *Vanity Fair*, March. Retrieved April 19, 2014, from http://www.vanityfair.com/politics/features/2007/03/spyagency200703.

Barstow, D. 2008. "Behind TV Analysts, Pentagon's Hidden Hand." *New York Times*, April 20. Retrieved December 20, 2013, from http://www.nytimes.com/2008/04/20/us/20generals.html.

Barstow, D., W. J. Broad, and J. Gerth. 2004. "How the White House Embraced Disputed Arms Intelligence." *New York Times*, October 3. Retrieved June 19, 2014, from http://www.nytimes.com/2004/10/03/international/middleeast/03tube.html.

Bauman, R., and C. L. Briggs. 1990. "Poetics and Performance as Critical Perspectives on Language and Social Life." *Annual Review of Anthropology* 19:59–88.

Beamish, T. D., H. Molotch, and R. Flacks. 1995. "Who Supports the Troops? Vietnam, the Gulf War, and the Making of Collective Memory." *Social Problems* 42 (3): 344–60.

Benaim, D., P. Motaparthy, and V. Kumar. 2003. "TV's Conflicted Experts." *Nation*, April 3. Retrieved April 19, 2014, from http://www.thenation.com/article/tvs-conflicted-experts.

Bennett, B. S., and S. P. O'Rourke. 2006. "A Prolegomenon to the Future Study of Rhetoric and Propaganda: Critical Foundations." In *Readings in Propaganda and Persuasion: New and Classic Essays*, edited by G. S. Jowett and V. O'Donnell, 51–71. Thousand Oaks, CA: SAGE.

Bennett, W. L. 1990. "Toward a Theory of Press-State Relations." *Journal of Communication* 40 (2): 103–25.

———. 2012. *News: The Politics of Illusion*. 9th ed. New York: Longman.

Bennett, W. L., R. G. Lawrence, and S. Livingston. 2007. *When the Press Fails: Political Power and the News Media from Iraq to Katrina*. Chicago: University of Chicago Press.

Bergen, P., and P. Cruickshank. 2007. "The Iraq Effect: War Has Increased Terrorism Sevenfold Worldwide." *Mother Jones*, March 1. Retrieved May 23, 2016, from http://www.mother jones.com/politics/2007/03/iraq-101-iraq-effect-war-iraq-and-its-impact-war-terrorism -pg-1.

Bernays, E. (1928) 2005. *Propaganda*. Reprint, New York: Ig Publishing.

Blitzer, W., reporter. 2002. "Interview with Condoleezza Rice; Pataki Talks About 9–11; Graham, Shelby Discuss War on Terrorism." *CNN Late Edition with Wolf Blitzer*, CNN, September 8. Retrieved June 19, 2014, from http://transcripts.cnn.com/TRANSCRIPTS/0209/08 /le.00.html. [Television broadcast transcript.]

Blommaert, J. 2005. *Discourse: A Critical Introduction*. Cambridge: Cambridge University Press.

Blum, W. 2004. *Killing Hope: U.S. Military and C.I.A. Interventions since World War II*. Monroe, ME: Common Courage Press.

———. 2010. "The Anti-empire Report #80: The United States Takes the Matter of Three-Headed Babies Very Seriously." *Anti-empire Report* (blog), April 5. Retrieved July 29, 2015, from http://williamblum.org/aer/read/80.

Borger, J. 2002. "Rumsfeld 'Offered Help to Saddam.'" *Guardian*, December 31. Retrieved July 8, 2015, from http://www.theguardian.com/world/2002/dec/31/iraq.politics.

Bourdieu, P. 1991. *Language and Symbolic Power*. Edited by J. B. Thompson. Translated by G. Raymond and M. Adamson. Cambridge, MA: Harvard University Press.

Boustany, N. 1990. "Iraqi Rebuffs Suggestions of Pullout." *Washington Post*, October 5, A30.

Boyle, F. 2002. Interview with D. Bernstein. *Covert Action Quarterly* 73:9–12, 27.

Breaux, J. 1991. 137 Congressional Record, S183 (January 11). Retrieved from ProQuest, http:// congressional.proquest.com.

Breazeale, K. 1994. "Bringing the War Back Home: Consuming Operation Desert Storm." *Journal of American Culture* 17 (1): 31–37.

Brookings Institution. 2002. Event: News Briefing—Brookings Institution (BI). *Federal News Service Daybook*, December 12.

Brooks, J. 2003. "Saddam Received Key to City of Detroit in 1980." *Detroit News*, March 26. Retrieved July 28, 2015, from http://www.timeenoughforlove.org/saved/SaddamReceived KeyToCityOfDetroit1980.htm.

Buchanan, P. 2003. *Buchanan and Press*, MSNBC, March 18. Retrieved from LexisNexis Academic. [Television broadcast transcript.]

Buchheit, P. 2014. "4 Shocking Examples of American Inequality." *AlterNet*, February 2. Retrieved July 21, 2015, from http://www.alternet.org/economy/4-shocking-examples-american -inequality.

Burke, K. 1954. *Permanence and Change*. 3rd ed. Berkeley: University of California Press.

Burton, D. 1991. 137 Congressional Record, H141 (January 10). Retrieved from ProQuest, http:// congressional.proquest.com.

Bush, G. H. W. 1990a. "Address on Iraq's Invasion of Kuwait." Miller Center, University of Virginia, August 8. Retrieved September 13, 2013, from https://millercenter.org/the-presidency /presidential-speeches/august-8-1990-address-iraqs-invasion-kuwait. [Television broadcast video and transcript.]

———. 1990b. "The President's News Conference." October 9. *American Presidency Project*. Retrieved September 13, 2013, from http://www.presidency.ucsb.edu/ws/?pid=18911. [Television broadcast transcript.]

———. 1990c. "Remarks at a Fundraising Luncheon for Gubernatorial Candidate Clayton Williams in Dallas, Texas." October 15. *American Presidency Project*. Retrieved September 13, 2013, from http://www.presidency.ucsb.edu/ws/?pid=18931. [Speech transcript.]

———. 1990d. "Remarks at a Republican Fundraising Breakfast in Des Moines, Iowa." October 16. *American Presidency Project*. Retrieved September 13, 2013, from http://www.presidency.ucsb.edu/ws/?pid=18934. [Speech transcript.]

———. 1990e. "Remarks at a Republican Fundraising Breakfast in Burlington, Vermont." October 23. *American Presidency Project*. Retrieved September 13, 2013, from http://www.presidency.ucsb.edu/ws/?pid=18954. [Speech transcript.]

———. 1990f. "Remarks at Republican Campaign Rally in Manchester, New Hampshire." October 23. *American Presidency Project*. Retrieved September 13, 2013, from http://www.presidency.ucsb.edu/ws/?pid=18955. [Speech transcript.]

———. 1990g. "Remarks to Officers and Troops at Hickam Air Force Base in Pearl Harbor, Hawaii." October 28. *American Presidency Project*. Retrieved September 13, 2013, from http://www.presidency.ucsb.edu/ws/?pid=18972. [Speech transcript.]

———. 1990h. "Remarks at a Republican Campaign Rally in Mashpee, Massachusetts." November 1. *American Presidency Project*. Retrieved September 13, 2013, from http://www.presidency.ucsb.edu/ws/?pid=18983. [Speech transcript.]

———. 1990i. "Remarks to Allied Armed Forces near Dhahran, Saudi Arabia." November 22. *American Presidency Project*. Retrieved September 13, 2013, from http://www.presidency.ucsb.edu/ws/?pid=19088. [Speech transcript.]

———. 1991a. "Remarks to the Reserve Officers Association." January 23. *American Presidency Project*. Retrieved September 20, 2014, from http://www.presidency.ucsb.edu/ws/?pid=19245. [Speech transcript.]

———. 1991b. "Address Before a Joint Session of the Congress on the State of the Union." January 29. *American Presidency Project*. Retrieved September 20, 2014, from http://www.presidency.ucsb.edu/ws/?pid=19253. [Speech transcript.]

———. 1991c. "Radio Address to United States Armed Forces Stationed in the Persian Gulf Region." March 2. *American Presidency Project*. Retrieved September 24, 2014, from http://www.presidency.ucsb.edu/ws/?pid=19355. [Speech transcript.]

Bush, G. W. 2001a. "Address to a Joint Session of Congress and the American People." September 20. National Archives. Retrieved July 28, 2015, from https://georgewbush-whitehouse.archives.gov/news/releases/2001/09/20010920-8.html. [Speech transcript.]

———. 2001b. "Address to the Nation from Atlanta on Homeland Security." November 8. *American Presidency Project*. Retrieved September 27, 2014, from http://www.presidency.ucsb.edu/ws/?pid=62836. [Speech transcript.]

———. 2002a. "President's Remarks at the United Nations General Assembly." September 12. National Archives. Retrieved April 11, 2013, from https://georgewbush-whitehouse.archives.gov/news/releases/2002/09/20020912-1.html. [Speech transcript.]

———. 2002b. "President Bush Outlines Iraqi Threat." October 7. National Archives. Retrieved April 19, 2013, from https://georgewbush-whitehouse.archives.gov/news/releases/2002/10/20021007-8.html. [Speech transcript.]

———. 2003. "Address Before a Joint Session of the Congress on the State of the Union." January 28. *American Presidency Project*. Retrieved April 11, 2013, from http://www.presidency.ucsb.edu/ws/index.php?pid=29645. [Speech transcript.]

———. 2004a. "Remarks at Fort Lewis, Washington." June 18. *American Presidency Project*. Retrieved September 27, 2014, from http://www.presidency.ucsb.edu/ws/?pid=63599. [Speech transcript.]

———. 2004b. "Remarks in Cuyahoga Falls, Ohio." October 2. *American Presidency Project*. Retrieved September 27, 2014, from http://www.presidency.ucsb.edu/ws/?pid=63387. [Speech transcript.]

———. 2007. "Address Before a Joint Session of the Congress on the State of the Union." January 23. *American Presidency Project*. Retrieved October 20, 2014, from http://www.presidency.ucsb.edu/ws/index.php?pid=24446. [Speech transcript.]

Butler, R. 2000. *The Greatest Threat: Iraq, Weapons of Mass Destruction, and the Crisis of Global Security*. New York: PublicAffairs.

———. 2002. Statement. *Hearing to Examine Threats, Responses, and Regional Considerations Surrounding Iraq Before the United States Senate Committee on Foreign Relations*, 107th Congress, July 31. Retrieved March 15, 2018, from https://www.gpo.gov/fdsys/pkg/CHRG-107shrg81697/html/CHRG-107shrg81697.htm. [Hearing Transcript.]

Calsamiglia, H., and C. López Ferrero. 2003. "Role and Position of Scientific Voices: Reported Speech in the Media." *Discourse Studies* 5 (2): 147–73.

Campbell, K. K., and K. H. Jamieson. 2008. *Presidents Creating the Presidency: Deeds Done in Words*. Chicago: The University of Chicago Press.

Cannon, G. 2001. "Cal Anti-war Rally Draws Vocal Crowd; Hundreds Attend a Walkout in Sproul Plaza with Signs and Slogans." *Contra Costa (CA) Times*, October 9, A3.

Cap, P. 2006. *Legitimisation in Political Discourse. A Cross-Disciplinary Perspective on the Modern US War Rhetoric*. Newcastle, UK: Cambridge Scholars Press.

———. 2013. *Proximization: The Pragmatics of Symbolic Distance Crossing*. Philadelphia: John Benjamins.

Carey, A. 1997. *Taking the Risk Out of Democracy: Corporate Propaganda versus Freedom and Liberty*. Urbana: University of Illinois Press.

Carpenter, T. G. 1995. *The Captive Press: Foreign Policy Crises and the First Amendment*. Washington, DC: Cato Institute.

Carvalho, A. 2008. "Media(ted) Discourse and Society: Rethinking the Framework of Critical Discourse Analysis." *Journalism Studies* 9 (2): 161–76.

Case, C. E. 1992. "Bumper Stickers and Car Signs: Ideology and Identity." *Journal of Popular Culture* 26 (3): 107–30.

CBS. 1992. "Testimony of Kuwaiti Ambassador's Daughter Sways Congress." *60 Minutes*, September 6. Retrieved from LexisNexis Academic. [Television broadcast transcript.]

———. 2000–2005. *CBS Evening News*. Produced by J. Murphy. Retrieved from the Vanderbilt Television News Archive, Vanderbilt University. [Television broadcast video.]

Center for Public Integrity. 2006. "U.S. Contractors Reap the Windfalls of Post-war Reconstruction." In *Crimes of War: Iraq*, edited by R. Falk, I. Gendzier, and R. J. Lifton, 279–92. New York: Nation Books.

Cheney, R. 2002. Interview by Tim Russert. *Meet the Press*, NBC, September 8. Retrieved March 15, 2018, from https://www.leadingtowar.com/PDFsources_claims_aluminum/2002_09_08_NBC.pdf. [Television broadcast transcript.]

———. 2003. Interview by Tim Russert. *Meet the Press*, NBC, March 16. Retrieved from ProQuest. [Television broadcast transcript.]

Chilton, P. A. 2003. "Deixis and Distance: President Clinton's Justification of Intervention in Kosovo." In *At War with Words*, edited by M. N. Dedaić and D. N. Nelson, 95–126. New York: Mouton de Gruyter.

Chomsky, N. 1991. "Gulf War Pullout." *Z Magazine*, February. Retrieved July 28, 2015, from https://chomsky.info/199102__/.

———. 1992. "Language in the Service of Propaganda." In *Stenographers to Power: Media and Propaganda*, edited by D. Barsamian, 63–85. Monroe, ME: Common Courage Press.

———. 2002. *Media Control: The Spectacular Achievements of Propaganda*. 2nd ed. New York: Seven Stories Press.

———. 2003. *Hegemony or Survival: America's Quest for Global Dominance*. New York: Metropolitan Books.

———. 2016. "American Power under Challenge: Masters of Mankind (Part 1)." *Tom Dispatch*, May 8. Retrieved May 23, 2016, from http://www.tomdispatch.com/post/176137/tomgram%3A_noam_chomsky%2C_the_challenges_of_2016/.

Chouliaraki, L. 2006. "Towards an Analytics of Mediation." *Critical Discourse Studies* 3 (2): 153–78.

Clarke, R. A. 2004. *Against All Enemies: Inside America's War on Terror*. New York: Free Press.

Cockburn, A. 1991. "Sifting for the Truth on Both Sides: War Brings Propaganda, All Designed to Protect Government." *Los Angeles Times*, January 17. Retrieved February 23, 2018, from http://articles.latimes.com/1991-01-17/local/me-68_1_amnesty-international.

Cockburn, P. 2014. "How the War on Terror Created the World's Most Powerful Terror Group." *Nation*, August 21. Retrieved May 20, 2017, from https://www.thenation.com/article/how-war-terror-created-worlds-most-powerful-terror-group/.

Coll, S. 2004. *Ghost Wars: The Secret History of the CIA, Afghanistan, and bin Laden, from the Soviet Invasion to September10, 2001*. New York: Penguin.

Collier, R. 2002. "Bush's Evidence of Threat Disputed; Findings Often Ambiguous, Contradict CIA." *San Francisco Chronicle*, October 12. Retrieved June 1, 2015, from http://www.sfgate.com/news/article/Bush-s-evidence-of-threat-disputed-Findings-2785731.php.

Condit, C. M., and J. L. Lucaites. 1993. *Crafting Equality: America's Anglo-African Word*. Chicago: University of Chicago Press.

Conetta, C. 2002. *Strange Victory: A Critical Appraisal of Operation Enduring Freedom and the Afghanistan War*. Research Monograph 6. Cambridge, MA: Project on Defense Alternatives, Commonwealth Institute. Retrieved July 29, 2015, from http://www.comw.org/pda/0201strangevic.html.

Coy, P. G., L. M. Woehrle, and G. M. Maney. 2008. "Discursive Legacies: The U.S. Peace Movement and 'Support the Troops.'" *Social Problems* 55 (2): 161–89.

Cramer, P. 2013. "Sick Stuff: A Case Study of Controversy in a Constitutive Attitude." *Rhetoric Society Quarterly* 43 (2): 177–201.

Creel, G. 1920. *How We Advertised America*. New York: Harper and Brothers.

Cunningham, S. B. 2001. "Responding to Propaganda: An Ethical Enterprise." *Journal of Mass Media Ethics* 16 (2–3): 138–47.

Cushing, L. 2009. "Political Graphics of the 'Long 1960s.'" In *New World Coming: The Sixties and the Shaping of Global Consciousness*, edited by K. Dubinsky, C. Krull, S. Lord, S. Mills, and S. Rutherford. Toronto: Between the Lines Press. Retrieved October 4, 2014, from http://www.docspopuli.org/articles/NewWorldComing.html.

Dahl, D. 1991. "House Backs Troops." *St. Petersburg (FL) Times*, January 19, 5A.

Damore, D. F. 2002. "Candidate Strategy and the Decision to Go Negative." *Political Research Quarterly* 55 (3): 669–85.

DeBenedetti, C., and C. Chatfield. 1990. *An American Ordeal: The Antiwar Movement of the Vietnam Era*. Syracuse, NY: Syracuse University Press.

Defense Science Board. 2004. *Report of the Defense Science Board Task Force on Strategic Communication*. Washington, DC: Office of the Under Secretary of Defense for Acquisition, Technology, and Logistics. Retrieved May 20, 2017, from https://fas.org/irp/agency/dod/dsb/commun.pdf.

Dewachi, O. 2011. *Insecurity, Displacement, and Public Health Impacts of the American Invasion of Iraq*. Providence: Costs of War Project, Watson Institute for International and Public Affairs, Brown University. Retrieved February 23, 2018, http://watson.brown.edu/costsofwar/files/cow/imcc/papers/2011/DewachiIraqiRefugees.pdf.

Dickinson, T. 2016. *Twitter-Search-API-Python*. GitHub. Retrieved October 18, 2016, from https://github.com/tomkdickinson/Twitter-Search-API-Python. [Computer software.]

Docherty, N., producer. 1992. "To Sell a War." *Fifth Estate*. Toronto: CBC Enterprises. [Television broadcast.]

Domke, D. S. 2004. *God Willing? Political Fundamentalism in the White House, the "War on Terror," and the Echoing Press*. London: Pluto Press.

Doob, L. W. 1989. "Propaganda." In *International Encyclopedia of Communications*, edited by E. Barnouw, G. Gerbner, W. Schramm, T. L. Worth, and L. Gross, 3:374–78. New York: Oxford University Press.

Drutman, L. 2015. "How Corporate Lobbyists Conquered American Democracy." *Atlantic*, April 20. Retrieved May 12, 2017, from https://www.theatlantic.com/business/archive/2015/04/how-corporate-lobbyists-conquered-american-democracy/390822/.

Dunmire, P. 2009. "'9/11 Changed Everything': An Intertextual Analysis of the Bush Doctrine." *Discourse and Society* 20 (2): 195–222.

———. 2011. *Projecting the Future Through Political Discourse: The Case of the Bush Doctrine*. Amsterdam: John Benjamins.

Egelko, B. 2006. "Pelosi's First Priority Is to Halt Iraq War; Speaker Taking Office Jan. 4 Comes Home to Talk Up Plans." *San Francisco Chronicle*, December 10. Retrieved October 27, 2014, from http://www.sfgate.com/politics/article/SAN-FRANCISCO-Pelosi-s-first-priority-is-to-2465706.php.

Ekman, P., and E. Rosenberg. 1997. *What the Face Reveals*. New York: Oxford University Press.

Elliot, S. 1991. "Ranking Pitches; Worst Efforts Rely on Misguided Wishes of Support." *USA Today*, February 26, 8B.

Ellul, J. 1965. *Propaganda: The Formation of Men's Attitudes*. Translated by K. Kellen and J. Lerner. New York: Vintage Books.

Endersby, J. W., and M. J. Towle. 1996. "Tailgate Partisanship: Political and Social Expression Through Bumper Stickers." *Social Science Journal* 33 (3): 307–19.

Entman, R. M. 2004. *Projections of Power: Framing News, Public Opinion, and U.S. Foreign Policy*. Chicago: University of Chicago Press.

Fairclough, N. 1992. *Discourse and Social Change*. Cambridge: Polity Press.

———. 1995. *Media Discourse*. New York: E. Arnold.

———. 1999. "Global Capitalism and Critical Awareness of Language." *Language Awareness* 8 (2): 71–83.

———. 2003. *Analyzing Discourse: Textual Analysis for Social Research*. London: Routledge.

Fairness and Accuracy in Reporting. 2003. "In Iraq Crisis, Networks Are Megaphones for Official Views." March 18. Retrieved February 23, 2018, from https://fair.org/take-action/action-alerts/in-iraq-crisis-networks-are-megaphones-for-official-views/.

Falk, R., and H. Friel. 2004. *The Record of the Paper: How the* New York Times *Misreports U.S. Foreign Policy*. London: Verso.

Fang, L. 2013. "The Reverse Revolving Door: How Corporate Insiders Are Rewarded upon Leaving Firms for Congress." *Nation*, May 4. Retrieved July 21, 2015, from http://www.thenation.com/article/reverse-revolving-door-how-corporate-insiders-are-rewarded-upon-leaving-firms-congres/.

Fashion Staff. 1991. "Dressed Up for a Notable Exit." *Los Angeles Times*, January 25. Retrieved October 18, 2014, from http://articles.latimes.com/1991-01-25/news/vw-582_1_hometown-beverly-hills.

Fellows, E. W. 1959. "'Propaganda': History of a Word." *American Speech* 34 (3): 182–89.

Fields, J. 1991. 137 Congressional Record, H179 (January 10). Retrieved from ProQuest, http://congressional.proquest.com.

FlagsOnCars. n.d. "Support Our Troops Products." Retrieved October 19, 2014, from http://www
.flagsoncars.com/support-our-troops-products.html.

Fleischer, A. 2002. "White House Press Briefing." December 5. *American Presidency Project.*
Retrieved June 18, 2014, from http://www.presidency.ucsb.edu/ws/index.php?pid=47459.
[Press briefing transcript.]

Forbes. n.d. "Manuel Moroun and Family." Retrieved October 18, 2014, from http://www.forbes.com
/profile/manuel-moroun/.

Foss, S. K., and C. L. Griffin. 1995. "Beyond Persuasion: A Proposal for an Invitational Rhetoric."
Communication Monographs 62 (1): 2–18.

Fox Broadcasting Company. 2013. *Support Our Troops.* Retrieved May 21, 2017, from https://www
.ispot.tv/ad/7ITu/fox-support-our-troops-feat-lea-michele-naya-rivera. [Television advertisement video.]

Frankel, G. 1990. "Iraq, Kuwait Waging an Old-Fashioned War of Propaganda." *Washington Post,*
September 10, A18. Retrieved February 23, 2018, from https://www.washingtonpost.com
/archive/politics/1990/09/10/iraq-kuwait-waging-an-old-fashioned-war-of-propaganda
/e681bc46-15c1-4be7-9e0b-a61b8aea74af/.

Franklin, H. B. 2000. *Vietnam and Other American Fantasies.* Amherst: University of Massachusetts Press.

Frantz, D. 2001. "A Nation Challenged: The Afghans; Taliban Say They Want to Negotiate with the
U.S. over bin Laden." *New York Times,* October 3. Retrieved July 29, 2015, from http://
www.nytimes.com/2001/10/03/world/nation-challenged-afghans-taliban-say-they-want
-negotiate-with-us-over-bin-laden.html.

Freeman, D. W. 2010. "Cigarette Warning Labels: Brazil's More Shocking than Ours." *CBS News,*
November 12. Retrieved July 18, 2015, from http://www.cbsnews.com/news/cigarette
-warning-labels-brazils-more-shocking-than-ours-pictures/.

Galtung, J. 1993. Preface to *Communication and Culture in War and Peace,* edited by C. Roach,
xi–xii. Newbury Park, CA: SAGE.

Gans, H. 1979. *Deciding What's News.* New York: Vintage Books.

Garofoli, J. 2005. "Blue and Red Divided over Yellow Ribbons; 'Support Our Troops' Car Magnets
Arrive—with Political Rebuttals." *San Francisco Chronicle,* January 1, A1. Retrieved October 11, 2014, from https://www.sfgate.com/politics/joegarofoli/article/Blue-and-red-divided
-over-yellow-ribbons-2740163.php.

Garver, E. 1994. *Aristotle's* Rhetoric: *An Art of Character.* Chicago: University of Chicago Press.

Garza, A. 2014. "A Herstory of the #BlackLivesMatter Movement." *Feminist Wire,* October 7.
Retrieved July 20, 2015, from http://www.thefeministwire.com/2014/10/blacklivesmatter
-2/.

Gellman, B. 1998. "Iraq Hasn't Cooperated, Arms Inspector Reports." *Washington Post,* December
16. Retrieved June 7, 2014, from http://www.washingtonpost.com/wp-srv/inatl/longterm
/iraq/stories/butler121698.htm.

———. 1999. "U.S. Spied on Iraq via U.N." *Washington Post,* March 2. Retrieved April 21, 2014,
from http://www.washingtonpost.com/wp-srv/inatl/daily/march99/unscom2.htm.

Gilbert, G. M. 1947. *Nuremberg Diary.* New York: Da Capo Press.

Gilens, M., and B. I. Page. 2014. "Testing Theories of American Politics: Elites, Interest Groups, and
Average Citizens." *Perspectives on Politics* 12 (3): 564–81.

Gilson, D., and C. Perot. 2011. "It's the Inequality, Stupid." *Mother Jones,* March/April. Retrieved
July 21, 2015, from http://www.motherjones.com/politics/2011/02/income-inequality
-in-america-chart-graph.

Gjelten, T., reporter. 1990. "Released Hostages Tell of Kuwait Terror." *All Things Considered,*
National Public Radio, produced by P. Breslow, September 7. [Radio broadcast
transcript.]

Glaister, D. 2004. "High-Profile Air Strikes 'Killed Only Civilians.'" *Guardian*, June 14. Retrieved July 31, 2015, from https://www.theguardian.com/world/2004/jun/14/iraq.usa.

Gold, M., and A. Narayanswamy. 2015. "2016 Fundraising Shows Power Tilting to Groups Backed by Wealthy Elite." *Washington Post*, July 15. Retrieved February 23, 2018, from https://www.washingtonpost.com/politics/2016-fundraising-shows-power-tilting-to-groups-backed-by-wealthy-elite/2015/07/15/4c915a74-2b05-11e5-a250-42bd812efc09_story.html.

Goodman, M. 2006. Interview. "The Dark Side." *Frontline*, Public Broadcasting Service. Retrieved April 18, 2013, from http://www.pbs.org/wgbh/pages/frontline/darkside/themes/nie.html#goodman.

Gordon, M. R., and J. Miller. 2002. "Threats and Responses: The Iraqis; U.S. Says Hussein Intensified Quest for A-Bomb Parts." *New York Times*, September 8. Retrieved June 19, 2014, from http://www.nytimes.com/2002/09/08/world/threats-responses-iraqis-us-says-hussein-intensifies-quest-for-bomb-parts.html.

Graham, P. 2004. "Predication, Propagation, and Mediation: SFL, CDA, and the Inculcation of Evaluative-Meaning Systems." In *Systemic Functional Linguistics and Critical Discourse Analysis: Studies in Social Change*, edited by L. Young and C. Harrison, 53–67. London: Continuum.

Graham, P., T. Keenan, and A. Dowd. 2004. "A Call to Arms at the End of History: A Discourse-Historical Analysis of George W. Bush's Declaration of War on Terror." *Discourse and Society* 15 (2–3): 199–221.

Greenwald, G. 2008. "Brian Williams' 'Response' to the Military Analyst Story." *Salon*, April 30. Retrieved February 23, 2018, from https://www.salon.com/2008/04/30/williams_7/.

Guilliard, J., L. Henken, K. Mellenthin, T. K. Takaro, R. M. Gould, A. Fatollah-Nejad, and J. Wagner. 2015. *Body Count: Casualty Figures after 10 Years of the "War on Terror."* Translated by A. Fatollah-Nejad. Berlin: International Physicians for the Prevention of Nuclear War; Washington, DC: Physicians for Social Responsibility; Ottawa: Physicians for Global Survival. Retrieved July 30, 2015, from http://www.ippnw.de/commonFiles/pdfs/Frieden/Body_Count_first_international_edition_2015_final.pdf.

Guriev, S., and D. Treisman. 2015. "The New Dictators Rule by Velvet Fist." *New York Times*, May 24. Retrieved July 3, 2015, from https://www.nytimes.com/2015/05/25/opinion/the-new-dictators-rule-by-velvet-fist.html.

Halliday, M. A. K. 1985. *An Introduction to Functional Grammar*. London: Edward Arnold.

Halliday, M. A. K., and C. M. I. M. Matthiessen. 2004. *An Introduction to Functional Grammar*. 3rd ed. London: Hodder Education.

Hallin, D. 1986. *The Uncensored War: The Media and Vietnam*. New York: Oxford University Press.

Harris, S., and J. Meyer. 1991. "Gulf Troops Welcomed with Hollywood Flair: Parade: Hundreds of Thousands Watch Them March in Festive Display. Veterans of All Conflicts Are Honored." *Los Angeles Times*, May 20. Retrieved October 18, 2014, from http://articles.latimes.com/1991-05-20/news/mn-1458_1_parade-route.

Hart, C. 2010. *Critical Discourse Analysis and Cognitive Science: New Perspectives on Immigration Discourse*. New York: Palgrave Macmillan.

Hart, P. 2003. "O'Reilly's War: Any Rationale—or None—Will Do." *Extra!*, May. Retrieved March 14, 2018, from https://fair.org/extra/oreillys-war/.

Hart, P., and N. Newhouse. 2008. *NBC News/Wall Street Journal Survey, Study #6084*, July 18–21. Retrieved November 2, 2014, from http://msnbcmedia.msn.com/i/msnbc/sections/news/080723_Released.pdf.

Hedges, C. 2003. *War Is a Force that Gives Us Meaning*. New York: Anchor Books.

Hedges, S. J. 1999. "Arms Aide: U.N. Helped U.S. to Spy on Iraqis." *Chicago Tribune*, January 10. Retrieved April 21, 2014, from http://articles.chicagotribune.com/1999-01-10/news/9901100180_1_unscom-australian-richard-butler-special-security-organization.

Heilbronn, L. M. 1994. "Yellow Ribbons and Remembrance: Mythic Symbols of the Gulf War." *Sociological Inquiry* 64 (2): 151–78.

Henderson, G. L., and M. J. Braun. 2016. "A Call for Renewed Attention to Propaganda in Writing Studies and Rhetoric." Introduction to *Propaganda and Rhetoric in Democracy: History, Theory, Analysis*, edited by M. J. Braun and G. L. Henderson, 1–25. Carbondale: Southern Illinois University Press.

Hepburn, K. 2004. "Crying: Notes on Description, Transcription, and Interaction." *Research on Language and Social Interaction* 37 (3): 251–90.

Herman, E. S., and N. Chomsky. 2002. *Manufacturing Consent: The Political Economy of the Mass Media*. New York: Pantheon.

Herold, M. W. 2003. "A Dossier on Civilian Victims of United States' Aerial Bombing of Afghanistan: A Comprehensive Accounting." Retrieved March 15, 2018, from https://web.archive.org/web/20171227062115/http://pubpages.unh.edu/~mwherold/dossier.

Hersh, S. 2000. "Overwhelming Force." Annals of War. *New Yorker*, May 22, 49–82.

———. 2003. "Selective Intelligence." Annals of National Security. *New Yorker*, May 12. Retrieved June 1, 2015, from http://www.newyorker.com/magazine/2003/05/12/selective-intelligence.

Hodges, A. 2008a. "The Dialogic Emergence of 'Truth' in Politics: Reproduction and Subversion of the 'War on Terror' Discourse." *Colorado Research in Linguistics* 21:1–12.

———. 2008b. "The Politics of Recontextualization: Discursive Competition over Claims of Iranian Involvement in Iraq." *Discourse and Society* 19 (4): 483–505.

———. 2011. *The "War on Terror" Narrative: Discourse and Intertextuality in the Construction and Contestation of Sociopolitical Reality*. New York: Oxford University Press.

———. 2013. "The Generic U.S. Presidential War Narrative: Justifying Military Force and Imagining the Nation." In *Discourses of War and Peace*, edited by A. Hodges, 47–68. New York: Oxford University Press.

———. 2014. "'Yes, We Can': The Social Life of a Political Slogan." In *Contemporary Critical Discourse Studies*, edited by C. Hart and P. Cap, 349–66. London: Bloomsbury.

———. 2015. "War Discourse." In *The International Encyclopedia of Language and Social Interaction*, edited by K. Tracy, 1545–50. New York: John Wiley and Sons. Retrieved March 15, 2018, from https://works.bepress.com/adamhodges/55/.

Hodges, A., and C. Nilep. 2007. Introduction to *Discourse, War, and Terrorism*, edited by A. Hodges and C. Nilep, 1–17. Philadelphia: John Benjamins.

Huckin, T. 2002. "Textual Silence and the Discourse of Homelessness." *Discourse and Society* 13 (3): 347–72.

———. 2010. "On Textual Silences, Large and Small." In *Traditions of Writing Research*, edited by C. Bazerman, R. Krut, K. Lunsford, S. McLeod, S. Null, P. Rogers, and A. Stansell, 419–31. New York: Routledge.

———. 2016. "Propaganda Defined." In *Propaganda and Rhetoric in Democracy: History, Theory, Analysis*, edited by M. J. Braun and G. L. Henderson, 118–36. Carbondale: Southern Illinois University Press.

Hyland, K. 2000. *Disciplinary Discourses: Social Interactions in Academic Writing*. Harlow, UK: Longman.

Institute for Propaganda Analysis. 1937. "How to Detect Propaganda." *Propaganda Analysis* 1 (2): 5–8.

Iraq Body Count. 2012. "Iraqi Deaths from Violence 2003–2011." January 2. Retrieved May 20, 2017, from https://www.iraqbodycount.org/analysis/numbers/2011/.

Irvine, J. T., and S. Gal. 2000. "Language Ideology and Linguistic Differentiation." In *Regimes of Language*, edited by P. V. Kroskrity, 35–83. Santa Fe: School of American Research Press.

Isenberg, N., O. Silbersweig, A. Engelien, S. Emmerich, K. Malavade, B. Beattie, A. C. Leon, and E. Stern. 1999. "Linguistic Threat Activates the Human Amygdala." *Proceedings of the National Academy of Sciences of the United States of America* 96 (18): 10456–59.

Isikoff, M., and D. Corn. 2006. *Hubris: The Inside Story of Spin, Scandal, and the Selling of the Iraq War*. New York: Crown.

Isocrates. 1992. *Antidosis*. In *Isocrates*, vol. 2, translated by G. Norlin, 179–365. Loeb Classical Library 229. Cambridge, MA: Harvard University Press.

Ivie, R. L. 1980. "Images of Savagery in American Justifications for War." *Communication Monographs* 47 (4): 279–94.

———. 2007. *Dissent from War*. Bloomfield, CT: Kumarian Press.

Jackson, B. 2008. "The Truth on Troop Support?" *FactCheck.org*, July 22. Retrieved October 21, 2014, from http://www.factcheck.org/2008/07/the-truth-on-troop-support/.

Jackson, J. 2014. "14th Annual Fear and Favor Review: Owners and Advertisers vs. Journalism." *Extra!*, February. Retrieved July 26, 2015, from http://fair.org/extra-online-articles/14th-annual-fear-and-favor-review/.

Jamieson, K. H., and P. Waldman. 2003. *The Press Effect: Politicians, Journalists, and the Stories that Shape the Political World*. New York: Oxford University Press.

Jarman, A. 2001. "People Gather to Remember, Mourn Those Lost on Sept. 11." *St. Louis Dispatch*, September 25, 1.

Jehl, D. 2003. "A Nation at War: Rallies; Across Country, Thousands Gather to Back U.S. Troops and Policy." *New York Times*, March 24, B15. Retrieved February 23, 2018, from http://www.nytimes.com/2003/03/24/us/nation-war-rallies-across-country-thousands-gather-back-us-troops-policy.html.

Jensen, R. 2001. *Writing Dissent: Taking Radical Ideas from the Margins to the Mainstream*. New York: Peter Lang.

———. 2016. "Writing Dissent in the Propaganda Flood." In *Propaganda and Rhetoric in Democracy: History, Theory, Analysis*, edited by M. J. Braun and G. L. Henderson, 264–72. Carbondale: Southern Illinois University Press.

Johnson, C. 2004. "Abolish the CIA!" *London Review of Books*, October 21, 25–28. Retrieved February 23, 2018, from https://www.lrb.co.uk/v26/n20/chalmers-johnson/abolish-the-cia.

Johnson, L. B. 1966. "Remarks upon Awarding the Medal of Honor to Sgt. Robert E. O'Malley, USMC." December 6. *American Presidency Project*. Retrieved September 13, 2014, from http://www.presidency.ucsb.edu/ws/?pid=28062. [Speech transcript.]

———. 1967. "Letter to the Speaker of the House Requesting Supplemental Appropriations in Support of Military Operations in Southeast Asia." January 24. *American Presidency Project*. Retrieved September 13, 2014, from http://www.presidency.ucsb.edu/ws/?pid=28161.

———. 1971. *Vantage Point: Perspectives of the Presidency, 1963–1969*. New York: Holt, Rinehart, and Winston.

Johnstone, B. 2005. "Discourse Analysis and Narrative." In *The Handbook of Discourse Analysis*, edited by D. Schiffrin, D. Tannen, and H. E. Hamilton. Malden, MA: Blackwell.

———. 2008. *Discourse Analysis*. 2nd ed. Malden, MA: Blackwell.

Jolidon, L. 1990. "U.S. Tails Iraqi Freighter; Gas Lines Form in Bagdad." *USA Today*, October 22, 4A.

Joseph, J. E. 2006. *Language and Politics*. Edinburgh: Edinburgh University Press.

Jowett, G. S., and V. O'Donnell. 2015. *Propaganda and Persuasion*. 6th ed. Thousand Oaks, CA: SAGE.

Kagan, R. 2014. "Superpowers Don't Get to Retire: What Our Tired Country Still Owes the World." *New Republic*, May 26. Retrieved July 27, 2015, from https://newrepublic.com/article/117859/superpowers-dont-get-retire.

Katz, A. 1992. "T-Talk." *Alcalde*, July/August, 24–25.

Kaufer, D. S., and K. M. Carley. 1993. "Condensation Symbols: Their Variety and Rhetorical Function in Political Discourse." *Philosophy and Rhetoric* 26 (3): 201–26.

Kay, D. 1998. Statement at Hearing Before the Senate Armed Services Committee, March 25. Retrieved March 15, 2018, from https://archive.li/ooJxe. [Speech transcript.]

———. 1999. Interview. "Spying on Saddam." *Frontline*, Public Broadcasting Service. Retrieved April 21, 2014, from http://www.pbs.org/wgbh/pages/frontline/shows/unscom/interviews/kay.html. [Interview transcript.]

———. 2002. Statement at Hearing Before the House Armed Services Committee on the Iraqi Weapons of Mass Destruction Program and the History of U.N. Inspection Efforts in Iraq, September 10. C-SPAN. Retrieved March 15, 2018, from https://www.c-span.org/video/?172551-1/iraqi-weapons-mass-destruction. [Video and broadcast transcript.]

Kazeniac, A. 2009. "Social Networks, Facebook Takes Over Top Spot, Twitter Climbs." *Compete Pulse Blog*, February 9. Retrieved March 15, 2018, from https://web.archive.org/web/20090213040901/http://networkings.over-blog.com:80/.

Kellner, D. 1992. *The Persian Gulf TV War*. Boulder, CO: Westview Press.

———. 2004a. "9/11, Spectacles of Terror, and Media Manipulation: A Critique of Jihadist and Bush Media Politics." *Critical Discourse Studies* 1 (1): 41–64.

———. 2004b. "The Persian Gulf TV War Revisited." In *Reporting War: Journalism in Wartime*, edited by S. Allan and B. Zelizer, 136–54. New York: Routledge.

King, M. L. 1963. *Why We Can't Wait*. New York: Mentor.

Kinzer, S. 2006. *Overthrow: America's Century of Regime Change from Hawaii to Iraq*. New York: Times Books.

Kipp, M., M. Neff, and I. Albrecht. 2007. "An Annotation Scheme for Conversational Gestures: How to Economically Capture Timing and Form." *Language Resources and Evaluation* 41 (3–4): 325–39.

Klien, S. A. 2005. "Public Character and the Simulacrum: The Construction of the Soldier Patriot and Citizen Agency in *Black Hawk Down*." *Critical Studies in Media Communication* 22 (5): 427–49.

Knightley, P. 2004. *The First Casualty: The War Correspondent as Hero and Myth-Maker from the Crimea to Iraq*. Baltimore: Johns Hopkins University Press.

Kockelman, P. 2005. "The Semiotic Stance." *Semiotica* 157 (1/4): 233–304.

Koenig, R. L. 1991. "Senate Vote Supports Forces: United Action Shows 'When Americans Go to War, We Go Together.'" *St. Louis Post-Dispatch*, January 18, 1A.

Kotcheff, T., director. 1982. *First Blood*. Los Angeles: Orion Pictures. [Motion picture.]

Krakauer, S. 2010. "GOP Florida Governor Candidate's New Campaign Ad: 'Obama's Mosque.'" *Mediaite*, August 17. Retrieved July 16, 2015, from http://www.mediaite.com/online/gop-florida-governor-candidates-new-campaign-ad-obamas-mosque/.

Krebs, B. 2001. "Patriotism Permeates Parade; Flags Prominent at Annual Glen Rock Halloween Event." *York (PA) Dispatch*, October 8.

Kress, G. R. 1993. "Against Arbitrariness: The Social Production of the Sign as a Foundational Issue in Critical Discourse Analysis." *Discourse and Society* 4 (2): 169–91.

———. 1995. "The Social Production of Language: History and Structures of Domination." In *Discourse in Society: Systemic Functional Perspectives*, edited by P. H. Fries and M. Gregory, 115–40. Norwood, NJ: Ablex.

Kress, G. R., and T. Van Leeuwen. 2001. *Multimodal Discourse: The Modes and Media of Contemporary Communication*. London: Arnold.

———. 2006. *Reading Images: The Grammar of Visual Design*. London: Routledge.

Labov, W. 1972. *Language in the Inner City*. Philadelphia: University of Pennsylvania Press.

Labov, W., and J. Waletzky. 1997. "Narrative Analysis: Oral Versions of Personal Experience." *Journal of Narrative and Life History* 7 (1–4): 3–38.

LaMay, C. 1991a. "By the Numbers I: The Bibliometrics of War." In *The Media at War: The Press and the Persian Gulf Conflict*, edited by C. LaMay and E. Dennis, 41–44. New York: Freedom Forum.

————. 1991b. "By the Numbers II: Measuring the Coverage." In *The Media at War: The Press and the Persian Gulf Conflict*, edited by C. LaMay and E. Dennis, 45–50. New York: Freedom Forum.

Lanham, R. A. 2007. *Style: An Anti-textbook*. 2nd ed. Philadelphia: Paul Dry Books.

Larsen, L. 1994. "The Yellow Ribboning of America: A Gulf War Phenomenon." *Journal of American Culture* 17 (1): 11–22.

Latour, B. 1987. *Science in Action: How to Follow Scientists and Engineers Through Society*. Harvard: Harvard University Press.

Lau, R. R., L. Sigelman, and I. Brown Rovner. 2007. "The Effects of Negative Political Campaigns: A Meta-analytic Reassessment." *Journal of Politics* 69 (4): 1176–209.

Lee, G., and J. Lancaster. 1991. "'Rape of Kuwait' Book, Ad Campaign Try to Make Case for Military Force; Major Lobbying Effort Underway by Supporters of Bush Policy." *Washington Post*, January 17, A29. Retrieved February 26, 2018, from https://www.washingtonpost.com /archive/politics/1991/01/17/rape-of-kuwait-book-ad-campaign-try-to-make-case-for -military-force/2f0e0be1-afb6-4f6c-88e4-8cd36ad6af83/.

Lee, M. A., and N. Solomon. 1990. *Unreliable Sources: A Guide to Detecting Bias in the News Media*. New York: Lyle Stuart.

Leff, L. 1990. "Weary, Wary Evacuees Bring Tales of Horror." *Washington Post*, September 11, A8. Retrieved February 26, 2018, from https://www.washingtonpost.com/archive/politics /1990/09/11/weary-wary-evacuees-bring-tales-of-horror/c9f5f29f-d17a-49c0-bd31 -34dc73632bf1/.

Leitz, L. 2011. "Oppositional Identities: The Military Peace Movement's Challenge to Pro-Iraq War Frames." *Social Problems* 58 (2): 235–56.

Lembcke, J. 1998. *The Spitting Image: Myth, Memory, and the Legacy of Vietnam*. New York: New York University Press.

Lemke, J. L. 1998. "Multiplying Meaning: Visual and Verbal Semiotics in Scientific Text." In *Reading Science*, edited by J. R. Martin and R. Veel, 87–113. London: Routledge.

Lempert, M., and M. Silverstein. 2012. *Creatures of Politics: Media, Message, and the American Presidency*. Bloomington: Indiana University Press.

Lewis, C., and M. Reading-Smith. 2008. "Iraq: The War Card. Orchestrated Deception on the Path to War." Center for Public Integrity, January 23. Retrieved July 30, 2015, from http://www .publicintegrity.org/politics/white-house/iraq-war-card.

Lilley, T. G., J. Best, B. E. Aguirre, and K. S. Lowney. 2010. "Magnetic Imagery: War-Related Ribbons as Collective Display." *Sociological Inquiry* 80 (2): 313–21.

Lincoln (NE) Journal Star. 2001. "Oppose War? Support Our Troops Anyway." October 12, 5.

Linell, P. 1998. "Discourse Across Boundaries: On Recontextualizations and the Blending of Voices in Professional Discourse." *Text* 18 (2): 143–57.

Lowell (MA) Sun. 2001. "Littleton Rallies for Our Troops." October 19.

Lozano-Reich, N. M., and D. L. Cloud. 2009. "The Uncivil Tongue: Invitational Rhetoric and the Problem of Inequality." *Western Journal of Communication* 73 (2): 220–26.

Lutz, A. 2012. "These 6 Corporations Control 90% of the Media in America." *Business Insider*, July 14. Retrieved July 21, 2015, from http://www.businessinsider.com/these-6-corporations -control-90-of-the-media-in-america-2012-6.

Lynch, J., and J. Galtung. 2010. *Reporting Conflict: New Directions in Peace Journalism*. St. Lucia: University of Queensland Press.

MacArthur, J. R. 1992. *Second Front: Censorship and Propaganda in the 1991 Gulf War*. Berkeley: University of California Press.

Machin, D. 2007. *Introduction to Multimodal Analysis*. New York: Oxford University Press.

Mackay, R. R. 2015. "Multimodal Legitimation: Selling Scottish Independence." *Discourse and Society* 26 (3): 323–48.

Manheim, J. B. 1994. "Strategic Public Diplomacy: Managing Kuwait's Image during the Gulf Conflict." In *Taken by Storm: The Media, Public Opinion, and U.S. Foreign Policy in the Gulf War*, edited by W. L. Bennett and D. L. Paletz, 131–48. Chicago: University of Chicago Press.

Marlin, R. 2013. *Propaganda and the Ethics of Persuasion*. 2nd ed. Toronto: Broadview Press.

Martin, J. R., and P. R. R. White. 2005. *The Language of Evaluation: Appraisal in English*. New York: Palgrave Macmillan.

Mason, A. 2013. "Iraq Policy 1990 to 2000 from the US Perspective." *Iraq Inquiry Digest*, August 11. Retrieved March 15, 2018, from https://web.archive.org/web/20170226190746/http://www .iraqinquirydigest.org/?p=14023.

Massing, M. 2004. "Now They Tell Us." *New York Review of Books*, February 26. Retrieved June 3, 2014, from http://www.nybooks.com/articles/archives/2004/feb/26/now-they-tell-us/.

Mayer, J. 2004. "The Manipulator." A Reporter at Large. *New Yorker*, June 7. Retrieved July 30, 2015, from https://www.newyorker.com/magazine/2004/06/07/the-manipulator.

Mayk, L. 2001. "Westampton to Send Notes of Support; About 540 Middle School Students Will Write Letters to Military Personnel from the Burlington County Area. Students to Send Letters of Support." *Philadelphia Inquirer*, October 28, BR01.

Mazid, B. M. 2007. "Presuppositions and Strategic Functions in Bush's 20/9/2001 Speech: A Critical Discourse Analysis." *Journal of Language and Politics* 6 (3): 351–75.

McCain, J. 1991. 137 Congressional Record, S183 (January 11). Retrieved from ProQuest, http:// congressional.proquest.com.

———. 2008. "Troop Funding." YouTube, July 18. Retrieved October 21, 2014, from http://www .youtube.com/watch?v=mm9IUfPZsX8. [Video advertisement.]

McChesney, R. W., and J. Nichols. 2010. *The Death and Life of American Journalism: The Media Revolution that Will Begin the World Again*. New York: Nation Books.

McFadden, R. D. 2003. "Threats and Responses: Overview; From New York to Melbourne, Cries for Peace." *New York Times*, February 16, A20. Retrieved February 26, 2018, from http:// www.nytimes.com/2003/02/16/nyregion/threats-and-responses-overview-from-new -york-to-melbourne-cries-for-peace.html.

McGee, M. 1980. "The 'Ideograph': A Link Between Rhetoric and Ideology." *Quarterly Journal of Speech* 66 (1): 1–16.

McGinniss, J. 1969. *The Selling of the President*. New York: Trident.

Metal Storm Limited. 2006. "Form 6-K: Report of Foreign Private Issuer Pursuant to Rule 13a-16 or 15d-16 under the Securities Exchange Act of 1934." November 1. United States Securities and Exchange Commission Archives. Retrieved April 19, 2014, from http://www.sec.gov /Archives/edgar/containers/fix060/1119775/000130901406000716/htm_1783.htm.

Miller, D. 2001. "World Opinion Opposes." *ZNet*, November 21. Retrieved July 29, 2015, from https://www.globalpolicy.org/component/content/article/154-general/26553.html.

Miller, D. W., and M. Toman. 2014. "An Analysis of Rhetorical Figures and Other Linguistic Devices in Corporation Brand Slogans." *Journal of Marketing Communications* 22 (5): 474–93.

Miller, J. 2002. "Threats and Responses: Inspections; Verification Is Difficult at Best, Say the Experts, and Maybe Impossible." *New York Times*, September 18, A18. Retrieved March 14, 2018, from http://www.nytimes.com/2002/09/18/world/threats-responses-inspections -verification-difficult-best-say-experts-maybe.html.

Miller, J., and M. R. Gordon. 2002. "Threats and Responses: Baghdad's Arsenal; White House Lists Iraq Steps to Build Banned Weapons." *New York Times*, September 13, A13. Retrieved June 19, 2014, from http://www.nytimes.com/2002/09/13/world/threats-responses-baghdad-s -arsenal-white-house-lists-iraq-steps-build-banned.html.

Miller, M. C. 2005. Introduction to *Propaganda*, by E. Bernays, 9–33. Reprint, New York: Ig Publishing.

Morrison, P. 2011. "Media Monopoly Revisited." *Extra!*, October. Retrieved July 21, 2015, from http://fair.org/extra-online-articles/media-monopoly-revisited/.

Moyers, B., host. 2012. "United States of ALEC." *Moyers and Company*, WNET, September 28. Retrieved July 21, 2015, from http://billmoyers.com/episode/united-states-of-alec/. [Television broadcast video and transcript.]

Mueller, J. 1994. *Policy and Opinion in the Gulf War*. Chicago: University of Chicago Press.

Murdoch, L. 2013. "US Tried to Napalm Truth in Justifying Iraq War." *Age* (Melbourne), March 19. Retrieved August 6, 2015, from http://www.theage.com.au/comment/us-tried-to-napalm -truth-in-justifying-the-iraq-war-20130318-2gbov.html.

Nagourney, A., and M. Thee. 2006. "With Election Driven by Iraq, Voters Want New Approach." *New York Times*, November 2. Retrieved October 20, 2014, from http://www.nytimes.com /2006/11/02/us/politics/02poll.html.

NBC. 1990. *NBC Nightly News*. Produced by S. Friedman. Retrieved from the Vanderbilt Television News Archive, Vanderbilt University. [Television broadcast video.]

———. 2001–5. *NBC Nightly News*. Produced by S. Capus. Retrieved from the Vanderbilt Television News Archive, Vanderbilt University. [Television broadcast video.]

Nemickiene, Z. 2013. "Slogan Linguistics in Life Cycle Revival of Trademarks." *Proceedings in Advanced Research in Scientific Areas* 2 (1): 327–31.

Newport, F. 2014. "More Americans Now View Afghanistan War as a Mistake." Gallup, February 19. Retrieved August 7, 2015, from http://www.gallup.com/poll/167471/americans-view -afghanistan-war-mistake.aspx.

New York Times. 1915. "German Atrocities Are Proved, Finds Bryce Committee." May 13, 6. Retrieved February 23, 2018, from https://www.nytimes.com/1915/05/13/archives/bryce -committees-report-on-deliberate-slaughter-of-belgian.html.

Nixon, R. 2015. "Turmoil at Voice of America Is Seen as Hurting U.S. Ability to Counter Propaganda." *New York Times*, April 15. Retrieved July 3, 2015, from http://www.nytimes.com /2015/04/16/us/signs-of-turmoil-seen-for-voice-of-america.html.

Nixon, R. M. 1969. "Nixon's 'Silent Majority' Speech." November 3. Watergate.info. Retrieved September 14, 2013, from http://watergate.info/1969/11/03/nixons-silent-majority-speech.html. [Television broadcast video and transcript.]

———. 1978. *RN: The Memoirs of Richard Nixon*. New York: Grosset and Dunlap.

Obama, B. H. 2009. "Remarks on Health Care Reform." July 21. *American Presidency Project*. Retrieved September 30, 2014, from http://www.presidency.ucsb.edu/ws/?pid=86446. [Speech transcript.]

———. 2013a. "Remarks at National Defense University." May 23. *American Presidency Project*. Retrieved September 30, 2014, from http://www.presidency.ucsb.edu/ws/?pid=103625. [Speech transcript.]

———. 2013b. "Remarks at the National Conference on Mental Health." June 3. *American Presidency Project*. Retrieved September 30, 2014, from http://www.presidency.ucsb.edu/ws /?pid=103644. [Speech transcript.]

Oddo, J. 2011. "War Legitimation Discourse: Representing 'Us' and 'Them' in Four U.S. Presidential Addresses." *Discourse and Society* 22 (3): 287–314.

———. 2013. "Discourse-Based Methods Across Texts and Semiotic Modes: Three Tools for Micro-rhetorical Analysis." *Written Communication* 30 (3): 236–75.

———. 2014a. *Intertextuality and the 24-Hour News Cycle: A Day in the Life of Colin Powell's U.N. Address*. East Lansing: Michigan State University Press.

———. 2014b. "Variation and Continuity in Intertextual Rhetoric: From the 'War on Terror' to the 'Struggle against Violent Extremism.'" *Journal of Language and Politics* 13 (3): 512–37.

Oddo, J., and P. Dunmire. 2016. "Privatized Propaganda and Broadcast News: Legitimizing the Call to Arms." In *Propaganda and Rhetoric in Democracy: History, Theory, Analysis*, edited by M. J. Braun and G. L. Henderson, 181–201. Carbondale: Southern Illinois University Press.

O'Dwyer's PR Services Report. 1991. "H&K Leads PR Charge in Behalf of Kuwaiti Cause." 5 (1): 8.

Operation Support Our Troops. 2005. "Mission Statement." Retrieved March 15, 2018, from https://web.archive.org/web/20060527074120/http://www.operation-support-our-troops.org/Mission-History.htm.

Orwell, G. 1949. *1984*. New York: Signet Classics.

O'Sullivan, C. D. 2009. *Colin Powell: American Power and Intervention from Vietnam to Iraq.* Lanham, MD: Rowman and Littlefield.

Page, R. 2012. "The Linguistics of Self-Branding and Micro-celebrity in Twitter: The Role of Hashtags." *Discourse and Communication* 6 (2): 181–201.

Parry-Giles, S. J. 1996. "'Camouflaged' Propaganda: The Truman and Eisenhower Administrations' Covert Manipulation of News." *Western Journal of Communication* 60 (2): 146–67.

———. 2002. *The Rhetorical Presidency, Propaganda, and the Cold War: 1945–1955.* Westport, CT: Praeger.

Parsons, G. E. 1991. "How the Yellow Ribbon Became a National Folk Symbol." *Folklife Center News* 13 (3): 9–11. Retrieved October 1, 2014, from http://www.loc.gov/folklife/ribbons/ribbons.html.

Peirce, C. S. 1955. "Pragmatism in Retrospect: A Last Formulation." In *Philosophical Writings of Peirce*, edited by J. Buchler, 269–89. New York: Dover.

Perelman, C., and L. Olbrechts-Tyteca. 1969. *The New Rhetoric: A Treatise on Argumentation.* Translated by J. Wilkinson and P. Weaver. Notre Dame, IN: University of Notre Dame Press.

Perlstein, R. 2008. *Nixonland: The Rise of a President and the Fracturing of America.* New York: Scribner.

Pershing, L., and M. R. Yocom. 1996. "The Yellow Ribboning of the USA: Contested Meanings in the Construction of a Political Symbol." *Western Folklore* 55 (1): 41–85.

Pew Research Center. 2002. *Midterm Election Preview: Americans Thinking About Iraq but Focused on the Economy.* Washington, DC: Pew Research Center for the People and the Press. Retrieved February 27, 2018, from http://www.people-press.org/2002/10/10/americans-thinking-about-iraq-but-focused-on-the-economy/.

———. 2008. "Public Attitudes Toward the War in Iraq: 2003–2008." March 19. Retrieved September 27, 2014, from http://www.pewresearch.org/2008/03/19/public-attitudes-toward-the-war-in-iraq-20032008/.

Pilger, J. 2000. "Squeezed to Death." *Guardian*, March 3. Retrieved May 23, 2016, from http://www.theguardian.com/theguardian/2000/mar/04/weekend7.weekend9.

Porter, E. 2013. "Inequality in America: The Data Is Sobering." *New York Times*, July 30. Retrieved July 21, 2015, from http://www.nytimes.com/2013/07/31/business/economy/in-us-an-inequality-gap-of-sobering-breadth.html.

Powell, C. 2003. "U.S. Secretary of State Colin Powell Addresses the U.N. Security Council." February 5. National Archives. Retrieved April 12, 2013, from http://georgewbush-whitehouse.archives.gov/news/releases/2003/02/20030205-1.html. [Speech transcript.]

Pratkanis, A. R., and E. Aronson. 2001. *Age of Propaganda.* 2nd ed. New York: W. H. Freeman.

Priest, D. 1990. "Evacuees Hail Kuwaitis for Their Aid, Comfort." *Washington Post*, December 12, A1. Retrieved February 26, 2018, from https://www.washingtonpost.com/archive/politics/1990/12/12/evacuees-hail-kuwaitis-for-their-aid-comfort/be59437c-a055-4078-8f9d-a87c37adaec0/.

Quaid, L. 2002. "Missouri Delegation Considers Iraq Resolution." Associated Press, October 3.

Quinn, E., and C. Young. 2015. "Who Needs Lobbyists? See What Big Business Spends to Win American Minds." Center for Public Integrity, January 15. Retrieved July 21, 2015, from http://www.publicintegrity.org/2015/01/15/16596/who-needs-lobbyists-see-what-big-business-spends-win-american-minds.

Quintanilla, M. 1991. "Retail of the Red, Hot, and Blue: Commerce: Patriotism Has a Sweet Ring for Business. After the Gulf Victory, Manufacturers Are Creating Items that Wave the Flag and Celebrate the U.S. Troops." *Los Angeles Times*, March 8. Retrieved September 29, 2014, from http://articles.latimes.com/1991-03-08/news/vw-2454_1_american-flag-shirts.

Radler, M. 2002. "Stateside—News from Jewish America." *Jerusalem Post*, September 27.

Raine, L., S. Fox, and D. Fallows. 2003. *The Internet and the Iraq War: How Online Americans Have Used the Internet to Learn War News, Understand Events, and Promote Their Views*. Washington, DC: Pew Internet and American Life Project. Retrieved February 26, 2018, from http://www.pewinternet.org/2003/04/01/the-internet-and-the-iraq-war/.

Rampton, S., and J. Stauber. 2003. *Weapons of Mass Deception: The Uses of Propaganda in Bush's War on Iraq*. New York: Tarcher.

Rauch, J. 1993. *Kindly Inquisitors: The New Attacks on Free Thought*. Chicago: University of Chicago Press.

Reagan, R. 1981. "Remarks on Presenting the Medal of Honor to Master Sergeant Roy P. Benavidez." February 24. *American Presidency Project*. Retrieved July 23, 2014, from http://www .presidency.ucsb.edu/ws/?pid=43454. [Speech transcript.]

Reece, B. B., B. G. Vanden Bergh, and H. Li. 1994. "What Makes a Slogan Memorable and Who Remembers It." *Journal of Current Issues and Research in Advertising* 26 (2): 41–57.

Reisigl, M., and R. Wodak. 2009. "The Discourse-Historical Approach (DHA)." In *Methods of Critical Discourse Analysis*, edited by R. Wodak and M. Meyer, 87–121. 2nd ed. London: SAGE.

Reuters. 1990. "171 Americans Fly to Freedom: Refugees Fear for Husbands, Tell of Iraqi Atrocities." *Los Angeles Times*, September 7. Retrieved September 16, 2013, from http://articles.latimes .com/1990–09–07/news/mn-864_1_iraqi-troops.

Richardson, J. E., and R. Wodak. 2009. "Recontextualising Fascist Ideologies of the Past: Right-Wing Discourses on Employment and Nativism in Austria and the United Kingdom." *Critical Discourse Studies* 6 (4): 251–67.

Ridolfo, J., and D. N. DeVoss. 2009. "Composing for Recomposition: Rhetorical Velocity and Delivery." *Kairos: A Journal of Rhetoric, Technology, and Pedagogy* 13 (2). Retrieved February 26, 2018, from http://kairos.technorhetoric.net/13.2/topoi/ridolfo_devoss/index.html.

Risen, J., and D. E. Sanger. 2003. "After the War: C.I.A. Uproar; New Details Emerge on Uranium Claim and Bush's Speech." *New York Times*, July 18. Retrieved May 21, 2014, from http:// www.nytimes.com/2003/07/18/world/after-the-war-cia-uproar-new-details-emerge-on -uranium-claim-and-bush-s-speech.html.

Roberts, J. 2007a. "Poll: Bush's Approval Rating at New Low." *CBS News*, January 22. Retrieved October 27, 2014, from http://www.cbsnews.com/news/poll-bush-approval-rating -at-new-low/.

———. 2007b. "CBS Poll: Speech Has Upside for Bush." *CBS News*, January 24. Retrieved November 2, 2014, from http://www.cbsnews.com/news/cbs-poll-speech-has-up-side -for-bush/.

Roberts-Miller, P. 2005. "Democracy, Demagoguery, and Critical Rhetoric." *Rhetoric and Public Affairs* 8 (3): 459–76.

Roosevelt, F. D. 1941. "President Franklin Delano Roosevelt Address over the Radio on Navy Day Concerning the Attack upon the Destroyer U.S.S. Kearny." October 27. *American Merchant Marine at War*. Retrieved July 14, 2015, from http://www.usmm.org/fdr/kearny.html.

Rowse, A. E. 1991. "Flacking for the Emir." *Progressive* 55 (5): 20–22.

———. 1992. "How to Build Support for War." *Columbia Journalism Review* 31 (3): 28–29.

S. Rep. No. 108–301. 2004. *Report of the Select Committee on Intelligence on the U.S. Intelligence Community's Prewar Intelligence Assessments on Iraq*. July 9. Retrieved February 26, 2018, from https://www.intelligence.senate.gov/sites/default/files/publications/108301.pdf.

Saad, L. 2008. "McCain vs. Obama as Commander in Chief." Gallup, June 25. Retrieved December 15, 2014, from http://news.gallup.com/poll/108373/McCain-vs-Obama-Commander -Chief.aspx.

Said, M. 1992. "The Mother of All Misinformations [*sic*] and Cover-ups: The Issue of Kuwaiti Premature Babies Dying Because of Iraqi Soldiers Pulling Incubators." January 21. Retrieved February 26, 2018, from https://drsaid.net/project/misinformation-in -kuwait/.

Salaita, S. 2013. "No, Thanks: Stop Saying 'Support the Troops.'" *Salon*, August 25. Retrieved August 11, 2014, from http://www.salon.com/2013/08/25/no_thanks_i_wont_support_the _troops/.

Santino, J. 1992. "Yellow Ribbons and Seasonal Flags: The Folk Assemblage of War." *Journal of American Folklore* 105 (415): 19–33.

Sasson, J. P. 1991. *The Rape of Kuwait: The True Story of Iraqi Atrocities against a Civilian Population*. New York: Knightsbridge.

Sawyer, D, host. 2002. "Weapons Declaration: Iraq Dossier Arrived at UN Last Night." Interview with Melissa Fleming. *Good Morning America*, ABC News, December 9. [Television broadcast transcript.]

Seal, C. 2003. "Cheryl Seal Reports Correction: Bush's Top WMD Inspector David Kay Is NOT a Scientist of Any Kind." *Baltimore Independent Media Center*, July 31. Retrieved February 26, 2018, from http://www.baltimoreimc.org/newswire/display/4522/index.php.

Second Gulf War (blog). 2009. "Opening Salvo: The Dora Farms Strike." October 4. Retrieved July 31, 2015, from http://secondgulfwar.blogspot.com/2010/10/opening-salvo-dora-farms -strike.html.

Sheridan, K. 2013. "Iraq Death Toll Reaches 500,000 since Start of U.S.-Led Invasion, New Study Says." *Huffington Post*, October 15. Retrieved July 31, 2015, from http://www.huffingtonpost .com/2013/10/15/iraq-death-toll_n_4102855.html.

Siddique, H. 2008. "Barack Obama Opens Nine-Point Lead over John McCain in Poll." *Guardian*, September 24. Retrieved December 15, 2014, from http://www.theguardian.com/world /2008/sep/24/uselections2008.barackobama1.

Silverstein, M., and G. Urban. 1996. "The Natural History of Discourse." In *Natural Histories of Discourse*, edited by M. Silverstein and G. Urban, 1–17. Chicago: University of Chicago Press.

Sirota, D. 2012. "The Myth of the Spat-Upon War Veteran." *Minneapolis Star Tribune*, June 7. Retrieved September 17, 2014, from http://www.startribune.com/opinion/commentaries /157945515.html.

Smagorinsky, P. 2008. "The Method Section as Conceptual Epicenter in Constructing Social Science Research Reports." *Written Communication* 25 (3): 389–411.

Small, M. 2002. *Antiwarriors: The Vietnam War and the Battle for America's Hearts and Minds*. New York: Oxford University Press.

Snow, T., reporter. 2002. "Colin Powell on Fox News Sunday." *Fox News Sunday,* Fox News, September 8. Retricved June 19, 2014, from http://www.foxnews.com/story/2002/09/09/transcript -colin-powell-on-fox-news-sunday/. [Television broadcast transcript.]

Snyder, R. C. 1999. *Citizen-Soldiers and Manly Warriors: Military Service and Gender in the Civic Republican Tradition*. Lanham, MD: Rowman and Littlefield.

Society of Professional Journalists. 2014. "Code of Ethics." Retrieved December 20, 2013, from http://www.spj.org/ethicscode.asp.

Soley, L. C. 1992. *The News Shapers: The Sources Who Shape the News*. New York: Praeger.

Solomon, N. 2005. "The Military-Industrial-Media Complex: Why War Is Covered from the War-riors' Perspective." *Extra!*, August. Retrieved February 26, 2018, from https://fair.org /extra/the-military-industrial-media-complex/.

Sontag, S. 1970. "Posters: Advertisement, Art, Political Artifact, Commodity." In *The Art of Revolu-tion: 96 Posters from Cuba, 1959–1970*, edited by D. Stermer, 7–23. New York: McGraw-Hill.

Sproule, J. M. 1987. "Propaganda Studies in American Social Science: The Rise and Fall of the Criti-cal Paradigm." *Quarterly Journal of Speech* 73 (1): 60–78.

————. 1989. "Progressive Propaganda Critics and the Magic Bullet Theory." *Critical Studies in Mass Communication* 6 (3): 225–46.

————. 1991. "Propaganda and American Ideological Critique." In *Communication Yearbook 14*, edited by J. A. Anderson, 211–38. Newbury Park, CA: SAGE.

————. 1994. *Channels of Propaganda*. Bloomington, IN: Edinfo Press.

Stadd, A. 2013. "The Median Twitter User Has One Follower." *Adweek*, December 26. Retrieved December 29, 2016, from http://www.adweek.com/socialtimes/median-twitter-user-1 -follower/494745.

Stahl, R. 2009. "Why We 'Support the Troops': Rhetorical Evolutions." *Rhetoric and Public Affairs* 12 (4): 533–70.

Stanley, J. 2015. *How Propaganda Works*. Princeton, NJ: Princeton University Press.

Stauber, J. C., and S. Rampton. 1995. *Toxic Sludge Is Good for You: Lies, Damn Lies, and the Public Relations Industry*. Monroe, ME: Common Courage Press.

Steele, J. E. 1995. "Experts and the Operational Bias of Television News: The Case of the Persian Gulf War." *Journalism and Mass Communication Quarterly* 72 (4): 799–812.

Strong, M. 1992. "Portions of the Gulf War Were Brought to You by the Folks at Hill and Knowlton." *TV Guide*, February 22, 11–13.

Sulzberger, C. L. 1971. "U.S. Now Faces Its Vincibility." *Miami News*, July 12, 17A. Originally published in the *New York Times*.

Sweeney, M. S. 2012. "Reporters and 'Willing Propagandists': AEF Correspondents Define Their Roles." *American Journalism* 29 (1): 7–31.

Taylor, A. 2015. "149,000 People Have Died in War in Afghanistan and Pakistan since 2001, Report Says." *Worldviews* (blog). *Washington Post*, June 3. Retrieved July 29, 2015, from https:// www.washingtonpost.com/blogs/worldviews/wp/2015/06/03/149000-people-have-died -in-war-in-afghanistan-and-pakistan-since-2001-report-says/.

Tian, Y. L., T. Kanade, and J. F. Cohn. 2005. "Facial Expression Analysis." In *Handbook of Face Recognition*, edited by S. Z. Li and A. K. Jain, 247–76. New York: Springer.

Thibault, P. J. 1991. *Social Semiotics as Praxis: Text, Social Meaning Making, and Nabokov's* Ada. Minneapolis: University of Minnesota Press.

Thompson, L. B. 1991. "The Media Versus the Military: A Brief History of War Coverage in the United States." In *Defense Beat: The Dilemmas of Defense Coverage*, edited by L. B. Thompson, 3–56. New York: Lexington Books.

Thompson, M. 2015. "The True Cost of the Afghanistan War May Surprise You." *Time*, January 1. Retrieved July 30, 2015, from http://time.com/3651697/afghanistan-war-cost/.

Tirman, J. 2011. *The Deaths of Others: The Fate of Civilians in America's Wars*. New York: Oxford University Press.

Tracy, K. 2010. *Challenges of Ordinary Democracy: A Case Study in Deliberation and Dissent*. University Park: Pennsylvania State University Press.

Tugend, A. 2003. "Pundits for Hire." *American Journalism Review*, May. Retrieved December 19, 2013, from http://ajrarchive.org///Article.asp?id=2995.

Tuohy, W. 1990. "Rights Group Tells of Iraqi Torture, Baby Deaths." *Los Angeles Times*, December 19. Retrieved February 26, 2018, from http://articles.latimes.com/1990-12-19/news/mn -6386_1_human-rights.

Unger, C. 2007. *The Fall of the House of Bush*. New York: Scribner.

Urban, G. 1996. "Entextualization, Replication, Power." In *Natural Histories of Discourse*, edited by M. Silverstein and G. Urban, 21–44. Chicago: University of Chicago Press.

U.N. General Assembly. 1948. Resolution 217, Universal Declaration of Human Rights, A/RES/217(III) (December 10).

U.N. Security Council. 1990. Hearing on Human Rights Violations in Kuwait, November 27. C-SPAN. Retrieved March 14, 2018, from https://www.c-span.org/video/?15141-1/human-rights -violations kuwait.

U.S. Congressional Human Rights Caucus. 1990. Hearing on Human Rights Violations in Kuwait, October 10. C-SPAN. Retrieved March 14, 2018, from https://www.c-span.org/video /?14441-1/human-rights-violations-kuwait.

U.S. Defense Intelligence Agency. 2001. *Iraq: Procuring Possible Nuclear-Related Gas Centrifuge Equipment.* Military Intelligence Digest Supplement, November 30. Nuclear Proliferation International History Project, Wilson Center. Retrieved June 19, 2014, from http://digital archive.wilsoncenter.org/document/119226.

U.S. Department of Defense. 2002a. "The President's Remarks—Talking Points." October. Washington, DC. [Memorandum.]

———. 2002b. *Pentagon Briefing.* October 30. Washington, DC.

———. 2002c. "United National Security Council Resolution Passage." November 8. Washington, DC. [Memorandum.]

———. 2002d. "Department of Defense Themes and Talking Points on Iraq." December 9. Washington, DC. [Memorandum.]

———. 2003a. "Department of Defense: Notable Quotes on Iraq." January 17. Washington, DC. [Memorandum.]

———. 2003b. "Talking Points on the Case for Military Action in Iraq." February. Washington, DC. [Memorandum.]

———. 2003c. "Talking Points on Iraq's al Samoud 2 Missiles." March. Washington, DC. [Memorandum.]

———. 2003d." Talking Points on Iraq's Ties to Terrorism." March. Washington, DC. [Memorandum.]

———. 2003e. "Talking Points on Iraqi and Weapons of Mass Destruction." March. Washington, DC. [Memorandum.]

———. 2003f. "Talking Points on Iraqi Regime's Assault on the Environment." March. Washington, DC. [Memorandum.]

———. 2003g. "Talking Points on Iraqis Who Surrender Will Be Treated Humanely." March. Washington, DC. [Memorandum.]

———. 2003h. "Talking Points on Overwhelming Force." March. Washington, DC. [Memorandum.]

———. 2003i. "Talking Points on Turkey." March. Washington, DC. [Memorandum.]

———. 2003j. *Pentagon Briefing.* Key Quotes. March 14. Washington, DC.

U.S. Department of Defense, Inspector General. 2011. *Review of Matters Related to the Office of the Assistant Secretary of Defense (Public Affairs) Retired Military Analyst Outreach Activities* (DoDIG-2012–025). November 21. Retrieved February 26, 2018, from https://media .defense.gov/2011/Nov/21/2001712365/-1/-1/1/RMATheFinalReport112111redacted.pdf.

U.S. Department of State. 2001. "Update on Efforts to Prevent Iraqi Procurement of Aluminum Tubes." June 29. Retrieved July 12, 2014, from http://www2.gwu.edu/~nsarchiv/NSAEBB /NSAEBB326/doc04.pdf. [Memorandum.]

———. 2003. "Iraq PD: Staying the Course." January. [Memorandum from American Embassy in Cairo.]

U.S. Department of State, Bureau of Public Affairs. 2003. *The Great Seal of the United States.* Retrieved October 18, 2014, from http://www.state.gov/documents/organization /27807.pdf.

U.S. National Security Council. 2015. *National Security Strategy.* National Archives. Retrieved February 26, 2018, from https://obamawhitehouse.archives.gov/sites/default/files/docs/2015 _national_security_strategy_2.pdf.

Van Dijk, T. A. 1986. *Racism in the Press.* London: Arnold.

———. 1993. "Principles of Critical Discourse Analysis." *Discourse and Society* 4 (2): 249–83.

———. 1998. *Ideology: A Multidisciplinary Approach.* London: SAGE.

———. 2006. "Discourse and Manipulation." *Discourse and Society* 17 (2): 359–83.

———. 2007. "War Rhetoric of a Little Ally: Political Implicatures and Anzar's Legitimization of the War in Iraq." In *The Soft Power of War*, edited by L. Chouliaraki, 61–84. Amsterdam: John Benjamins.

———. 2008. *Discourse and Context: A Sociocognitive Approach*. Cambridge: Cambridge University Press.

Van Leeuwen, T. 1996. "The Representation of Social Actors." In *Texts and Practices: Readings in Critical Discourse Analysis*, edited by C. R. Caldas-Coulthard and M. Coulthard, 32–70. London: Routledge.

———. 2005. *Introducing Social Semiotics*. London: Routledge.

———. 2007. "Legitimation in Discourse and Communication." *Discourse and Communication* 1 (1): 91–112.

———. 2008. *Discourse and Practice: New Tools for Critical Discourse Analysis*. New York: Oxford University Press.

Varadarajan, S. 1998. "'UNSCUM' vs. 'Bunny-Huggers' in Iraq." *Times of India*, February 26. Retrieved July 30, 2015, from http://svaradarajan.blogspot.com/1998/02/unscum-vs-bunny-huggers-in-iraq.html.

Volosinov, V. N. 1973. *Marxism and the Philosophy of Language*. Translated by L. Matejka and I. R. Titunik. Cambridge, MA: Harvard University Press.

Walton, D. 1995. "Appeal to Pity: A Case Study of the *Argumentum ad misericordiam*." *Argumentation* 9 (5): 769–84.

Warrick, J. 2002. "Evidence on Iraq Challenged: Experts Question if Tubes Were Meant for Weapons Program." *Washington Post*, September 19, A18. Retrieved February 26, 2018, from https://www.washingtonpost.com/archive/politics/2002/09/19/evidence-on-iraq-challenged/2ef6ddac-cfff-4b14-8d57-0fe6fb6993c3/.

Webb, S. 2008. "Iraq Signs Billion-Dollar Power Deals with GE, Siemens." Reuters, September 28. Retrieved May 2, 2013, from http://www.reuters.com/article/2008/09/28/us-iraq-ge-siemens-idUSTRE48Q30Y20080928.

Weiler, H. N. 1983. "Legalization, Expertise, and Participation: Strategies of Compensatory Legitimation in Educational Policy." *Comparative Education Review* 27 (2): 259–77.

Weldon, C. 1991. 137 Congressional Record, H175 (January 10). Retrieved from ProQuest, http://congressional.proquest.com.

West, M. 1990. "Amnesty International: Iraq Has Tortured, Killed Hundreds in Kuwait." Associated Press, December 18.

Westley, B. H., and M. S. MacLean, Jr. 1977. "A Conceptual Model for Communications Research." In *Foundations of Communication Theory*, edited by K. K. Sereno and C. D. Mortensen, 73–83. New York: Harper and Row.

Wien, C. 2001. "The Reference to Expert Sources in Danish Newspapers." Paper presented at Nordmediakonferens, Reykjavik.

Willis, W. N. 1914. *The Kaiser and His Barbarians*. London: Anglo-Eastern Publishing. Reprinted in *European War Pamphlets, 1914–1918*, vol. 55.

Wilson, P. 1983. *Second-Hand Knowledge: An Inquiry into Cognitive Authority*. Westport, CT: Greenwood.

Wittenauer, C. 2002. "Former Chief Weapons Inspector Discusses Homeland Security." Associated Press, October 24.

Wittenburg, P., H. Brugman, A. Russel, A. Klassmann, and H. Sloetjes. 2006. "ELAN: A Professional Framework for Multimodality Research." In *Proceedings of LREC 2006, Fifth International Conference on Language Resources and Evaluation*. Retrieved February 27, 2018, from http://www.lrec-conf.org/proceedings/lrec2006/pdf/153_pdf.pdf.

Wolfowitz, P. 2003. "Deputy Secretary Wolfowitz Interviews with Karen DeYoung." *Washington Post*, May 28. Retrieved March 15, 2018, from https://web.archive.org/web/20140929152903/http://www.defense.gov/transcripts/transcript.aspx?transcriptid=2676.

Wolin, S. 2008. *Democracy Incorporated: Managed Democracy and the Specter of Inverted Totalitarianism*. Princeton, NJ: Princeton University Press.

Zaller, J., and D. Chiu. 1996. "Government's Little Helper: U.S. Press Coverage of Foreign Policy Crises, 1945–1991." *Political Communication* 13 (4): 385–405.

Zinn, H. 2001. "The Uses of Scholarship." In *Howard Zinn on History*, 177–88. New York: Seven Stories Press.

———. 2002. *Terrorism and War*. New York: Seven Stories Press.

———. 2003. *A People's History of the United States: 1492–Present*. New York: Harper Perennial.

———. 2006. "After the War." *Progressive*, January 27. Retrieved September 17, 2014, from http://www.progressive.org/news/2006/01/2915/howard-zinn-after-war.

———. 2007. "A Just Cause, Not a Just War." *Progressive*, July 16. Retrieved May 16, 2015, from http://www.progressive.org/news/2007/07/5084/just-cause-not-just-war.

———. 2011. "One Iraqi's Story." In *Howard Zinn on War*, 237–40. New York: Seven Stories Press.

Zinn, H., M. Konopacki, and P. Buhle. 2008. *A People's History of American Empire*. New York: Metropolitan Books.

Index

Central Intelligence Agency (CIA) *(continued)*
    and Taliban, 47
    and Vietnam, 161
characterological voice, 117–18, 120, 137
Cheney, Dick, 144, 145, 146, 262n4 (chap. 7)
    on Saddam Hussein, 30, 145
Citizens for a Free Kuwait (CFK), 59–60, 63, 70,
    73, 100, 260n5
    campaign by, 71–72, 75, 77, 81, 84, 99
civic rhetoric, 33, 34, 38, 218, 220–22
Clarke, Richard, 48
Clarke, Victoria, 107
classic propaganda. *See* vertical propaganda
Clinton, Bill, 50, 172, 263n8 (chap. 8)
coercion, 4, 214, 220
    emotional, 28, 31, 33, 38
    slogans and, 209
collectivization, 121
commodification, 185–210. *See also*
    merchandise
    semiotics of, 10, 185–98
    and SOT slogan, 187–98
counterappeals, 201, 208, 209
counterargument, 141, 217
counterinsurgency (COIN) strategy, 178, 185
critical discourse analysis (CDA), 6–7, 211, 218,
    224–25, 259n4 (Intro.)
critical discourse studies (CDS), 5, 217–18,
    259n4 (Intro.)
cues, 22–23, 89, 93, 103, 213

debate
    classified, 140–48
    democratic, 15, 24, 29–31, 32, 216–217, 225
    public, 149–52, 164, 170, 220, 221
deflection, 160–61, 169
dehumanization, 38, 218, 251
deliberate propagandists, 14, 16, 20–22, 25, 27,
    37–38, 92, 99, 103, 139, 140, 152, 213, 224
democracy and propaganda, 4, 16, 215–17
Desert Storm, 44–46, 160, 169, 170, 172
    commodities during, 185, 187–90
detachability, 3, 4, 6, 22, 25, 37, 58, 70, 80, 213,
    226–27
disciplinary appeals, 201, 205–6, 208
discourse of betrayal. *See* narrative of betrayal
disinformation, 2, 4
dissemination, 2, 19–20, 37, 259n2 (chap. 1)
dissent, among intelligence community, 150–52
dissociation, 161, 163, 169
doublespeak, 28, 214, 259n7 (chap. 1)

Downing, Wayne, 108, 112, 119, 127, 238, 244
Duelfer, Charles, 110, 125–28, 132, 134, 237, 243

E Pluribus Unum, 189
eagle, bald, 188–90
elite actors, 4, 9, 20, 24–25, 137, 176, 210
    corporate, 209
    and incubator story, 79, 100
    and news media, 104, 219
    and recontextualization, 213–14
    symbolic elites, 24–27, 37
elite institutions, 2, 16, 24, 35, 104, 181, 213, 218
elite propaganda, 14–16, 165, 177, 212, 217, 222,
    259n3 (Concl.)
Ellul, Jacques, 2, 6, 15–16, 19, 176
    pre-propaganda, 209
emotional appeals, 69
emotional coercion, 28, 31, 33, 38
emotional semiotics, 70
entextualization, 6, 22, 24, 37, 124, 139, 223
    and G. H. W. Bush, 91
    and G. W. Bush, 150
    and expert voice, 120, 122
    and incubator story, 59, 70, 80, 94
    slogans and, 32
    and VNRs, 71
erasure, 139, 152
expertise, 105, 113–16, 132
    semiotic production of, 118–29

films, war, 167–68, 171–72
FlagsOnCars, 194, 195, 264n7
Fleischer, Ari, 137
focalization, 139, 140, 145, 150, 152
Free Kuwait campaign, 71, 75, 77
"Free Kuwait," 3, 60, 84, 160

gatekeeper, 17–18
general appeals, 200, 201, 207
genericization, 121
Germany
    propaganda about, 14, 29, 57–58
    propaganda by, 14, 29
Göering, Hermann, 57
Goering, Kurt, 95–96
Gordon, Michael, 144, 148, 149–50
Great Seal of the United States, 188–90

Hamza, Khidir, 111–12, 151–52, 237, 244
hero appeals, 201, 203–4
Hill & Knowlton (H&K), 59–60, 71, 73, 83–84

horizontal propaganda, 16, 19–20, 176–77, 185–87, 194, 199, 209, 213
Human Rights Caucus (HRC). *See* U.S. Congressional Human Rights Caucus
Hussein, Saddam, 70, 76, 122, 127, 136, 137
and incubator story, 90, 97
and relationship with U.S., 41–44, 45, 46, 49–51
and weapons, 3, 50, 110, 137, 144–46, 147, 216

Institute for Propaganda Analysis (IPA), 15
list of common devices, 2
integration appeals, 201, 205, 208
International Atomic Energy Agency (IAEA), 114–15, 149, 262n1 (chap. 7)
Iran
and the U.S., 41–42, 43, 46, 260n1 (chap. 2)
revolution, 41, 46
war with Iraq, 3, 42, 136–37
ironic appeals, 208

Johnson, Lyndon B., 161–63, 166, 169, 170, 175, 263n5 (chap. 8)
Joulwan, George, 130, 135, 238, 244
journalist code of ethics, 104–5

Kay, David, 104, 109–15, 119, 122, 127, 129–30, 134, 147–52, 237, 243, 261nn7, 10 (chap. 5), 262n11, 263nn6, 8 (chap. 7)
King, Martin Luther, Jr., 2, 4, 34, 161
Kuwait
G. H. W. Bush on, 89–90
invasion and occupation by Iraq, 42–44, 58, 76, 187
media accounts, 80–82, 92–94, 98–99
and the U.N., 80
and U.S., 59–60, 136. *See also* Citizens for a Free Kuwait; "Free Kuwait"

Lantos, Tom, 60, 61, 70, 98, 260n8 (chap. 3)
Los Angeles Times, 80, 81, 97, 170, 228

manipulation, 4, 5, 13–15, 26–36, 214–15
manipulative silence, 29, 30, 61, 118, 120, 152
mass media, 15, 24–25, 168, 176, 213–14, 220
mass scale, and recontextualization, 3, 20, 26, 37, 58, 79, 138, 152, 139, 199, 211, 214, 220, 222, 259n4 (chap. 1)
Massing, Michael, 130

McCaffrey, Barry, 45, 108, 113, 115, 119, 135–36, 238, 244
McCain, John, 181–85
mediation, 5
Meigs, Montgomery, 114, 127, 137, 238, 244
merchandise, 160, 177, 185–86, 194–95, 199. *See also* commodification
message and messaging, 3, 4, 17, 18–19, 22–23
and communication, 17–18, 19
as propaganda, 8, 19, 20, 22
methodology, limits of, 211–13
Middle East Watch, 87, 92, 97, 261n14
military analysts, 104, 106–9, 112, 113–15, 129, 133–36, 237, 239
Miller, Judith, 144, 148, 149–50, 151
misleading argument, 27, 28–29
Mitchell, Andrea, 125–26, 129, 131, 146–47
mobility, 140, 156. *See also* semiotic mobility
model appeals, 201, 206–7
Morella, Constance, 70, 260n8 (chap. 3)
mujahadeen, 46–47
multimodal semiotics. *See* semiotics, multimodal

Nachmanoff, Elena, 112–13, 129
narrative of betrayal, 166, 169, 182, 209
National Public Radio (NPR), 76–77, 82, 228
All Things Considered, 76, 81, 95
Weekend Edition Sunday, 81
Nayirah, transcript of, 230–33
need appeal, 202
network news, 239–42
New York Times, 58, 107, 109, 113, 144–45, 148–51, 165, 228, 258, 262n4 (chap. 7)
news analysts, 9, 104–6, 124–29, 131–36, 237–42
newspapers. *See also* titles of individual newspapers
newspeak, 30
9/11 attacks, 29, 48, 51, 113, 172, 186, 191, 194, 216, 224
Nixon, Richard, 163–67, 169, 263n5 (chap. 8)

Oak Ridge National Laboratory, 150
Obama, Barack, 21
and Afghan war, 202, 203, 208
negative ads about, 182, 183–85
and SOT slogan, 172, 174–75, 202–3, 208
tweets against, 203, 206–7, 208
objectivation, 121
oil, 42–44, 47, 51, 54, 60, 260n1 (chap. 2)
Operation Desert Fox, 50

truth, 3, 4, 14, 27, 70, 75, 99–100, 198, 215, 219

tweets. *See* Twitter

Twitter, 10, 18, 21, 31, 177, 264n10
    SOT slogan and, 198–210, 212
    and sociological appeals, 199–210

U.N. Resolution 1441, 132, 251, 254, 255

U.N. Resolution 687, 49–50, 260n4 (chap. 2)

U.S. Congressional Human Rights Caucus
    (HRC), 60–61, 72, 73, 76, 78, 84, 230

United Nations Special Commission
    (UNSCOM), 49–51, 109, 237–238

United Nations, on Iraq invasion of Kuwait,
    42–44

United States Central Command (CENTCOM),
    110, 114

universal appeals, 201, 207, 208

Unocal, 47. *See also* oil

unwitting propagandists, 4, 16, 20–21, 22, 37, 38,
    59, 92, 213, 259n4 (chap. 1)

uranium, 111
    depleted, 44, 53
    highly enriched (HEU), 140–41, 143,
        144–46, 149, 151–52

vertical propaganda, 15, 19, 20, 25–26, 176–77,
    181, 194, 209, 213

victory appeals, 201, 204–5

video news release (VNR), 71, 73, 227, 229

"Vietnam Syndrome," 165–68, 171

Vietnam Veterans Against the War (VVAW),
    163–64

visual semiotics, 61

Voice of America (VOA), 1

voice, 23–24, 30, 219
    authoritative, 24, 79–80, 107 (*see also* elites)
    believability, 76–77

characterological, 117–18

defined, 117

dissenting, 31, 33, 99, 150–52, 216

expert voice, 9, 118–38, 213

military, 135–36

Nayirah's, 63–65, 69–71, 76

on-air, 115, 118, 129–30, 132, 148 (*see also*
    analysts)

Warrick, Joby, 151–52

Washington Post, 50, 82, 83, 98, 151, 228, 258

weapons analysts, 103–4, 109–12, 115, 118, 132–36,
    237–42

weapons inspectors, 9, 51, 109, 110, 128

weapons of mass destruction (WMDs), 30, 50,
    111, 137, 216
    Iraq and, 50, 51–52, 54, 108, 112–14, 132–35,
        138, 152, 173, 243

weapons, 53. *See also* weapons of mass
    destruction (WMDs)
    chemical, 3, 44, 130
    Iraqi, 50–51, 54, 109–15, 130, 140–44, 151,
        243, 249. *See also* WMDs
    nuclear, 51, 109, 140, 142–43, 144, 145–46.
        See also aluminum tubes
    precision-guided, 52
    U.S. as supplier of, 41, 46

Weldon, Curt, 97

Westmoreland, William, 163

WMDs. *See* weapons of mass destruction

World War I, 14–15, 42, 57

World War II, 15, 167

yellow ribbons, 45, 170, 171, 187–88, 190

Zippe centrifuge, 143, 144, 150, 262n2 (chap. 7),
    263n7 (chap. 7)